FLORENCE

THE BLUE GUIDES

ENGLAND
SCOTLAND
IRELAND
WALES AND THE MARCHES
LONDON
THE CHANNEL ISLANDS
MALTA
GREECE
ATHENS AND ENVIRONS
CRETE
CYPRUS
PORTUGAL
PARIS AND ENVIRONS
LOIRE VALLEY, NORMANDY, BRITTANY
NORTHERN ITALY
SOUTHERN ITALY
ROME AND ENVIRONS
SICILY
FLORENCE
VENICE
HOLLAND
SPAIN: THE MAINLAND
BELGIUM AND LUXEMBOURG
MOSCOW AND LENINGRAD

BLUE GUIDE

FLORENCE

ALTA MACADAM

*Atlas of 16 pages and 15 other maps and plans drawn
by John Flower*

ERNEST BENN LIMITED/LONDON
W.W. NORTON & COMPANY INC./NEW YORK

FIRST EDITION 1957
SECOND EDITION 1982

Published by Ernest Benn Limited
25 New Street Square, London EC4A 3JA

Printed in Great Britain

Published in the United States of America by
W.W. Norton & Company Inc.
500 Fifth Avenue, New York, N.Y. 10036

ISBN *Library* 0 510-01650-2   0 393-01538-6 (U.S.A.)
ISBN *Paperback* 0 510-01649-9   0 393-00091-5 (U.S.A.)

PREFACE

Florence has remained a city of human dimension, *a misura d'uomo,* a quality appreciated by both visitors and residents alike. It is sustained by a remarkable history, and a tradition of excellence remains in the life of the city. This is still true despite the need to rebuild part of the city and provide housing for an expanding population in the post-war years, the disastrous flood of the Arno in 1966, and the requirements of some 2½ million tourists a year.

Changes and improvements in the museums and monuments of the city are taking place all the time. In Florence it is rare to find a church closed indefinitely for restoration or a museum awaiting rearrangement, a situation now sadly familiar in many other Italian cities. This is partly explained by the great interest Florentines retain in their city, and also because of the policy (particularly tenaciously upheld in the last year or two) of the authorities to replace restored works of art to their original positions as soon as possible. Before the end of this edition the description of many of the most famous museums (the Galleria dell'Accademia, the Museo di San Marco, the Pitti, the Uffizi, and Palazzo Vecchio) may be out-of-date.

Since the flood of the Arno in 1966 great advances have been made in conservation work, and chemically inert substances are being studied as a means of protecting stone exposed to the elements. Some statues made to stand outside may have to be brought in under cover. Among the most remarkable restorations in recent years has been that of the huge 14C frescoes by Nardo di Cione in the Cappella Strozzi in Santa Maria Novella. The fame and skill of the Florentine restoration laboratories was confirmed with the arrival in the city of two more than life-size Greek bronze statues which were fished up off the coast of Calabria at Riace in 1972. Their exhibition in Florence after their restoration there at the end of 1980 aroused the greatest interest among the Florentines themselves, before their fame reached the whole world and the exhibition was prorogued until the summer of 1981. Ghiberti's bronze East Doors of the Baptistery are at present being restored, panel by panel. The famous frescoes in the Cappella Brancacci in S.M. del Carmine are at last getting the attention they deserve; they are being cleaned and restored in situ. Work on the structure of the chapel itself has exposed the original window, and some exciting revelations may be made there in the next year or so. One of the most significant discoveries of a work of art in this century was made in 1975 in San Lorenzo when mural drawings by Michelangelo were brought to light.

The guide has been arranged in itineraries in conformity with other volumes in the series. Florence lends itself to exploration on foot because of its size, and the closure of the centre of the city to through traffic has made this a pleasanter occupation. Much of the city remains as it was laid out in the 13C and 14C, and one route, entitled 'Medieval Florence' has attempted to provide a picture of the city at that time. No visitor should leave Florence without having seen the city from a raised vantage point (from the top of the Duomo or the Campanile, and from one of the surrounding hills).

The author is particularly grateful to **John Flower** who undertook the cartography for this book with his usual skill and enthusiasm. The author's training as assistant to *Stuart Rossiter,* author of many Blue Guides, continues to stand her in good stead, particularly when undertaking a new guide. In the preparation of this guide the author is indebted in the first instance to *Marco Chiarini,* who generously agreed to contribute an introductory article on the Florentine Renaissance, which has greatly enhanced the book. He also read the draft of Palazzo Pitti and the Bóboli gardens and made many helpful comments. *Giorgio Bonsanti* was always ready with precise information about the restoration of paintings in the city, and about the museums under his direction (the Accademia, the Cappelle Medicee, and the Museo di San Marco). His friendly help and invaluable advice were greatly appreciated.

Much of the research for the book was carried out at the library of the Kunsthistorisches Institut in Florence; the author would like to thank the director, and the staff for their efficiency and kindness. Friends at Villa I Tatti were always helpful, and in particular the author is indebted to *Padre Salvatore Camporeale. Sandra Corti Malchiodi* and *Alessandra Baldanzi,* both friends and former colleagues at Fratelli Alinari, provided assistance on numerous occasions. *Sig. Enzo Settesoldi* of the Opera del Duomo was most courteous and helpful when the author bothered him with questions about the cathedral and its museum. *Dottoressa Maria Fossi Todorow* kindly read the text for Palazzo Davanzati and made several suggestions for its improvement. Thanks also go to *Dott. Gianfranco Boninsegni* of the Azienda Autonoma del Turismo, who gave help on several occasions and assistance in the preparation of the practical information section of the book. The author wishes to record her debt to all her friends in Florence, too numerous to mention by name, who provided help in countless ways. Many delightful mornings in Florence were spent with *Giovanni Colacicchi* visiting galleries and churches, during which familiar works of art were seen with fresh enthusiasm.

Illustrations

The illustrations are reproduced by kind permission of Fratelli Alinari, Florence.

CONTENTS

		Page
PREFACE		5
THE FLORENTINE RENAISSANCE by *Marco Chiarini*		9
HISTORICAL SKETCH OF FLORENCE		29
GLOSSARY		40
EXPLANATIONS		42

PRACTICAL INFORMATION

I	APPROACHES TO FLORENCE	43
II	HOTELS AND PENSIONS	44
III	RESTAURANTS AND CAFÉS	46
IV	TRANSPORT	52
V	USEFUL ADDRESSES	53
VI	CHURCHES	54
VII	AMUSEMENTS	55
VIII	MUSEUMS, COLLECTIONS, AND MONUMENTS	56
IX	GENERAL INFORMATION	59

FLORENCE

Route		Page
1	THE BAPTISTERY AND THE DUOMO	61
2	PIAZZA SAN GIOVANNI AND PIAZZA DEL DUOMO	71
3	PIAZZA DEL DUOMO TO PIAZZA DELLA SIGNORIA	75
4	PIAZZA DELLA SIGNORIA	78
5	PALAZZO VECCHIO	80
6	GALLERIA DEGLI UFFIZI	88
7	GALLERIA DEGLI UFFIZI TO PALAZZO PITTI	98
8	PALAZZO PITTI AND THE BÓBOLI GARDENS	100
9	GALLERIA DELL'ACCADEMIA AND SANTISSIMA ANNUNZIATA	112
10	SAN MARCO, PALAZZO MEDICI-RICCARDI, AND SAN LORENZO	121
11	SANTA MARIA NOVELLA AND OGNISSANTI	133
12	VIA TORNABUONI: SANTA TRÍNITA AND PALAZZO STROZZI. PALAZZO RUCELLAI	139
13	MUSEO NAZIONALE DEL BARGELLO	143
14	FROM THE BADIA FIORENTINA TO SANTA MARIA NUOVA	150
15	SANTA CROCE AND CASA BUONARROTI	152
16	SANT'AMBROGIO AND SANTA MARIA MADDALENA DEI PAZZI	162
17	THE ARNO BETWEEN PONTE ALLA CARRAIA AND PONTE ALLE GRAZIE	164
18	THE OLTRARNO: SANTO SPIRITO AND SANTA MARIA DEL CARMINE	171
19	THE OLTRARNO: PORTA SAN FREDIANO TO PORTA SAN NICCOLÒ	176
20	FORTE DI BELVEDERE AND THE BASILICA OF SAN MINIATO	180
21	MEDIEVAL FLORENCE	186
22	THE VIALI	196

ENVIRONS OF FLORENCE

23	FIÈSOLE AND SAN DOMENICO	200
24	SETTIGNANO	206
25	THE MEDICI VILLAS OF CAREGGI, LA PETRAIA, AND CASTELLO. SESTO FIORENTINO	207
26	THE CERTOSA DEL GALLUZZO AND IMPRUNETA	210
27	MONTEOLIVETO AND BELLOSGUARDO. BADIA A SETTIMO AND LASTRA A SIGNA	212
28	POGGIO A CAIANO	214

INDEX OF PRINCIPAL ITALIAN ARTISTS — 215
INDEX — 225

MAPS AND PLANS

ROUTES — *Atlas* 2-3
FLORENCE — *Atlas* 4-11
FIÈSOLE — *Atlas* 12-13
ENVIRONS OF FLORENCE — *Atlas* 14-15
CENTRE OF FLORENCE — *Atlas* 16

PLANS

ANCIENT CITY WALLS AND FORTIFICATIONS — 30-31
BÓBOLI GARDENS — 111
DUOMO — 65
MUSEO NAZIONALE DEL BARGELLO — 145
MUSEO DI SAN MARCO: GROUND FLOOR — 123
                    FIRST FLOOR — 125
PALAZZO PITTI — 103
PALAZZO VECCHIO: GROUND FLOOR — 81
                    FIRST FLOOR — 83
                    SECOND FLOOR — 86
SS. ANNUNZIATA — 119
S. CROCE — 156-57
S. LORENZO — 129
S.M. NOVELLA — 135
S. MINIATO AL MONTE — 185
S. SPIRITO — 173

THE FLORENTINE RENAISSANCE

by MARCO CHIARINI
Director of the Pitti Gallery

The City. Seen from the circle of hills which surrounds the city, Florence gives an impression of completeness of design, its medieval and Renaissance architecture dominated by Brunelleschi's immense terracotta dome 'erta sopra e cieli, ampla da coprire chon sua ombra tucti e popoli toscani'* (as Leon Battista Alberti described it in his 'Trattato della Pittura' with its celebrated dedication to 'Filippo di Ser Brunellesco'). The city is a perfect whole to which nothing can be added or removed without altering the harmony which it has been given by man over a span of about eight centuries. In perhaps no other city are the intention of man and the design of nature so bound up together. The city is born out of the valley, its monuments enclosed by an amphitheatre of hills. Its architecture has been created by the human mind in imitation of its natural setting, and Brunelleschi cemented this relationship for ever with his great cupola, a poetic masterpiece of engineering.

I advise any visitor, before penetrating the streets and piazze of the city, to take himself 'without the city gates', up onto the circle of hills, so as to perceive the physical unity which embraces the spirit of Florentine art. Probably the most remarkable of all Florentine views is that from the hillside of Bellosguardo, approached by a winding road from which the natural landscape can be seen blending with that of the city. The view from the top of the hill takes in the façades of the most important buildings in an almost unconscious summary of the beauties of Florence, to paraphrase one of the oldest guides to the city. Thousands of modest roofs covered by simple terracotta tiles remind us of the humble but highly skilled craftsmanship which is still an important characteristic of daily life in the city. Above these rise the principal monuments of the city which testify to the presence of exceptional artists, from the Romanesque period onwards, who made Florence the centre to which the art world looked for inspiration and guidance.

The Birth of Florentine Art. The continuity of figurative language which accompanies the evolution of Florentine art is its most distinctive feature—not only in architecture, sculpture, and painting, but also in the decorative arts. This logical development results in a clearly defined style of a consistently high standard. It is as if there were no break in time between the works of the anonymous architects of the Baptistery, Santi Apostoli, and San Miniato al Monte, and the later buildings of Brunelleschi, Michelozzo and Michelangelo: they all represent an unmistakable, uniquely Florentine style. This style is based on forms of such essential simplicity that it lends itself to endless repetitions and variations, without ever becoming stale, reaffirming, on the banks of the Arno, the simple perfection of the civilization of Athens at the time of Pericles and Phidias.

*'Soaring above in the sky, large enough to cover with its shadow all the Tuscan people'.

The orientation of the centre of the city, based on the Roman encampment which preceded it, still follows a plan according to the cardinal points: the religious centre with the Duomo and the political centre with the town hall and its piazza at either end of one axis; and on the other axis the two most important conventual houses, the Dominicans in Santa Maria Novella to the N.W., and the Franciscans in Santa Croce to the S.E. In these two different worlds some of the most important developments in the artistic history of the city have taken place over the centuries.

The first buildings in Florence to signal the birth of a characteristic style, with a clarity of design based on classical elegance, are the Baptistery, Santi Apostoli, and San Miniato al Monte, built during the eleventh and twelfth centuries. The octagonal Baptistery surmounted by a dome and lantern, clearly takes its inspiration from the centrally planned Pantheon in Rome. It became the prototype for the centralized churches of the Renaissance which were modelled on Brunelleschi's incomplete project for the church of Santa Maria degli Angeli. The green and white marble facing of the Baptistery emphasizes the geometric design of the structure, and this relationship between structure and decoration had a fundamental influence on contemporary architecture as well as later buildings, such as the Duomo and the 15C façade of Santa Maria Novella designed by Alberti. The rhythmical arrangement of architectural elements which characterizes Florentine Romanesque architecture is applied with particular elegance to the distinctive, luminous façade of San Miniato al Monte. Here the beautiful arches show a study of proportion and an understanding of harmonic rhythms which were later important elements in Brunelleschi's artistic language. The same attempt to find a rhythmic proportion, rescinding the gigantic forms which characterized the architecture of the late Roman Empire, can be seen in the interior of Santi Apostoli where the double line of columns, derived from the basilican form, is surmounted by Romanesque arches in a spatial synthesis which was to find its ultimate refinement in the basilicas of Brunelleschi.

But it was at the end of the thirteenth century, possibly because of the Gothic influence spreading throughout Europe from France, that a series of building and decorative enterprises was started in Florence, which had no equal in any other part of Italy. They not only gave a new face and character to the city, but also determined the beginnings of a new figurative language in art which would eventually become common to other Italian cities. At the end of the 13C the great religious and civic monuments of the city were begun; building continued in the 14C, and, in some cases, such as Santa Maria Novella, was not completed until the 15C. The 13C city was expanding both politically and economically, despite the strife between Guelfs (supporters of the Pope) and Ghibellines (supporters of the Emperor). Thanks to its flourishing commerce and the shrewdness of Florentine businessmen Florence took up a central position in the Tuscan economy. The rich merchants, rather than the aristocracy, now began to come to the forefront of the political scene, and they determined the new plan of the city which was seeing its commerce grow alongside its territorial expansion. The religious orders, too, had their moment of particular importance in the civic and cultural history of the city, and the two convents of Santa Maria Novella and Santa Croce were to become the scene of the great triumphs of Florentine painting. These two 14C buildings offered space for the great families of Florence to build the chapels which would bear their names and be dedicated to their patron saints, and soon rich citizens were competing with each other to have their chapels decorated by the best artists of the day. In the sombre but elegant architecture of these two churches the Gothic style is evident, but it is reinterpreted in the Florentine manner with the accent on perspective and spatial relationships, and on light, which was absent in the great cathedrals of the North. On the white walls of the side aisles and chapels, fresco cycles illustrated some of the important features and stories of religion for the people. The technique of fresco was to play a vital part in Florentine art throughout at least two centuries.

Cimabue and Giotto, on their return from Assisi where they had decorated the transept and nave of the upper church, and had there been influenced by the classical tendencies in the work of the Roman artists involved in the same project, were the creators of a new pictorial language which, according to Vasari, translated painting 'from Greek to Latin'. A memorable event of the time, related by the same historian, was the people's procession in honour of **Cimabue**'s Maestà, painted for the church of Santa Trinita (now in the Uffizi), around the year 1285, an event which signalled the advent of a new spirituality in pictorial forms, unknown in the Byzantine art which had been predominant until then in Europe. This altarpiece and the one painted at about the same time for the Rucellai chapel in Santa Maria Novella by the Sienese master, **Duccio,** mark the birth of the two important schools of Florentine and Sienese painting, which were to contend for predominance in 14C art.

The Fourteenth Century. The painter who first put the accent on the continuity between classical and medieval art, creating new forms which were clearly a prelude to Humanism and the Renaissance, was **Giotto,** Cimabue's great pupil. Dante Alighieri noted this when he wrote his famous lines:

> Credette Cimabue nella pintura
> Tener lo campo, ed ora ha Giotto il grido,
> Sì che la fama di colui è oscura.*

Giotto became the protagonist, not only of Florentine art but of all Italian art of the 14C. Active as a painter, architect, and inspirer of sculptural forms, he embodied the idea of the 'universal' artist which was to culminated in the High Renaissance with Leonardo, Michelangelo, and Raphael. It is significant that some of Giotto's most important works, from his early youth to his full maturity, lie outside Florence: his fame was such that he was called on to work in northern Italy (at Padua his cycle of frescoes for the Scrovegni chapel is considered to be the masterpiece of his mature years), in central Italy, at Rimini, and in the south, in Rome (St Peter's) and Naples. This is an unmistakable sign of the diffusion of his pictorial language, which must have touched all the most important centres of the 14C

*Cimabue thought he held the field.
In painting, and now Giotto is the cry,
The other's fame obscured.

Italian school. His style was a synthesis of the exalted dramatic qualities of Cimabue (as can be seen by comparing Cimabue's Crucifix now in the Museo dell'Opera di Santa Croce with that by Giotto in the sacristy of Santa Maria Novella) and the classical influence he had encountered in Assisi, and perhaps directly in Rome.

Giotto sought a return in painting to the realism which finds a parallel in the poetry of his friend and admirer, Dante Alighieri. The simplicity of Giotto's style can be seen in the Maestà, a work with origins in the Byzantine tradition, painted for the church of Ognissanti in Florence in the first decade of the 14C (now in the Uffizi). In this work, one of three large paintings to be dedicated to the Madonna in Florence, Giotto affirms a new humanity in the grave but smiling face of the Madonna, and in the upward movement of the figures of the angels and saints which surround her. Here we find the same highly religious but deeply human spirit which pervades the 'Divina Commedia', which was absent from the paintings of the same subject thirty years earlier by Cimabue and Duccio. In Giotto's Maestà the regal, Byzantine qualities of Cimabue and Duccio are softened by contact with a sense of human realities which was to be the leading characteristic of Florentine art from now on, eventually influencing the whole of Italian art. It is difficult to put into words the spirit which pervades Giotto's frescoes in the two chapels (Bardi and Peruzzi) which he decorated in Santa Croce, rediscovered after centuries of critical oblivion by John Ruskin. In these and in Giotto's other Florentine works we see the beginning of a style which was to be continued by his followers, though in a progressively more diluted form, as the Gothic style gained influence during the second half of the 14C.

Giotto's influence was also felt in architecture and sculpture: the early project for the Campanile of the cathedral was entrusted to him and there is evidence of his style in some of the relief panels which decorate the base, although they were probably executed by Andrea Pisano. Giotto's most able follower was **Arnolfo di Cambio,** the architect and sculptor who played a prominent part in the reconstruction of the city under the Republic. The building which was to become the symbol of Florence and its government, the Palazzo dei Priori, today known as Palazzo Vecchio, is associated with him. This was the residence of the 'Priori', elected from the rich and powerful city Guilds, whose rule superseded that of the 'Capitano del Popolo' and the 'Podestà', as power gradually shifted from the nobility to the rich merchants and bankers. Begun during the last year of the 13C, the tower was probably completed by 1323, and the rest of the building was enlarged and enriched over the course of the century. As P. Toesca, the Italian art historian, wrote: 'Rappresenta il palazzo dei Priori, non meno della Cattedrale, l'essere della città e dell'arte fiorentina: fermezza e agilità, austerità e finezza; e già vi si esalta quel senso di movimento che è anima di tutte le più grandi creazioni fiorentine'.* ('Il Treccento', 1951). Two and a half centuries after the building of Palazzo Vecchio, Vasari emphasized its political and social importance when he framed it in a view from the river with the long

*'Like the cathedral, Palazzo Vecchio represents the essence of the city and of Florentine art; it has a strength and agility, an austerity and finesse which already demonstrates that sense of movement which enlivens all the greatest Florentine works of art.'

arcades of his Uffizi building. Its imposing rusticated exterior, lightened by elegant mullioned windows, was to be used during the Renaissance as a model by Brunelleschi and Michelozzo when they designed the first great houses for the rich and powerful families of the city. Arnolfo, who was an engineer (he built a circle of city walls), as well as a sculptor and architect, also designed other buildings in those years of fundamental importance to the face of Florence: the cathedral of Santa Maria del Fiore, built on the site of the older and much smaller Santa Reparata, and, very probably also Santa Croce, the Franciscan church which, more than any other, sums up the spatial and structural qualities of Florentine architecture in the late 14C and early 15C. Arnolfo had envisaged an elaborate marble façade for Santa Maria del Fiore, populated with statues and reliefs, but, like the interior, it was left incomplete at his death. The drawings which survive of the façade, and the sculptures preserved in the Museo dell'Opera del Duomo are testimony to the powerful imagery and clarity of form in the work of Arnolfo which place him, as an artist, on a level with Giotto.

We do not know exactly how Arnolfo planned the interior of the cathedral as it was continued after his death in a new spirit, and the architectural framework was put to different use. However Santa Croce, probably based on Arnolfo's designs, seems to preserve his sense of monumental yet lithe clarity in the wide bays between the pilasters of pietra forte and the Gothic arches above them. Santa Croce, although fundamentally Gothic in form and influenced by contemporary architecture north of the Alps, is still characteristically Florentine in its use of light, in the width of its nave, and in the prominence given to the carrying structure in relation to the decorative details in the apse and the side chapels.

Other churches besides Santa Croce underwent alteration and enlargement at this time, including the Badia whose bell tower rises beside the tower of the Bargello and competes with the heavier, more imposing campanile of Santa Maria Novella, and Santa Trinita and San Remigio, both with more overtly Gothic interiors. Meanwhile, alongside Arnolfo's façade of the Duomo rose the Campanile which traditionally bears Giotto's name, even though he only built the first story. It is an imposing structure framed by corner buttresses. The tower rises without diminishing in volume towards the upper stories (completed in the second half of the 14C) where the structure is lightened by large Gothic windows. Giotto here repeated the Romanesque style of green and white marble decoration, adding pink marble, a colour scheme which was later copied on the exterior of the Duomo.

The classicism of Giotto and Arnolfo had enormous influence not just in Florence but throughout Italy. Although it was of short duration, it was taken up again in the 15C by Donatello and Masaccio. The various interpretations given to Giotto's art by his immediate followers can be seen in the decoration of Florence's most important churches, Santa Croce and Santa Maria Novella. We must imagine these interiors as they were then, almost completely covered by frescoes depicting religious subjects, arranged in a way which took into account the organic divisions of the wall space determined by the architectural structure. In the Baroncelli Chapel in Santa Croce, **Tad-**

deo Gaddi rendered his narrative more complex (showing the influence of Giotto's work in Padua), by an insistence on the use of perspective in the painted niches on the lower part of the walls where the liturgical objects give a strong impression of illusionism. In his scenes from the life of Mary, above, the buildings and landscapes are given more satisfying proportions in relation to the figures, even though they lack the coherent stength of Giotto's works. **Maso di Banco** produced yet another personal interpretation of Giotto's style in his stories from the life of St Sylvester in the Bardi di Vernio chapel in Santa Croce. He gave a remarkable chromatic emphasis to the plastic qualities of Giotto's painting, as can be seen also in his 'Deposition' for San Remigio (now in the Uffizi; also attributed to 'Giottino'). The delicate works of **Bernardo Daddi,** in particular his small religious paintings and polyptychs, show the influence of the Giottesque school. He approached the dazzling colours of the Sienese school, and the gracefulness that marked his work won him great popularity during his lifetime.

In sculpture, **Andrea Pisano,** though following Giotto's design in the relief panels on the base of the Campanile, moved away from his influence when the bronze doors for the Baptistery were commissioned from him by the Opera del Duomo. The doors, produced between 1330 and 1336, are a masterly piece of metal casting and signal the rebirth of bronze sculpture in which the Florentines were to emulate the art of Ancient Rome. Furthermore, the architecture of these doors was later to serve as a model for the second pair made by Ghiberti during the first quarter of the 15C, the competition for which marked the change from Gothic to Renaissance art. Andrea, in his work on the Campanile begun by Giotto, opened large Gothic niches for statues in the second story, which found an echo later in the external tabernacles of Orsanmichele, which was already under construction nearby. The sculpture of Andrea Pisano, and even more so that of his son Nino (who, however, worked mostly in Pisa), derived its elegance of style from Gothic forms but at the same time made obvious reference to the powerful plastic qualities to be found in the work of Giotto. This is evident particularly in the solidity of the four prophets sculpted for the niches of the Campanile, and also in his bronze reliefs for the Baptistery doors.

Meanwhile, the commercial and political power of Florence continued to flourish and the conquest of Prato, Pistoia, and San Miniato firmly established the autonomy and sovereignty of the independent Commune. Notwithstanding the great famines of 1346 and then the plague which broke out in 1348, which reduced the populations of Florence and Siena by half, the Florentines did not cease to embellish their city with imposing works of art, including buildings destined for practical use. The church of Orsanmichele, begun in 1337 as a loggia for the storage of grain and only completed in 1404, summarizes, especially in its sculptural decoration, more than half a century of Florentine art, and it is witness to the passage from the Gothic to the Renaissance style. **Andrea Orcagna,** one of the most important figures in Florentine art during the second half of the 14C, built for the interior a Gothic tabernacle dedicated to the Madonna in the area which was by then enclosed for use as a chapel. This represented a definitive break with the clarity and simplicity of Giotto's style, and the adoption of a flowery, decorative language. This taste for affected elegance and decorative richness later developed into the 'International Gothic' style. It is possible that this radical change in Florentine art owed much to the effects of the plague which caused an accentuation of religious feeling. In what can be seen of the remains of Orcagna's frescoes of the 'Triumph of Death' from the left nave of Santa Croce (now detached and exhibited in the Museo dell'Opera di Santa Croce), the characterization of the figures achieves a dramatic force that is almost expressionistic. Churches were enriched by more and more decoration, inspired not only by the life of Christ and of the saints, but also by allegories exalting the function of religion and of the saints in daily life. Whilst the simpler style of **Giovanni da Milano**, in his frescoes in the Rinuccini chapel in Santa Croce, looked back to Giotto, and **Giovanni del Biondo** filled churches throughout Florence and her surrounding territories with polyptychs that were easy to understand and bright with colour highlighted with gold, Orcagna and his brothers, **Nardo** and **Jacopo di Cione**, together with **Andrea di Bonaiuto**, evolved a more inspired pictorial language, solemn and allegorical, in its overtly didactic intent.

A large part of Andrea Orcagna's frescoes in Santa Croce were destroyed and those in the choir of Santa Maria Novella were replaced a century later by the frescoes of Ghirlandaio, so that the most important surviving work by Orcagna is probably the triptych in the Strozzi Chapel of Santa Maria Novella. The walls of the chapel were painted by his brother, Nardo, with a rather crowded but picturesque representation of 'The Last Judgement', 'Paradise', and 'Inferno'. The allegorical style of Nardo's work, with its throng of figures, leaves little space for any clarity of concept. This pictorial style was carried still further in the frescoes by And. di Bonaiuto in the Chapter House of Santa Maria Novella, known as the Cappellone degli Spagnuoli. The general effect is most impressive; the colours are extremely well-preserved and the decoration is complete in every detail. This is one of the few decorative schemes of the 14C to have reached us intact, complete with its altarpiece, a polyptych by Bernardo Daddi. A particularly interesting element present in these frescoes, which depict the work of the Dominicans for the Church, is the inclusion of a representation of the Duomo, then under construction, showing it complete with its three polygonal tribunes and dome, which would suggest that the E. end had already been given this plan by Arnolfo.

Agnolo Gaddi, Taddeo's son, continued in the wake of Orcagna and Bonaiuto. In his cycle dedicated to the Legend of the Cross in the choir of Santa Croce he exhibits an even more narrative style, completely removed from that of Giotto, in which bright colours tend to substitute formal structure. Landscapes in pictures of this time show increasingly the influence of the Gothic style, while the individuality of Giotto disappears, and the late-Gothic poetical imagination found in Lorenzo Monaco and Gentile da Fabriano had yet to be developed. Another personality active in Florence at the end of the 14C was **Spinello Aretino** who, with his beautifully preserved frescoes depicting stories of St Benedict in the sacristy of San Miniato al Monte, has left us a work rich in poetry and pictorial values which anticipates the delicacy and elegance to be found in the art of Lorenzo Monaco.

But it was, above all, around the workshops of the Opera del

Duomo that the creative energies of the city were concentrated. The Duomo was to be the largest and most important church of Tuscany, more imposing even than the cathedral of Siena which was at that time being enlarged according to very ambitious plans, and which was in fact left unfinished. The chief architect in the second half of the Trecento was **Francesco Talenti,** who had already completed the last three stories of the Campanile, decorating them with double and triple mullioned windows which unite the styles of his predecessors with Gothic motifs. In fact, as was always the case in Florentine art (in direct contrast to the Sienese school), the Gothic style was classicized. The exterior decoration of the Duomo recalls the Romanesque style with its different coloured marble facing, and the Gothic element is more apparent in the sculptural decoration of the doors and windows on its two flanks. But it is at the E. end of the cathedral, with its harmonious rhythm of the architectural elements and volumes, that the originality of the architects is fully revealed. The apsidal structure, with its tribunes, appears almost independent from the nave, and provides a fitting prelude to the cupola which rises abruptly and is only fully revealed from this end of the church. The huge dome, already planned by this time, was to defy construction until the time of Brunelleschi.

In the interior of the Duomo there is the same structural emphasis, the same clarity of conception and spatial amplitude as in Santa Croce, but the nave is higher owing to the use of Gothic vaulting. This Florentine interpretation of Gothic architecture is further emphasized by the use of massive pilasters crowned by capitals designed by Francesco Talenti. These pilasters were copied by Benci di Cione and Simone Talenti in the Loggia della Signora where the three great round arches and horizontal frieze are motifs derived from the two major ecclesiastical buildings of Florence. It seems that no pictorial decoration was envisaged for the solemn and bare interior of the cathedral, as it was for Santa Maria Novella and Santa Croce; instead, all the decoration was concentrated on the exterior. The carvings and statues in the tympanum above each of the doors, and on the pinnacles and buttresses, repeated the decorative style of the Campanile (which was further enriched with statues after the turn of the century).

The building generally considered to be next in importance to the cathedral as regards sculptural decoration is Orsanmichele, where there was a parallel development of Florentine sculpture in the late 14C and 15C, a development which did not have its equal in painting until the advent of Masaccio. The individuality of Florentine art seemed to follow the political vicissitudes of the city where power was increasingly concentrated in the hands of a few families who fought for control of the 'Signoria', always within the limits of the law. The emergence of the Medici family as leaders through their financial supremacy and their ability to govern was accompanied by an extraordinary blossoming of brilliant artists who also made their contribution to the field of humanistic studies, already awakening in Florence. Whereas in the 14C, the writings of Dante, Petrarch, and Boccaccio predominated amongst a multitude of followers of the 'dolce stil novo', the 15C saw a series of developments which were to make Florence, as in the days of Giotto and Arnolfo, the artistic centre not only of Italy but of the whole of Europe.

Humanism. Although the Renaissance is usually considered to have begun in 1401, the year of the competition for the second Baptistery doors, it was only very slowly that the new ideas inspired by the Classical world made any headway in Florentine art and literature. These were linked to a new conception of the representation of space for which Brunelleschi was primarily responsible. The time was ripe for this turning point and the first signs of its arrival were to be seen in the cathedral workshop and at Orsanmichele. **Nanni di Banco** demonstrated an evident interest in classical sculpture in the 'Porta della Mandorla' on the left side of the cathedral and in his statues of St Eligius and of the Four Soldier Saints (the 'Quattro Santi Coronati') in two of the Orsanmichele tabernacles. In painting, however, the International Gothic style, which first made its appearance with the work of the Sienese artist **Simone Martini,** became established throughout the first quarter of the 15C with the works of Lorenzo Monaco and Masolino, and the presence in Florence of **Gentile da Fabriano** who, in 1423, painted his 'Adoration of the Magi' (now in the Uffizi) for the Strozzi chapel in Santa Trinita. For this same chapel Fra Angelico was soon to paint his 'Deposition' (now in the Museum of San Marco), in full Renaissance style.

But it was, above all, Brunelleschi in architecture and Donatello in sculpture who determined the real change in style which was to mark the epoch known, from Vasari onwards, as the 'Renaissance'. By this term is meant the rebirth of the laws of ideal beauty and perfection of the Classical world. **Brunelleschi**'s artistic personality matured slowly, as he became increasingly subject to the influence of Antique models. If we look at the relief (now in the Bargello) executed by him for the competition for the Baptistery doors, we realize that his concepts of space and structure are still Gothic, even if they are seen in the light of a new sense of rationality and realism, consciously in contrast with the superficial linear elegance of the late-Gothic style. In the event, the doors were commissioned from Ghiberti who worked on them throughout the first quarter of the fifteenth century, winning the acclaim of the Florentine people. Brunelleschi had to wait patiently to realize the triumph of his engineering genius in the creation of the cathedral dome, the commission for which he managed to obtain only in 1423. He had already proved his originality as an architect with the building of the Ospedale degli Innocenti and the sacristy of San Lorenzo (known as the 'Old Sacristy' to distinguish it from the later one built by Michelangelo). At this time the Medici began to rebuild San Lorenzo, which was later to become their family mausoleum. Brunelleschi, in fact, became increasingly involved with Giovanni and then with Cosimo de' Medici, the founders of the great power and fortune of the family, which, from then on, was to play a vital role in the political, cultural, and artistic life of the city.

Brunelleschi's style, based on a uniquely personal interpretation of classical forms (columns, capitals, arches, central or basilican plans, all of which he brought back into use), was expressed through a harmonious and well-proportioned use of internal and external space. This was emphasized by his typical use of pietra serena underlining the architectural forms, and alternating with plain white plastered surfaces, apparently inspired by the geometrical quality of Romanesque architecture. But the most important aspect of Brunelleschi's architecture is his treatment of perspective; it was he who first used regular mathematical proportions in the elevation of his buildings, giving them an appearance of geometrical perfection. The laws which he studied and systematically applied revolutionized architecture which, like all the visual arts, had been dominated especially in the late-Gothic period by an abstract use of form and colour, tending to create a completely transfigured image of reality. Brunelleschi emphasized instead the real, tangible values of representation, indicating to his contemporaries and successors a way forward that was followed for the next five centuries of Western culture.

The Early Renaissance. The impression made by Brunelleschi's buildings (San Lorenzo, Santo Spirito, the Pazzi Chapel, Santa Maria degli Angeli, etc.), rising harmoniously out of the medieval fabric of the old city, was tremendous. For the first time, not only architects, but painters and sculptors as well, realized the possibilities that the use of perspective offered in the representation of reality. **Donatello,** who studied with Brunelleschi the ruins of Ancient Rome, entered with him the intellectual circle under the protection of the Medici. He immediately mastered the idea of perspective and gave its first interpretation in sculpture in the statue and bas-relief which he made for the tabernacle of the armourers' guild for Orsanmichele. In the statue of the young St George, and even more in the 'schiacciato' relief representing the Saint freeing the Princess, he applied Brunelleschi's principles of a unified point of vision and perspective (which were to be so important in the work of the young Michelangelo). Donatello's style appears rougher and less sophisticated than that of Brunelleschi; in some of his sculptures he seems to have drawn inspiration from the intense realism found in certain Etruscan portraits. Indeed Donatello strove to resuscitate the aesthetic ideals of classic sculpture: his cherubs full of life and energy; his bronzes, in which he revived for the first time a technique of sculpture which had not been employed since Antiquity; his use of very low 'schiacciato' relief which brings to the metal or marble surface a completely new pictorial quality, using Brunelleschi's principles of perspective to create an illusion of depth —these were all innovations which must have had great impact on the younger generation.

The purpose of the sculptures themselves also changed. They were no longer works intended simply to decorate public buildings, they began to stand alone as refined products bought by the rich bourgeoisie for their palaces, villas, or gardens, buildings which were now being constructed according to the new principles of Brunelleschi. For their palaces the great families adopted new Renaissance forms. The first notable example was the palace built by Brunelleschi's pupil, **Michelozzo,** in Via Larga (now Via Cavour) for Cosimo il Vecchio. Cosimo appointed Michelozzo as architect having rejected as too expensive a plan drawn up for him by Brunelleschi. We can be almost certain, however, that the design was inspired at least in part by Brunelleschi (although on a simplified scale). Cosimo also employed Michelozzo on more modest building projects, and he commissioned from him the convent of San Marco, built in Florence for the use of the Dominicans of Fièsole, and the villa of Careggi, and castle of Cafaggiolo.

The third great personality of the Early Renaissance, who completes the Florentine artistic panorama, was **Masaccio** who effected the same revolution in painting as Brunelleschi had achieved in architecture and Donatello in sculpture, despite his death at the early age of twenty seven. Although younger than his two colleagues, he was yet able to impose great changes on the artistic world through the work he did in collaboration with **Masolino** (a painter who still belonged to the International Gothic school) in the Brancacci Chapel in the church of the Carmine. The decoration consisted of a cycle of frescoes depicting scenes from the life of St Peter, and in the parts painted by Masaccio we can see a spiritual parallel with the work of Donatello, especially the Donatello of the 'Prophets' made for the Campanile. Masaccio's figures are powerful, sculptural and simple, free of the linear and chromatic grace that had distinguished the Gothic style. Colour is here used by the painter not to please the eye but to construct form, and this he evidently derived from Giotto's frescoes in Santa Croce (which also provided the young Michelangelo the model for his earliest drawings). Masaccio's figures express the same profound sentiments as those of Giotto, but within a structure derived from Brunelleschi's use of perspective which offered greater possibilities of concentration and realism. Masaccio remained excluded from the protected circle of the Medici and had to seek work outside Florence during the years which saw the ascent of the Medici to power. He was already dead when Cosimo il Vecchio returned, triumphant, to govern Florence after a year of exile in Padua. But the first direct followers of Masaccio, Donatello, and Brunelleschi, had already appeared, establishing the predominance of the new language of the Renaissance with the help of the most powerful family in Florence.

The artists' patrons were still, for the most part, the religious orders, the cathedral workshop, and the 'Signoria'. For these the artists produced the works which unmistakably characterize the Florentine Renaissance. **Luca della Robbia,** who was a follower of Donatello and like him collaborated on the decoration of Brunelleschi's buildings, created a new medium, that of enamelled terracotta, which was to be the speciality of his family workshop until the 16C. Using transparent glazes over red clay which had been simply coloured with white and blue slip, Luca della Robbia was able to achieve effects which were quite unique and which harmonized perfectly with the grey and white of Brunelleschi's buildings. Luca also created purely decorative forms inspired by motifs taken from classical sculpture, such as garlands of flowers, fruit, and leaves which encircle his reliefs, and the coats-of-arms of the Guilds (on Orsanmichele) or noble families, all of which became extremely popular. The rather severe dramatic language of Donatello was now neglected by the younger generation who looked more to his joyful, vigorous works such as the reliefs of the cathedral 'Cantoria', and the Prato pulpit, and the so-called 'Atys-Amorino' made for the Doni, and now in the Bargello (the same family were later to commission works from Michelangelo and Raphael). Donatello's affectionate reliefs of the Madonna anticipate the paintings of the young Raphael. These works were to inspire **Antonio** and **Bernardo Rossellino, Desiderio da Settignano, Mino da Fiesole, Benedetto da Maiano,** and **Agostino di Duccio,** each of whom created his own individual interpretation of Donatello's art.

This was also the moment of the revival of portraiture, realistically drawn from life or from death masks. Portraits were used in funerary monuments, for which the Renaissance model was Rossellino's tomb of Leonardo Bruni in Santa Croce.

In painting, Masaccio's work had breached the Gothic tradition, imposing the new laws of perspective in drawing and a rigorous, three-dimensional composition. But some of his followers could not forget the more colourful, lively aspects of the Gothic style, still present in the second decade of the 15C in the elegant work, so full of colour and narrative sense, of **Lorenzo Monaco.** Lorenzo's work brings us to that of **Beato Angelico** who managed to transform the preciousness of the Gothic style of colouring into a luminosity, derived from his study of natural light, which is innovative even when compared with the work of Masaccio. His great 'Deposition', painted for the Strozzi chapel in Santa Trinita (now in the Museum of San Marco), as well as the altarpieces he painted for several of the religious houses in Florence (especially the Dominican convent where he took his vows), and the frescoes he painted in the convent of San Marco, place Fra Angelico among the most spiritually rich and talented interpreters of Masaccio's style. Beside him stands another great interpreter of Masaccio's ideas in terms of light and colour, **Domenico Veneziano,** the master of Piero della Francesca, who transmitted the Renaissance style throughout central Italy. In this group of painters may also be included **Filippo Lippi,** a Carmelite friar of indifferent vocation (he eventually left the Order to marry an ex-novice, and their son, Filippino, became a talented follower of his father). Filippo painted a fresco in the cloister of the Carmine directly inspired by Masaccio but with a sense of humour and a closeness to the realities of everyday life which were quite new. In his mature works, notably his frescoes in the choir of Prato cathedral, Lippi was to find a balance between draughtsmanship, colour, and the expression of movement which was to have great importance for his most gifted pupil, Sandro Botticelli.

But the time also seemed ripe for experimentation, even of an extreme kind, as **Paolo Uccello** demonstrated. He was one of the most relentless investigators of the laws of perspective and illusionism in painting. He, too, was connected with the Medici and it was for them that he painted the three paintings of the 'Battle of San Romano', today distributed between the Uffizi, the Louvre, and the National Gallery, London. In the biblical fresco cycle he painted for the Chiostro Verde of Santa Maria Novella, he gives a Renaissance interpretation to this medieval decorative practice. As an historical painter (the 'Battle of San Romano' is one of the first paintings to depict an actual event) he was asked by the 'Signoria' to paint a memorial to John Hawkwood in the cathedral. Hawkwood was an English mercenary who led the Florentine army into battle against the Sienese. A bronze equestrian statue had been planned for his tomb, but this was never carried out because of the expense. Uccello's fresco, on the left wall of the nave, depicts the bronze horse and rider that should have been there, and its greenish colour imitates the patina of bronze. Uccello also painted the cathedral clock and supplied the cartoon for one of the windows in the drum of the dome.

Andrea del Castagno, the youngest of Masaccio's followers, played a similar role to that of Uccello. Primarily a fresco painter, he rigorously applied Brunelleschi's rules of perspective in his great fresco of the Last Supper in the refectory of the convent of Sant' Apollonia, animating it with nervously drawn, grandiose figures in an 'heroic' style, a style which could not fail to impress the young Michelangelo. Similar monumental figures appear in Andrea's frescoes of 'illustrious men and women' painted in a room of the Carducci villa and now in the Uffizi, and in the equestrian painting of Niccolò da Tolentino next to Uccello's John Hawkwood in the cathedral. In all these works, the vitality and sculptural feeling of the forms take precedence over the harsh, metallic colour.

Cosimo il Vecchio, after his triumphant return in 1434, increasingly came to be the enlightened 'ruler' of the city, even though he maintained the governmental structures unaltered. His strong personality was evident in all public works and he determined the development of Florentine culture. He surrounded himself with the most talented artists of the day to whom he entrusted important commissions for his family or for the state, and he began to form the rich Medici art collections which were to become celebrated. The houses of wealthy Florentines became more and more luxurious. They were filled with elaborate furniture, gilded and painted (notably 'cassone', or marriage chests), even the beds were often decorated with paintings. The walls were hung with pictures, often of very large dimensions, and sometimes in the form of a roundel (comp. the celebrated tondoes by Filippo Lippi and Sandro Botticelli), and they were enriched by elaborate carved frames recalling the wreaths of Luca della Robbia, with their flowers and foliage. It seems, indeed, as though there were hardly enough painters available to satisfy the demands of the rich families who competed with each other and with the Medici. Some of the most beautiful palaces of the city were built during these years, such as those designed for the Pazzi and the Antinori by **Giuliano da Maiano;** the Pitti which was probably based on plans by Brunelleschi, and Palazzo Rucellai designed by Leon Battista Alberti, who was also commissioned by Giovanni Rucellai to complete the façade of Santa Maria Novella, and to build the chapel of the Holy Sepulchre in San Pancrazio. The rivalry between families also extended to the various family chapels built and renovated in the most important churches as a testimony to the increasing prosperity of the bourgeois city. One of the finest funerary chapels of this period is that of the Cardinal of Portugal in San Miniato al Monte, which is an exceptional example of collaboration between painters and sculptors (Rossellino, Pollaiolo, and Baldovinetti).

The arts were codified by **Leon Battista Alberti** who established himself, before Leonardo da Vinci, as a 'universal' artist and theoretician of Renaissance art whose ideas were to become law for anyone wanting to follow the new Renaissance style. The figure of the artist became increasingly more complex; and the researches in the artistic field going on in all three arts were on a theoretical and intellectual level unknown to the medieval world. Artists now tended to work in a number of different fields, and, very often, their careers began in the goldsmiths' workshop because of the ever increasing demand for precious objects. It is not strange, then, that Pollaiolo and Verrocchio not only produced paintings and sculpture for their patrons, but also armour, crests and jewels for display in parades, festivals, and tournaments, such as that held in 1471 in which Giuliano and Lorenzo de' Medici distinguished themselves.

The stability of the government of Cosimo il Vecchio (who died in 1464) ensured the city's great prosperity, a prosperity founded on commerce. In Florence at this time the principal desire seems to have been to brighten life with all that was most beautiful and precious in art and nature. Even the subject matter of works of art changed and artists increasingly drew inspiration from mythological subjects of antiquity, in the same way as allusions to the classical world abounded in the literature of the time. 'The Procession of the Magi', by Benozzo Gozzoli in the chapel of the Medici palace, is almost a manifesto of this new ideal. Here there are portraits of members of the family, richly dressed and surrounded by pages and courtiers, set against an imaginary landscape. There is little emphasis on the mystical aspect of the event, more on the worldly one, the atmosphere being that of a cavalcade for a tournament or some fairy-tale procession. But Florence at this time reached the apex of her political importance, and it was in Florence that the meeting of the Council of the Eastern and Western Churches took place in 1439, underlining the socio-political function of the city. The house of the Medici had by now become a royal palace, its rooms decorated with works of art by Paolo Uccello, Filippo Lippi, Benozzo Gozzoli, Pollaiolo and Verrocchio. Cosimo's treasury, with all its marvellous antiques which he passed on to Lorenzo, had its vault decorated with enamelled terracotta tiles by Luca della Robbia (now in the Victoria and Albert Museum).

The 'Crisis' of the 1460s. Around 1460, Florentine art reached a turning point: the **Pollaiolo** brothers sought, above all, new expressive values and imparted a dynamic force to line and form. They were masters at casting bronze, and they imposed on sculpture a new artistic canon based on elegance of line and a swirling, vortical movement and added an expression of force and balance which emulated the art of the Ancient World. **Verrocchio** was also at work at this time, and he was for long favoured by the Medici as a painter and sculptor. He reached a measured perfection and a monumentality even in small-scale works (see, for example, his 'David' in the Bargello), and marked the advent of a new figurative and aesthetic concept which was to be fully realized by his greatest pupil, Leonardo da Vinci. Verrocchio's high degree of intellectuality is evident in his creation of the tomb destined for the father and uncle of Lorenzo and Giuliano de' Medici in the Old Sacristy of San Lorenzo: the sumptuous sarcophagus, devoid of figure decoration, is framed by a bronze grille of studied simplicity. The importance of Pollaiolo and Verrocchio can also be measured by the role they assumed outside Florence: two Popes' tombs in St Peter's were commissioned from Pollaiolo, and Verrocchio was responsible for the equestrian statue of Colleoni in Venice, a superb sequitor to Donatello's Gattamelata monument in Padua, and directly inspired by the heroic world of Antiquity.

Not even the conspiracy devised by the Pazzi in 1478 against Lorenzo and Giuliano seemed to interrupt this period of incredible creative activity in the artistic life of Florence. Moreover, despite the murder of Giuliano, Lorenzo emerged from the fray even stronger, the absolute ruler of the city, establishing himself as the greatest political and diplomatic genius of the time, besides being something of a poet.

He surrounded himself with men of letters, poets, and philosophers, and his 'round table' of Humanists, based at the villa of Careggi, seemed to have brought the culture of Periclean Athens to life in Florence. In the figurative arts the most evident reflection of this was in the mythologies painted by **Sandro Botticelli** which, in their play of line taken from Pollaiolo, carried the rhythmic capacity of drawing to its utmost limit. Botticelli worked mostly for private patrons, and his paintings, even those of religious subjects, reach an almost abstract intellectual level that seems to be in direct antithesis to the world of intensely human images created by Donatello and Masaccio.

Renaissance architecture left little space for the large mural decorations which had been so important a feature of 14C Florentine art. The masters of the new style, although interested in the traditional techniques of their predecessors (with the exception of Botticelli who made only very limited use of this medium), either had to content themselves with a secondary part in the economy of the new architecture or re-use the existing surfaces in older buildings. The latter was often the case, and **Domenico Ghirlandaio** was among the painters who dedicated themselves to fresco painting, reawakening the glories of the 14C. Indeed, he was said to have wanted to cover even the city walls with frescoes! Ghirlandaio typifies, in the best possible way, the bourgeois spirit now increasingly dominant in Florentine society, setting his stories from the past against a background of contemporary Florence. He adapted perfectly the new style to the pre-exisiting Gothic spaces, and there is no discrepancy in style in the narratives painted by him and his assistants spread over the vast areas available. His works include the stories of the life of St Francis in the Sassetti chapel of Santa Trinita, and life of the Virgin and St John the Baptist in the Tornabuoni chapel of Santa Maria Novella; the decoration of the Sala dei Gigli in the Palazzo Vecchio; and a series of vividly coloured altarpieces reminiscent of Flemish painting. He was an accomplished draughtsman and a painter of supreme technical skill, and his easy and pleasing style made him a popular artist in his day.

During these years Florence increasingly became the meeting place of some of the most fundamental tendencies in Italian art. **Pietro Perugino**, the Umbrian artist who taught Raphael, preceded him in leaving some of his greatest works in Florentine churches and private collections. **Filippino Lippi** and **Piero di Cosimo**, who were also active in Florence then, anticipated to a certain extent the restless aspect of Mannerism.

In the field of architecture **Giuliano da Sangallo** built the villa at Poggio a Caiano for Lorenzo il Magnifico, and Santa Maria delle Carceri at Prato, two buildings which reiterated the fundamental teachings of Brunelleschi, though with some original developments. Within the city, new buildings sprang up to embody the wealth and ambitions of the richest families; the Gondi palace by Giuliano da Sangallo, the Guadagni palace by Cronaca, and, above all, Palazzo Strozzi, also by Cronaca. Although he did not complete it, this palace represents the most ambitious and perfect example of a palatial residence of the Renaissance. In sculpture, however, after the death of Pollaiolo and Verrocchio Sansovino lacked the capacity for innovation. It required the nascent genius of Michelangelo to show that in this field—and not only in this field!—art was to take a new direction.

But in the meantime, the genius who, more than anyone else, embodied the Renaissance ideal of the 'universal' artist, **Leonardo da Vinci,** was born near Florence. A pupil of Verrocchio, he was undoubtedly influenced by him in his early works but developed, as he matured, an entirely personal vision which, together with his writings, made him a celebrated figure not only in art but in every field of knowledge. His tireless researches and ingenious engineering, his rare pictorial works, his wanderings throughout Italy, his exile in France, and his unique style which opened new horizons in painting and sculpture (thanks to his anatomical studies), all served to make an almost mythical figure of him. Strange, then, that his genius went unremarked by Lorenzo il Magnifico, who, however, towards the end of his life was increasingly involved with the political problems then troubling Italy. Possibly, Leonardo's subtle and introverted spirit had little appeal to one of Lorenzo's temperament who was drawn instead to the sort of conceptual clarity derived from Platonism, and to the Classicism evident in the sculptural works he had collected over the years in the garden of San Marco.

The artist who embodied Lorenzo's ideals was the very young **Michelangelo Buonarroti,** a pupil of Ghirlandaio and Bertoldo. Legend has it that he came to the notice of Lorenzo when he sculpted the head of a faun in the garden of San Marco. It is certain, however, that the young genius who began his career under the wing of the Medici, represents, more than any other Florentine artist of the time, the aesthetic ideal on which the whole century's art was based; that mythicized vision of the Ancient World which represented absolute perfection, the highest embodiment of human genius. Michelangelo soon established himself as the artist who, more than any other, could offer Florence that continuity in art which summarized the possibilities of so many generations, and that universality so sought after by his predecessors. Sculptor, painter, and architect, poet and philosopher, his solitary personality was recognized for its importance, not only in Florence but throughout Italy and all of Europe. His prodigious working capacity allowed him to develop from his early Florentine works in which he reabsorbed 15C experiences, towards the creation of an artistic idiom, which, although indebted to Masaccio and Luca Signorelli, Donatello and Verrocchio, Brunelleschi and Sangallo, had the capacity of evolving a highly individual style which bridges the centuries to reach the heroic, monumental conception of the art of Imperial Rome.

The early period of this indefatigable artist, which can be defined as 'classical', culminated in his 'David'. At this time certain 15C motifs, such as the use of the tondo in both painting and sculpture, reappear (see, for instance his reliefs for the Pitti and Gaddi, and his painting for the Doni, the married couple whose portraits Raphael was painting at about the same time). Next follows a more complex phase in Michelangelo's art, to which belong works such as his 'St Matthew', and the first 'prisoners' (now in the Louvre) for the tomb of Julius II, in which there are clear signs of the disturbed state of mind of the artist, so sensitive to the difficulties that Florence was undergoing at this period. Dividing his time between Florence and Rome, Michelangelo seemed to reflect in his constantly changing projects an instability that was to become typical of his art and similarly cause him so often to leave his works unfinished.

There is no doubt that with Michelangelo came the break with 15C Humanism, with the serene, joyous style which had characterized the works of the Early Renaissance. Although he still used some of the elements which had distinguished those works, he forged a new style that seemed deliberately to disrupt that balance so carefully sought by his predecessors. An obvious example of this is the construction of the New Sacristy in San Lorenzo, a mausoleum for the Medici family. Here the graceful shapes, reminiscent of Brunelleschi, are reinforced by elements taken from Roman architecture and, above all, by the massive sculptures, conceived as an essential complement to the design. In these figures, as in those of the 'prisoners' (now in the Accademia) for the second project for the tomb of Julius II, Michelangelo eschewed the 15C forms which had occupied him up to then, in favour of dynamic, articulated forms, turning in on themselves, which were to be the model for all the 'serpentine figures' of the Mannerist sculpture of the 16C. In the staircase of the vestibule of the Laurentian Library, the same instability of form is evident, the same desire to break up the centralized perspective which had been Brunelleschi's great innovation, with alternating plays of light and points of view, which were clearly a prelude to the Baroque.

After the demise of the short-lived Florentine Republic, Michelangelo expressed his disillusionment and disapproval of the Medici by leaving Florence for good, leaving behind many of his works incomplete. Nevertheless, it was his example which determined the birth of a new style known as 'Mannerism' in Florence. This style interpreted that aspect of Michelangelo's art which seemed to break away from the classical forms that had been the concern of Florentine artists since Giotto and Arnolfo.

The High Renaissance. Despite the disturbances which troubled Florence after the death of Lorenzo il Magnifico in 1492, the city still remained the centre of some of the most important developments in Italian art between the end of the 15C and the beginning of the 16C. Apart from Michelangelo, who after 1508 was increasingly occupied with commissions from the Pope in Rome, other important artists worked in Florence and created a mature, grandiose language, complex in form and colour, which was to characterize the High Renaissance. With the arrival in the city of the young **Raphael,** who here developed his unique, pure classical style, local artists were influenced towards an evolution of form based primarily on drawing, a medium in which the Florentines excelled. **Fra Bartolomeo** and **Andrea del Sarto** were the two greatest exponents of this trend. Andrea del Sarto, whom Vasari christened 'the faultless painter', undertook important public works, including altarpieces and frescoes of masterly execution, and created a school of painting which dominated Florentine art in the first half of the 16C. His pupils included **Pontormo** and **Rosso Fiorentino,** who were important for their original interpretation of Mannerism, a style which became increasingly intellectualized and refined, very far removed from the rationalism of the Early Renaissance. In their unique forms and colours, they re-elaborated the teachings of Michelangelo who was still looked to as the supreme master, but in an even more pronounced stylized and almost abstract language.

This period of Mannerism at its most original was soon to come to an end. After the assassination of Duke Alessandro in 1537, a distant cousin, Cosimo de' Medici, took over the government of the city. He brought about rapid changes in its cultural life, as the political ideas of the new Duke prevailed in everything, including the arts. The commissioning of great public works which had characterized the regimes of the Republic and later the Medici 'Signoria' now ceased almost entirely. Even the cathedral workshops fell silent and work on the embellishment of the interior proceeded only sporadically. Artistic manifestations were now almost entirely controlled by the absolute ruler who determined their nature. The face of the city was changed by the talented work of **Giorgio Vasari** and of **Bartolomeo Ammannati,** the two architects to whom the Grand-duke entrusted most of the important works of the period. Vasari constructed the new centre of government, the Uffizi, which, with its arcades still inspired by Brunelleschi, frames the view of Palazzo Vecchio on one side and the Arno on the other. He also built (in five months) the Corridor which bears his name to connect the Uffizi with the Grand-ducal residence. Ammannati enlarged the palace, which, after its purchase from the Pitti family, became the home of the reigning families of Florence for the next three centuries. The bridge of Santa Trinita is also the work of Ammannati.

Cosimo continued the tradition of enlivening the city with statuary, but in a way which gave Florence the aspect which it still has today, of a great, open-air museum of sculpture. Piazza della Signoria was peopled with works by the most prestigious sculptors of the day: Ammannati made the fountain of Neptune, assisted by some of the most important protagonists of Mannerism in Florence, such as **Giambologna, Vincenzo de' Rossi,** and **Vincenzo Danti; Bandinelli** sculpted the 'Hercules and Cacus' which can be seen almost as a challenge to Michelangelo's 'David' nearby; **Benvenuto Cellini** made his beautiful bronze 'Perseus', poised on an exquisite marble base decorated with bronze statuettes; Giambologna sculpted the 'Rape of the Sabines', one of the finest examples of a 'serpentine figure' borrowed from Michelangelo's mature period. The equestrian monuments to Cosimo I (by Giambologna) and to Ferdinando I (by Tacca) are an attempt to recreate the climate of Imperial Rome.

Garden architecture was becoming more complicated, enriched as it was with statuary, fountains and artificial grottoes which gave ample opportunity for the full expression of the talent and refinements of Florentine architects and sculptors. Art became, increasingly, the private expression of the Duke, who dictated the fashion and imposed the tastes of his Court on the great families of Florence. Interiors became more and more sumptuous and loaded with decoration. **Bronzino** came to the fore in painting with a very personal form of classicism seen through the formal refinements of Pontormo's Mannerism. His use of gem-like and enamelled colours give his paintings an almost surreal aspect, and his portraits represent the social standing of the sitters rather than their personalities.

The reworking of all the motifs which had characterized 15C Florentine art seemed to find its conclusion in the historical events taking place in the city from the 16C onwards. Ably governed by Cosimo I and his successors, Florence became increasingly a centre of cultural elaboration rather than of original creativity as it had been for three centuries. Even Mannerism, which in its early phase had influenced the whole of European art with its sophisticated style, began to show an irreversible involution, merely repeating the talented inventions of its early protagonists. Court art reflected more and more the private nature of the artist's product, even in fresco—now chiefly used in the decoration of great houses—which had been the glory of Florentine art for three centuries. Once the echoes of Michelangelo's direct influence were spent, Florentine art was no longer capable of formulating its own original language; the city became a provincial centre reflecting pictorial trends from other, more important centres such as Rome, Bologna, and Venice. Basically, Florentine art continued to follow forms which had their roots in the past and especially in the 16C. Even in the so-called Baroque period, architecture, sculpture, and painting reflect the ideas of the great Renaissance tradition, and as late as the 19C, with the enlargement of the city during its brief period as the capital of Italy, there is the same recourse to an eclectic architecture making use of all the styles developed by the great artists of the Renaissance, except when, a little later, mock-Gothic becomes the fashion. But by this time we are dealing with a history of taste rather than the history of the art of a city that has given an unequalled contribution to European civilization.

HISTORICAL SKETCH OF FLORENCE

The plain of the Arno was first inhabited in Neolithic times when Italic tribes from the north settled here towards the end of the 10C B.C. Although some Etruscan tombs have been found on the plain towards Sesto, there is no evidence of an Etruscan city preceding Florence. The Etruscans preferred to build their stronghold on the hill of Fièsole (5C B.C. or earlier). The Roman colony of 'Florentia' was founded in 59 B.C. by Julius Caesar, and the city was built on the Arno where the crossing is narrowest. The river, navigable up to this point, had great importance in the early economic development of the city. The Roman city, which was enlarged in the Augustan era, flourished in the 2C and 3C A.D., when it probably contained over 10,000 inhabitants.

By the early 5C the city was already threatened by Ostrogoth invaders. Despite the Byzantine walls erected in 541-545, Totila was able to inflict considerable damage on the city in 552. By the end of the 6C Florence had followed the fate of the rest of central and Northern Italy and was firmly held under Lombard dominion. Charlemagne visited the city in 781 and 786 and the Carolingian circle of walls was set up in 869-896. By this time Florence was the largest county in Tuscany and had made considerable economic progress. In the 11C Florence was one of the principal centres of Christianity. The city was favoured by Matilda, Margrave of Tuscany, who saw to the building of a fourth circle of walls in 1078 as a defence against the Emperor Henry IV. Thus the Florentines, who espoused the cause of the Pope, were able to withstand a siege of Imperial troops for 10 days. In 1125 the rival town of Fièsole was finally overcome after a fierce battle.

The 'Comune' of Florence came into being in the first decades of the 12C, with a college of officials, a council of some 100 men, and a 'Parlamento' which was called regularly to approve government policy. The Commune protected the business interests of Florentine merchants who had begun to prosper through the cloth trade and money-lending. The fifth line of walls, which now included the Oltrarno, was built in 1173–75. In 1207 the consular regime was replaced, and a 'Podestà' installed who held executive power in the government. The post was traditionally reserved for a foreigner. At this time the first guilds ('Arti') were formed to protect the commercial interests of the merchant and banking community. During the course of the 13C three new bridges were built over the Arno, the Palazzo del Popolo (Bargello) was erected, and the two great mendicant Orders, the Franciscans and Dominicans, came to Florence to found Santa Croce and Santa Maria Novella.

The political life of the 13C was dominated by the long drawn-out struggle between the Guelfs and Ghibellines. This was sparked off by the feuds arising from the murder of one of the Buondelmonti by the Amidei in 1215. The Ghibelline faction, which supported the Emperor, derived its name from Weiblingen, the Castle of the Hohenstaufen, and the Guelfs, who supported the Pope, from the family name ('Welfs') of Otto IV. By the middle of the century Florentine merchants, who travelled as far afield as England and the Near East, were established in a privileged and independent position

30

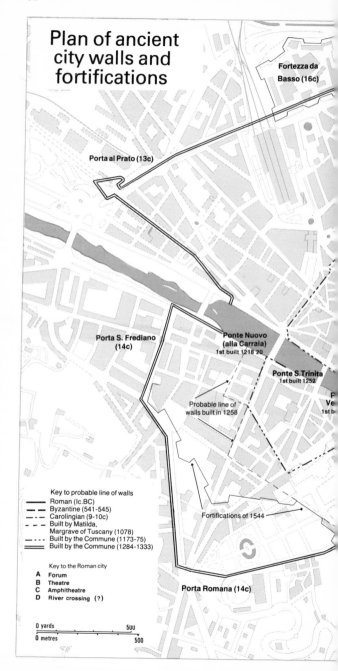

Plan of ancient city walls and fortifications

Fortezza da Basso (16c)

Porta al Prato (13c)

Porta S. Frediano (14c)

Ponte Nuovo (alla Carraia)
1st built 1218-20

Ponte S.Trinita
1st built 1252

P
Ve
1st b

Probable line of walls built in 1258

Fortifications of 1544

Porta Romana (14c)

Key to probable line of walls
— Roman (1c.BC)
– – Byzantine (541-545)
–·–· Carolingian (9-10c)
– – Built by Matilda, Margrave of Tuscany (1078)
··–··– Built by the Commune (1173-75)
═══ Built by the Commune (1284-1333)

Key to the Roman city
A   Forum
B   Theatre
C   Amphitheatre
D   River crossing (?)

0 yards   500
0 metres   500

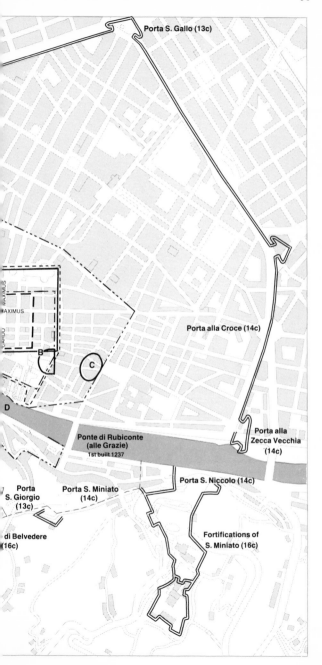

Porta S. Gallo (13c)

MAXIMUS

MAXIMUS

CARDO

B

C

D

Porta alla Croce (14c)

Ponte di Rubiconte
(alle Grazie)
1st built 1237

Porta alla
Zecca Vecchia
(14c)

Porta S. Niccolo (14c)

Porta
S. Giorgio
(13c)

Porta S. Miniato
(14c)

di Belvedere
(16c)

Fortifications of
S. Miniato (16c)

in trade and commerce. The florin, first minted in silver c. 1235, and soon after in gold, was used as the standard monetary unit in Europe. The regime of the 'Primo Popolo' (1250–60), supported by the Guelfs, now included the merchant class. The towers of the great noble families in Florence were reduced in height by order of the government. The city was victorious in battles against Pisa, Pistoia, and Siena.

In a renewed war against Siena (and the German army led by Manfred) the Florentines were defeated at Montaperti in 1260. However, the city was spared from destruction at the hand of the Ghibellines, through the generosity of their leader, Farinata degli Uberti, a member of one of the oldest noble families of Florence. Count Guido Novello took up residence in the Bargello as 'Podestà' of the Ghibelline government. After continuous struggles between the two factions, the regime of the 'Secondo Popolo' was set up in 1284 by the 'Arti Maggiori' (Greater Guilds). In 1292 Giano della Bella became 'Priore' and through his famous 'ordinamenti di giustizia' the Florentine nobility were excluded from high political office. The last circle of walls was begun in 1284, and the centre of government was moved from the Bargello to Palazzo della Signoria (begun in 1294), the residence of the 'Priori'. By the beginning of the 14C Florence was among the five largest cities in Europe with a population of c. 100,000. Her prosperity was based largely on the woollen-cloth industry which had accounted for her significant economic growth in the 13C.

The internal struggles within the Guelf party were renewed with the rival factions known as the Neri (Blacks) and Bianchi (Whites), being led respectively by the Cerchi and Donati families. Charles of Valois, called in as a peacemaker by Boniface VIII, favoured the Blacks and sent 600 Whites into exile (1302), among them Dante. In 1342 Walter de Brienne, Duke of Athens, was elected 'Signore' for life and given absolute power, but an insurrection led to his expulsion from the city a year later. The Florentine economy suffered a severe crisis in the 1340s with the bankruptcy of the two most powerful banking families, the Bardi and the Peruzzi (the Mozzi bank had already failed in 1311) partly due to the inability of Edward III of England to repay his debts during the disastrous 100 Years War, and with the Black Death, a catastrophe in which the population was reduced by more than half (and which was to recur seven times between 1350 and 1430). The rising of the Ciompi, or wool-carders, in 1378 under Michele di Lando represented a high point in labour unrest in Florence's chief industry. The demands for recognition and the right to form a guild were met with the creation of three new guilds and direct representation in government for a very brief time. However in 1382 the 'popolo grasso', united with the Guelf party, succeeded in establishing an oligarchic form of government, and the power of the guilds lost ground in the political life of the city after nearly a century of pre-eminence.

The regime of the 'popolo grasso' in which a relatively small group of wealthy middle-class merchant families succeeded in holding power, ruled Florence for 40 years. Every so often the heads of rival families were exiled in order to lessen the risk of power being concentrated in the hands of any one man. Benedetto degli Alberti, one of the wealthiest men in the city, and leader of a moderate faction in the government, was banished in 1387; he was followed into exile by the Strozzi, and finally the Medici. During these turbulent years of warfare against the Visconti in Milan, the government still conducted an ambitious foreign policy. Florence at last gained direct access to the sea when she conquered Pisa in 1406.

At the beginning of the 15C Florence was established as the intellectual and artistic centre of Europe. Cultivated Florentines adopted the civic ideal and the city proclaimed herself heir to Rome. In the city, 'a misura d'uomo', of human dimension, there was a profound involvement in political life on the part of intellectuals and artists. A new conception of art and learning symbolized the birth of the Renaissance. Chancellors of the Republic now included humanist scholars such as Coluccio Salutati, Leonardo Bruni, Poggio Bracciolini, and Carlo Marsuppini.

In 1433 Cosimo de' Medici was exiled for 10 years by Rinaldo degli Albizi since his popularity had been growing among the merchant faction in the city, in opposition to the oligarchic regime. But his return just a year later was unanimously acclaimed by the people, and he at once became the first citizen of Florence. His prudent leadership of the city lasted for 30 years. He adhered to the constitutional system of the old regime and managed to dominate the policy of the government abroad as well as at home. He usually avoided holding public office himself, but was careful to keep the support of a wide circle of friends. At the same time he increased the immense wealth of his family banking business which had been founded by his father, Giovanni di Bicci. In 1439 Cosimo succeeded in having the Council which led to the brief union of the Greek and Roman churches transferred to Florence from Ferrara. The city, now at the height of her prestige in Europe, played host to the emperor John Paleologus, the Patriarch of Constantinople, and pope Eugenius IV with their huge retinues of courtiers and scholars. Cosimo, perhaps the greatest figure in the history of Florence, symbolized the Renaissance ideal of the 'universal man'; a successful businessman and brilliant politician, he was also patron of the arts and an intellectual (he founded in Florence the first modern libraries in Europe).

On the death of Cosimo il Vecchio, 'Pater Patriae', his son Piero automatically took over his position in the government of the city. Known as 'Piero il Gottoso' because of his ill-health, his brief rule was characterized by his great interest in the arts, and a number of notable monuments of the Renaissance were commissioned by him. His son, Lorenzo, called 'Il Magnifico', was another famous Medici ruler during the Renaissance. His princely 'reign' fostered a revival of learning which led to the foundation of the Platonic Academy at Careggi, whch included among its members Lorenzo's friends Marsilio Ficino, Angelo Poliziano, and Pico della Mirandola. Lorenzo himself was a humanist scholar and poet of considerable standing. In a famous conspiracy in 1478 the Pazzi, old rivals of the Medici, with the help of pope Sixtus IV, attempted to assassinate Lorenzo. His brother Giuliano was killed, but Lorenzo escaped, with the result that his position in the government of the city was even more secure. Francesco de' Pazzi and the other conspirators were hung from a window of Palazzo Vecchio. In 1489 Lorenzo succeeded in having his son Giovanni (later

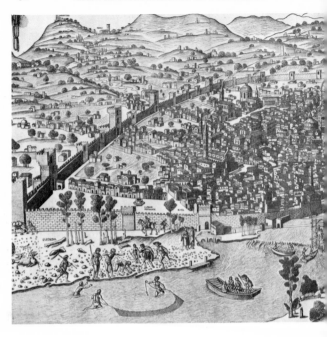

The 'Pianta della Catena', the first known view of the entire city, a woodcut of c. 1472 attributed to Francesco Rosselli. (Berlin, Kupferstich Kabinett)

pope Leo X) created a cardinal at the tender age of 13, one of his most significant political achievements. However he was a less able businessman than his grandfather and was unable to save the Medici bank from failure before he died at the age of 44 in 1492.

Lorenzo il Magnifico's eldest son Piero was driven out of the city after his surrender to Charles VIII of France at Sarzana (1494), and the people, under the inspiration of the oratory of the Dominican Girolamo Savonarola, rebelled against the Medici, and a Republican government with a Great Council was formed. Savonarola was burnt at the stake as a heretic (1498) but the Republic continued, and in 1502, under Piero Soderini, succeeded in retaking Pisa. After the defeat of Florence in battle by the Spanish army in 1512 Giuliano and Giovanni de' Medici returned to the city with the support of the Pope. However, in 1527 when Rome had been sacked by the troops of Charles V, they were again sent into exile. The new Republican government led by Niccolò Capponi lasted only until 1529 when a peace treaty between the Emperor and Pope provided for the reinstatement of the Medici in the government of Florence. The Florentines resisted their return in a last bid for independence but finally succumbed after a famous siege in which not even the new fortifications hastily erected by Michelangelo were able to withstand the

united armies of Pope and Emperor. The great-grandson of Lorenzo il
Magnifico, Alessandro, was married to Charles V's daughter
Margaret of Parma, and appointed Duke of Florence in 1530.

Alessandro's unpopular rule, in which he was opposed by those
who had supported the Republican regime, and by the patricians who
saw their power in the government diminished, came to an abrupt end
with his murder in 1537 by a cousin, Lorenzaccio. He was succeeded
by Cosimo de' Medici, son of the famous condottiere, Giovanni delle
Bande Nere. A last attempt by the Republican exiles (led by the rich
aristocrat Filippo Strozzi) to abolish the Medici principate ended in
their defeat at the battle of Montemurlo. During his long despotic
rule, Cosimo I brought the subject cities of Tuscany under Florentine
dominion, but his active and enlightened reign assured the independence of the Tuscan State from both Emperor and Pope. In
1570 Cosimo received the title of Grand-Duke of Tuscany from pope
Pius V and the Medici absolutist principate continued for another two
centuries. Cosimo I commissioned numerous works of art and architectural works to embellish the city and glorify his name, and this
patronage was continued by his successors (who also amassed
remarkable private eclectic collections). The Medici grand-dukes were
responsible for the Uffizi collection, which they augmented over the
centuries, particularly Ferdinando II and his brother Cardinal
Leopoldo. The last of the Medici, Anna Maria Lodovica, settled her
inheritance on the people of Florence.

Two years before the death of Anna Maria de' Medici in 1737, the
succession of Francesco of Lorraine, afterwards Francis I of Austria,

A view of Florence c. 1735 from a copper engraving by F. B. Werner. (Museo di Firenze com'era)

had been arranged by treaty, and Tuscany became an apendage of the Austrian Imperial house. The reign of Pietro Leopoldo, grand-duke in 1765–90, stands out for his remarkable scientific interests and the agricultural reforms he introduced to Tuscany (it was at this time that many of the handsome 'case coloniche' were built in the Tuscan countryside). In 1799 the French expelled the Austrians, and, after an ephemeral appearance as the Kingdom of Etruria (1801–02), under the Infante Louis of Bourbon, the grand duchy was conferred in 1809 upon Elisa Bonaparte Baciocchi. The Bourbon restoration (1814) brought back the Lorrainers, whose rule, interrupted by the revolution of 1848, ended in 1859. In March 1860, Tuscany became part of united Italy and from 1861 to 1875 Florence was the capital of the Italian kingdom.

Despite the efforts to prevent it by Gerhard Wolf, the wartime German consul (later made a freeman by grateful Florentines), all the bridges except the Ponte Vecchio were blown up by the Germans in the Second World War; the city was occupied by the Allies in August 1944, after considerable desultory fighting.

In 1966 the Arno overflowed its banks and severely damaged buildings and works of art. This was treated as an international disaster, and most historical buildings and works of art have now been restored. Reconstruction was necessary, too, of hundreds of houses and artisans' workshops, and it is not clear if sufficient precautions have since been taken to prevent another flood.

A. MACADAM

Among the many famous names that Florence has contributed to Italian culture the following stand out: the poets *Brunetto Latini* (1212–94), master of Dante, *Guido Cavalcanti* (c. 1225–1300), and the great *Dante Alighieri* (1265–1321), whose 'Divina Commedia' established Tuscan as the literary vernacular of Italy. *Petrarch* (1304–74), son of a Florentine father, was a famous poet and the first great humanist. *Boccaccio* was born in Paris in 1312 but lived and died (1375) in Florence. The father of Italian prose, he described Florentine life in his 'Decameron', a brilliant secular work. Other Florentines include: the historians and statesmen *Niccolò Machiavelli* (1469–1527) and *Francesco Guicciardini* (1482–1540); the writers *Giovanni Rucellai* (1403–81), *Benvenuto Cellini* (1500–71), whose memoirs rival his goldsmith's work, *Giorgio Vasari* (born in Arezzo; 1511–74), art historian and author of the 'Lives of the Artists' as well as a painter and architect, and *Bernardo Davanzati* (1529–1606). The explorer *Amerigo Vespucci* (1451–1512) gave his name to America. *Galileo Galilei* (1564–1642) was born in Pisa but lived and died in Florence, and was succeeded by his pupil *Vincenzio Viviani* (1622–1703). Among the multitude of great Florentine artists *Leon Battista Alberti* (1404–72), *Michelangelo Buonarroti* (1475–1564) and *Leonardo da Vinci* (1452–1519) stand out not only for their artistic achievements but also for their writings and 'universal' talents.

Music. The change of style between Iacopo Peri's musical drama 'Dafne', performed in Palazzo Corsi in 1597, and his 'Euridice' composed in 1600 to honour the marriage in Florence of Maria de' Medici to Henri IV of France, is generally held to mark the beginning of opera. The pianoforte was invented in Florence in 1711 by Bart. Cristofori (1655–1731). The composers Jean-Baptiste Lully (1632–87) and Luigi Cherubini (1760–1842) were natives of Florence.

Anglo-American Associations. Florence was one of the principal goals of the 'Grand Tour' and throughout the 18C and 19C was visited by almost every traveller of note. Prince Charles Edward Stuart lived in the city in 1774–85, where he was known to Florentines as the Count of Albany. His wife, the Countess of Albany, entertained Chateaubriand, Shelley, Byron and Von Platen in her 'salon'. Florence Nightingale (1820–1910) was born in Florence. John Sargent, R.A. (1856–1925), son of a Boston physician, was likewise a native. Landor had several addresses in the city in 1821–28 before settling at Fièsole; while at the Villa Castiglione (3 km beyond Porta S. Niccolò) he met Lamartine, entertained Hazlitt, and was drawn by Bewick. He died in Via della Chiesa behind the Carmine. Leigh Hunt lived for a time in Via Magliabechi in 1823–25. Robert and Elizabeth Barrett Browning rented a flat in the Casa Guidi after their marriage in 1846 and lived in Florence until Elizabeth's death in 1861. Mark Twain finished 'Pudd'n-head Wilson' in 1892 at Settignano, and later lived at Quarto in a villa earlier occupied by Jerome Bonaparte. Princess Mary of Teck, later Queen Mary, lived here with her family 'in exile' in 1884–85, mainly at the Villa I Cedri near Bagno a Ripoli.

The Medici Family

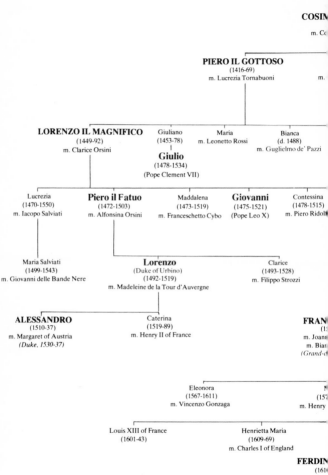

COSIM

m. Co

PIERO IL GOTTOSO
(1416-69)
m. Lucrezia Tornabuoni   m.

LORENZO IL MAGNIFICO   Giuliano   Maria   Bianca
(1449-92)   (1453-78)   m. Leonetto Rossi   (d. 1488)
m. Clarice Orsini   m. Guglielmo de' Pazzi
                         Giulio
                        (1478-1534)
                      (Pope Clement VII)

Lucrezia   **Piero il Fatuo**   Maddalena   **Giovanni**   Contessina
(1470-1550)   (1472-1503)   (1473-1519)   (1475-1521)   (1478-1515)
m. Iacopo Salviati   m. Alfonsina Orsini   m. Franceschetto Cybo   (Pope Leo X)   m. Piero Ridolf

Maria Salviati   **Lorenzo**   Clarice
(1499-1543)   (Duke of Urbino)   (1493-1528)
m. Giovanni delle Bande Nere   (1492-1519)   m. Filippo Strozzi
                     m. Madeleine de la Tour d'Auvergne

ALESSANDRO   Caterina   **FRAN**
(1510-37)   (1519-89)   (1:
m. Margaret of Austria   m. Henry II of France   m. Joan
(Duke, 1530-37)   m. Biar
                                                (Grand-c

                    Eleonora   I
                   (1567-1611)   (157
                 m. Vincenzo Gonzaga   m. Henry

Louis XIII of France   Henrietta Maria
(1601-43)   (1609-69)
                         m. Charles I of England

                                        FERDIN
                                        (1610
                                    m. Vittoria
                                    (Grand-de

                                        COSI
                                        (164
                                    m. Marguerite-L
                                    (Grand-duk

GIAN GASTONE
(1671-1737)
m. Anna Maria of Saxe-Lauenburg
(Grand-duke, 1723-37)

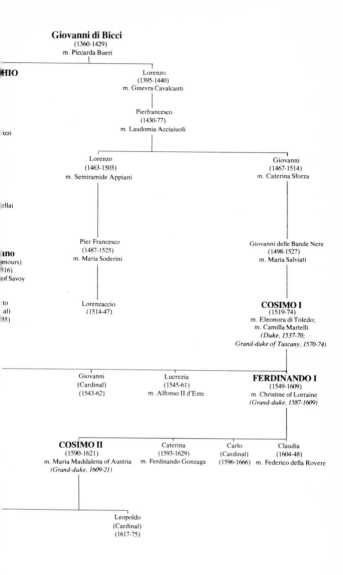

Giovanni di Bicci
(1360-1429)
m. Piccarda Bueri

...HIO

Lorenzo
(1395-1440)
m. Ginevra Cavalcanti

Pierfrancesco
(1430-77)
m. Laudomia Acciaiuoli

...izzi

Lorenzo
(1463-1503)
m. Semiramide Appiani

Giovanni
(1467-1514)
m. Caterina Sforza

...ellai

Pier Francesco
(1487-1525)
m. Maria Soderini

Giovanni delle Bande Nere
(1498-1527)
m. Maria Salviati

...ano
mours)
516)
of Savoy

to
al)
5)

Lorenzaccio
(1514-47)

COSIMO I
(1519-74)
m. Eleonora di Toledo;
m. Camilla Martelli
*(Duke, 1537-70;
Grand-duke of Tuscany, 1570-74)*

Giovanni
(Cardinal)
(1543-62)

Lucrezia
(1545-61)
m. Alfonso II d'Este

FERDINANDO I
(1549-1609)
m. Christine of Lorraine
(Grand-duke, 1587-1609)

COSIMO II
(1590-1621)
m. Maria Maddalena of Austria
(Grand-duke, 1609-21)

Caterina
(1593-1629)
m. Ferdinando Gonzaga

Carlo
(Cardinal)
(1596-1666)

Claudia
(1604-48)
m. Federico della Rovere

Leopoldo
(Cardinal)
(1617-75)

Anna Maria
(1667-1743)
m. William, Elector Palatine

GLOSSARY

AEDICULE. Small opening framed by two columns and a pediment, originally used in classical architecture

ARCHITRAVE. Lowest part of an entablature, horizontal frame above a door

ARTE (pl. *Arti*). Guild or Corporation (see p 76)

ATTIC. Topmost story of a classical building, hiding the spring of the roof

BADIA, *Abbazia,* Abbey

BALDACCHINO. Canopy supported by columns, usually over an altar

BASILICA. Originally a Roman building used for public administration; in Christian architecture an aisled church with a clerestory and apse and no transepts

BORGO. A suburb; a street leading away from the centre of a town

BOTTEGA. The studio of an artist; the pupils who worked under his direction

BOZZETTO. Sketch, often used to describe a small model for a piece of sculpture

CALDARIUM. Room for hot or vapour baths in a Roman bath

CAMPANILE. Bell-tower, often detached from the building to which it belongs

CANTORIA. Singing-gallery in a church

CAPOMAESTRO. Director of Works

CARTOON. From *cartone,* meaning large sheet of paper. A full-size preparatory drawing for a painting or fresco

CASSONE. A decorated chest, usually a dower chest

CAVEA. The part of a theatre or amphitheatre occupied by the rows of seats

CENACOLO. Scene of the Last Supper (often in the refectory of a convent)

CHIAROSCURO. Distribution of light and shade, apart from colour, in a painting

CIBORIUM. Casket or tabernacle containing the Host

CIPPOLINO. Onion marble; greyish marble with streaks of white or green

CIPPUS (pl. *Cippae*). Sepulchral monument in the form of an altar

CONTRAPPOSTO. A pose in which the body is twisted. First used in classical statuary, it is characteristic of Michelangelo's sculpture and works by the Mannerist school

CORBEL. A projecting block, usually of stone

CRENELLATIONS. Battlements

CUPOLA. Dome

DIPTYCH. Painting or ivory tablet in two sections

DUOMO. Cathedral

EXEDRA. Semi-circular recess

EX-VOTO. Tablet or small painting expressing gratitude to a Saint

FRESCO (in Italian, *affresco*). Painting executed on wet plaster. On the wall beneath is sketched the *sinopia,* and the *cartone* (see above) is transferred onto the fresh plaster (*intonaco*) before the fresco is begun either by pricking the outline with small holes over which a powder is dusted, or by means of a stylus which leaves an incised line on the wet plaster. In recent years many frescoes have been detached from the walls on which they were executed

FRIGIDARIUM. Room for cold baths in a Roman bath

GRAFFITI. Design on a wall made with an iron tool on a prepared surface, the design showing in white. Also used loosely to describe scratched designs or words on walls

GREEK-CROSS. Cross with the arms of equal length

GRISAILLE. Painting in various tones of grey

GROTESQUE. Painted or stucco decoration in the style of the ancient Romans (found during the Renaissance in Nero's Golden House in Rome, then underground, hence the name, from 'grotto'). The delicate ornamental decoration usually includes patterns of flowers, sphynxes, birds, human figures, etc., against a light ground

INTARSIA. Inlay of wood, marble, or metal

INTRADOS. Underside or soffit of an arch

LATIN-CROSS. Cross with a long vertical arm

LAVABO. Hand-basin usually outside a refectory or sacristy

LOGGIA. Covered gallery

LUNETTE. Semi-circular space in a vault or ceiling, or above a door or window, often decorated with a painting or relief

LUNGARNO (pl. *Lungarni*). The roads which follow the banks of the Arno in Florence

MACIGNO. Quartz, used as a building material in Florence

MAESTÀ. Madonna and Child enthroned in majesty

MEDALLION. Large medal; loosely, a circular ornament

MONOCHROME. Painting or drawing in one colour only

MONOLITH. Single stone (usually a column)

NIELLO. Black substance used in an engraved design

OCULUS. Round window

OPERA (DEL DUOMO). The office in charge of the fabric of a building (i.e. the Cathedral)

OPUS TESSELLATUM. Mosaic formed entirely of square tesserae

PALA. Large altarpiece

PALAZZO. Palace; any dignified and important building

PAX. Sacred object used by a priest for the blessing of peace and offered for the kiss of the faithful, usually circular, engraved, enamelled, or painted in a rich gold or silver frame

PENDENTIVE. Concave spandrel beneath a dome

PIETÀ. Group of the Virgin mourning the dead Christ

PIETRE DURE. Hard or semi-precious stones, often used in the form of mosaics to decorate cabinets, table-tops, etc.

PIETRA FORTE. Fine-grained limey sandstone used as a building material in Florence, and often for the rustication of palace façades

PIETRA SERENA. Fine-grained dark sandstone, easy to carve. Although generally not sufficiently resistent for the exterior of buildings, it was used to decorate many Renaissance interiors in Florence

PLUTEUS (pl. *plutei*). Marble panel, usually decorated; a series of them used to form a parapet to precede the altar of a church

POLYPTYCH. Painting or panel in more than three sections

PORTONE. Main entrance (large enough for carriages) to a Palazzo or Villa

PREDELLA. Small painting or panel, usually in sections, attached below a large altarpiece, illustrating the story of a Saint, the Life of the Virgin, etc.

PRESEPIO. Literally, crib or manger. A group of statuary of which the central subject is the Infant Jesus in the manger

PULVIN. Cushion stone between the capital and the impost block

PUTTO (pl. *putti*). Figure sculpted or painted, usually nude, of a child

QUATREFOIL. Four-lobed design

ROOD-SCREEN. A screen below the Rood or Crucifix dividing the nave from the chancel of a church

SCHIACCIATO. Term used to describe very low relief in sculpture, where there is an emphasis on the delicate line rather than the depth of the panel

SINOPIA. Large sketch for a fresco made on the rough wall in a red earth pigment called sinopia (because it originally came from Sinope on the Black Sea). By detaching a fresco it is now possible to see the sinopia beneath and detach it also

SPANDREL. Surface between two arches in an arcade or the triangular space on either side of an arch

SPORTI. Overhang, or projecting upper story of a building, characteristic of medieval houses in Florence

STELE (AI). Upright stone bearing a monumental inscription

STEMMA. Coat-of-arms or heraldic device

STOUP. Vessel for Holy Water, usually near the W. door of a church

TEPIDARIUM. Room for warm baths in a Roman bath

TERM. Pedestal or terminal figure tapering towards the base in the form of a human figure, etc.

TERRAVERDE. Green earth pigment, sometimes used in frescoes

TESSERA. Small cube of marble, glass, etc. used in mosaic work

THERMAE. Roman Baths

THOLOS. A circular building

TONDO. Round painting or relief

TRANSENNA. Open grille or screen, usually of marble, in an early Christian church

TRIPTYCH. Painting or tablet in three sections

TROMPE L'OEIL. Literally, a deception of the eye. Used to describe illusionist decoration, painted architectural perspectives, etc.

VILLA. Country house with its garden

The terms QUATTROCENTO, CINQUECENTO (abbreviated in Italy, '400, '500 etc.) refer not to the 14C and 15C, but to the 'fourteen-hundreds' and 'fifteen-hundreds', i.e. the 15C and 16C, etc.

EXPLANATIONS

Type. Smaller type is used for historical and preliminary paragraphs, and (generally speaking) for descriptions of greater detail or minor importance.

Asterisks indicate points of special interest or excellence.

Heights are given in metres.

Abbreviations. In addition to generally accepted and self-explanatory abbreviations, the following occur in the guide:

Abp.	=	Archbishop
A.C.I.	=	Automobile Club Italiano
Adm.	=	Admission
Bp.	=	Bishop
C	=	century
c.	=	circa
C.I.T.	=	Compagnia Italiana Turismo
d	=	died
E.N.I.T.	=	Ente Nazionale Italiano per il Turismo
E.P.T.	=	Ente Provinciale per il Turismo
exc.	=	except
fest.	=	*festa*, or festival (i.e. holiday)
fl.	=	floruit (flourished)
incl.	=	including
km	=	kilometre(s)
l.	=	lira (pl. lire); left
m	=	metre(s)
min.	=	minutes
Pal.	=	Palazzo
Pl.	=	atlas plan
P.za	=	Piazza
r.	=	right
R.	=	room(s)
Rte	=	Route
SS.	=	Saints (in English); Santissimo, -a (in Italian)
T.C.I.	=	Touring Club Italiano
tel.	=	telephone

For abbreviations of Italian Christian names, see p 215; for glossary see p 40.

References in the text (Pl. 1; 1) are to the 16-page Atlas at the back of the book, the first figure referring to the page, the second to the square. Ground plan references are given as a bracketed single figure or letter.

PRACTICAL INFORMATION

I APPROACHES TO FLORENCE

The Approaches from the North are described in the 'Blue Guide Northern Italy'.

Information Bureaux. General information may be obtained in London from the *Italian State Tourist Office* (*E.N.I.T., Ente Nazionale Italiano per il Turismo*), 201 Regent St., W1R 8AY, who distribute free an invaluable 'Traveller's Handbook' (revised c. every year), a list of hotels and pensions in Florence, etc. The information office of the *Azienda Autonoma di Turismo* in Florence is at No. 15 Via Tornabuoni (Pl. 16; 3). The headquarters of the *Ente Provinciale per il Turismo* (E.P.T.), with an information office, is at No. 16 Via Manzoni (Pl. 7; 8). A Hotel Booking Office (I.T.A.) is open daily (10–20.30) at the railway station of Santa Maria Novella, and (in summer) at the 'Firenze Nord' exit of the 'autostrada del Sole'.

Travel Agents (most of whom belong to the Association of British Travel Agents) sell travel tickets and book accommodation, and also organize inclusive tours and charter trips to Florence. These include: *C.I.T.,* 10 Charles II St., SW1 (agents for the Italian State Railways), *Thomas Cook & Son,* 45 Berkeley St, W1, and other branches, *American Express,* 9 Suffolk Place, SW1, etc.

Passports or **Visitors Cards** are necessary for all British travellers entering Italy and must bear the photograph of the holder. American travellers must carry passports. British passports valid for ten years are issued at the Passport Office, Clive House, Petty France, London SW1, or may be obtained for an addtional fee through any tourist agent. No visa is required for British or American travellers to Italy.

Currency Regulations. Exchange controls have been suspended by the British Government since 1979. There are now no restrictions on the amount of sterling travellers may take out of Great Britain.

There are frequent variations in the amount of Italian notes which may be taken in or out of Italy. Since there are normally strict limitations, the latest regulations should be checked before departure. At present, only 100,000 in lira notes can be taken in or out of Italy.

Money. In Italy the monetary unit is the Italian lira (pl. lire). Notes are issued for 500, 1000, 2000, 5000, 10,000, 20,000, 50,000 and 100,000 lire. Coins are of 5, 10, 20, 50, 100 and 200 lire. The rate of exchange in 1981 is approximately 2,200 lire to the £ and 1,100 lire to the U.S. dollar.

Police Registration is required within three days of entering Italy. For travellers staying at a hotel the management will attend to the formality. The permit lasts three months, but can be extended on application.

Airport

The nearest international airport is at **Pisa**, 85 km W. of Florence. Daily direct flights from London are run by *British Airways* and *Alitalia*. All services have a monthly excursion fare. Considerable reductions are normally available on scheduled return flights by booking one month in advance. There is a special reduced fare for full-time students and young people. Charter companies also run services to Pisa from London at modest prices, and 'package' holidays, including charter flight and hotel accommodation, are often an advantageous arrangement.—Alitalia also operate a direct flight three times a week between Pisa and Frankfurt and Paris, and direct internal services to Rome, Milan, Verona, Palermo, Cagliari, Alghero, and Olbia.

There is a frequent COACH SERVICE in under 2 hours (in connection with flights) run by *Lazzi* (Pl. 5; 6) and *S.I.T.A.* (Pl. 5; 5), both with terminals close to Florence railway station.—The TRAIN SERVICE (less convenient) from Pisa takes c. 1½ hrs. There is a town bus (No. 5) or taxi from Pisa airport to the railway station. Work has begun on extending the railway line from Pisa to the airport and there are long-term plans to improve the rail connection with Florence.

The airport of **Peretola**, a few kilometres N. of Florence, is at present used only by light aircraft, but there are plans to re-open it for regular domestic flights to Rome and Milan.

Railway Station

Stazione di Santa Maria Novella (Pl. 5; 6), very close to the centre of the city. It has a restaurant, an 'albergo diurno' (day hotel; comp. p 46), a left-luggage office (always open), a bank, and a tourist information office with hotel booking facilities (see above). The station is well served by buses (comp. p 52), and there is a taxi rank on the E. side of the building.—A few fast trains to the S. depart from **Campo di Marte** station (beyond Pl. 7; 4), which may become the terminus for the new railway line (the 'direttissima') for express trains between Rome and Florence.

European Bus Service. A bus service now operates in two days between London and Rome viâ Florence. Information in London from the National Travel Office at Victoria Coach Station, and in Florence at the S.I.T.A. office.

Car Parks

The road approaches to Florence are described in the 'Blue Guide Northern Italy'. British drivers in Italy will find the speed of the traffic much faster than in Britain. Most of the centre of Florence (see Plan 16) has been closed to private cars (from 8-20), except for access (which includes the hotels in this area). As a result, the main traffic arteries, such as the Viali and the Lungarni, are extremely congested, but public transport functions well. Florence has various car parks and garages, and the city is best explored on foot (using public transport when necessary). Large car parks near the centre of the city include the Fortezza da Basso and P.za del Carmine. An hourly tariff is charged at P.za Pitti, P.za Stazione, and P.za Libertà, and numerous smaller car parks (all with a parking attendant). Waiting in other areas is severely restricted, and on roads where parking is permitted it is usually very difficult to find a vacant place. Cars have to be removed once a week when the street is cleaned overnight (otherwise they are towed away to 19 Via Circondaria, Rifredi).

II   HOTELS AND PENSIONS

Florence has numerous hotels and pensions all over the city. These are all listed with charges in the annual (free) publication of the E.P.T. and Azienda Autonoma del Turismo of Florence: *'Firenze: tariffe alberghiere'* (available from their offices). *It is essential to book well in advance* in summer and at Easter; to confirm the booking a deposit should be sent. Information about hotels in Florence may be obtained in London from the E.N.I.T. office, and on arrival at the tourist office at the railway station, or at the offices of the E.P.T. or Azienda Autonoma.

Every hotel or pension has its fixed charges agreed with the Provincial Tourist Board. In all hotels the service charges are included in the rates. V.A.T. is added at a rate of 9 per cent (14 per cent in De Luxe hotels). However the total charge is exhibited on the back of the door of the hotel room. Breakfast is a separate charge and not included in the price of the room. Pensions are entitled to impose half-board terms (room, breakfast, and one meal); visitors requiring accommodation only should use hotels. Hotels are now obliged by law (for tax purposes) to issue an official receipt to customers, who should not leave the premises without this document ('ricevuta fiscale').

There are five official categories of hotels and three official categories of pensions in Italy: de luxe, first, second, third, and fourth class. In the following list, the category of the hotel or pension has been given. Hotels with more than 100 rooms (100 R) have been indicated. Florence has over 250 hotels and pensions and it has been thought necessary to give only a small selection; omission does not imply any derogatory judgement.

Florence also contains about 100 modest (and usually very small) 'locande' (inns) which are recommended to visitors satisfied with the simplest accommodation since they are considerably cheaper than hotels or pensions. Many of them (often called 'Soggiorno') are situated near the Station, in Via Faenza, Via Nazionale, Via Fiume, etc.

ACCOMMODATION IN FLORENCE AND ENVIRONS

DE LUXE HOTELS. **Excelsior Italie** (*1*; Pl. 5; 7), 3 P.za Ognissanti (210 R); **Savoy** (*2*; Pl. 16; 4), 7 P.za della Repubblica (100 R); **Villa Medici** (*3*; Pl. 4; 6), 42 Via il Prato (100 R), with swimming pool.

FIRST CLASS HOTELS. **Astoria Etap** (*4*; Pl. 16; 1), 9 Via del Giglio (100 R); **Croce di Malta** (*5*; Pl. 5; 7), 7 Via della Scala (100 R); **De la ville e Florence** (*6*; Pl. 16; 3), 1 Piazza Antinori; **Grand Hotel Baglioni** (*7*; Pl. 5; 6), 6 Piazza Unità Italiana (200 R); **Grand Hotel Majestic** (*8*; Pl. 5; 6), 1 Via del Melarancio (100 R); **Grand Hotel Minerva** (*9*; Pl. 5; 8), 16 Piazza Santa Maria Novella (110 R); **Kraft** (*10*; Pl. 4; 6), 2 Via Solferino; **Londra** (*11*; Pl. 5; 5), 16 Via Iacopo da Diacceto (100 R); **Lungarno** (*12*; Pl. 9; 2), 14 Borgo San Jacopo; **Plaza e Lucchesi** (*13*; Pl. 11; 3), 38 Lungarno della Zecca Vecchia (100 R).

SECOND CLASS HOTELS. **Ambasciatori** (*14*; Pl. 5; 5), 3 Via Alamanni (100 R); **Balestri** (*15*; Pl. 10; 4), 7 Piazza Mentana; **Berchielli** (*16*; Pl. 16; 5), 14 Lungarno Acciaiuoli; **Bonciani** (*17*; Pl. 5; 8), 17 Via Panzani; **Cavour** (*18*; Pl. 16; 4), 3 Via Proconsolo (100 R); **Continental** (*19*; Pl. 16; 5), 2 Lungarno Acciaiuoli; **Della Signoria** (*20*; Pl. 16; 5), 1 Via delle Terme; **Helvetia e Bristol** (*21*; Pl. 16; 3), 2 Via de' Pescioni; **Jennings Riccioli** (*22*; Pl. 10; 4), 2 Lungarno delle Grazie; **Milano Terminus** (*23*; Pl. 16; 3), 10 Via Cerretani.

THIRD CLASS HOTELS. **Aprile** (*24*; Pl. 5; 8), 6 Via della Scala; **Columbia-Parlamento** (*25*; Pl. 16; 6), 29 P.za San Firenze (100 R); **Delle Nazioni** (*26*; Pl. 5; 5), 15 Via Alamanni (130 R); **Melegnano** (*27*; Pl. 5; 7), 1 Via Maso Finiguerra; **Porta Rossa** (*28*; Pl. 16; 5), 19 Via Porta Rossa; **Rapallo** (*29*; Pl. 6; 3), 7 Via Santa Caterina d'Alessandria; **Royal** (*30*; Pl. 6; 4) 52 Via delle Ruote; **Universo** (*31*; Pl. 5; 8), 20 Piazza Santa Maria Novella.

FOURTH CLASS HOTELS. **Morandi** (*32*; Pl. 6; 7), 3 P.za SS Annunziata; **Santa Croce** (*33*; Pl. 10; 2), 3 Via Bentaccordi.

FIRST CLASS PENSION. **Beacci Tornabuoni** (*34*; Pl. 16; 5), 3 Via Tornabuoni.—SECOND CLASS PENSIONS. **Annalena** (*35*; Pl. 9; 3) 34 Via Romana; **Ariele** (*36*; Pl. 4; 6), 11 Via Magenta; **Bretagna** (*37*; Pl. 9; 2), 6 Lungarno Corsini; **Cen-

trale (*38*; Pl. 5; 8), 3 Via dei Conti; **Consigli** (*39*; Pl. 4; 8), 50 Lungarno Vespucci
Hermitage (*40*; Pl. 16; 5), 1 Vicolo Marzio; **La Cupola** (*41*; Pl. 16; 2), 1 Piazza
Duomo; **La Residenza** (*42*; Pl. 16; 3), 8 Via Tornabuoni; **Medici** (*43*; Pl. 16; 4), €
Via dei Medici; **Monna Lisa** (*44*; Pl. 7; 7), 27 Borgo Pinti; **Pendini** (*45*; Pl. 16; 3)
2 Via Strozzi; **Quisisana Ponte Vecchio** (*46*; Pl. 16; 5), 4 Lungarno Archibusieri
Rigatti (*47*; Pl. 16; 8), 2 Lungarno Diaz.—THIRD CLASS PENSIONS. **Alessandra**
(*48*; Pl. 16; 5), 17 Borgo SS Apostoli; **Antica** (*49*; Pl. 6; 8), 27 Via Pandolfini
Bandini (*50*; Pl. 9; 3), 9 Piazza Santo Spirito; **Bartolini** (*51*; Pl. 9; 1), 1 Lungarno
Guicciardini; **Bellettini** (*52*; Pl. 5; 8), 7 Via dei Conti; **Boboli** (*53*; Pl. 9; 3), 63 Via
Romana; **La Scaletta** (*54*; Pl. 9; 4), 13 Via Guicciardini; **Le Due Fontane** (*55*; Pl
6; 6), 14 Piazza SS Annunziata; **Norma** (*56*; Pl. 16; 5), 8 Borgo SS Apostoli.

HOTELS OUTSIDE THE CENTRE OF FLORENCE with gardens (and convenient for
visitors with cars). *On the S. bank of the Arno:* **Grand Hotel Villa Cora** (*57*; Pl
9; 7), 18 Viale Machiavelli (with swimming pool), **1**; **David** (*58*; Pl. 11; 6), 1 Viale
Michelangelo, and **Villa Belvedere** (S. of Pl. 8; 8), 3 Via Castelli (with swimming
pool), both **2**.—*On the N. outskirts of the city:* **Villa Park San Domenico** (N. of
Pl. 7; 2), 53 Via della Piazzola, and **Villa Le Rondini** (N. of Pl. 7; 1), 224 Via
Bolognese (with swimming pool), both **2**. **Villa Meridiana** (near the Villa di
Careggi), 30 Via Cosimo il Vecchio.
    HOTELS AND PENSIONS IN FIÈSOLE (within easy reach of Florence, and conve-
nient for visitors with cars). All of them have gardens and are in good positions
(especially pleasant in summer). Hotels: *Villa San Michele,* **1**; *Aurora,* **2**; *Villa
Bonelli,* **3**. *Bencistà* and *Pensionato Villa San Girolamo,* both Second-Class Pensions.

Youth Hostel and **Students' Hostels.** *Italian Youth Hostels Association*
(Associazione Italiana Alberghi per la Gioventù), Palazzo del Civiltà del Lavoro
E.U.R., 00144 Rome. In Florence, the headquarters of the A.I.G. is at 2 Viale A
Righi (Tel. 600315). A membership card of the A.I.G. or the International
Youth Hostel Federation is required for access to Italian Youth Hostels. A
'Guide for Foreign Students' giving detailed information on students' hostels
students' facilities, etc., can be obtained from the Italian Ministry of Education
Viale Guidoni.—The main camping site in Florence 'PARCO COMUNALE DI
'Villa Camerata'), 2 Viale A. Righi, is in a good position in a park at the bottom
of the hill of San Domenico (500 beds). Bus No. 17C from the Station and
Duomo.—Other hostels, some run by religious organizations, are shown in the
annual hotel list supplied by the E.P.T. These include the *Centro Ospitalità Santa Monica,* 6 Via S. Monica, and the *Casa di Sette Santi,* 11 Viale dei Mille.

Camping. Guides to sites and general information are published by the
Federazione Italiana del Campeggio; available from the *Centro Nazionale
Campeggiatori Stranieri,* Casella Postale 649, 50100 Florence (at Calenzano near
the motorway exit). The *Campeggio Club Firenze e Toscana* has offices at 143
Viale Guidoni.—The main camping site in Florence 'PARCO COMUNALE DI
CAMPEGGIO' is at 80 Viale Michelangelo (Pl. 11; 5), which takes 500 tents (closed
Nov-March). Another site, 'VILLA CAMERATA' is at 2 Viale Righi in the park of
the Youth Hostel at the bottom of the hill of San Domenico.—In Fièsole
'CAMPING PANORAMICO' in Via Peramondo, Borgunto (see Atlas p 13) is another
site in a good position. There are also camping sites in the environs, at *Im-
pruneta,* in the *Mugello,* etc.

ALBERGO DIURNO, 'day hotel', at the Railway Station with bathrooms, hairdressers, cleaning services, and other amenities. The Albergo Diurno at 28 Via
dei Pepi has bathrooms and hairdressers, and the Diurno Centrale, 5 Via de
Pecori has bathrooms.

III   RESTAURANTS AND CAFÉS

Restaurants (*Ristoranti, Trattorie*) of all kinds and categories
abound in Florence. The least pretentious restaurant often provides
the best value. Prices on the menu generally do not include a cover
charge (*coperto,* shown separately on the menu) which is added to the
bill. The service charge is now almost always automatically added at

the end of the bill. Tipping is therefore not strictly necessary, but a few hundred lire are appreciated. The menu displayed outside the restaurant indicates the kind of charges the customer should expect. However, many simpler establishments do not offer a menu, and here, although the choice is usually limited the standard of cuisine is often very high. Lunch is normally around 1 o'clock and is the main meal of the day, while dinner is around 8 or 9 o'clock.

Restaurants are now obliged by law (for tax purposes) to issue an official receipt to customers, who should not leave the premises without this document ('ricevuta fiscale'). Many restaurants in Florence close down for part of the month of August (or July).

In the list below a selection of restaurants has been given grouped according to price range.

1. Luxury-class, well-known restaurants, mostly with international cuisine. Not cheap. **Harry's Bar**, 22 Lungarno Vespucci (Pl. 5; 7); **Enoteca Nazionale**, 87 Via Ghibellina (Pl. 10; 2); **Doney**, 46 Via Tornabuoni (Pl. 16; 3); **Lo Zodiaco da Sante**, 2 Via delle Casine (specializing in fish; Pl. 11; 1); **Buca Lapi**, 1 Via del Trebbio (Pl. 16; 3); **Celestino**, 4 Piazza Santa Felicita (Pl. 16; 7); **Oliviero**, 51 Via delle Terme (Pl. 16; 5); **Cammillo**, 57 Borgo San Jacopo (Pl. 16; 7); **Sabatini**, 41 Via Panzani (Pl. 16; 1); **Il Coccodrillo**, 5 Via della Scala (Pl. 5; 7); **Lorenzaccio**, 42 Via il Prato (Pl. 4; 6).

2. First-class Restaurants. **Mamma Gina**, 36 Borgo San Jacopo (Pl. 16; 7); **La Loggia**, 1 Piazzale Michelangelo (Pl. 11; 5); **Coco Lezzone**, 26 Via del Parioncino (Pl. 9; 2); **Buca dell' Orafo**, 28 Volta de Gerolami (Pl. 16; 5); **Campidoglio**, 8 Via del Campidoglio (Pl. 16; 3); **Natalino**, 17 Borgo degli Albizi (Pl. 10; 2); **Trattoria Sostanza ('Il Troia')**, 29 Via Porcellana (Pl. 5; 7); **Antico Fattore**, 1 Via Lambertesca (Pl. 16; 6); **Fagioli**, 47 Corso dei Tintori (Pl. 10; 4).

3. Well-known restaurants and trattorie. **Latini**, 6 Via Palchetti (Pl. 5; 8); **Otello**, 28 Via Orti Oricellari (Pl. 5; 5); **13 Gobbi**, 9 Via Porcellana (Pl. 5; 7); **Cavallino**, P.za Signoria (6 Via delle Farine), with tables outside in summer (Pl. 16; 6); **Paoli**, 12 Via dei Tavolini (Pl. 16; 4); **Le Rampe**, 1 Viale Giuseppe Poggi (Pl. 11; 3); **Ottorino**, 6 Via S. Elisabetta (Pl. 16; 4); **Calandrino**, Via Guicciardini (Pl. 16; 7); **La Posta**, 20 Via Lamberti (Pl. 16; 5); **Al Pescatore**, 54 Via Ponte alle Mosse (specializing in fish; Pl. 4; 4); **Il Pennello**, 4 Via Dante Alighieri (Pl. 16; 4); **Cantinetta Antinori**, Palazzo Antinori, Piazza Antinori (Pl. 16; 3); **Buca Mario**, 16 P.za Ottaviani (Pl. 5; 8); **Cafaggi**, 33 Via Guelfa (Pl. 6; 5); **Il Fagiano**, 57 Via dei Neri (Pl. 16; 6); **Giannino**, 35 Borgo San Lorenzo (also self-service; Pl. 16; 2); **La Nandina**, 64 Borgo SS Apostoli (Pl. 16; 5); **Coq d'Or**, Lungarno del Tempio (Pl. 11; 4); **Antico Crespino**, 15 Largo Fermi (just beyond Pl. 9; 7); **Alfredo**, Viale Don Minzoni (Pl. 7; 1); **Il Bronzino**, Via delle Ruote (Pl. 6; 4); **Le Cantine**, 4 Via Pucci (Pl. 16; 2); **Osteria No. 1**, 1 Borgo Ognissanti (Pl. 5; 7); **L'Orologio**, P.za Ferrucci (Pl. 11; 4); **Il Profeta**, Via della Scala (Pl. 5; 7); **Angiolino**, 138 Via Guelfa (Pl. 6; 5); **Il Cibrèo**, 118 Via dei Macci (Pl. 11; 1).

4. Simple Trattorie of good value. **Tito**, 112 Via San Gallo (Pl. 6; 4); **Nella**, 19 Via delle Terme (Pl. 16; 5); **Angiolino**, 36 Via S. Spirito (Pl. 9; 1); **Da Benvenuto**, 16 Via Mosca (Pl. 16; 6); **Le Sorelle**, 30 Via San Niccolò (Pl. 11; 3); **Trattoria del Carmine**, 18 Piazza del Carmine (with tables outside in summer; Pl. 9; 1); **Antico Barile**, 40 Via dei Cerchi (Pl. 16; 6); **Pinocchio**, 28 Via della Scala (Pl. 5; 5).

5. 'Vinai' (who sell wine by the glass and good simple food) and cheap eating places (usually crowded and often less comfortable than normal trattorie). **Mario**, 2 Via Rosina (lunch only; Pl. 6; 5); **Palle d'Oro**, 42 Via S. Antonino (Pl. 6; 5); **Nello**, 21 Borgo Tegolaio (Pl. 9; 3); **da Niccolino**, Volta dei Mercanti, Mercato Nuovo (with tables outside in summer, otherwise no seating accommodation; Pl. 16; 5); **Vinaio in Via Alfani** (No. 70; Pl. 6; 6); **Sabatino**, 39 Borgo S. Frediano (Pl. 9; 1); **Quattro Leoni**, Via Toscanella (1 Via Vellutini; Pl. 16; 7); **Sergio Gozzi**, Piazza San Lorenzo (Pl. 16; 1); **La Casalinga**, 41 Via Michelozzi; **Trattoria & Rosticceria Le Cure** (Fratelli Leonessi), Piazza delle Cure (Pl. 7; 2); **Mossacce**, 55 Via Proconsolo (Pl. 16; 4); **Spaghetteria Tarrocchi**, Via de' Renai (Pl. 10; 4).—The following are small wine bars ('Vinai') which serve snacks (but have no seating accommodation): **Fratellini**, 38 Via dei Cimatori (Pl. 16; 6); **Donatello**, Via de' Neri (corner of Via dei Benci; Pl. 10; 2); **Cantina Ristori**, 6

Volta di San Piero (Pl. 10; 2); **Vinaio**, 25 Piazza Castellani (Pl. 16; 6); **Vinaio** inside the Mercato Centrale (open until 13; Pl. 16; 1).

There are a number of self-service restaurants in the centre of the city (**Giannino**, Borgo San Lorenzo; **Leonardo**, 5 Via de' Pecori, etc.). Pizzas and other good hot snacks are served in a *Pizzeria, Rosticceria,* and *Tavola Calda*. Some of these (in Via Cavour, Via dell'Ariento, the Corso, etc.) have no seating accommodation and sell food to take away or eat on the spot. Tripe, a Florentine speciality, is sold in sandwiches from barrows on the street (at the Arco di San Piero, Via dell'Ariento, P.za San Frediano, P.za del Porcellino, P.za de' Frescobaldi, etc.). *Friggitorie* are small shops where fried snacks (sweet and savoury) are sold (in Via dell'Albero, Via S. Antonino, Volta di S. Piero, Borgo Pinti, Via dei Neri, Via Serragli, etc.). Sandwiches ('panini') can be ordered from some *Pizzicherie* and *Alimentari* (grocery shops), and *Fornai* (bakeries) often sell individual pizze, cakes, etc.

STUDENTS' CANTEENS ('MENSE') are open at 25 Via San Gallo, Via dei Servi (No. 66), 2 Piazza SS. Annunziata (Casa di S. Francesco), 51 Viale Morgagni, and the Mensa del Dopolavoro Ferroviario, 6 Via Alamanni.

Chinese Restaurants (not cheap) include: **Fior di Loto**, 35 Via dei Servi; **Pino e Bambù**, 12 Lungarno Corsini; **Il Pavone**, 18 Via Cavour; **Il Mandarino**, 17 Via Condotta; **Peking**, 21 Via del Melarancio.
Kosher Restaurant: 3 Via Farini.

Restaurants in the environs of Florence. Rte 23. **Fièsole:** *Trattoria 'Il Lordo',* 13 P.za Mino da Fièsole; *La Romagnola,* Via Gramsci. **Olmo:** Torre di Buiano, *Casa del Prosciutto, Da Mario.* **Maiano:** *Le Cave di Maiano* (with tables outside). **Via Bolognese:** *Alessi* (necessary to book in advance).—Rte 24. **Settignano** (Ponte a Mensola): *Osvaldo.*—Rte 25. **Cercina** (N. of Careggi): *Trianon, I Ricchi* (both with tables outside).—Rte 26. **Galluzzo:** *Da Bibe,* 1 Via delle Bagnese, Ponte all'Asse. **Sant'Andrea in Percussina:** *Scopeti.*—Rte 28. *Villa di Artimino.*—Rte 20. **Arcetri:** *Omero,* 11 Via Pian dei Giullari (with tables outside).

Cafés (*Bar*) which are open from early morning to late at night, serve numerous varieties of excellent refreshments which are usually eaten standing up. The cashier should be paid first, and the receipt given to the barman in order to get served. It has become customary to leave a small tip of 50 lire for the barman. If the customer sits at a table the charge is considerably higher (about double) and he will be given waiter service (and should not pay first). Black coffee (*caffè* or *espresso*) can be ordered diluted (*lungo* or *alto*), with a dash of milk (*macchiato*), with a liquor (*corretto*), or with hot milk (*cappuccino* or *caffè-latte*). In summer cold coffee (*caffè freddo*) and cold coffee and milk (*caffè-latte freddo*) are served.

The best known cafés in the city which often serve good snacks and all of which have tables (some outside) include: *Rivoire,* P.za Signoria; *Le Giubbe Rosse, Gilli,* both in P.za della Repubblica; *Giacosa, Doney,* both in Via Tornabuoni; *San Firenze,* P.za S. Firenze.—Cafès without tables, but well-known for their cakes, pastries, and confectionary, include: *Robiglio,* Via dei Servi and Via Tosinghi; *Giurovich,* Viale Don Minzoni; *Procacci,* Via Tornabuoni (famous for truffle sandwiches); *Gambrinus,* Via Brunelleschi; *Sieni,* Via dell'Ariento; *Maioli,* Via Giucciardini; and *Scudieri,* Via Cerretani.
Among the best ICE-CREAM SHOPS in Florence are: *Vivoli,* 7 Via Isola delle Stinche (near Santa Croce); *Badiani,* 20 Viale dei Mille; *Cavini,* 22 P.za delle Cure; and *Perchè no?,* 19 Via dei Tavolini.

Food and Wine

As elsewhere in Italy traditional local dishes have become more difficult to find, and Florentine cookery is now similar to that to be found all over the country. The chief speciality of Italian cookery is the *pasta* served in various forms with different sauces and sprinkled with cheese. A well-known Tuscan soup is *minestrone* made with a variety of vegetables. *Ribollita* or *Zuppa di pane* is a thick soup of bread, white beans, cabbage, herbs, etc. In summer, *panzanella* is a tasty dish, made of bread, tomatoes, capers, basil, etc. As a main course, *bistecca alla fiorentina* is famous, a large T-bone steak which can be grilled in one piece and served to 2 or 3 people. Tripe (*trippa*) is also a traditional Florentine dish, usually cooked in tomato sauce and parmesan cheese. *Baccalà* (salt cod) is an acquired taste; it is boiled or fried *'alla Livornese'* with tomato sauce. Another unusual fish dish is *'nzimino,* cuttlefish cooked with vegtables. White beans (*fagioli*) are a favourite Florentine speciality, cooked with sage, in a tomato sauce *fagioli all'uccelletto*).

Wines. The cheapest wine is always the 'house wine' (*vino della casa*), which varies a great deal, but is normally a drinkable 'vin ordinaire'. In Tuscany the red table wine is usually of better quality than the white. The most famous Tuscan wine is *Chianti* (the name is protected by law, and only those wines from a relatively small district which lies between Florence and Siena are entitled to the name 'Chianti Classico'). *Chianti Classico 'Gallo Nero'* (distinguished by a black cock on the bottle) is usually considered the best, but *Chianti 'Putto'* and *Chianti 'Grappolo'* are also very good. Other wines in Tuscany such as *Vino nobile di Montepulciano, Vernaccia* (white, from San Gimignano), *Aleatico* (a dessert wine from Elba), and *Brunello di Montalcino* (not cheap) are particularly good.

The MENU which follows includes many dishes that are likely to be available in Florentine restaurants:

Antipasti, Hors d'oeuvre

Prosciutto crudo o cotto, Ham, raw or cooked
Prosciutto e melone, Ham (usually raw) and melon
Salame, Salami
Finocchiona, Salami cured with fennel
Crostini, Fresh liver paste served on bread
Salame con funghi e carciofini sott'olio, Salami with mushrooms and
    artichokes in oil
Tonno, Tunny fish
Salsicce, Dry sausage
Frittata, Omelette
Verdura cruda, Raw vegetables
Carciofi o finocchio in pinzimonio, Raw artichokes or fennel with a dressing
Antipasto misto, Mixed cold hors d'oeuvre
Antipasto di mare, Seafood hors d'oeuvre
Panzanella, A summer salad made with bread, tomatoes, capers, basil,
    etc.
Insalata Russa, Russian salad

Minestre e Pasta, Soups and Pasta

Minestra, zuppa, Thick soup
Brodo, Clear soup
Stracciatella, Broth with beaten egg
Minestrone alla toscana, Tuscan vegetable soup
Taglierini (or *Tagliolini*) *in brodo,* Thin pasta in broth
Ribollita, Thick soup made with bread, white beans, cabbage, etc.
Spaghetti al sugo or *al ragù,* Spaghetti with a meat sauce
Spaghetti al pomodoro, Spaghetti with a tomato sauce
Penne all'Arrabbiata (or *Strascicata*), Short pasta with a rich spicy sauce
Tagliatelle, Flat spaghetti-like pasta, almost always made with egg
Lasagne, Layers of pasta with meat filling and cheese and tomato sauce
Cannelloni, Rolled pasta 'pancakes' with meat filling and cheese and tomato
    sauce
Ravioli, Pasta filled with spinach and ricotta cheese (or with minced veal)

Tortellini, Small coils of pasta, filled with a rich stuffing served either in broth or with a sauce

Fettuccine, Ribbon noodles

Spaghetti alla carbonara, Spaghetti with bacon, beaten egg, and black pepper sauce

Spaghetti alla matriciana, Spaghetti with salt pork and tomato sauce

Spaghetti alle vongole, Spaghetti with clams

Agnolotti, Ravioli filled with meat

Pappardelle alla lepre, Pasta with hare sauce

Cappelletti, Form of ravioli often served in broth

Gnocchi, A heavy pasta made from potato, flour, and eggs

Risotto, Rice dish

Risotto di mare, . . . with fish

Polenta, Yellow maize flour, usually served with a meat or tomato sauce

Pappa di pomodoro, a thick tomato 'soup' with bread, seasoned with basil, etc.

Pesce, Fish

Zuppa di pesce, Various types of fish usually in a sauce (or soup)

Fritto misto di mare, Various types of fried fish

Pesce arrosto, Pesce alla griglia, Roast, grilled fish

Pescespada, Sword-fish

Aragosta, Lobster (an expensive delicacy)

Calamari, Squid

Baccalà, Salt cod (*alla Livornese*) fried and cooked in a tomato sauce

Sarde, Sardines

Coda di Rospo, Angler fish

Dentice, Dentex

Orata, Bream

Triglie, Red mullet

Sgombro, Mackerel

Cefalo, Grey mullet

Anguilla, Eel

Sogliola, Sole

Tonno, Tunny fish

Trota, Trout

Cozze, Mussels

Gamberi, Prawns

Polipi, Octopus

Seppie, Cuttlefish

Acciughe, Anchovies

Pietanze, Entrèes

Bistecca alla fiorentina, T-bone steak, (usually cooked over charcoal)

Vitello, Veal

Manzo, Beef

Agnello, Lamb

Maiale (arrosto), Pork (roast)

Pollo (bollito), Chicken (boiled)

Petto di Pollo, Chicken breasts

Pollo alla cacciatora, Chicken with herbs, and (usually) tomato and pimento sauce

Costoletta alla Bolognese, Veal cutlet with ham, covered with melted cheese

Cotolette Milanese, Veal cutlets, fried in breadcrumbs

Saltimbocca, Rolled veal with ham

Bocconcini, Rolled veal with cheese

Scaloppine al marsala, Veal escalope cooked in wine

Ossobuco, Stewed shin of veal

Coda alla vaccinara, Oxtail cooked with herbs and wine

Stufato, Stewed meat served in pieces in a sauce

Polpette, Meat balls (often served in a sauce)

Involtini, Thin rolled slices of meat in a sauce

Spezzatino, Veal stew, usually with pimento, tomato, onion, peas, and wine

Cotechino e Zampone, Pig's trotter stuffed with pork and sausages

Stracotto, Beef cooked in a sauce, or in red wine

Trippa, Tripe

Fegato, Calf's liver

Fegatini alla salvia, Chicken livers cooked with sage
Tacchino arrosto, Roast turkey
Cervello, Brains
Rognoncini trifolati, Sliced kidneys in a sauce
Animelle, Sweetbreads
Bollito, Stew of various boiled meats
Arista, Pork chop
Rosticciana, Grilled spare ribs
Coniglio, Rabbit
Lepre, Hare
Cinghiale, Wild boar
Piccione, Pigeon

Contorni, Vegetables

Insalata verde, Green salad
Insalata mista, Mixed salad
Pomodori, Tomatoes
Funghi, Mushrooms
Spinaci, Spinach
Broccoletti, Tender broccoli
Piselli, Peas
Fagiolini, Beans (French)
Fagioli (all'uccelletto), White beans (in a tomato sauce)
Carciofi, Artichokes
Asparagi, Asparagus
Zucchini, Courgettes
Melanzane, Aubergine
Melanzane alla parmigiana, Aubergine in cheese sauce
Peperoni, Pimentoes
Peperonata, Stewed pimentoes, often wth aubergine, onion, tomato, potato, etc.
Finocchi, Fennel
Patatine fritte, Fried potatoes

Dolci, Sweets

Torta, Tart
Monte Bianco, Mont Blanc (with chestnut flavouring)
Saint Honorè, Rich meringue cake
Gelato, Ice cream
Cassata, Ice cream cake
Zuppa Inglese, Trifle
Torta della nonna, Cream flan with almonds
Castagnaccio, Chestnut cake with pine nuts and sultanas
Crostata, Fruit flan
Bongo-Bongo, Chocolate cream éclairs

Frutta, Fruit

Macedonia di frutta, Fruit salad
Fragole (con panna), Strawberries (and cream)
Fragole (al limone), . . . with lemon
Fragole (al vino), . . . with wine
Fragoline di bosco, Wild strawberries
Mele, Apples
Pere, Pears
Arance, Oranges
Ciliege, Cherries
Pesche, Peaches
Albicocchi, Apricots
Uva, Grapes
Fichi, Figs
Melone, Melon
Popone, Water melon

IV TRANSPORT

Buses provide an excellent and fast means of transport in Florence where most of the centre of the city has been closed to private traffic. The servce is run by *A.T.A.F.* (Information office, 57 red P.za del Duomo, Tel. 212301). Tickets are obtained from tobacconists and most bars, or A.T.A.F. offices (P.za del Duomo, the Station, etc.). In 1981 a single ticket costs 300 lire; a book of 12 costs 3300 lire. Tickets must be stamped at an automatic machine on board (they remain valid for 70 minutes on any bus). Because of one-way streets, return journeys do not always follow the same route as the outward journey. In 1981 an experimental tourist bus service ('T') was introduced in the summer with a ticket valid for one day. A selection of the more important routes is given below.

Bus Services

15 Fortezza da Basso (car park) — P.za Indipendenza — P.za S. Marco — Via Proconsolo — Ponte alle Grazie — Piazza Pitti — P.za Santo Spirito — P.za del Carmine — Viale Petrarca — Porta Romana (the return journey from Porta Romana follows Via Maggio) — Ponte Santa Trinita — Via Porta Rossa — Via Calzaioli — Via dei Servi — P.za Indipendenza — Fortezza da Basso.

1 P.za Stazione — Via Panzani — P.za Duomo — Via Cavour — P.za Libertà, etc.

11 Via Ricasoli — P.za Duomo — P.za della Repubblica — Ponte alla Carraia — Via Serragli — Porta Romana

17C Cascine — P.za Stazione — P.za Duomo — Via Lamarmora — Viale dei Mille — Salviatino (Youth Hostel)

13 red (circular) P.za Stazione — Ponte alla Vittoria — Viale Rafaello Sanzio — Porta Romana — Viale Michelangelo — Piazzale Michelangelo — Ponte alle Grazie –- Via dei Benci — Via Bufalini — P.za Duomo — P.za Stazione

13 black (circular)—as above, but in the opposite direction

38 Porta Romana — Piazzale Galileo — Pian dei Giullari

7 P.za Stazione — P.za Duomo — San Marco — Domenico — Fièsole

10 P.za Stazione — P.za Duomo — P.za San Marco — Ponte a Mensola — Settignano

28 P.za Stazione — Via Reginaldo Giuliani — Il Sodo —Castello — Sesto Fiorentino

14C Via Ghibellina — P.za Duomo — P.za Stazione — Viale Morgagni — Careggi

25 P.za Stazione — P.za S. Marco — P.za Libertà — Via Bolognese

12 Via Pacinotti — P.za delle Cure — Via Faentina — Ponte alla Badia — Le Caldine — La Querciola

37 P.za S.M. Novella — Ponte alla Carraia — Porta Romana — Galluzzo — Certosa — Tavarnuzze

31 P.za Stazione — P.za Duomo — Lungarno della Zecca Vecchia — Ponte da Verrazzano — Badia a Ripoli — Ponte a Ema — Grassina

32 P.za Stazione — P.za Duomo — Lung. della Zecca Vecchia — Ponte da Verrazzano — Badia a Ripoli — Ponte a Ema — Antella

Country Buses

From Florence a wide network of bus services in Tuscany is operated by *Lazzi,* 4 P.za Stazione (Tel. 215155), *S.I.T.A.,* 15 Via S. Caterina da Siena (Tel. 284661), *CO.PI.T.,* 22 P.za S.M. Novella (Tel. 215451), *C.A.P,* 13 Via Nazionale (Tel. 214637), and *C.A.T.,* 15 Via Nazionale (Tel. 283400). Details of the main services of interest to the visitor are given in the text of the environs (pp 199-214).

Taxis

Taxis (yellow or white in colour) are provided with taximeters. They are hired from ranks; there are no cruising taxis. There are ranks at the Station, P.za S.M. Novella, P.za S. Marco, P.za S. Trinita, P.za del Duomo, P.za della Signoria, P.za della Repubblica, Porta Romana, etc. For Radio taxis dial 4390 or 4798. A supplement for night service, and for luggage is charged. Modest tipping is expected.—HORSE CABS are used exclusively by tourists. The fare must be established before starting the journey. In summer, they can usually be hired in P.za del Duomo and P.za della Signoria.

Car Hire

The principal car-hire firms have offices at Pisa airport as well as in Florence. *Avis,* 128 Borgo Ognissanti; *Hertz,* 33 Via Maso Finiguerra; *Maggiore,* 11 Via Maso Finiguerra, etc.

Sight-seeing Tours of Florence and environs

Tours of Florence, Pisa, and Siena and San Gimignano are organized by *C.I.T.* (57 Via Cerretani), starting at 51 P.za Stazione (corner of P.za della Unità Italiana), and other travel agents in Florence (see below).—*Agriturist* (10 Via del Proconsolo) organize day trips by coach in the Tuscan countryside (on Sundays, April-Oct), and visits to the gardens of Florentine villas (on Mon, Tues, Thurs, & Sat afternoons from April-June). These depart from Piazza Strozzi and can be booked at any tourist agency in Florence. The tours are announced in the local newspapers.

V   USEFUL ADDRESSES

Information Bureaux and Tourist Agents. *E.P.T.* (*Ente Provinciale per il Turismo*), 16 Via Manzoni (Tel. 678841). *Azienda Autonoma di Turismo,* 15 Via Tornabuoni (Tel. 217459).—Among the numerous tourist agents in Florence are: *C.I.T.,* 57 Via Cerretani and 51 P.za Stazione; *Wagons-Lits Turismo,* 14 P.za Strozzi; *Eyre & Humbert,* 4 P.za Rucellai; *Universalturismo,* 7 Via Speziali.—*Centro Turistico Universitario* (*C.T.U.*), 12 Via San Gallo (also for student travel facilities); *Centro Turistico Studentesco e Giovanile,* 53 Via delle Terme.

Head Post Office, 53 Via Pietrapiana (Pl. 11; 1), and Via Pellicceria (Pl. 16; 3), with the telephone exchange (always open) and 'Poste Restante' (open 8.15–19.30). Post Offices are open from 8.15–14 incl. Sat.

Public Offices. For all emergencies, Tel. 113. *Questura* (Central Police Station), 2 Via Zara; *Carabinieri* (flying squad), 48 Borgo Ognissanti (Tel. 212121). *Lost Property Office,* 22 Lungarno delle Grazie (Tel. 367943).—HOSPITALS: *Santa Maria Nuova,* 1 P.za S.M. Nuova; *Careggi,* Viale Morgagni; *S. Giovanni di Dio,* 20 Borgo Ognissanti (to be transferred to Torregalli, Scandicci), etc. For emergency medical service at night and on holidays, Tel. 477891. Ambulance service of the Misericordia, Tel. 212222. Some chemists (*farmacie*) remain open all night and on holidays (listed in the local newspapers, or Tel. 192).

RAILWAY STATION, Information office, Tel. 278785.—*Automobile Club d'Italia* (*A.C.I.*), 36 Viale Amendola. Breakdown service, Tel. 116 (in Florence, Tel. 666500).—*Pisa Airport,* Tel. (050) 28088;

Peretola Airport, Tel. 370123. *Alitalia,* 10 Lungarno Acciaioli; *British Airways,* 36 Via Vigna Nuova.

Banks (usually open Mon-Fri 8.20–13.20; Sat & holidays closed). *Banca Commerciale Italiana,* 8 Via Strozzi; *Cassa di Risparmio di Firenze,* 4 Via Bufalini; *Banca d'Italia,* 37 Via Oriuolo; *Banca d'America e d'Italia,* 16 Via Strozzi; *Banca C. Steinhauslin & Co.,* 4 Via dei Sassetti; *American Express Bank,* 2 Via della Vigna Nuova.

Consulates. *British Consulate,* 2 Lungarno Corsini (Pl. 9; 2); *American Consulate,* 38 Lungarno Vespucci (Pl. 4; 8).

Learned Institutions and Cultural Societies. *British Institute,* 2 Via Tornabuoni (Italian language courses), with a library and reading room at 9B Lungarno Guicciardini. *Institut Français,* 2 Piazza Ognissanti; *German Institute of Art History,* 44 Via Giuseppe Giusti (with excellent art history consulting library open to graduate students); *Dutch Institute,* 5 Viale Torricelli; *Harvard Center for Renaissance Studies,* Villa I Tatti, Ponte a Mensola, Settignano (with a fine arts consulting library open to graduate students). *Centro Linguistico Italiano 'Dante Alighieri',* 12 Via de' Bardi (Italian language courses); *Centro di Cultura per Stranieri* (courses in Italian language, history of art, etc.) attached to the University of Florence, Villa Fabbricotti; *Centro di incontro per Stranieri,* Palazzo Strozzi; *Istituto Nazionale di Studi sul Rinascimento,* Palazzo Strozzi; *Società Dantesca Italiana,* 1 Via Arte della Lana; *Accademia della Crusca,* Villa Medicea di Castello; *Amici dei Musei,* 10 Via del Proconsolo, *Italia Nostra,* 9 Viale Gramsci.

Libraries. *Biblioteca Nazionale Centrale,* 1 Piazza Cavalleggeri; *Archivio di Stato,* Palazzo degli Uffizi (to be moved to a new building under construction in P.za Beccaria); *Gabinetto Scientifico Letterario G.B. Vieusseux,* Palazzo Strozzi; *Biblioteca Medicea Laurenziana,* 9 P.za S. Lorenzo; *Biblioteca Riccardiana & Moreniana,* 10 Via Ginori; *Biblioteca Marucelliana,* 43 Via Cavour; *Biblioteche delle Facoltà Universitarie Fiorentine,* 31 Via degli Alfani; *Biblioteca Comunale,* 21 Via S. Egidio.—*Istituto Geografico Militare,* 14 Viale Strozzi (a cartography library, where excellent maps of Italy may be obtained).

VI   CHURCHES

The opening times of churches vary a great deal but the majority are open from 7 to 12. In the afternoons many remain closed until 15, 16 or even 17 and close again at about 18; some do not reopen at all in the afternoon. A few churches open for services only. The opening times of the major churches in Florence have been given in the text. The sacristan will usually show closed chapels, crypts, etc., and a small tip should be given. Many pictures and frescoes are difficult to see without lights which are often coin operated (100 lire). A torch and a pair of binoculars are especially useful to study fresco cycles, etc. Some churches now ask that sightseers do not enter during a service, but normally visitors may do so, provided they are silent and do not approach the altar in use. Churches in Florence are very often not orientated. In the text the terms N. and S. refer to the liturgical N. (left) and S. (right), taking the high altar as at the E. end.

Roman Catholic Services. On Sun and, in the principal churches, often on weekdays, Mass is celebrated up to 12 o'clock and from 18 until 19 in the evening. Confessions are heard in English on Sunday at the Duomo, S. Lorenzo, S. Marco, S. Trinita, S. Croce, Orsanmichele, and S. Miniato al Monte.—CHURCH FESTIVALS. On Saints' days mass and vespers with music are celebrated in the churches dedicated to the saints concerned. On the feast of the patron Saint of Florence, San Giovanni (24 June), a local holiday, special services are held. On Easter Day the *Scoppio del Carro* is held in and outside the Duomo (see below).

Non-Catholic churches. *Anglican,* St Mark's, 16 Via Maggio; *American Episcopalian,* St James's, 13 Via B. Rucellai; *Lutheran,* 11 Lungarno Torrigiani; *Waldensian,* Via Micheli; *Greek Orthodox,* 76 Viale Mattioli; *Russian Orthodox,* 8 Via Leone X.—*Jewish Synagogue,* 4 Via Farini.

VII   AMUSEMENTS

Concerts, drama performances, exhibitions, and conferences are organized throughout the year and advertised in the local press, on wall posters, and in 'Florence Today', issued every two months and available (free) from the Azienda Autonoma del Turismo, hotels, etc. In recent years new theatres have been opened and there has been a notable increase in the cultural activitity of the city.

Theatres. *La Pergola* (Pl. 6; 8), 12 Via della Pergola (drama season); *Niccolini,* Via Ricasoli; *Affratellamento,* 73 Via G. Orsini; *Oriuolo,* 31 Via dell'Oriuolo; *Rondò di Bacco,* P.za Pitti; *Sangallo,* 45 Via Sangallo (English theatre); *Teatro Tenda,* Lungarno Aldo Moro.—The *Teatro Comunale Metastasio* in Prato has a renowned theatre season Oct-April (tickets also available in Florence at No. 7 P.za Ottaviani), and a music festival Oct-Dec.

Music. *Teatro Comunale* (Pl. 4; 6), 16 Corso Italia, symphony concerts and opera. Here is held the MAGGIO MUSICALE, an annual music festival (May-July). Some of the concerts are held at the Pergola theatre and the courtyard of Palazzo Pitti (tickets from the Teatro Comunale and Universalturismo, 7 Via degli Speziale).—Excellent chamber music concerts given by famous musicians from all over the world are organized by the *'Amici della Musica'* in Jan-April and Oct-Dec at the Pergola Theatre. The *'Musicus Concentus'* hold chamber music concerts in S.M. del Carmine (Salone Vanni) and the Auditorium of Palazzo dei Congressi, 2 Viale Strozzi. Occasional concerts are also held at the Villa di Poggio Imperiale and the Certosa di Galluzzo, and in churches (San Lorenzo, Santa Croce, etc.).—The ESTATE FIESOLANA is an annual festival of music, drama, and films held from the end of June to the end of Aug. Performances in the Teatro Romano in Fièsole, at the Badia Fiesolana, Santa Croce, the courtyard of Pal. Pitti, etc.

EXHIBITIONS are held in Forte di Belvedere, Pal. Strozzi, Orsanmichele, Pal. Medici-Riccardi, Pal. Pitti (Sala Bianca), Pal. Vecchio (Sala d'Armi), Pal. di Parte Guelfa, the Accademia di Belle Arti (P.za S. Marco), etc.—The material owned by the Biblioteca Laurenziana and the Gabinetto Disegni e Stampe degli Uffizi is mounted in regular exhibitions of great interest.

Popular annual festivals and exhibitions. *Scoppio del Carro,* on Easter Day, an annual traditional religious festival held in and outside the Duomo at mid-day. A 'dove' is sent from the high altar through the cathedral to ignite a bonfire of fireworks on a 'carro' led by white oxen outside the W. door.—*Festa del Grillo,* on Ascension Day, a large fair in the Cascine where crickets are sold.—On 24 June, St John's Day, the patron saint of Florence, a local holiday is celebrated with fireworks at Piazzale Michelangelo. A 'football' game in 16C costume (*'Calcio in costume'*) is held three times during St John's week in the Boboli gardens, P.za Signoria, or P.za S. Croce. The teams represent the four 'quartiere' of the city (San Giovanni, Santa Croce, S.M. Novella, and S. Spirito) and the game is played with few rules and considerable violence.—On 25 March, the festival of the Annunziata, a fair is held in Piazza Santissima Annunziata.

An Antiques Fair (the *Mostra Mercato Internazionale dell' Antiquariato*) is held biennially (next in 1983) in the autumn in Palazzo Strozzi. Numerous annual exhibitions are held at the FORTEZZA DA BASSO, notably *'Pitti-Donna',* an international fashion show, and the *'Mostra dell'Artigianato',* an exhibition of artisans' products from all over the world.—In May, in a garden just below Piazzale Michelangelo, an *Iris festival* is held.

Sport. SWIMMING-POOLS: *Amici del Nuoto,* 38 Via del Romito; *Tropos,* 20 Via Orcagna.—OPEN-AIR: *Le Pavoniere,* Viale degli Olmi (Cascine); *Costoli,* Viale Paoli (Stadio); *Bellariva,* 8 Lungarno Colombo.—TENNIS: Viale Michelangelo, Il Poggetto (Via Michele Mercati), the Cascine, etc.—GOLF COURSE (18 holes) at Ugolino, 12 km S.E. of Florence on the Strada Chiantigiana, beyond Grassina.

VIII   MUSEUMS, COLLECTIONS, AND MONUMENTS

Below will be found a table giving the hours of admission to the various museums, galleries, and monuments in Florence in force in 1981. *Opening times vary and often change without warning;* those given below should therefore be accepted with reserve. All State museums, etc. are closed on the main public holidays: 1 Jan, Easter Day, 25 April, 1 May, 1st Sun in June, 15 Aug, and Christmas Day. On other holidays (see below) they open only in the morning (9–13). Almost all State-owned museums and galleries have a standard time-table for the whole year, namely weekdays 9–14, Sun & fest. 9–13, Monday closed. In Florence, an exception has been made for the Galleria degli Uffizi and the Cappelle Medicee which both stay open from 9–19 on weekdays (Sun 9–13). A current list of opening times is usually available at the Azienda Autonoma di Turismo in Via Tornabuoni.

In 1980 the admission charges to State galleries and museums were greatly increased (they had remained unchanged since 1958). At the same time, museum cards for tourists, and other facilities for free admission (such as membership of Italia Nostra, T.C.I., etc.) were abolished. An exception was made for Italian citizens under the age of 20 or over the age of 60 who are still entitled to free admission (and all children under the age of 12 accompanied by a teacher). However, there remain four days a month when entrance is free: 1st and 3rd Sat and 2nd and last Sun of the month. The new charges for the State museums (marked 'S' in the Museum table) in Florence are as follows: Uffizi, Lire 1250; Palazzo Pitti (Galleria Palatina, Museo degli Argen-

ti, and Appartamenti Monumentali), Lire 1000; Palazzo Pitti
(Galleria d'Arte Moderna, Collezione Contini-Bonacossi), Lire 1000;
Galleria dell'Accademia, Bargello, Museo di S. Marco, Pal. Davan-
zati, Cappelle Medícee, and the Museo Archeologico, all Lire 750.
The Museums owned by the Comune of Florence (marked 'C' in the
Museum table) charge between Lire 250-500 entrance fee (free on
Sun); a ticket (valid 1 week) which gives adm to all these museums
may be purchased at a reduced price.

HOURS OF ADMISSION TO THE MUSEUMS, COLLECTIONS, AND MONUMENTS OF FLORENCE

Name	Open (see note a)	Page
Bargello, see Museo Nazionale		
Biblioteca Mediceo Laurenziana	9–17; closed Sun	130
Bóboli Gardens	(S) Daily 9 to sunset	109
Campanile of the Duomo	Daily 8.30–12, 14.30–17.30	70
Cappelle Medicee	(S) 9–19; fest. 9–13; closed Mon	131
Cappella dei Pazzi	9–12.30, 15–17 (18.30 in summer); closed Wed	159
Cappella di San Sepolcro	10–13, 15–17; fest. 10–13; closed Mon	142
Casa Buonarroti	9–13 closed Tues	160
Casa di Dante	9–12.30, 15.30–18; fest. 9.30–12.30; closed Wed	193
Cenacolo di Foligno	(S) ring for adm (sometimes granted on request) see note b	132
Cenacolo di Ognissanti	(S) ring for adm (9–12, 15.30–17.30)	139
Cenacolo di Sant'Apollonia	(S) ring for adm (sometimes granted on request) see note b	126
Cenacolo di San Salvi	(S) temporarily closed for restoration (see note b)	198
Cenacolo di Santo Spirito	(C) 9–13; closed Mon	174
Certosa di Galluzzo	9–12, 15 or 16–18 or 19 (winter 14.30–17) temporarily closed, but normally open	211
Chiostri Monumentali di S.M. Novella	(C) 9–14; fest. 9–13; closed Fri	137
Chiostro dello Scalzo	(S) temporarily closed for restoration	125
Collezione Alberto della Ragione	(C) 9–14. fest. 9–13; closed Tues	80
Collezione Contini-Bonacossi see Palazzo Pitti		
Corridoio Vasariano	adm by previous appointment at the Uffizi	
Cupola of the Duomo	Daily 8.30–12, 14.30–17.30	67
Fiesole Roman Theatre, Archaeological Excavations and Museum	9.30–12.30, 14–17; closed Mon	203
Fondazione Salvatore Romano	(C) 9–13; closed Mon	174
Forte di Belvedere	Daily 9–20 (ramparts and terrace only)	181
Galleria dell'Accademia	(S) 9–14; fest. 9–13; closed Mon	112
Galleria d'Arte Moderna see Palazzo Pitti		
Galleria Corsini	adm only by previous appointment	164
Galleria Palatina	(S) 9–14; fest. 9–13; closed Mon	101
Galleria degli Uffizi	(S) 9–19; fest. 9–13; closed Mon	88
Giardino dei Semplici	Mon, Wed, & Fri 9–12	122

Name	Open (see note a)	Page
'La Specola' see Museo Zoologico		
Medici Chapels see Cappelle Medicee		
Museo dell'Angelico see Museo di San Marco		
Museo Archeologico	(S) 9–14; fest. 9–13; closed Mon	119
Museo degli Argenti see Palazzo Pitti		
Museo Bandini (Fièsole)	10–12 or 12.30, 14 or 15–18 or 19; closed on fest.	204
Museo Bardini	(C) 9–14; fest. 9–13; closed Wed	168
Museo del Bigallo	14–19 exc Sun & fest.	71
Museo Botanico	Mon, Wed, & Fri 9–12	122
Museo della Casa Fiorentina Antica	(S) 9–14; fest. 9–13; closed Mon	187
Museo Fiorentina di Preistoria	9.30–12.30; closed Sun	152
Museo di Firenze com'era	(C) 9–14; fest. 9–13; closed Thurs	151
Museo della Fondazione Horne	(S) 9–13; closed Sat & 2nd & last Sun of month	167
Museo di Geologia	Mon 14–17.30, Thurs & Sat 10–13	122
Museo di Mineralogia	weekdays 9–12	122
Museo Nazionale di Antropologia ed Etnologia	temporarily closed; when open Mon, Wed, & Fri 9–13	151
Museo Nazionale del Bargello	(S) 9–14; fest. 9–13; closed Mon	143
Museo dell'Opera del Duomo	daily 9.30–12.30, 14–17; summer, 9.30–13, 15–17.30; fest. 10–13	72
Museo dell'Opera di Santa Croce	9–12.30, 15–17 (18.30 in summer); closed Wed	159
Museo di Palazzo Strozzi	Mon, Wed & Fri 16–19	141
Museo delle Procellane (Bóboli)	(S) 9–14; fest. 9–13; closed Mon	112
Museo delle Porcellane di Doccia (Sesto Fiorentino)	9.30–13, 15.30–18.30; closed Sun & Mon	210
Museo di San Marco	(S) 9–14 fest. 9–13; closed Mon	122
Museo Stibbert	9–14; fest. 9–13; closed Thurs	197
Museo di Storia della Scienza	10–13, 14–16; fest. 10–13; closed last Sun of the month	166
Museo di Strumenti Musicale	closed indefinitely	114
Museo Zoologico 'La Specola'	Sun 9–12, Tues 9–12.30; Sat 14–17 (winter 15–18; anatomy section on Sat 14–17; 15–18 in summer)	179
Opificio delle Pietre Dure	(S) 9–13; closed Sun	114
Ospedale degli Innocenti (Galleria)	9–13; closed Mon (April-September 9–19)	116
Palazzo Davanzati see Museo della Casa Fiorentina Antica		
Palazzo Medici-Riccardi	9–13, 15–17; fest. 9–12; closed Wed	127
Palazzo Pitti:		
Appartamenti Monumentali:	(S) 9–14, fest. 9–13; closed Mon	106
Galleria Palatina	(S) 9–14, fest. 9–13; closed Mon	101
Galleria d'Arte Moderna	(S) 9–14, fest. 9–13; closed Mon	107
Museo degli Argenti	(S) 9–14, fest. 9–13; closed Mon	107
Collezione Contini-Bonacossi	adm only with special permission	109
Palazzo Vecchio	(C) 9–19; fest 9–13; closed Sat	80
Poggio a Caiano (Villa Medicea)	closed for restoration; adm to gardens 9–17.30 exc. Mon	214
Santa Maria Maddalena dei Pazzi (Chapter House)	(S) 9–12, 15–18	163

Name	Open (see note a)	Page
San Martino del Vescovo	10–12, 15–17; Sat 15–16 closed Sun & fest.	193
Santa Reparata excavations (Duomo)	9.30–11.30, 14.30–17.30; fest. 9.30–12.30	67
Science Museum *see* Museo di Storia della Scienza		
Spanish Chapel *see* Chiostri Monumentali di S.M. Novella		
Uffizi *see* Galleria degli Uffizi		
Villa Medicea di Careggi	adm only with special permission from the administration of S.M. Nuova	208
Villa di Castello	gardens only 9–dusk; closed Mon	209
Villa della Petraia	villa 9–14; park and garden 9–dusk; closed Mon	208
Villa di Poggio Imperiale	Thurs & Sat 9–12	210

NOTES

a The opening hours for Sundays apply also to holidays (*giorni festivi*)
b Apply for adm at the Soprintendenza per i Beni Artistici, 5 Via della Ninna
(S) Museums owned by the State (Soprintendenza per i Beni Ambientali e Architettonici, Pal. Pitti, Tel. 292174, Soprintendenza per il Beni Artistici e Storici, 5 Via della Ninna, Tel. 218341).
(C) Museums owned by the Comune of Florence (Ufficio Belle Arti e Musei Comunali, 21 Via S. Egidio, Tel. 217305).

IX GENERAL INFORMATION

Season. The changeable climate of Florence is conditioned by its position in a small basin enclosed by hills. It can be extremely hot and oppressive in summer. Perhaps the most pleasant months to visit the city are June and October when the temperature is often still quite high. Spring can be unexpectedly wet and cold until well after Easter. The most crowded months are at Easter and July and September. The winter in Florence can be as cold as an English winter.

Plan of Visit. The 28 itineraries in the Guide correspond to at least a month's (leisurely) sight-seeing. For visitors with only a short time at their disposal, the following areas and monuments in the city should not be missed:

1. The Baptistery, Duomo, and Campanile (including a climb to the top of the cupola or the campanile), all described in Rte 1, and the Museo dell'Opera del Duomo (Rte 2).

2. Orsanmichele (Rte 3), Piazza della Signoria (Rte 4), and Palazzo Vecchio (Rte 5).

3. Galleria degli Uffizi (Rte 6).

4. Palazzo Pitti (Galleria Palatina) and the Bóboli gardens (Rte 8).

5. Galleria dell'Accademia, and Piazza Santissima Annunziata (Rte 9), and the Museo di San Marco (Rte 10).

6. Palazzo Medici-Riccardi (the Chapel frescoed by Benozzo Gozzoli), San Lorenzo, Biblioteca Laurenziana, and the Cappelle Medicee (Rte 10).

7. Santa Maria Novella (and the Spanish Chapel; Rte 11), Santa Trinita, and the exterior of Palazzo Strozzi and Palazzo Rucellai (Rte 12).

8. Museo Nazionale del Bargello (Rte 13), Santa Croce (and the Pazzi Chapel), and the Casa Buonarroti (Rte 15).

9. Santo Spirito and Santa Maria del Carmine (the Brancacci Chapel; Rte 18), and San Miniato al Monte (Rte 20).

10. Fièsole (Rte 23).

Public Holidays. The main holidays in Italy, when offices, shops, and schools are closed are as follows: New Year's Day, 25 April (Liberation Day), Easter Monday, 1 May (Labour Day), 15 Aug (Assumption), 1 Nov (All Saints' Day), 8 Dec (Conception), Christmas Day, and 26 Dec (St Stephen). In addition the festival of the patron Saint of Florence, St John, is celebrated on 24 June as a local holiday in the city.

Telephones and Postal Information. Stamps are sold at tobacconists (displaying a blue 'T' sign) and post offices (open 8.15–14, Mon–Sat). It is always advisable to post letters at Post Offices or the Railway Station; collection from letterboxes is erratic. There are numerous public telephones all over the city, in bars and restaurants, etc. These are operated by metal discs known as 'gettone', rather than coins, which are bought (100 lire each) from tobacconists, bars, some newspaper stands, and post offices (and are considered valid currency). For long-distance calls the telephone exchange at the Post Office in Via Pellicceria is always open. Most cities in Europe can now be dialled direct from Italy (prefix for London, 00441).

Newspapers. The Italian newspapers which carry local news of Florence are 'La Nazione', 'La Città' and 'Paese Sera'. Other national newspapers include 'Corriere della Sera', 'La Repubblica', and 'La Stampa'. Foreign newspapers can be purchased at most kiosks.

Working Hours. Government offices usually work weekdays from 8–13.30 or 14. Shops are open from 8 or 9–13 and 16.30 or 17.30–19.30 or 20. Most of the year, food shops are closed on Wednesday afternoon, and other shops (clothes, hardware, hairdressers, etc.), are closed on Monday morning. From mid-June to mid-September all shops are closed instead on Saturday afternoon. For banking hours, see p 54.

FLORENCE

FLORENCE, in Italian *Firenze,* has been famous for centuries as one of the principal centres of art and learning in Italy. In the later Middle Ages and the early Renaissance it was the intellectual capital of the peninsula, well meriting its designation 'the Italian Athens'. The city remains a treasury of art, not only on account of the priceless collections in its museums and galleries, but also by virtue of its rich endowment of medieval monuments and Renaissance buildings, in which it is rivalled by Rome alone. Today, Florence, with 458,000 inhabitants, is still one of the most beautiful cities in Italy, and the historical centre and the hills in the immediate vicinity have been largely preserved from new buildings. It lies in a delightful position in a small basin enclosed by low hills (which accounts for its changeable climate and high temperatures in summer). It is important as the trading centre for the fertile valleys of Tuscany, and since 1970 has been the capital of the new 'region' of Tuscany. It has for long been favoured as a residence by scholars, artists, and others from abroad. The river Arno, a special feature of the city, is a mountain torrent, subject to sudden floods and droughts.

1 THE BAPTISTERY AND THE DUOMO

The ****Baptistery of San Giovanni** (Pl. 16; 4; closed 12–14.30) is one of the oldest and most revered buildings in the city. Called by Dante his 'bel San Giovanni', it has always held a special place in the history of Florence. The date of its foundation is uncertain; in the Middle Ages it was thought to be a Roman building. Most scholars now consider it to have been built in the 6C or 7C, and anyway not later than the 9C. A Roman palace of the 1C A.D. has been discovered beneath its foundations. It is a domed octagonal building of centralized plan derived from Byzantine models. The EXTERIOR was entirely encased in white and green marble from Prato in a classical geometrical design in the 11–12C, at the charge of the 'Arte di Calimala', the most important Guild of the medieval city (comp. pp 75-6). The decoration became a prototype for numerous other Tuscan Romanesque religious buildings. At the end of the 13C the striped angle pilasters were added, and the semicircular apse was probably replaced at this time by the rectangular 'scarsella'. The cupola was concealed by an unusual white pyramidal roof probably in the 13C (and the 11C lantern placed on top). The larger arch which marks the main East entrance faces the Duomo. The two porphyry columns here were a gift from Pisa in 1135; they proved to be unsound and therefore could not be used as architectural elements.

The building is famous for its three sets of gilded bronze doors at its three entrances. The earliest by Andrea Pisano (1336) was followed by those on the N. and E. sides erected a century later by Lorenzo Ghiberti after a competition held by the 'Arte di Calimala' in which his work was preferred to that of many of the greatest artists of the

61

Quattrocento, including Brunelleschi and Jacopo della Quercia. Thi
competition of 1401 is often taken as a convenient point to mark th
beginning of the Florentine Renaissance, and it is significant that th
Baptistery should have been the monument chosen for adornment
Two trial reliefs for the competition, entered by Brunelleschi an
Ghiberti, are preserved in the Bargello (comp. p 147).

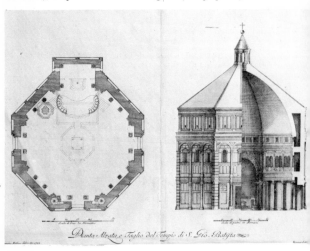

The Baptistery, drawn by C. B. Clemente Nelli
and published by Bernardo Sgrilli in 1755.
(Museo di Firenze com'era)

The ***South Door**, by *Andrea Pisano*, was erected in 1336 at the main entranc
facing the Duomo. It was moved to its present position in 1424 to make way fo
Ghiberti's new doors. It has 28 compartments containing reliefs within Gothi
quatrefoil frames of the history of St John the Baptist and the theological an
cardinal Virtues. The decorations of the bronze frame were added by *Vitt
Ghiberti* (1452–64), son of Lorenzo.—Over the doorway are bronze figures o
the Baptist, the Executioner, and Salome, by *Vinc. Danti* (1571).

The ***North Door**, by *Lorenzo Ghiberti* (1403–24), is again divided into 2
compartments, and the scenes of the Life of Christ, the Evangelists, and th
Doctors of the Church, are contained within Gothic frames copied from th
earlier Pisano doors. The chronological sequence of the scenes from the Life o
Christ begins on the left-hand door on the 3rd panel from the bottom and con
tinues towards the top, running left to right. The two lower registers depict th
Evangelists and Doctors. Ghiberti's self-portrait appears in the 5th head from
the top of the left door (middle band); he is wearing an elaborate hat. Th
beautiful decoration of the frame is also by Ghiberti.—The bronze figures abov
are St John the Baptist preaching, the Levite, and the Pharisee, by *Fr. Rustic
(1506–11), from a design by *Leonardo* (mentioned by Vasari).

The ****East Door** is the most celebrated work of *Lorenzo Ghiberti*, the com
pletion of which took him most of his life (1425–52). It is said to have been calle
by Michelangelo the 'Gate of Paradise'. The 10 separate panels contain reliefs o
scriptural subjects, the design of which probably owes something to Ghiberti'
contact with the humanists. The artist was assisted by *Michelozzo, Benozzo Goz
zoli*, and others. The pictorial reliefs, no longer restricted to a Gothic frame
depict each episode with great conciseness, and the workmanship of the carvin
is masterly, with scenes in low relief extending far into the background. The us
of perspective here is of great importance, and typical of the new Renaissanc
concept of art. The panels are being removed one by one for restoration. Th

ubjects from above downwards are: 1. The Creation and Expulsion from
Paradise; 2. Cain and Abel; 3. Noah's Sacrifice and Drunkenness; 4. Abraham
nd the Angels and the Sacrifice of Isaac; 5. Esau and Jacob; 6. Joseph sold and
ecognized by his Brethren (temporarily removed for restoration); 7. Moses
eceiving the Tables of Stone; 8. The Fall of Jericho; 9. Battle with the
Philistines; 10. Solomon and the Queen of Sheba. In the framing are 24 very fine
tatuettes of Prophets and Sibyls, and 24 medallions with portraits of Ghiberti
imself (the 4th from the top in the middle row on the left) and his principal con-
emporaries. The splendid bronze door-frame is by Ghiberti also.—Above the
loor the sculptural group of the Baptism of Christ, formerly attrib. to *And. San-
ovino,* may instead be the work of *Vinc. Danti.* The Angel was added by *In-
ocenzo Spinazzi* in the 18C. The sculptures have been removed for restoration
ince 1975.

The interior is at present (1981) open only in the afternoon (12–17.30) since
ervices are held here while restoration work is going on in the Duomo.

The harmonious INTERIOR is designed in two orders, of which the
ower has huge granite columns from a Roman building, with gilded
Corinthian capitals, and the upper, above a cornice, a gallery with
livided windows. The walls are in panels of white marble divided by
pands of black, in the dichromatic style of the exterior. The beautiful
lecoration has survived intact, despite the evident signs of the 1966
lood on the lower part of the walls. The centre of the building was
ormerly occupied by a large font; the Gothic font on the r. of the en-
rance dates from 1371. The oldest part of the splendid mosaic *PAVE-
MENT (begun 1209) is near the font. The decoration in 'opus
essellatum', which recalls that of San Miniato (see Rte 20), includes
geometrical designs, oriental motifs, the signs of the Zodiac, etc.
Beside the high altar (13C; reconstructed) is an elaborate paschal
candlestick delicately carved by *Agostino di Iacopo* (1320). To the r. is
he *Tomb of the antipope John XXIII (Baldassarre Coscia, who died
n Florence in 1419) by *Donatello* and *Michelozzo,* one of the earliest
Renaissance tombs in the city. Apart from the exquisite carving, this
monument is especially remarkable for the way it is inserted into a
narrow space between two huge Roman columns, and in no way
listurbs the architectural harmony of the building. The bronze effigy
of the pope is generally attrib. to *Donatello.* On the l. of the apse are
wo late-Roman sarcophagi adapted as tombs (one showing a wild
boar hunt, and the other, the tomb of Bp Giov. da Velletri, 1230, with
cenes of Roman life). The statue of Mary Magdalen by Donatello has
been removed to the Museo dell'Opera del Duomo (Rte 2).

The *MOSAICS (light) in the vault are remarkably well preserved.
The earliest (c. 1225) are in the 'scarsella' above the altar; they are
signed by the monk *'Iacopo',* a contemporary of St Francis, and show
he influence of the mosaic decoration of San Marco in Venice. In the
vault, an elaborate wheel with the figures of the Prophets surrounds
he Agnus Dei. This is supported by four caryatids kneeling on Corin-
hian capitals. On either side are the Virgin and St John the Baptist en-
hroned. On the entrance arch is a frieze of Saints, and, on the outer
ace, half-figures of Saints flank a striking image of the Baptist. The
ame artist is thought to have begun the main dome, the centre of
vhich is decorated with paleochristian motifs surrounded by a band of
angels. Above the apse is the Last Judgement with a huge figure of
Christ (8 metres high), attrib. to *Coppo di Marcovaldo.* The remain-
ng section of the cupola is divided into four bands: the inner one il-
ustrates the Story of Genesis (beginning on the N. side); the 2nd

band, the Story of Joseph (the design of some of the scenes has recent
ly been attrib. to the *'Maestro della Maddalena'*); the 3rd band, th
Story of Christ; and the outer band, the Story of St John the Baptis
(some of the early episodes are attrib. to *Cimabue*). Work on th
mosaics was well advanced by 1271, but probably continued into th
14C. The marble rectangular frames at the base of the dome contai
mosaic Saints.

The gallery, and the foundations of the Roman building which formerly stoo
on this site, may only be visited with special permission. A medieval cemeter
was found between the Baptistery and the Duomo in 1972–73 (since covere
over).

The ***Duomo** (Pl. 16; 4; closed 12–14.30), the cathedral dedicated t
the Madonna of Florence, *Santa Maria del Fiore,* fills Piazza de
Duomo; a comprehensive view of the huge building is difficult in th
confined space. It produces a memorable effect of massive grandeur
especially seen from its southern flank, lightened by the colour an
pattern of its beautiful marble walls (white from Carrara, green fron
Prato, and red from the Maremma). The famous dome, one of th
masterpieces of the Renaissance, rising to the height of the surroun
ding hills (from which it is nearly always visible), holds sway over th
whole city.

History. The paleochristian church dedicated to the Palestinian sain
Reparata, is thought to have been founded in the 6–7C, or possibly earlier. It wa
several times reconstructed in the Romanesque period. Considerable remains c
this church were found in 1965–74 beneath the present cathedral (comp. p 67)
The Bishop's seat, formerly at San Lorenzo (comp. Rte 10) is thought to hav
been transferred here in the late 7C. By the 13C a new and larger cathedral wa
deemed necessary. In 1294 *Arnolfo di Cambio* was appointed as architect, and
is not known precisely how far building had progressed by the time of his deat
in the first decade of the 14C. In 1331 the 'Arte della Lana' (Guild of Wool Mer
chants) took over responsibility for the cathedral works and *Giotto* was ap
pointed 'capomaestro'. He began the campanile in 1334. It was not until 135
that work was taken up again on the cathedral itself, this time by *Francesc
Talenti.* It seems he followed Arnolfo's original design of a vaulted basilica wit
a domed octagon flanked by three polygonal tribunes. During the 14C *Albert
Arnoldi, Giovanni d'Ambrogio, Giov. di Lapo Ghini, Neri di Fioravante, Or
cagna,* and others, all joined Talenti as architects, and the octagonal drum wa
substantially finished by 1417. The construction of the cupola had for long bee
recognised as a major technical problem. A competition was held an
Brunelleschi and *Ghiberti* were appointed jointly to the task in 1418
Brunelleschi soon took over full responsibility for the work and the dome wa
finished up to the base of the lantern by 1436 when pope Eugenius IV con
secrated the cathedral.

EXTERIOR. The majestic ****CUPOLA**, the greatest of all *Brunelleschi'*
works (1420–36), is a feat of engineering skill. It was the first dome tc
be projected without the need for a wooden supporting frame to sus
tain the vault during construction. This was possible partly becaus
the upper section was built in bricks in consecutive rings in horizonta
courses, bonded together in a herring-bone pattern. However the ex
act constructional technique used by Brunelleschi has still not bee
satisfactorily explained. The dome was the largest and highest of it
time. Its pointed shape was probably conditioned by the octagona
drum which already existed over the crossing and from which the eigh
marble ribs ascend to the lantern. The cupola has two concentric
shells, the octagonal vaults of which are evident both on the exterio
and interior of the building. This facilitated construction and lessene
the weight; the outer shell is thinner than the inner shell. Some of th

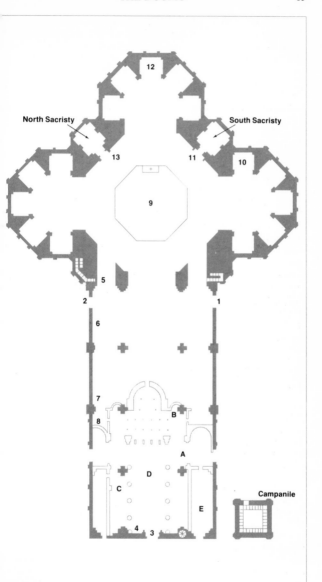

The Duomo

apparatus invented by Brunelleschi which may have been used during the building of the dome survives in the Museo dell'Opera (p 73).—On the completion of the cupola Brunelleschi was subjected to another competition as his ability to crown it with a lantern was brought into question. It was begun a few months before the architect's death in 1446, and carried on by his friend *Michelozzo*. In the late 1460s *Verrocchio* placed the bronze ball and cross on the summit. Brunelleschi also designed the four decorative little exedrae with niches which he placed around the octagonal drum between the three domed tribunes. The balcony at the base of the cupola, covering the brick work, on the S.E. side, was added by *Baccio d'Agnolo,* on a design by *Giul. da Sangallo* and *Cronaca* in 1507–15. According to Vasari, it was never completed because of Michelangelo's stringent criticism that it reminded him of a crickets' cage.

The building of the cathedral was begun on the S. side where the decorative pattern of marble can be seen to full advantage. Here, high above a doorway near the campanile are 14C sculptures. The PORTA DEI CANONICI (1) has fine sculptured decoration by *Lor. d'Ambrogio* and *Piero di Giov. Tedesco* (1395–99). On the N. side, the *PORTA DELLA MANDORLA (2) dates from 1391–1405. The lower part was sculpted by *Giov. d'Ambrogio, Piero di Giov. Tedesco, Iac. di Piero Guidi,* and *Nic. Lamberti*. In the gable is an *Assumption of the Virgin in an oval almond-shaped frame (or 'mandorla') by *Nanni di Banco* (c. 1418–20), continued after his death by his workshop. The busts in relief on the inside of the gable of a Prophet and Sibyl are considered early works by *Donatello*. The sculptures have been blackened by the polluted air and are difficult to appreciate from this distance; they had an important influence on early Renaissance sculpture. In the lunette is an Annunciation in mosaic by *Dom.* and *Dav. Ghirlandaio* (1491).—The FAÇADE, erected to a third of its projected height by 1420, was demolished in 1587–88 (comp. p 72), and the present front in the Gothic style was designed by *Emilio De Fabris* and built in 1871–87. The bronze doors date from 1899–1903.

The Gothic INTERIOR is somewhat bare and chilly after the warmth of the colour of the exterior, whose splendour it cannot match. The huge grey stone arches of the nave reach the clerestory beneath an elaborate sculptured balcony. The massive pilasters which support the stone vault have unusual composite capitals. Three dark tribunes with a Gothic coronet of chapels surround the huge dome. During restoration work on the frescoes of the dome (expected to take a number of years), only the S. aisle of the cathedral is open and, during the day, services are held in the Baptistery. The beautiful marble pavement was designed by *Baccio d'Agnolo, Fr. da Sangallo* and others (1526–1660).—WEST WALL. Mosaic of the Coronation of the Virgin, attrib. to *Gaddo Gaddi* (3). *Ghiberti* designed the three round stained glass windows. The frescoes of the angel musicians are by *Santi di Tito*. The huge clock, restored in 1973, uses the 'hora italica' method of counting the hours; the last hour of the day (XXIV) ends at sunset or Ave Maria (a system used in Italy until the 18C). *Paolo Uccello* decorated it and painted the four heads of prophets in 1443. The recomposed tomb (4) of Antonio d'Orso, Bp of Florence (d 1321) by *Tino da Camaino,* includes a fine statue. The painting of St Catherine of Alexandria is by the school of *Bernardo Daddi*.

SOUTH AISLE. The simple tomb slab (*E*) of Brunelleschi has been placed in the floor here above the spot where it was found in 1972 in the crypt of Santa Reparata (see below). The architect of the cupola was the only Florentine granted the privilege of burial in the cathedral. In the tondo above is his bust by *Buggiano,* his adopted son (1446; probably taken from his death mask). In the first 'marble' side altar, *Nanni di Banco,* Statue of a Prophet (1408). The bust of Giotto (1490) by *Benedetto da Maiano* bears an inscription by Poliziano. By the nave pillar, is an elaborate Gothic stoup (c. 1380), attrib. to *Urbano da Cortona.* The angel and basin are copies; the originals are in the Opera del Duomo (p 72).

Steps lead down to the entrance (*A*) to the **Excavations of Santa Reparata** (adm see p 59). During 1965–74 the ancient cathedral of Santa Reparata (comp. p 64) was uncovered beneath the present cathedral (see the Plan on p 65). The complicated remains, on various levels, include Roman edifices on which the early Christian church was built, a fine mosaic pavement of the paleochristian church, and remains of the pre-Romanesque and Romanesque reconstructions. Since only a few column bases and parts of the pavement of the earliest church were discovered, its precise plan is not known; the excavated area corresponds to the plan of the Romanesque church with its five apses. Four of the massive nave pilasters of the present cathedral above intrude into this area. The excavations are explained by a detailed model (*C*).

At the entrance, cases of finds from the excavations: gilded bronze sword and spurs of Giovanni de' Medici (comp. below); Roman sculpture, paving tiles, etc; Romanesque architectural fragments; majolica and unglazed pottery from earth fills and tombs dating from the period of the construction of the present cathedral (1296–1375). Beyond is the Romanesque crypt of Santa Reparata with 13C tomb slabs in the floor. The fresco fragments include a 14C Christ in Passion (*B*). In the area towards the N. aisle is part of the mosaic pavement from the first church with a fragment of Romanesque pavement above it. Plutei of the 8–9C are displayed near the base of the stairs which led up to the raised choir. Beyond the huge square base of one of the nave pillars of the present cathedral are some fragments of Roman buildings below the floor level. A model here (*C*) explains in detail the various levels of excavations. Nearby is part of a pavement thought to be from the pre-Romanesque period and several tomb slabs. From here a walkway leads across the best preserved part of the paleochristian mosaic floor, interrupted here and there by fragments of brick, marble, and pietra serena from later buildings. The walkway leads back across a wall of the Roman period to the imposing raised tomb (*D*) of Giovanni de' Medici, buried here in 1351. Nearby are five plans of the excavations. On the other side of the entrance stairs is the S.E. apse of the church; in the S. aisle (closed but seen through a grille) Brunelleschi's tomb (*E*) was discovered.

By the S. door, St Bartholomew enthroned by *Rossello di Jac. Franchi* (early 15C). On the 2nd altar, statue of Isaiah, by *Ciuffagni* (1427), between two painted sepulchral monuments of Fra' Luigi Marsili and Cardinal Pietro Corsini, by *Bicci di Lorenzo.* The stained glass windows, with six saints, were designed by *Agnolo Gaddi* (1394–5). Beneath the second window is a bust of Marsilio Ficino (1433–99), holding a volume of Plato, the famous philosopher and friend of Cosimo il Vecchio, by *And. Ferrucci* (1521).—Beyond the second S. door is an entrance to the steps which ascend the cupola; during restoration work on the dome (comp. above) the E. end of the church (described below) is closed to visitors.

*Ascent of the Dome (adm see p 57). At present access is from the N. aisle (5), but during restoration work the door in the S. aisle may sometimes be used. The climb (463 steps) is not specially arduous, and is highly recommended (except for those who suffer from vertigo); it follows a labyrinth of corridors, steps, and spiral staircases (used by the builders of the cupola) as far as the lantern at the top of the dome. During the ascent the structure of the dome (comp. p 64) can be examined, and the views of the inside of the cathedral from the balcony around the drum, and of the city from the small windows and from the lantern, are remarkable.—At the top of the steps which ascend the pier is the interior of one of the small exedrae which Brunelleschi added beneath the drum. From here a spiral staircase continues, at the top of which there is a view of the huge market building of S. Lorenzo next to the dome of the Chapel of the Princes. A corridor emerges on the balcony which encircles the octagonal drum. It provides an interesting, if dizzy, view of the inside of the cathedral. The frescoes by Vasari and Zuccari (comp. p 69) on the cupola are covered with scaffolding while being restored. The 7 stained glass windows in the roundels can be seen to advantage; they were designed in 1443–5 by the following artists; *Paolo Uccello*, Nativity; *And. del Castagno*, Deposition; *Paolo Uccello*, Resurrection; *Donatello*, Coronation of the Virgin; *Ghiberti*, Ascension, Prayer in the Garden, and Presentation in the Temple. When Brunelleschi was commissioned to construct the cupola the building of the cathedral had already reached this height; from here can be appreciated the huge space (45½ metres in diameter) which the architect was required to vault.

A spiral staircase leads to the base of the double dome, the curve of which can clearly be seen. The ascent continues between the two shells, and the little windows frame views of the monuments of the city. The distinctive herring-bone pattern of the bricks (which vary in size; comp. p 64) used in the construction of the dome can here be examined. On the right a steep flight of steps scales the uppermost part of the inner dome. Iron steps continue out on to the lantern, beautifully carved in marble. Access to the bronze ball has been closed for many years; it is large enough to hold about 10 people at a time. The view from here (91 metres) embraces the city; the most conspicuous buildings include (r. to l.): the campanile, Palazzo Strozzi, and the church of the Carmine in the distance; Santo Spirito with its dome and campanile and the huge Palazzo Pitti, and (nearer) the tall Orsanmichele. At the foot of the cathedral is a group of small medieval houses and towers. The Forte di Belvedere can be seen in the distance on its hill behind Palazzo Vecchio, the Uffizi, and the Loggia della Signoria. Farther left is the Badia with its tall tower and the Bargello; the marble façade of Santa Croce with its campanile, and, on the hill behind, San Miniato. Beyond the arcaded façade of the hospital of Santa Maria Nuova rises the green dome of the Synagogue. The straight Via dei Servi leads to the SS. Annunziata, to the right of which are the extensive buildings of the Innocenti with a garden, and nearer at hand the octagonal rotunda of Santa Maria degli Angeli, also by

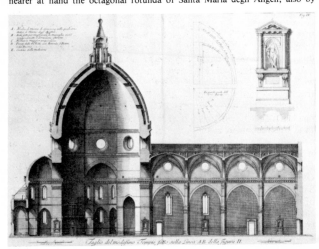

The Duomo and Cupola, section drawn by G. B. Nelli (1661–1725), surveyor of the Opera del Duomo, and published by Bernardo Sgrilli in 1755. (Museo di Firenze com'era)

Brunelleschi. In the distance rises the hill of Fiesole. The long façade of Palazzo Medici Riccardi on Via Cavour can be seen near the tall iron roof of the 19C market building beside the domed church of San Lorenzo. Near the station is Santa Maria Novella with its cloisters and campanile.

NORTH AISLE (6) *Dom. di Michelino,* Dante and the 'Divina Commedia' which illuminates Florence (1465; showing the drum of the cupola before it was faced with marble); *Bicci di Lorenzo,* SS. Cosmas and Damian. The two stained glass windows were designed by *Agnolo Gaddi.* On the side altar, *Bern. Ciuffagni,* King David (1434; designed for the old façade of the Cathedral). Beyond are two splendid *Equestrian memorials (7 and 8) to the famous 'condottieri', the Englishman Sir John Hawkwood ('Giovanni Acuto'), who commanded the Florentine army from 1377 until his death in 1394, and Nic. da Tolentino (d 1434). They are both frescoes giving the illusion of sculpture: the former by *Paolo Uccello* (1436) and the latter by *And. del Castagno* (1456). The bust of the organist Ant. Squarcialupi is by *Benedetto da Maiano* (1490; the epigraph is thought to be by Poliziano). On the last altar, *Donatello* (attrib.), the prophet Joshua (traditionally thought to be a portrait of the humanist friend of Cosimo il Vecchio, Poggio Bracciolini), originally on the façade of the Duomo. On the nave pillar, *Giov. del Biondo,* St Zenobius (late 14C).

EAST END OF THE CHURCH. Above the octagon the great dome soars to a height of 91 metres. The fresco of the Last Judgement by *Vasari* and *Fed. Zuccari* (1572–79) is covered for restoration (comp. p 66). The 15C stained glass in the round windows of the drum is described on p 68. Against the pillars dividing the nave from the transepts stand eight 16C statues of Apostles: (clockwise from the nave) *Iac. Sansovino,* St James; *Vinc. de' Rossi,* St Thomas; *And. Ferrucci,* St Andrew; *Baccio Bandinelli,* St Peter; *Benedetto da Rovezzano,* St John; *Giov. Bandini,* St James the Less, St Philip; *Vinc. de' Rossi,* St Matthew.—The marble SANCTUARY (9) by *Bandinelli* (1555) with bas-reliefs by himself and *Bandini,* encloses the High Altar, also by Bandinelli, with a wood crucifix by *Bened. da Maiano.*

Each of the three apses is divided into five chapels with stained glass windows designed by *Lor. Ghiberti.* In the right and left apse are frescoes beneath the windows after Paolo Schiavo (c. 1440; heavily restored). Right Apse: 5th Chap. (10) 'Madonna del Popolo', fragment of a Giottesque fresco. Above the entrance to the SOUTH SACRISTY (11), large lunette of the Ascension in enamelled terracotta by *Luca della Robbia.* The interesting interior is usually closed.—Central Apse: 3rd Chap. (12). On the altar, two graceful kneeling angels by *Luca della Robbia.* Beneath the altar, *Bronze reliquary urn, by *Lor. Ghiberti* with exquisite bas-reliefs.—Over the door into the NORTH SACRISTY (13; 'delle Messe') is another fine relief by *Luca della Robbia* of the *Resurrection. This was his earliest important work (1442) in enamelled terracotta. The iconographical composition was copied by later artists. The doors were Luca's only work in bronze (1446–67); he was assisted by *Michelozzo* and *Maso di Bartolomeo.* It was in this sacristy that Lorenzo il Magnifico took refuge on the day of the Pazzi conspiracy in 1478 in order to escape the death which befell his brother, Giuliano. The interior has been closed since 1972, but there are plans to reopen it after restoration. The inlaid cupboards were begun by *Ant. Manetti* and others and continued by *Giul.* and *Bened. da Maiano, Aless. Baldovinetti,* and *Ant. del Pollaiolo.* The lavabo was designed by *Brunelleschi* and made by *Buggiano.*—Left Apse. In the pavement (usually hidden by pews) is Toscanelli's huge Gnomon (1475) for solar observations (related to a window in the lantern of the cupola). Toscanelli, a famous scientist, mathematician, and geographer, discussed his calculations concerning perspective with his friend Brunelleschi. Michelangelo's famous Pietà, formerly displayed in the first chapel, has been removed to the Museo dell'Opera del Duomo (p 73). The adjoining chapel has a dossal painted on both sides (much ruined) by the school of *Giotto.*

The **Campanile* (Pl. 16; 4; nearly 85 metres high) was begun by *Giotto* in 1334 when, as the most distinguished Florentine artist, he was appointed city architect. It was continued by *And. Pisano* (1343), and completed by *Fr. Talenti* in 1348–59. It is built of the same coloured marbles as the Duomo, in similar patterns, in a remarkably well-proportioned design. Between the various stories are horizontal bands of green, white, and pink inlay. The lowest story bears two rows of bas-reliefs which have been replaced by copies. The originals, now in the Museo dell'Opera, are described on p 73. The lowest row are contemporary with the building, and some of them are thought to have been designed by *Giotto.* They were executed by *And. Pisano* and illustrate the Creation of Man, and the Arts and Industries. Five reliefs on the N. face were added by *Luca della Robbia.* The upper register has reliefs by pupils of *And. Pisano.* The row of niches in the second story contains casts of the statues of Prophets and Sibyls by *Donatello* and others (1415–36) also removed to the Museo dell'Opera (see p 73). Above are two stories, each with a pair of beautiful double-arched windows in each side, then the highest story, with large and triple-arched openings, and the cornice. The campanile was partly closed for restoration in 1981.

The **Ascent of the bell-tower** by 414 steps (adm see p 57) is interesting for its succession of views of the Duomo, the Baptistery, and the rest of the city. Although lower than the cupola, the climb is steeper.—The third and fourth stories, with their Gothic windows, overlook the Duomo and the Baptistery. The terracotta pots along the roof of the aisle of the Duomo serve to protect the building from the direct fall of rainwater from the gutters. On the highest story, with its beautiful slender windows, the modern bells can be seen hanging above the original ones (the 'Apostolica' bell, displayed on a platform, dates from the beginning of the 15C). The steps become steeper before emerging beside the simple tiled roof above the cornice.—The splendid panorama of the city includes (r. to l.): Piazza della Repubblica (with its conspicuous advertisements), with Pal. Strozzi behind, and the Carmine in the distance. Farther l. is Santo Spirito; then Pal. Pitti with the Boboli gardens stretching as far as the Forte di Belvedere on its hill. Nearer at hand rises the tall Orsanmichele. Farther l. is the Loggia della Signoria beside Pal. Vecchio and the Uffizi, and, at the foot of the campanile, is a group of medieval houses with red tiled roofs and towers. The Badia is marked by its tall bell-tower next to the Bargello. Beyond Santa Croce, the Synagogue can be seen just to the r. of the cupola. On the other side of the dome the long straight Via Ricasoli leads out of the city towards the hills of Fiesole in the distance. On the parallel Via Cavour stands Pal. Medici-Riccardi. The huge 19C market building is near San Lorenzo with its dome; the large church of Santa Maria Novella can be seen beside the railway station.

2   PIAZZA SAN GIOVANNI AND PIAZZA DEL DUOMO

The Baptistery and the Duomo fill P.za San Giovanni and P.za del Duomo (Pl. 16; 4). Between the Baptistery and the Campanile is the little Gothic *LOGGIA DEL BIGALLO* built for the Misericordia (comp. below) in 1351–58 probably by *Alberto Arnoldi,* who carved the reliefs and the lunette of the Madonna and Child (1361) above the door into the Oratory (facing the Baptistery). The Compagnia del Bigallo, founded in 1245, and involved in similar charitable works to the Misericordia, moved to this seat in 1425 when the two confraternities were merged. Beneath the Loggia lost and abandoned children were exposed for three days before being consigned to foster-mothers. The three 14C statues in tabernacles high up on the façade were moved here from the Bigallo's former headquarters near Orsanmichele. The **Museo del Bigallo** (Pl. 16; 4; No. 1 P.za San Giovanni; adm see p 58) is the smallest museum in the city, but one of the most charming, often neglected by visitors. It preserves most of the works of art commissioned over the centuries by the Misericordia and the Bigallo from Florentine artists.

The SALA DEI CAPITANI is approached through fine inlaid doors (c. 1450) which bear the arms of the Misericordia and the Bigallo. The *Madonna of the Misericordia,* by an artist in the circle of *Bernardo Daddi,* dates from 1342. The fresco includes the earliest known view of Florence, with the marble Baptistery prominent in the centre near the incomplete campanile and façade of the Duomo. The relief in pietra serena with the Altoviti coat-of-arms is by *Desiderio da Settignano.* Above two wall cupboards containing the archives of the company, is the Madonna in glory with two orphans in adoration, and Charity, both by *Carlo Portelli* (c. 1570). Between the windows: *School of Orcagna,* St Peter Martyr giving the standard to twelve captains of the Bigallo (with an inscription on the reverse), c. 1360, recording the foundation of the company. Above, *School of Botticelli,* Madonna and Child. The twelve charming frescoed scenes (damaged) from the life of Tobias, patron saint of the Misericordia (c. 1360) were detached from the Udienza Vecchia. The fresco fragment of the Captains of the Misericordia consigning lost and abandoned children to foster-mothers outside the Loggia del Bigallo (1386) is by *Niccolò di Pietro Gerini* and *Ambrogio di Baldese.* It was detached from the outside of the building in 1777 (the complete fresco is shown in its original position in the small 18C water-colour).—In the CORRIDOR, Tondo of the Nativity in terracotta (Tuscan, end of 15C).

SACRISTY. *'Maestro di San Miniato',* Madonna and Child; *Bernardo Daddi,* Portable triptych, dated 1333, one of his most important early works; *Dom. di Michelino,* *Madonna of Humility with two angels; *Alunno di Benozzo,* Madonna enthroned with Saints.—ORATORY. The Madonna and Child and two angels by *Alberto Arnoldi* (1359–64), were placed in a gilded wood tabernacle by *Noferi di Ant. Noferi* in 1515. Beneath the statues, predella by *Ridolfo del Ghirlandaio,* including a scene of Tobias burying a corpse in front of the Loggia del Bigallo with hooded members of the Misericordia in their black habits (comp. below) in the background. *Jacopo del Sellaio,* Tondo of the Madonna and Saints in a beautiful contemporary frame; *Alberto Arnoldi* (attrib.), Statuette of the Madonna and Child. High up in the lunette above the door, detached sinopia of Christ between angels by *Nardo di Cione,* whose workshop painted the fresco fragment opposite. The 13C painted Crucifix is attrib. to the *'Maestro del Bigallo'.* The original base for the statues by Arnoldi is the work of *Ambrogio di Renzo* (1363).

Across Via dei Calzaiuoli (which leads to Piazza Signoria) is the MISERICORDIA, a charitable institution which gives gratuitous help to those in need, and runs an ambulance service. The Order, thought to have been founded in the 13C, moved to this site in 1576 from the

Bigallo across the road. In the Middle Ages the brotherhood was
specially active during the plague years when they gave medical care to
the poor and attended to their burial. The lay confraternity continues
its work through some 2000 volunteers who are a characteristic sight
of Florence in their black capes and hoods. The pretty little *Oratory*
(left of the main door) contains an altarpiece by And. della Robbia,
and a statue of St Sebastian by Bened. da Maiano. Outside is a
modern painting by Pietro Annigoni.—In Via del Campanile a tabernacle, lit by a lamp, contains a good 15C painting of the Madonna and
Child between two Saints. In the piazza is *Palazzo dei Canonici* with
its heavy columns and colossal 19C statues of Arnolfo and
Brunelleschi. From this corner of the piazza (by Via del Proconsolo),
there is a good view of the cathedral and dome. On the corner of Via
dell' Oriuolo (which leads to the Museo di Firenze com'era, see Rte
14) is the large 17C *Palazzo Guadagni-Riccardi*.

At No. 9 Piazza del Duomo is the ***Museo dell'Opera del Duomo**
(Pl. 16; 4; adm see p 58), in a building which has been the seat of the
Opera del Duomo (responsible for the maintenance of the cathedral)
since the beginning of the 15C. Over the entrance is a bust of Cosimo I
by Bandini. One of the pleasantest museums in the city, it contains
material from the Duomo, the Baptistery, and the Campanile, including important sculpture.

COURTYARD. Baroque statues by *Girol. Ticciati,* and two large
Roman sarcophagi (mid-3C), from the Baptistery.—GROUND FLOOR.
In the entrance hall, marble bust of Brunelleschi, attrib. to *Giov. Ban-
dini.* This is thought to have been commissioned by the Opera del
Duomo for its present position. The enamelled terracotta relief of the
Madonna and Child is by *And. della Robbia;* the flat lunette of God
the Father between two angels is also attrib. to *Andrea.* The marble
panels from the choir of the Duomo (1547) are fine works by *Baccio
Bandinelli* and *Giov. Bandini.*—The room beyond contains sculptures
and architectural fragments from the Duomo and a lunette of St
Zenobius by *And. della Robbia* (1496).

ROOM I. The drawing (r.) of the old façade (never completed) of the
Duomo designed by Arnolfo di Cambio was made shortly before its
demolition in 1587 by *Bernardino Poccetti* (and is the most detailed illustration of it which has survived). On the wall opposite are
numerous sculptures from the old façade by *Arnolfo di Cambio,* including a *Madonna and Child (a somewhat enigmatic work with
striking glass eyes), *St Reparata, St Zenobius, the *Madonna of the
Nativity, and (at the end of the room) Boniface VIII (restored). The
statuettes from the main door (1362–77) are the work of *Piero d.
Giovanni Tedesco.* On the other long wall are the four seated
Evangelists which were added to the lower part of the façade in the
early 15C: *Nanni di Banco,* St Luke; *Donatello,* *St John the
Evangelist; *Bernardo Ciuffagni,* St Matthew; *Niccolò di Piero
Lamberti,* St Mark.—In the centre of the room, is the tomb of Piero
Farnese (14C) which includes a relief from a Roman sarcophagus of
the late 2C A.D., and the angel and basin of the 14C stoup (attrib. to
Urbano da Cortona) from the Duomo (comp. p 67). In the recess are
sculptural fragments inluding an Etruscan cippus (5C B.C.), showing

musicians and dancers, and a Roman sarcophagus with the story of Orestes. The two small rooms beyond are devoted to *Brunelleschi.* His death mask is displayed beside models in wood of the cupola (probably made by a contemporary of Brunelleschi), and the lantern (thought to date from 1436 and to be by the architect himself). The apparatus which may have been used in the construction of the cupola, including pulleys, ropes, technical instruments, etc. is displayed here. It was found in a storeroom at the foot of the cupola, together with Brunelleschi's original brick moulds.—Steps lead up to ROOM II which displays antiphonals, and three wood models entered in the competition of 1587 for the new façade of the Duomo. They are the work of *Giambologna, Don Giovanni de' Medici,* and *Buontalenti.* The roundel of the Agnus Dei, the 'stemma' of the 'Arte della Lana' who supervised work in the Duomo, has probably always been here since it was commissioned from the workshop of *And. della Robbia.*—In the CHAPEL are reliquaries by *Pier Giov. di Matteo* and other artists of the 14–16C. The Madonna between SS. Catherine and Zenobius, above the altar, is attrib. to *Bernardo Daddi* (1334).

On the Stair landing is the *Pietà of *Michelangelo* which has been placed here while restoration work is in progress in the Duomo (it was formerly in a chapel at the E. end). A late work, it was intended for Michelangelo's own tomb. According to Vasari, the head of Nicodemus is a self-portrait. Unsatisfied with his work, the sculptor destroyed the arm and left leg of Christ, and his pupil, Tiberio Calcagni, restored the arm and finished the figure of Mary Magdalen.—At the top of the stairs are two frescoed heads (SS. Peter and Paul) by *Bicci di Lorenzo.*

FIRST FLOOR. ROOM I is dominated by the two famous *Cantorie made in the 1430s by *Luca della Robbia* and *Donatello,* probably as organ-lofts (rather than singing galleries) above the two sacristy doors in the Duomo. The one on the left, by *Luca della Robbia,* was his first important commission. The original panels are displayed beneath the reconstructed Cantoria. As the inscription indicates, the charming sculptured panels illustrate Psalm 150. The children (some of them drawn from Classical models), dancing, singing, or playing musical instruments, are exquisitely carved within a beautiful architectural framework. *Donatello's* Cantoria, opposite, provides a striking contrast, with a frieze of running putti against a background of coloured inlay. Beneath it is displayed his expressive statue in wood of *St Mary Magdalen (formerly in the Baptistery), thought to be a late work. It has been beautifully restored after damage in the flood of 1966.—Around the walls are the 16 statues (most of them in poor condition) formerly in the niches on the Campanile (comp. p 70): *Donatello,* Bearded Prophet, Abraham and Isaac (part of the modelling is attributed to *Nanni di Bartolo*); *Nanni di Bartolo* (attrib.), Prophet; *Donatello,* Beardless Prophet; *And. Pisano* (attrib.), four Prophets; *Nanni di Bartolo,* Abdia; *Donatello,* 'Geremiah', *Habbakuk ('lo zuccone'), St John the Baptist (attrib.); *And. Pisano,* two Sibyls, Solomon, and David.—The adjoining room exhibits the original *Bas-reliefs (also badly worn) which decorated the two lower registers of the Campanile. The lower row, which date from the early 14C, are charming works by *And. Pisano* (some perhaps designed by *Giotto*);

they illustrate the Creation of Man, and the Arts and Industries. Starting on the wall opposite the entrance and going l.: Creation of Adam, Creation of Eve, Labours of Adam and Eve, Jabal (the Pastoral life), Jubal (Music), Tubalcain (the Smith), Noah, Gionitus (Astronomy), The Art of Building, Medicine, Hunting, Weaving, Phoroneus the Lawgiver, Daedalus, Navigation, Hercules and Cacus, Agriculture, Theatrica, Architecture, Phidias (Sculpture), Apelles (Painting). The last five reliefs (on the r. wall) were made in the following century by *Luca della Robbia* (1437–39) to fill the frames on the N. face of the Campanile: Grammar, Philosophy, Orpheus (representing Poetry or Rhetoric), Arithmetic, and Astrology (with the figure of Pythagoras).—The upper row of smaller reliefs by pupils of *Pisano,* illustrate the seven Planets, the Virtues, and the Liberal Arts. The seven Sacraments (r. wall) are by *Alberto Arnoldi.* In the middle of this wall is a lunette of the Madonna and Child by *And. Pisano,* formerly over a door of the Campanile.

Room II. To the r., two Byzantine mosaic tablets of exquisite workmanship, thought to date from the early 14C; *'Maestro del Bigallo',* St Zenobius enthroned and stories from his life; paintings of the 14–15C Florentine school; *And. Pisano,* statuettes of Christ and St Reparata; (in cases) 27 needlework *Panels (in poor condition) from a liturgical tapestry with scenes from the life of St John the Baptist worked by the craftsmen of the 'Arte di Calimala' designed by *Ant. del Pollaiolo.* At the foot of the steps, Madonna and Angel, formerly attrib. to *Nanni di Banco* (possibly by *Jac. della Quercia*). *Tino da Camaino,* Female bust; *Giov. di Balduccio* (or *And. Pisano*), Crucifix in wood (from the Baptistery); Florentine paintings including a Triptych of the Martyrdom of St Sebastian by *Giov. del Biondo.* Above the door, *Bened. Buglioni,* Mary Magdalen in the Desert.—At the end of the room is the magnificent *Altar of silver-gilt, from the Baptistery, a Gothic work by Florentine goldsmiths finished in the 15C, illustrating the history of St John the Baptist. The statuette of the Baptist is by *Michelozzo;* the reliefs (at the sides) of the Beheading of the Saint, and of his birth are by *Verrocchio* and *Ant. del Pollaiolo.* The altar is surmounted by a silver *Cross by *Betto di Francesco* (1455), *Ant. del Pollaiolo,* and probably other artists (*Bernardo Cennini?*). On the walls, *Monte di Giovanni,* mosaic of St Zenobius (1505); *Pagno di Lapo Portigiani* (attrib.), bas-relief of the Madonna and Child; *Jac. del Casentino* (attrib.), Processional painting of St Agatha (painted on both sides).

The piazza follows the curve of the Duomo. At No. 28 (red) the 16C Palazzo Strozzi-Niccolini stands on the site of a house where Donatello had his studio (19C plaque and bust). At the end of Via dei Servi can be seen Piazza SS. Annunziata with the equestrian statue of the grand-duke Ferdinando I. In Piazza del Duomo are several medieval houses with coats-of-arms (some of them put up in 1390), and one (No. 5) with a pretty loggia. Opposite a side door (the Porta della Mandorla, see p 66) of the Duomo, the long straight Via Ricasoli leads towards San Marco. Piazza San Giovanni is regained across the busy Via de' Martelli (view of Palazzo Medici-Riccardi). Beside the Baptistery is the *Pillar of St Zenobius,* erected in the 14C to commemorate an elm which came into leaf here when the body of the bishop saint (died c. 430) was translated from San Lorenzo to Santa Reparata in the 9C. In the piazza, at No. 7 is the *Casa dell'Opera di San Giovanni,* with a copy in the lunette of a statuette of St John by Michelozzo (the original is now in the Bargello). The interesting medieval courtyard is used by a florist. The W. end of the square is occupied by the huge *Palazzo Arcivescovile.* It incorporates the church of San Salvatore al Vescovo (adm sometimes on request) with frescoes by Ferretti (18C). The little romanesque façade (very worn) of the earlier church can be seen behind, in Piazza dell'Olio.

3 PIAZZA DEL DUOMO TO PIAZZA DELLA SIGNORIA

Between the Baptistery and the Campanile the straight VIA DE' CALZAIOLI (Pl. 16; 4,6; a pedestrian precinct) leads due S. towards Piazza Signoria. On the line of a Roman road, this was the main thoroughfare of the medieval city, linking the Duomo to Palazzo Vecchio, and passing the guildhall of Orsanmichele. Although many of the shops on the ground floors of the buildings still have arches, the street was transformed when it was widened in the 1840s. Via degli Speziali diverges r. for **Piazza della Repubblica** (Pl. 16; 3), on the site of the Roman forum, and still in the centre of the city. It was laid out at the end of the 19C after the demolition of many medieval buildings, the Mercato Vecchio, and part of the Ghetto (which was created in 1571 and extended from the N. side of the present square to Via dei Pecori). Much criticised at the time, it remains a disappointing intrusion into the historical centre of the city, with its sombre colonnades and undistinguished buildings disfigured by advertisements. The *Colonna dell'Abbondanza,* a granite Roman column, was first set up here in 1428. Several large cafès have tables outside, including the 'Giubbe Rosse', famous meeting place in the first decades of the century of writers and artists. Beneath the arcades is the central Post Office and (on Thusdays) a flower and plant market. The Cinema Edison, beneath the portico, was opened here in 1901. The huge triumphal arch on the W. side of the piazza leads into Via Strozzi (comp. p 142).

On the other side of Via de' Calzaioli is the narrow Via del Corso (comp. p 193). Farther on, opposite Via dei Tavolini (with a view of a medieval tower) rises the tall rectangular church of ***Orsanmichele** (Pl. 16; 6), on the site of *San Michele ad hortum* founded in the 9C and destroyed in 1239. It is thought that a grain market was erected here c. 1290 by *Arnolfo di Cambio* which was burnt down in 1304. The present building was built as a market by *Fr. Talenti, Neri di Fioravante,* and *Benci di Cione* in 1337. The arcades were enclosed by huge three-light windows by *Simone Talenti* in 1380. These, in turn, were bricked up shortly after they were finished (but their superb Gothic tracery can still be appreciated). The upper story, completed in 1404, was intended to be used as a granary. The decoration of the exterior was undertaken by the Guilds (or 'Arti') who commissioned statues of their patron saints for the canopied niches. They competed with each other to command work from the best artists of the age, and the statues are an impressive testimony to the skill of Florentine sculptors over a period of some two hundred years.

The 'Arti Maggiori' or Greater Guilds took over control of the government of the city at the end of the 13C and the regime of the 'secondo popolo' lasted for nearly a century. Merchants in the most important trades, bankers, and professional men were members of these guilds: the *'Calimala'* (the first guild, named from the street where the wholesale cloth-importers had their warehouses), the *'Giudici e notai'* (judges and notaries), the *'Cambio'* (bankers), the *'Lana'* (woollen-cloth merchants and manufacturers), the *'Por Santa Maria'* (named from the street which led to the workshops of the silk-cloth industry), the *'Medici e speziali'* (physicians and apothecaries, the guild to which painters belonged), and the *'Vaiai e pellicciai'* (furriers). The other corporations, the 'Arti Minori', created in the 13C, represented shopkeepers and skilled artisans.

The tabernacles, and the Guilds to whom they belonged, are described below, beginning at Via de' Calzaioli (corner of Via de' Lamberti) and going round to the right: 1. 'CALIMALA' (wholesale cloth-importers). Tabernacle and St John the Baptist (1414–16) by *Lor. Ghiberti*. This was the first life-size statue of the Renaissance to be cast in bronze.—Beyond the door, 2. 'TRIBUNALE DI MERCANZIA' (the merchants' court, where guild matters were adjudicated). Bronze group of the *Incredulity of St Thomas (1466–83) by *Verrocchio*. The tabernacle was commissioned earlier by the 'Parte Guelfa'; it is the work of *Donatello*, and formerly contained his St Louis of Toulouse now in the Museo dell'Opera di Santa Croce, comp. p 159. Above is the round 'stemma' of the 'Mercanzia' in enamelled terracotta by *Luca della Robbia* (1463).—3. 'GIUDICI E NOTAI' (judges and notaries). Tabernacle by *Niccolò Lamberti* (1403–06), with a bronze statue of St Luke (1601) by *Giambologna*.—4. 'BECCAI' (butchers). St Peter (1408–13) attrib. to *Donatello*.—5. 'CONCIAPELLI' (tanners). Tabernacle and St Philip (c. 1415) by *Nanni di Banco*.—6. 'MAESTRI DI PIETRA E DI LEGNAME' (stonemasons and carpenters, the guild to which architects and sculptors belonged). Tabernacle and statues of *Four soldier saints (the 'Quattro Santi Coronati'), modelled on Roman statues, by *Nanni di Banco* (c. 1415). The *Relief, by the same artist, illustrates the work of the Guild. Above is their 'stemma' in inlaid terracotta by *Luca della Robbia*.—7. 'ARMAIUOLI' (armourers). St George by *Donatello* (copies of the original statue of 1417 now in the Bargello, comp. p 146, and the bas-relief which has been removed for restoration).—8. 'CAMBIO' (bankers). Tabernacle and bronze statue of *St Matthew (1419–22), by *Ghiberti*.—Beyond the door, 9. 'LANAIUOLI' (wool manufacturers and clothiers). Bronze *St Stephen by *Ghiberti* (1428).—10. 'MANISCALCHI' (farriers). St Eligius and bas-relief of the Saint in a smithy by *Nanni di Banco*.—11. 'LINAIOLI E RIGATTIERI' (linen merchants and used clothes' dealers). *St Mark (1411–13) by *Donatello* (removed for restoration).—12. 'PELLICCIAI' (furriers). St James the Greater, with a bas-relief of his beheading, attrib. to *Niccolò Lamberti*.—13. 'MEDICI E SPEZIALI' (physicians and apothecaries). Gothic tabernacle attrib. to *Simone Talenti* (1399), with a *Madonna and Child (the 'Madonna delle Rose') thought to be the work of *Giov. Tedesco* (also attrib. to *Niccolò di Pietro Lamberti* or *Simone Ferrucci*). Above, '*Stemma' by *Luca della Robbia*.—14. 'SETAIUOLI E ORAFI (silkweavers and goldsmiths). St John the Evangelist by *Baccio da Montelupo* (1515).

The INTERIOR of the dark rectangular hall (best light in the morning) now serves as a church. It is divided into two aisles by two massive pillars, and on a raised platform at one end are the two altars. The vaults and central and side pilasters are decorated with interesting frescoes of patron saints (many of them damaged, restored, or difficult to see) painted in the late 14C or early 15C by *Jac. del Casentino, Giov. del Ponte, Niccolò di Pietro Gerini, Ambrogio di Baldese*, and *Smeraldo di Giovanni*. In the 15–16C more frescoes were added (and some panel paintings) by *Giov. Ant. Sogliani, Il Poppi, Lorenzo di Credi*, and *Mariotto Albertinelli*. The fine Gothic stained glass windows include one (St Jacob among the shepherds) designed by *Lor. Monaco*.—The Gothic *TABERNACLE (light on r.) by *And. Orcagna* (1349–59), is a masterpiece of all the decorative arts, ornamented with marble and coloured glass, as well as with reliefs and statuettes. This is the only important sculptural work by this artist who was also a

detail of the 'Pianta della Catena' of c. 1472, showing the Baptistery, Duomo, Orsanmichele, and the Palazzo and Loggia della Signoria

painter and architect. Around the base are reliefs of the life of th
Virgin (including, in front, the Marriage of the Virgin, and the An
nunciation). Behind the altar (facing the entrance) is an elaborat
sculptured relief of the Transition and Assumption of the Virgin. A
beautiful frame of carved angels encloses a painting on the altar of th
*Madonna by *Bern. Daddi.*—On the other altar is a statue of th
Madonna and Child with St Anne, by *Fr. da Sangallo* (1522).

The two large Gothic halls on the upper floors of Orsanmichele ar
now used for exhibitions. They are approached from an overhea
passageway (1569) from *Palazzo dell'Arte della Lana,* described i
Rte 21. In Via Orsanmichele is *Palazzo dell'Arte dei Beccai,* see p 186
One of the best known coffee merchants in the city has its shop an
cafè in Via de' Lamberti.—On the other side of Via de' Calzaioli is th
church of *San Carlo dei Lombardi* (1349–1404) with a severe (muc
ruined) façade. In the unattractive interior is a Deposition by Niccol
di Pietro Gerini (very poorly lit). The road ends in Piazza dell
Signoria, see Rte 4.

4   PIAZZA DELLA SIGNORIA

Piazza della Signoria (Pl. 16; 6), dominated by Palazzo Vecchio, th
town hall, has been the political centre of the city since the Middl
Ages. Here, from the 13C onwards, the 'popolo sovrano' met i
'parlamento' to resolve crises of government, and here in 1530 th
return of the Medici was acclaimed by the people. It was the scene o
public ceremonies, but also a gathering place in times of trouble. A
the instigation of Savonarola, 'immoral luxuries' including works o
art were burnt in the piazza, before the Inquisition denounced th
Prior of San Marco as a heretic and he, and his two companions, wer
burnt at the stake here on 23 May 1498. In the life of the city today
the piazza is still the focus of political manifestations. It is now a
pedestrian precinct (heavy traffic was banned from the piazza as earl
as 1385), and usually crowded with tourists as well as Florentines. O
Fridays it is a meeting place for factors and agricultural dealers from
the surrounding countryside. Several cafès and restaurants have table
outside.

The history of the square has followed that of Palazzo Vecchio. The area a
the foot of the palace was laid out as 'Piazza del Popolo' in 1307. During the 14C
houses were demolished nearby in order to expand the size of the piazza. B
1385, when it was paved, it had nearly reached its present dimensions. Excava
tions in 1973 (since covered over), near the statue of Cosimo I, revealed remain
of private Roman baths (2C A.D.).

Beside the splendid Palazzo Vecchio (described in Rte 5) is the hug
*Loggia della Signoria** (Pl. 16; 6; also known as *Loggia dei Lanzi* an
Loggia dell'Orcagna), with its three beautiful lofty arches. Thei
semicircular form, breaking free from Gothic shapes, anticipates th
Renaissance. The loggia was built in 1376–82 by *Benci di Cione* an
Simone Talenti (probably on a design by *Orcagna*) to be used b
government officials during public ceremonies, and as an ornament t
the square. In the spandrels are statues of Virtues (1384–89) against a
blue-enamelled ground, designed by *Agnolo Gaddi.* The columns ar

decorated with (worn) statuettes and lions' heads and have composite capitals; there are two elaborate corbels on the back wall. It received its alternative name 'Loggia dei Lanzi' from the bodyguard (the 'Lanzichenecchi') of Cosimo I who were stationed here.

It is only since the end of the 18C that the loggia has been used as an open-air museum of sculpture. In front, on the left, is *Cellini's* magnificent bronze Perseus trampling Medusa and exhibiting her severed head. This was commissioned by Cosimo I in 1545 and placed under the loggia near Donatello's Judith (see below); it is considered Cellini's masterpiece. He provides a graphic description in his 'Autobiography' of the great difficulties he encountered while casting it (during which time his studio caught fire and he retired to bed with a fever). He saved the situation at the last moment by sieżing all his pewter plates and bowls and throwing them into the melting-pot. The elaborate pedestal, using classical motifs, incorporates bronze statuettes and a bas-relief of Perseus rescuing Andromeda which have been replaced by copies (the originals are in the Bargello, see p 144). On either side of the central arch is a lion, that on the right a Greek work, and the other a 16C copy. Beneath the r. arch is *Giambologna's* last work, the *Rape of the Sabine (1583), a three-figure group. One of the most successful Mannerist sculptures, the elaborate serpentine composition is designed to be seen from every side. The pedestal bears a bronze bas-relief. Under the loggia are Hercules and the Centaur, by *Giambologna;* Ajax with the body of Patroclus, a Roman copy of a Greek original, and the Rape of Polyxena, by *Pio Fedi* (1866), against the back wall are Roman statues.

Beyond the corner of the piazza with the Uffizi buildings (see Rte 6) is the main entrance to Palazzo Vecchio. In front stands a copy of *Michelangelo's* famous DAVID. The huge statue was commissioned by the city of Florence in 1501 and set up here in 1504 as a political symbol representing the victory of Republicanism over tyranny. When it was unveiled it was heralded as a masterpiece and at once established Michelangelo as the greatest Florentine artist of his age. It was removed to the Accademia in 1873 (comp. p 113). The colossal statue of HERCULES AND CACUS was sculpted in 1534 by *Bandinelli;* it is an unhappy imitation of the David, all the defects of which were pointed out by Cellini to Cosimo I in the presence of the sculptor. Farther to the left, in front of the palace, is the base for the statue of Judith and Holofernes by Donatello, recently removed to the Sala d'Udienza in Palazzo Vecchio (see p 87), where it can be seen to advantage and is no longer dwarfed by the colossal statues on either side. Beyond a copy of Donatello's 'Marzocco', the heraldic lion of Florence (the original is in the Bargello, see p 146) is the NEPTUNE FOUNTAIN 1560–75). The colossal flaccid figure of Neptune, known to Florentines as 'il Biancone', has been restored. It was carved from a block of marble which, despite the efforts of Cellini, was first offered to Bandinelli and on his death to *Ammannati.* In the more successful elegant bronze groups on the basin, Ammannati was assisted by *Giambologna, And. Calamech,* and others. The porphyry disk in the pavement in front of the fountain marks the spot where Savonarola was burnt at the stake (see above). On a line with the statues across the front of Palazzo Vecchio is the fine bronze equestrian monument to Cosimo I by *Giambologna* (1595).

At the end of the piazza (which opens out towards Piazza San Firenze, see Rte 14), and opposite the long flank of Palazzo Vecchio described on p 82) is the *Tribunale di Mercanzia* (or Merchants' Court), founded in 1308 and established in this building in 1359. Guild matters were discussed here. *Palazzo Uguccioni* (No. 7) has an unusual but handsome façade attrib. to Mariotto di Zanobi Folfi (1550; awaiting restoration), and a bust of Francesco I by Giov. Bandini. Above a bank at No. 5, is displayed the COLLEZIONE DELLA RAGIONE (Pl. 16; 6; adm see p 57), a representative collection of 20C Italian art left to the city in 1970 by Alberto Della Ragione.

It is at present the only public collection open in Florence illustrating this period of Italian art. It includes mostly representational works by *Arturo Tosi, Carlo Carrà, Giorgio Morandi, Ottone Rosai, Gino Severini, Mario Sironi, Felice Casorati, Giorgio De Chirico, Arturo Martini, Virgilio Guidi, Massimo Campigli, Filippo De Pisis, Lucio Fontana, Marino Marini, Carlo Levi, Mario Mafai, Scipione, Giacomo Manzù, Corrado Cagli, Renato Guttuso,* and many others.

Savonarola burnt at the stake in Piazza della Signoria, a detail of a picture by an unknown Florentine painter, c. 1500, probably an eye-witness of the event. (Museo di S. Marco)

5 PALAZZO VECCHIO

*Palazzo Vecchio (Pl. 16; 6; adm see p 58; also know as *Palazzo della Signoria*), the medieval Palazzo del Popolo, is still the town hall of Florence. On a design traditionally attrib. to *Arnolfo di Cambio* (1298–1302), it is an imposing fortress-palace built in pietra forte on a trapezoidal plan. The façade has remained virtually unchanged: it has graceful divided windows and a battlemented gallery. It became the prototype of many other Palazzi Comunali in Tuscany. It was the tallest edifice in the city until the 15C; the tower (1310; recently restored), asymmetrically placed, is 95 metres high. Many of the rooms on the upper floors are open to the public.

The palace stands on part of the site of the Roman theatre of Florence built in the 1C A.D. Here the 'priori' lived during their two months' tenure of office in the government of the medieval city. The bell in the tower summoned citizens to 'Parlamento' in times of trouble in the square below. Cosimo il Vecchio was imprisoned in the 'Alberghetto' in the tower in 1433 before being exiled. The building became known as Palazzo della Signoria during the Republican governments of the 15C, and alterations were carried out inside by *Michelozzo, Giul.* and *Bened. da Maiano* and *Dom. Ghirlandaio*. After the expulsion of the Medi in 1494 a huge hall (later known as the Sala dei Cinquecento) was built by *Cronaca* to house the new legislative body, the Consiglio Maggiore, which represented the aristocratic character of the new regime. Savonarola, at first a supporter of this government, was imprisoned in the Alberghetto in 1498 before being burnt at the stake in the piazza outside. One of the most significant

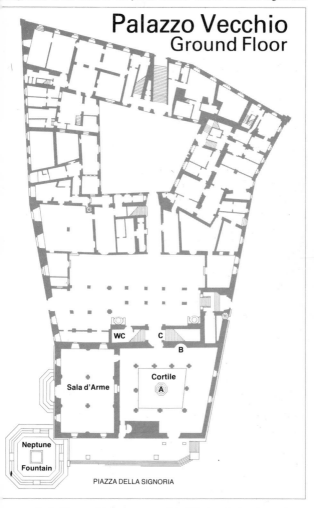

Palazzo Vecchio
Ground Floor

WC

C

B

Cortile

(A)

Sala d'Arme

Neptune
Fountain

PIAZZA DELLA SIGNORIA

moments in the history of the palace occured in 1540 when Cosimo I moved here from the private Medici palace in Via Larga (now Via Cavour). *Battista del Tasso, Vasari,* and later *Buontalenti* were called in to redecorate the building, now called Palazzo Ducale, and extend it at the back, for the early Medici dukes, without, however, altering the exterior aspect on Piazza della Signoria. It became known as Palazzo Vecchio only after 1549 when the Medici grand-dukes took up residence in Palazzo Pitti. The Provisional Governments of 1848 and 1859 met here, and from 1865 to 1871 it housed the Chamber of Deputies and the

Foreign Ministry when Florence was capital of the Kingdom of Italy. Since 1872 it has been the seat of the municipal government.—The flank of the building on Piazza Signoria includes the battlemented 14C *Salone dei Cinquecento*, with a hipped roof and marble window, and the handsome façade added by *Buontalenti* in Via de' Gondi. The 16C additions on the other flank, and at the back of the building on Via dei Leoni, incorporate medieval houses.

The room numbers given below refer to the plans in the text. It is likely that the itinerary of the visit to the upper floors will be changed when more of the building is opened to the public. The description below does not take into account the final arrangement of the rooms which was not completed in 1981.

The ENTRANCE is guarded by two bizarre terms by *Bandinelli* and *Vinc. de' Rossi* (the other sculptures outside the palace are described on p 79). Above is a frieze (1528) dedicated to 'Cristo Re' with the monogram of Christ flanked by two symbolic lions. The CORTILE was reconstructed by *Michelozzo* (1453). The elaborate decorations were added in 1565 by *Giorgio Vasari* on the occasion of the marriage between Francesco, son of Cosimo I, and Joanna of Austria. The columns were covered with stucco and the vaults and walls painted with grotesques and views (now very faded) of Austrian cities. The fountain (A) designed by Vasari bears a copy of *Verrocchio's* popular putto holding a dolphin (c. 1470), a bronze made for a fountain at the Medici villa at Careggi. The original is preserved inside the palace (see p 87). The statue of Samson killing the Philistine (B) is by *Pierino da Vinci*. In the large rectangular SALA D'ARME, the only room on this floor which survives from the 14C structure, occasional exhibitions are held. The rest of the ground floor is taken up with busy local government offices. Just beyond the Courtyard the monumental GRAND STAIRCASE (C) by *Vasari* ascends (r.) in a scenographic double flight to the first floor (where tickets are purchased).

The immense **Salone dei Cinquecento* (53½ x 22 metres, and 18 m high) was built by *Cronaca* in 1495 for the meetings of the Consiglio Maggiore of the Republic (addressed here in 1496 by Savonarola). *Leonardo da Vinci* was commissioned in 1503 by the government to decorate one of the two long walls with a huge mural representing the Florentine victory at Anghiari over Milan in 1440. He experimented, without success, with a new technique of mural painting and completed only a fragment of the work before leaving Florence for Milan in 1506. It is not known whether this had disappeared or was destroyed (probably by order of Cosimo I) before the present frescoes were carried out under the direction of Vasari. *Michelangelo* was asked to do a similar composition on the opposite wall, representing the battle of Cascina between Florence and Pisa in 1364, but he only completed the cartoon before being called to Rome by Julius II. The cartoons of both works and the fragment painted by Leonardo were frequently copied and studied by contemporary painters before they were lost (comp. p 85). The room was transformed by Vasari in 1563–65 when the present decoration (designed with the help of Vincenzo Borghini) was carried out in celebration of Cosimo I. In the centre of the elaborate ceiling is the Apotheosis of the Duke surrounded by the 'stemme' of the Guilds. The other panels, by *Vasari, Giov. Stradano, Jac. Zucchi,* and *G.B. Naldini,* represent allegories of the cities of Tuscany under Florentine dominion, the foundations and early growth of Florence, and the victories over Siena (1554–55) and Pisa

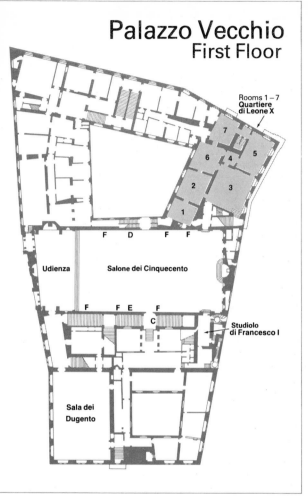

Palazzo Vecchio
First Floor

Rooms 1–7
Quartiere
di Leone X

7
6 4 5
2 3
1

F D F F

Udienza   Salone dei Cinquecento

F   F E   F

C

Studiolo
di Francesco I

Sala dei
Dugento

(1496–1509). On the walls are huge frescoes by the same artists illustrating three more episodes in the wars with Pisa (entrance wall)
and Siena. The decoration was completed on the end walls by *Jac.
Ligozzi, Dom. Passignano,* and *Cigoli.* The raised tribuna
('UDIENZA') contains statues by *Bandinelli* and *Vinc. de' Rossi* (finished in the following century by *Giov. Caccini*) of distinguished
members of the Medici family. *Michelangelo's* *Victory (D), a
strongly-knit two-figure group, was intended for a niche in the tomb
of Julius II in Rome. It was presented to Cosimo I by Michelangelo's
nephew in 1565 and set up here by Vasari as a celebration of the victory of Cosimo I over Siena. The serpentine form of the principal

figure was frequently copied by later Mannerist sculptors. On the entrance wall (E) is *Giambologna's* original plaster model for Virtue overcoming Vice (or 'Florence victorious over Pisa') commissioned as a 'pendant' to Michelangelo's Victory. The other statues, representing the Labours of Hercules (F), are *Vincenzo de' Rossi's* best works. On the end wall, opposite the tribune, are antique Roman statues.

A door in the entrance wall, to the right (inconspicuous as it is usually kept closed, but adm freely granted) gives access to the charming *Studiolo of Francesco I. This tiny study (with no windows) was created by *Vasari* and his school in 1570–75 on an iconographical scheme devised by Vincenzo Borghini. It is a masterpiece of Florentine Mannerist decoration.

The present entrance is modern; it was formerly accessible only by the door on the end wall from the private rooms of the dukes. It is entirely decorated with paintings and bronze statuettes celebrating Francesco's interest in the natural sciences and alchemy. The lower row of paintings conceal cupboards in which he kept his treasures. On the barrel vault, by *Il Poppi,* are allegories of the four Elements and portraits by *Bronzino* of Francesco's parents, Cosimo I and Eleonora di Toledo. The four walls, symbolizing the four Elements, include: left wall, ('Water'): *Vinc. Danti,* Venus (bronze); *Vasari,* Perseus liberating Andromeda; *Santi di Tito,* Crossing of the Red Sea; *G.B. Naldini,* Finding of amber; *Giov. Stradano,* Circe and the companions of Ulysses; *Aless. Allori,* Pearl fishing.—On the end wall ('Air'): *Giov. Bandini,* Juno (bronze); *Maso di San Friano,* Diamond mine, Fall of Icarus.—Right wall ('Fire'): *Giambologna,* Apollo, *Vincenzo de' Rossi,* Vulcan (both bronzes); *Giov. Maria Butteri,* Glass-blowing factory; *Aless. Fei,* Goldsmiths' workshop; *Giov. Stradano,* Alchemist's laboratory.—Entrance wall ('Earth'): *Bart. Ammannati,* Opi (bronze); *Jac. Zucchi,* Goldmine.—A small staircase leads up to the Tesoretto (adm only to scholars with special permission), the richly decorated private study of Cosimo I. The stuccoes are by *Tommaso Boscoli* and *Leonardo Ricciarelli* and the vault frescoes by *Il Poppi* (1559–62).

Also off the Sala dei Cinquecento (to the left of the dais) is a Vestibule (the coved ceiling of which has painted grotesque decorations) which leads into the **Sala dei Dugento** (usually closed), where the town Council meets. This was reconstructed in 1472–77 by *Benedetto* and *Giul. da Maiano* who also executed the magnificent wood ceiling (with the help of *Dom., Marco,* and *Giul. del Tasso*). The name is derived from the council of 200 citizens who met here. On the walls are *Tapestries made in Florence in 1546–53 with the story of Joseph, designed by *Bronzino, Pontormo, Salviati,* and *Allori.*

The door opposite the Studiolo leads into the **Quartiere di Leone X** (1–7) decorated by *Vasari* and assistants (including *Marco da Faenza* and *Giov. Stradano*) in 1555–62 for Cosimo I. The mural paintings illustrate the political history of the Medici family. Some of the rooms are usually closed. The Sala di Cosimo il Vecchio (1) has a ceiling painting showing Cosimo's return from exile, by *Vasari.*—The Sala di Lorenzo il Magnifico (2) shows Lorenzo receiving the homage of the ambassadors.—To the r. the Sala di Leone X (3) illustrates the life of cardinal Giovanni de' Medici, later Leo X. It has a good terracotta pavement and a fireplace by *Ammannati.*—In the CHAPEL (4) the wedding between Isabella, daughter of Cosimo I, and Alfonso d'Este was celebrated, and the secret marriage between Francesco I and Bianca Cappello took place. The altarpiece is an old copy of the Madonna dell'Impannata by Raphael now in the Pitti (p 106). It is flanked by Duke Cosimo as St Damian and Cosimo il Vecchio as St Cosma, the Medici patron saints, both good works by *Vasari.*—The SALA DI CLEMENTE VII (5) contains a mural painting of the siege of Florence by Charles V (1529–30) traditionally attrib. to *Vasari* (but now thought to be by *Giov. Stradano*), with a splendid panorama of the city.—The SALA DI COSIMO I (6) has the most elaborate historical paintings, with, in the centre, the prisoners from the battle of Montemurlo brought before Cosimo I.

Stairs lead up to the SECOND FLOOR past an interesting fresco (c. 1558) by *Giov. Stradano* of the fireworks in Piazza Signoria celebrating the feast-day of St John the Baptist. At the top of the stairs (left) is the **Quartiere degli Elementi,** five rooms (8-13) decorated with complicated allegories of the Elements by *Vasari* and assistants (including *Crist. Gherardi*). These rooms will probably be furnished and hung with paintings. The SALA DEGLI ELEMENTI (8) has good panel paintings set into the deeply recessed ceiling.—The TERRAZZA DI SATURNO (9) was sadly reduced in size in the last century. The ceiling was painted by *Stradano* on a design by *Vasari.* The fine view of Florence to the south-east includes the back of the Uffizi with the little round roof and lantern of the tribuna. Across the Arno, on the skyline, stands Forte di Belvedere, and the walls can be seen on the green hillside. San Miniato is prominent with its tower, and, lower down at the foot of the hill, Porta San Niccolò. Farther to the left is Santa Croce with its campanile.—The little bronze demon by *Giambologna* was removed from the exterior of Palazzo Vecchietti.—The rooms beyond are destined to become a MUSEUM of works of art recovered from abroad (many of them having been exported illegally during the last War). The paintings to be exhibited here will probably include works by *Memling* (Portrait of a Gentlemen), *Masaccio* (attrib.; Madonna and Child), *Bronzino, Rubens, Veronese, Tintoretto,* and *Seb. Ricci.* A painting of Leda attrib. to *Leonardo da Vinci* (formerly in the Spiridon collection), and the Discobolos of Myron, the finest and best preserved replica of this famous statue (formerly belonging to the Lancelotti), may also be displayed here.

A balcony leads across the end of the Sala dei Cinquecento. Here is a painting of 1557 which shows the lost fragment of the Battle of Anghiari by Leonardo (comp. above), probably the best copy that has survived. The painting may be moved to another room in the palace. The following rooms (14-19) form part of the **Quartiere di Eleonora di Toledo,** the apartments of the wife of Cosimo I. At present bare of furniture, they are also awaiting re-arrangement. The vault in the CAMERA VERDE (14) was painted with grotesques by *Rid. del Ghirlandaio* (c. 1540). The *CAPPELLA DI ELEONORA (15), entirely decorated by *Bronzino* in 1540–45, is one of his most famous works. The little study has a ceiling painted by *Salviati.*—The next four rooms were decorated in 1561–2 with ceilings by *Battista Botticelli* and paintings (illustrating allegories of the female Virtues) by *Vasari* and *Giov.*

Stradano. The SALA DI ESTER (17) has a pretty frieze of putti intertwined in the letters of the name of Eleonora, and a 15C lavabo from Palazzo di Parte Guelfa. In the SALA DI GUALDRADA (19) there is a series of charming views of the celebrations held in the streets and piazze of Florence.

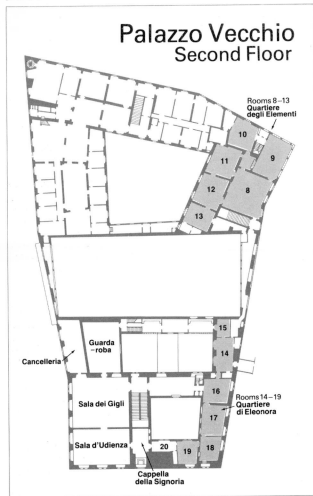

A passage (20) where remains of the old 14C polychrome ceiling, and parts of the ancient tower are visible, leads into the older rooms of the palace. The CAPPELLA DELLA SIGNORIA (or DEI PRIORI; 1511–14) was decorated by *Rid. del Ghirlandaio,* including an Annunciation with a view of the church of Santissima Annunziata in the background (before the addition of the portico). The altarpiece is by his pupil, *Fra*

Mariano da Pescia.—The **Sala d'Udienza** has a superb *Ceiling by *Giul. da Maiano* and assistants. Above the door from the chapel, designed by *Baccio d'Agnolo,* is a dedication to Christ (1529). The *Doorway crowned by a statue of Justice is by *Bened.* and *Giul. da Maiano.* The intarsia doors, with figures of Dante and Petrarch, are by *Giul. da Maiano* and *Francione.* The huge mural paintings illustrating stories from the life of the Roman hero Marco Camillus, were added c. 1545–8 by *Salviati;* they are one of the major works by this typically Mannerist painter. *Donatello's* bronze statue of *Judith and Holofernes has recently been removed from Piazza della Signoria and placed here. One of his last and most sophisticated works, it was commissioned by the Medici and used as a fountain in the garden of their palace. On their expulsion from the city in 1495 it was expropriated by the government and placed under the Loggia della Signoria with an inscription warning against tyrants.

The **Sala dei Gigli** takes its name from the lilies, symbol of the city, which decorate the walls and ceiling. It contains another magnificent *Ceiling, and the other face of the doorway with a statue of the young St John the Baptist and putti by *Bened.* and *Giul. da Maiano.* The fresco by *Dom. Ghirlandaio* shows St Zenobius enthroned between SS. Stephen and Lawrence and two lions, and lunettes with six heroes of ancient Rome. From the window can be seen Orsanmichele, the Campanile and cupola of the Duomo, the tower of the Badia, and the top of the Bargello.—A window of the old palace serves as a doorway into the CANCELLERIA, built in 1511 and used as an office by Niccolò Machiavelli during his term as government secretary. He is here recorded in a fine bust (16C) and a painting by *Santi di Tito.* Here, too, is displayed the *Putto with a dolphin, by *Verrocchio,* the original removed from the courtyard below (p 82). The stone bas-relief of St George (attrib. to *Arnolfo di Cambio*) used to decorate the Porta San Giorgio (comp. p 181).—The GUARDAROBA or SALA DELLE CARTE GEOGRAFICHE was decorated with a fine ceiling and wooden cupboards in 1563–65 by *Dionigi di Matteo Nigetti.* On the presses are 57 maps illustrating the entire known world with a remarkable degree of accuracy. Of great scientific and historical interest, they were painted by *Fra Egnazio Danti* for Cosimo I (1563) and completed by *Stef. Bonsignori* by 1581 for Francesco I. The map on the left of the entrance shows the British Isles. The huge globe in the centre is also designed by *Danti.*—From here a door (closed indefinitely) gives access to the Gallery, a covered walk encircling the 13C part of the palace.

The **Quartiere del Mezzanino** (at present closed to the public) contains the COLLEZIONE LOESER. It was left to the Commune of Florence in 1928 by the distinguished American art critic and connoisseur, and contains works of the Tuscan school from the 14C-16C (including a splendid portrait by *Bronzino* of Laura Battiferri, wife of Bartolomeo Ammannati).—The *Alberghetto,* used as a political prison, and the TOWER (*View) have been closed indefinitely to visitors.

6   GALLERIA DEGLI UFFIZI

The massive ***Palazzo degli Uffizi** (Pl. 16; 6) extends from Piazza della Signoria to the Arno. Houses were demolished to create this long narrow site next to Palazzo Vecchio, and *Vasari* commissioned by Cosimo I to erect a building here to serve as government offices ('uffici', hence 'uffizi'). The unusual U-shaped building with a short 'façade' on the river front was begun in 1560 and completed, according to Vasari's design, after his death in 1574 by *Alf. Parigi the Elder* and *Bern. Buontalenti* (who also made provision for an art gallery here for Francesco I). Resting on unstable sandy ground, it is a feat of engineering skill. The use of iron to reinforce the building permitted extraordinary technical solutions during its construction, and allowed for the remarkably large number of apertures. A long arcade supports three upper stories pierced by numerous windows and a loggia in pietra serena. In the niches of the pilasters are 19C statues of illustrious Tuscans. Beneath the arcades are the stalls of a market for leather goods and souvenirs (open all day exc. Mon in winter & Sat in summer). The building now houses the famous Art Gallery and the Tuscan State Archives.

The **Archivio dello Stato,** on the 2nd floor, is entered by the 8th door under the left-hand colonnade. Founded in 1582, the archives occupy over 400 rooms and date back to the 8C. They provide scholars with a wealth of information on the political and economic history of the city. They are to be moved to a new building under construction in P.za Beccaria (Pl. 11; 2).

The ground floor of *Palazzo della Zecca* is incorporated into the fabric of the building (r.; with well protected windows). The famous gold 'florins', first issued in 1252, were minted here.—At the end of Via Lambertesca is the Porta delle Suppliche added after 1574 by Buontalenti and surmounted by a bust of Francesco I by Bandini.

In Via della Ninna, incorporated into the building, are some of the nave columns of the church of *San Pier Scheraggio* (comp. below). Here also can be seen the beginning of the Corridoio Vasariano, forming a bridge between Palazzo Vecchio and the Uffizi (comp. p 99).

The ****Galleria degli Uffizi** is the most important collection of paintings in Italy and one of the great collections of the world. It is at present entered by the first door on the left under the colonnade (although there are plans to move the entrance to Via de' Castellani). Admission, see p 57.

The origins of the collection go back to Cosimo I. The galleries were enlarged and the collection augmented by Francesco I. The Medici dynasty continued to add numerous works of art in the following centuries: Ferdinando I transferred sculptures here from the Villa Medici in Rome; Ferdinando II inherited paintings by Raphael, Titian, and Piero della Francesca from Fr. Maria della Rovere of Urbino; and Cardinal Leopoldo began the collection of drawings and self-portraits. The last of the Medici, Anna Maria Lodovica, widow of the Elector Palatine, through a family Pact (1737) settled her inheritance on the people of Florence. The huge collection was partly broken up during the last century when much of the sculpture went to the Bargello and other material was transferred to the Archaeological Museum. This century many paintings from Florentine churches have been removed to the gallery.

The following description includes only some of the most important paintings and sculptures (and asterisks have been used sparingly). All the works are well labelled, and the collection is arranged chronologically by schools. Visitors are strongly recommended not to attempt to see the entire collection, for the first time, in one day; the first rooms (up to Room 15) include the major works of the Florentine Renaissance; the later rooms can be combined in a second visit.

Ground Floor. Beyond the ticket office is a room (not always open) which incorporates remains of the church of San Pier Scheraggio, founded c. 1068, and one of the largest churches of its time in Florence. It was altered when the Uffizi was built. Remains have also been found of an 8C Lombard church on this site. Here are displayed detached *Frescoes (c. 1450) by *And. del Castagno* of illustrious Florentines including Boccaccio, Petrarch, and Dante. These splendid monumental figures decorated a loggia of the Villa Pandolfini at Legnaia (and were later housed in the monastery of S. Apollonia). The room beyond (where the apse of the church has traces of damaged frescoes, c. 1294–99) contains the Madonna 'della Ninna' by the *'Maestro di San Martino alla Palma'* (c. 1340), and a predella with scenes from the life of St Peter by *Giov. del Ponte,* both painted for the church. In an adjacent corridor, *Fresco of the Annunciation by *Botticelli* (from the church of San Martino della Scala), and a column of the church with a 14C fresco of St Francis.—There is a LIFT for the picture galleries on the third floor. At the foot of the staircase is a colossal statue (very damaged), attrib. to the 16C Tuscan school, from the destroyed Medici theatre. The STAIRCASE, lined with antique busts and statues (including Venus Genetrix, and a Roman Vestal), leads up past part of the huge theatre built in the building by Buontalenti for Francesco I in 1586–89 (over the central door is a bust of Francesco by Giambologna or his workshop). On the left the old entrance now serves as the entrance to the **Prints and Drawings Rooms** (open to scholars with special permission, 9-13). The collection is one of the finest in the world and is particularly rich in Renaissance and Mannerist works. *Exhibitions are held periodically.

On the **Third Floor,** the VESTIBULE (A) contains antique sculpture including a statue of *Augustus, and two dogs, well preserved Greek works, perhaps of the Pergamenian School. Beyond is the long U-shaped gallery painted with grotesques in 1581 and lined with tapestries; it provides a fine setting for the superb collection of antique sculptures (mostly Hellenistic works). Opposite the windows overlooking the narrow piazza are doors leading into the numerous galleries of paintings (the collection begins in Room 2, to the left).

EAST CORRIDOR. ROOM 1, to the right (not always open), contains two copies of the Doryphoros of Polykleitos. Outside is (77.) Hercules and the Centaur, a late Hellenistic work restored by G.B. Caccini in 1589. Also in this part of the corridor: Roman sarcophagi, and statues of an Athlete (100.) and a Guardian Deity (252.), both from classical Greek originals. Among the tapestries which stretch the whole length of the corridor, those with grotesques on a yellow ground, by *Bachiacca,* are notable for the liveliness and imagination of the designs, and the 16C Flemish series (lives of Catherine de' Medici and Henri III) is interesting.

ROOM 2. TUSCAN SCHOOL OF THE 13C. Three huge *Paintings of the Madonna enthroned (the 'Maestà') dominate the room and provide a fitting introduction to the painting galleries. On the r. (8343.) the Madonna by *Cimabue* (c. 1285), painted for the church of Santa Trìnita, marks a final development of the Byzantine style of painting, where a decorative sense still predominates. On the l. is another exquisite version of this subject, the so-called 'Rucellai Madonna' from

Santa Maria Novella. Painted in 1285 it was traditionally attrib. to Cimabue, but is now recognised as the work of the younger Sienese artist, *Duccio di Boninsegna,* who is known to have worked in Cimabue's studio. The Madonna (8344.) in the centre of the room, painted some 25 years later for the church of Ognissanti by *Giotto,* heralds a new era in Western painting. Here there is a new idea of the monumentality of the figures in a more clearly defined space.—The Polyptych of the Badia (Madonna and four Saints) is also by *Giotto.* Other works from the Florentine, Lucchese, and Pisan schools of the 13C include St Luke, by the *'Maestro della Maddalena'* (3493.).

Room 3 (left). Sienese School of the 14C. 8346. *Ambr. Lorenzetti,* Presentation in the Temple (1342); 8348, 8349. Four scenes from the life of St Nicholas (restored in 1975); two small panels: 3157. *Niccolò Bonaccorsi,* Presentation in the Temple, and 3475. *Simone de' Crocifissi,* Nativity. 8347. *Pietro Lorenzetti* (brother of Ambrogio), panels of a dossal with the Story of the Blessed Umiltà; *451-453. *Simone Martini,* Annunciation (1333). The Gothic elegance of the two figures make this one of the masterpieces of the Sienese school. The Saints are by his brother-in-law, *Lippo Memmi.* 8439. *Niccolò di Ser Sozzo,* Madonna and Child; *Ambr. Lorenzetti,* 6411. Madonna and Child, St Nicholas of Bari and St Proculus (a triptych painted for the church of San Procolo recomposed when the central panel was left to the Gallery by Bernard Berenson). 445. *Pietro Lorenzetti,* Madonna in glory, signed and dated 1340.

Room 4. Florentine School of the 14C. 3073. *Bern. Daddi,* Madonna between SS. Matthew and Nicholas (1328); 3515. *Nardo di Cione,* Crucifixion; 454. *Giottino* (attrib.), Deposition (from the church of San Remigio); 8564. *Bern. Daddi,* Madonna and Child with Saints; 3163. *Orcagna,* St Matthew with scenes from his life (1367–8, completed by his brother, *Jacopo di Cione*); 459. *Giov. da Milano,* 10 panels of Saints, Martyrs, and Virgins.

Rooms 5 and 6. Later Gothic Schools. 447. *Gherardo Starnina,* The Thebaid, a charming panel telling the story of the life of these hermits. 885. *Lor. Monaco,* Coronation of the Madonna (1413); *Gentile da Fabriano,* 887. Mary Magdalen, St Nicholas of Bari, St John and St George (1425; from the Quaratesi polyptych), *8364. Adoration of the Magi (1423), with a fairy-tale quality, and a striking use of gold. The predella is exquisitely painted. 464. *Agnolo Gaddi,* Crucifixion; *466. *Lor. Monaco,* Adoration of the Magi.—From the window there is a view of Santa Croce and the hill of San Miniato.—Room 7, Florentine School of the early 15C. *Fra' Angelico,* 1612. Coronation of the Virgin, 143. Madonna and Child; *884. *Dom. Veneziano,* Madonna enthroned with SS. Francis, John the Baptist, Zenobius, and Lucy, one of the few works known by this artist, painted in beautiful soft colours. 8386. *Masaccio* and *Masolino,* Madonna and Child with St Anne. Masaccio is thought to have added the Madonna and Child to his master's painting, which has, however, otherwise been completely repainted. *1615. *Piero della Francesca,* a panel with the portraits of Federico di Montefeltro and his duchess, Battista Sforza, with their allegorical triumph on the reverse. Profoundly humanist in spirit, they are exquisite works with detailed landscapes in a transparent light. They were painted in Urbino c. 1465 in celebration

Uffizi Gallery

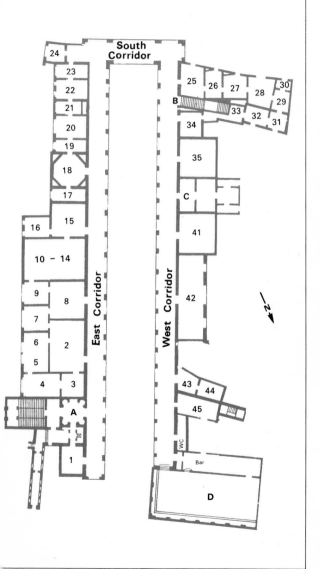

of this famous Renaissance prince. *479. *Paolo Uccello,* Battle of San
Romano, an amusing exercise in perspective. Together with its compan-
nions, now in the Louvre and National Gallery, London, it decorated
Lorenzo il Magnifico's bedroom in Palazzo Medici-Riccardi in 1492.

ROOM 8. FLORENTINE SCHOOL OF THE EARLY 15C (FILIPPO LIPPI)
*8351. *Filippo Lippi,* Predella of the Barbadori altarpiece (now in the
Louvre), with a remarkable sense of space; *483. *Aless. Baldovinetti,*
Annunciation; 8354. *Filippo Lippi,* Madonna enthroned with Saints.
8355. *Fr. Pesellino,* Predella of No. 8354. 487. *Aless. Baldovinetti,*
Madonna and Child with Saints; *Filippo Lippi,* *8352. Coronation of
the Virgin, 8350, 8353. Adoration of the Child, *1598. Madonna and
Child with two Angels (c. 1465), justly one of the most famous works
by this artist.

ROOM 9. POLLAIOLO. 495-499, 1610. *Piero del Pollaiolo,* Six Virtues
(including Charity, with a preparatory study on the back by his elder
brother *Antonio*); 1606. *Botticelli,* Fortitude, an early work. In the
case, four exquisite small *Panels: 1478, 8268. *And. del Pollaiolo,*
Labours of Hercules, and 1487, 1484. *Botticelli,* Story of Judith and
Holofernes (Judith returning from the camp of Holofernes, and the
discovery of the decapitated Holofernes in his tent), c. 1470. 1491.
Ant. del Pollaiolo, Portrait of a lady in profile; 1490. *Filippino Lippi,*
Young man in a red hat (of doubtful attribution); *1617. *Ant. de*
Pollaiolo, Saints Vincent, James, and Eustace, one of the best works
by this artist (formerly in the Chapel of the Cardinal of Portugal in
San Miniato, where it has been replaced by a copy); 1492. *Ant.* and
Piero del Pollaiolo, Portrait of Galeazzo Maria Sforza.

ROOMS 10-14 have recently been converted into one huge room and
the rafters of the stage of the old Medici theatre have been exposed. The mistaken illumination has been justly criticised. Here the
masterpieces of BOTTICELLI are displayed. 1488. *Botticelli,* Man with a
red hat holding a medallion of Cosimo il Vecchio; *Filippino Lippi,*
1566. Adoration of the Magi, 1568. Madonna painted for the Sala
degli Otto in Palazzo Vecchio (restored); *1608. *Botticelli,* Annunciation, showing an extraordinary spiritual bond between the two
figures; 881. *Dom. Ghirlandaio,* Madonna enthroned with Saints;
Botticelli, 1497. St Augustine in his study (a small work), 8361. Pala di
San Barnaba, with its predella (8390-8393). 1619. *Dom. Ghirlandaio,*
Tondo with the Adoration of the Magi; *Lor. di Credi,* *3094. Venus,
one of his best works; 8399. Adoration of the Shepherds; *Filippino
Lippi,* 8652. St Jerome, 3246. Adoration of the Child. *Botticelli's*
*Adoration of the Magi (882.) includes portraits of the Medici cour-
tiers with Lorenzo il Magnifico and a self-portrait on the extreme
right. The *Primavera (8360.) is one of *Botticelli's* most important
and most famous paintings. It has been temporarily removed for
cleaning (1981).

It was painted probably between 1477–78 for Lorenzo di Pierfrancesco de'
Medici, Lorenzo il Magnifico's younger cousin. An allegory of Spring, it is
thought to have been inspired by a work of Poliziano, although its precise
significance is still discussed. There is a rhythmical contact between the figures
who are placed in a meadow of flowers within a dark orange grove, the Garden
of Hesperides of classical myth. To the r. Zephyr chases Flora and transforms
her into Spring, who is shown bedecked with flowers. In the centre stands Venus
with Cupid above her, and beyond the beautiful group of the Three Graces
united in dance, is the figure of Mercury (perhaps an idealized portrait of Lorenzo

zo il Magnifico). The work is richly painted on poplar wood.

Botticelli, *1496. Calumny (after 1487). The subject of this very elaborate small painting is taken from Lucian's account of a picture by Apelles described in Alberti's treatise on painting. 1607. Tondo of the Madonna of the Pomegranate (1487; restored); *29. Pallas and the Centaur, probably intended as an allegory, the significance of which has been much discussed. The *Birth of Venus (878.) is perhaps the most famous of all the works of Botticelli.

This was also probably painted for Lorenzo di Pierfrancesco and hung in the Medici villa of Castello. The pagan subject is taken from a poem by Poliziano and illustrates Zephyr and Chloris blowing Venus ashore while Hora, her fluttering dress decorated with cornflowers and daisies, hurries to cover her nakedness. The elegant figures are painted with a remarkable lightness of touch in a decorative linear design. The classical nude figure of Venus balances on the edge of a beautiful scallop shell as it floats ashore. A strong wind blows through this harmonious Graeco-Roman world.

*1609. *Botticelli,* Madonna of the Magnificat (removed for restoration); *Filippino Lippi,* 1711. Self portrait (a fresco painted on a terracotta roof tile), 1485. Portrait of an old man; 8389. *Botticelli,* Predella of the Pala of San Marco.—In the centre of the room is the huge *Triptych (3191-3.) of the Adoration of the Shepherds, commissioned by the Medici agent in Bruges Tommaso Portinari from *Hugo van der Goes,* and shipped back to Florence in 1475. On the wings are Saints and members of the Portinari family. The painting had an important influence on contemporary Florentine artists. Behind (1114.), *Rogier van der Weyden,* Deposition.

ROOM 15 has recently been reopened. It displays the early Florentine works of LEONARDO DA VINCI, together with paintings by his master VERROCCHIO. 8368. *Luca Signorelli,* Crucifixion; *1618. *Leonardo da Vinci,* Annunciation, painted in Verrocchio's studio. The extent of his master's intervention is unclear: it is thought he was probably responsible for the design, and for the figure of the Madonna and the classical sarcophagus. 506. *Piero di Cosimo,* Immaculate Conception; *8358. *Verrocchio,* Baptism of Christ (begun c. 1470), according to Vasari and Albertini, the angel on the left was painted by the young Leonardo. *1594. *Leonardo,* Adoration of the Magi (1481). This huge crowded composition is remarkable for its figure studies and unusual iconography. The painting was left unfinished when Leonardo left Florence for Milan; it remains in its preparatory stage of chiaroscuro drawn in a red earth pigment (or 'sinopia', from Sinope in Asia Minor). *8359. *Verrocchio,* Tobias and three Archangels (recently cleaned; also attrib. to *Botticini*); 1597. *Lor. di Credi,* Annunciation; 1536. *Piero di Cosimo,* Perseus liberating Andromeda (1589); 8369. *Luca Signorelli,* Trinity, with the Madonna and Saints; 8365. *Perugino,* Pietà; 8371. *Signorelli,* Predella of the Trinity.—The walls of the SALA DELLE CARTE GEOGRAFICHE (16) are painted with maps of Tuscany by *Stef. Bonsignori* (1589). The rich ceiling is ascribed to *Iac. Zucchi.* Here are displayed paintings by *Hans Memling:* 1100. Benedetto Portinari, 1090. St Benedict, 1101-2. Portraits, 1024. Madonna with angels.

ROOM 18. The beautiful octagonal *TRIBUNA was designed by *Buonalenti* (1584) to display the most valuable objects in the Medici collection. It has a mother-of-pearl dome, a fine pavement in pietre dure, and an inlaid table of 1633. Since the 17C it has contained the most important sculptures owned by the Medici. The *Medici Venus, the most famous statue in the Uffizi, is a marble copy (probably of the 1C B.C.) of the Praxitelean Aphrodite of Cnidos, formerly in the Villa Medici in Rome. The other *Sculptures are: 230. 'Arrotino' (the knife-grinder), now thought to represent a Scythian as part of a group of Apollo and Marsias. It is the only surviving replica of an original by the school of Pergamum (3C or 2C B.C.), and it was purchased by Cosimo I in 1558 on Vasari's advice. 216. Wrestlers, a restored copy of a bronze original of the school of Pergamum; 220. Dancing Faun, a beautifully restored work; and 229. 'Apollino' (Young Apollo) derived from an Apollo of Praxiteles.—Around the walls are a remarkable series of distinguished court portraits, many of them of the family of Cosimo I commissioned from Bronzino. 28. *Bronzino,* Cosimo I; *783. *And. del Sarto,* Girl with a book of Petrarch; *Bronzino,* *748 Eleonora di Toledo, Cosimo I's wife, with their son Giovanni de' Medici, a fine portrait which speaks eloquently of its period. *Bronzino,* 1475. Giovanni de' Medici as a boy; *1575. Portrait of a Man, an intellectual typical of his time; 1472. Isabella de' Medici, daughter of Cosimo I; 1508. *Rosso Fiorentino,* Angel musician; 1446. *Raphael,* Young St John; 1445. *Franciabigio,* Madonna 'del Pozzo' (showing the influence of Raphael); *Bronzino,* 1571. Francesco I de' Medici, son of Cosimo I; *741, *736. Bartolomeo and Lucrezia Panciatichi, 2155. *Rid. del Ghirlandaio,* Young man; 770. *Bronzino,* Young girl with a book; 3574. *Pontormo,* Cosimo il Vecchio, and 1578. *Vasari,* Lorenzo il Magnifico, both posthumous and idealized portraits. 1500 *Aless. Allori,* Bianca Cappello, a mural.—Room 17, the SALA DELL'ERMAFRODITO (not always open) contains a Sleeping Hermaphrodite, copy of a Greek original of the 2C B.C., and small bronzes. Also, an exquisite small painted Triptych by *Mantegna.*

ROOM 19. PERUGINO AND SIGNORELLI. *1435. *Perugino,* Madonna enthroned with SS. John the Baptist and Sebastian; 3282. *Lor. Costa,* St Sebastian; 3341, 3343. *Melozzo da Forlì,* Annunciatory angel, and Madonna annunciate; 1535. *Girol. Genga,* Martyrdom of St Sebastian; 1444. *Fr. Francia,* Portrait of Evangelista Scappi; *Perugino,* 1474. Portrait of a young man (possibly Raphael); the work is also attrib. to *Costa,* *1700. Portrait of Francesco delle Opere (1494), a Florentine artisan, 8375, 8376. Don Biagio Milanesi and Baldassare Vallombrosano, two monks. *Luca Signorelli,* *502. Tondo of the Madonna and Child, one of his best works. In the background are allegorical figures, and prophets in the small roundels above; *1605 Tondo of the Holy Family, in a beautiful frame.—ROOM 20. DÜRER AND THE GERMAN SCHOOL. *1459, *1458. *Cranach,* Adam and Eve (1528); 1083. *Jan Breughel the Elder,* Calvary; *Dürer,* 8406. Calvary (a drawing in chiaroscuro, 1505), 1089, 1099. St James and St Philip the Apostles, *1434. Adoration of the Magi (1504), 1086. Portrait of the artist's father (painted at the age of 19, his first known work) 1645. *Joos van Cleve,* Portrait of a young man; *Cranach,* 512. Portrait of Luther (1543), 1056. St George (a tiny work), 1631, Self portrait (1550), 1160, 1139. Luther and his wife.—ROOM 21. VENETIAN SCHOOL (BELLINI AND GIORGIONE). 901. *Vittore Carpaccio,* Halberdiers (a fragment); 1863. *Giov. Bellini,* Portrait of a entleman; 3346. *Bart. Vivarini,* St Louis of Toulouse; 902. *Cima da* ʼoneɡliano, Madonna and Child; 3273. *Cosmè Tura,* St Dominic, a ʼrange, late work; *Giov. Bellini,* *631. Sacred Allegory. An exquisite ʼainting of uncertain meaning, it is infused with an exalted humanist uality. 943. Lamentation over the Dead Christ (an unfinished pain- ing left at the chiaroscuro stage). *Giorgione,* 947. Judgement of olomon (showing the influence of Bellini), 911. Warrior, the 'Gat- amelata', doubtfully attrib. to Giorgione, 945. Infant Moses brought ɔ Pharoah.—ROOM 22 contains GERMAN AND FLEMISH works. 1460. uca di Leida, Christ crowned with thorns; *1120. *Holbein,* Supposed ʼortrait of Thomas More (attrib. to his School); Dep. N. 5. *Albrecht* ʼltdorfer, Scenes from the life of St Florian; *Holbein,* 1630. Self- ʼortrait, *1087. Sir Richard Southwell (1536); *1643, 1644. *Joos van* ʼleve the Elder, Portrait of a man and his wife; 1152. *Gerard David,* ʼeposition; 1140, 1161. *Bernaert van Orley,* Portrait of a man and his ʼife; 1084. *Joos van Cleve the Elder,* Mater dolorosa; *1029. *Gerard* ʼavid, Adoration of the Magi; 1019. *'Maestro di Hoogstraeten',* ʼadonna enthroned with St Catherine of Alexandria and St Bar- ʼholomew.—ROOM 23. 3348. *Giov. Fr. Mainieri,* Christ bearing the ʼross; 1454. *Bern. Luini,* Head of St John the Baptist presented to ʼerod; 738. *Sodoma,* Derision of Christ; 2184. *Giov. Ant. Boltraffio,* ʼarcissus; *Raphael* (attrib.), 1441. Elizabeth Gonzaga, 8538. ʼuidobaldo da Montefeltro (very ruined); *Correggio,* 1329. Madonna ʼ glory; 1455. Rest on the Flight, 1453. Madonna in adoration of the ʼhild.—ROOM 24 is occupied by the COLLECTION OF MINIATURES 5-18C), but is not normally open.

The short SOUTH CORRIDOR commands a splendid view of Florence: ʼn the extreme left is San Miniato and Forte di Belvedere, in the cen- ʼe, beyond the Uffizi building is Palazzo Vecchio and the cupola of ʼe Duomo; at the far end the tiled roof of the Corridoio Vasariano ʼan be seen on its way from the Uffizi to Ponte Vecchio. The Arno ʼows downstream beneath Ponte Santa Trìnita and the bridges ʼeyond. On the S. bank the dome and campanile of Santo Spirito are ʼrominent, and, beyond, the dome of San Frediano.—Some of the ʼest pieces of sculpture are displayed here: *Roman matron, seated; ʼeres, the so-called 'Night' draped with black marble; Boy with a ʼhorn in his foot, replica of the 'Spinario' in the Capitoline Museum in ʼome; *Pedestal for a candelabrum; Sarcophagus with the Fall of ʼhaeton and chariot-races; *Crouching Venus, and Seated Girl ʼreparing to dance, both from Hellenistic originals of the 3C B.C.; ʼars, Roman copy of a Greek original; and a series of fine busts ʼhowing Marcus Aurelius from a very young boy to a middle-aged ʼan. The sculpture is continued in the WEST CORRIDOR: two *Statues ʼf Marsyas, from Hellenistic originals of the 3C B.C.; Nereid on a sea- ʼorse, Hellenistic; bust of Cicero and of Julia Severus; athletes, war- ʼors, and gods; and, at the far end of the corridor, Laocoön, a copy ʼy *Bandinelli* of the Vatican group.

ROOM 25 (MICHELANGELO). Opposite the entrance is the famous 'Tondo Doni' (1456.) of the Holy Family, the only finished oil pain- ing by *Michelangelo.* It was painted for the marriage of Agnolo Doni ʼith Maddalena Strozzi (1504–05), when the artist was 30 years old. ʼlthough owing much to Signorelli (comp. Room 19) it signals a new moment in High Renaissance painting, and points the way forward to the Sistine chapel frescoes. The contemporary frame by *Domenico de Tasso* is noteworthy. Also in this room: 1587. *Mariotto Albertinelli* Visitation (1503), probably his best work; 8455. *Fra' Bartolomeo,* Apparition of the Virgin to St Bernard (much repainted, but particularly interesting for the landscape); 1482. *Raphael* (attrib.), Portrait of Perugino; 8380. *Giul. Bugiardini,* Portrait of a lady; 2152. *Rosso Fiorentino,* Moses defending the children of Jethro (possibly a fragment). The geometrical forms of the nudes in the foreground display a very original and modern tendency. 2152. *Fr. Granacci,* Joseph and his brothers.

ROOM 26 (RAPHAEL). *1557. *And. del Sarto,* Madonna of the Harpies (1517); *Pontormo,* 1480. Portrait of a lady, 1843. Portrait of a man; *Raphael,* *1447. Madonna del Cardellino (of the Goldfinch, 1506). Painted for the marriage of the artist's friend, Lorenzo Nasi, it was shattered by an earthquake in 1547, but carefully preserved and repaired by the owner. *40p. Leo X with cardinals Giulio de' Medici (afterwards Clement VII) and Luigi de' Rossi (1518–19), one of his most powerful portrait groups which was to influence Titian, painted shortly before his death. It provides a vivid picture of the Medici Pope's world. 1450. Julius II, a replica (restored in 1975) of inferior quality to the painting in the National Gallery of London; 1706. Self portrait; 8760. Francesco Maria della Rovere. *Pontormo,* 1525. Martyrdom of St Maurice and the eleven Martyrs, 8379. St Anthony Abbot; 1583. *And. del Sarto,* St James and two children.

ROOM 27 (PONTORMO). 8381. *Franciabigio,* Portrait of a young man with gloves; 8377. *Bronzino,* Holy family, commissioned by Bartolomeo Panciatichi (comp. Room 18); 8740. *Pontormo,* Supper at Emmaus (1525), painted for the Certosa di Galluzzo, and an uncharacteristic work by this artist. Above the head of Christ is a surrealist symbol of God the father. 8545. *Bronzino,* Pietà; *Pontormo,* 743. Portrait of the musician Fr. Dell'Ajolle, 3565. Portrait of Maria Salviati, widow of Giovanni delle Bande Nere; 9449. *Vasari,* Adoration of the Shepherds; 3245. *Rosso Fiorentino,* Portrait of a girl.—ROOM 28 is devoted to TITIAN. *1462. Flora; *1437, Venus of Urbino, commissioned by Guidobaldo della Rovere, later duke of Urbino, in 1538. One of the most beautiful nudes ever painted, it has had a profound influence on European painting. *942. Knight of Malta, a portrait charged with religious fervour. 919. Eleonora Gonzaga della Rovere, duchess of Urbino, and her husband (926.), Francesco Maria della Rovere; 1431. Venus and Cupid (c. 1560, a late work); and work by *Palma Vecchio.*

ROOMS 29 and 30 are devoted to the 16C EMILIAN SCHOOL, notably *Parmigianino:* *230 p. Madonna 'dal collo lungo' ('with the long neck'). This work (1534–36), of extreme elegance and originality, is a fundamental painting of the Mannerist school. 1328. Madonna and Saints (including St Zacharias). Also small works by: *Il Garofalo, Girol. da Carpi, Lo Scarsellino, Mazzolino,* and *Luca Cambiaso.*—R 31 (VENETO SCHOOL) has a view of Palazzo Vecchio, the Duomo, and the top of Orsanmichele. 1481. *Lor. Lotto,* Head of a young boy; *Seb del Piombo,* 1443. 'La Fornarina', formerly attrib. to Raphael and thought to be a portrait of his mistress; *2183. Portrait of a sick man also attrib. to *Titian;* works by *Dosso Dossi.*—ROOM 32 (VENETO SCHOOL) is dominated by (916.) *Death of Adonis, by *Seb. del. Piombo,* in an autumnal Venetian landscape. Also displayed here are works by *Lor. Lotto,* and portraits by *Paris Bordone* and *Romanino.*

ROOM 33. 37. *Jean Perréal* (attrib.), Portrait of a lady; *987. *François Clouet,* Equestrian portrait of Francis I; 3112. *Luis de Morales,* Christ carrying the Cross; 1108. *Frans Pourbus il vecchio,* Portrait of Virgilio van Aytta; 1637. *Ant. Moro,* Self portrait; 4338. *16C French School,* Christine of Lorraine; 763. *Aless. Allori,* Torquato Tasso.—In the corridor the small 16C paintings include several works by *Aless. Allori,* and a Head of Medusa (1479.) by the *16C Flemish school.*

ROOM 34. VERONESE AND THE VENETIAN SCHOOL. 1343. *Paolo Veronese,* Crowning of St Agatha, a tiny work; *Giulio Campi,* 1796. Portrait of a man, 958. Guitar player; 1387. *Jac. Tintoretto,* Portrait of a man; *G.B. Moroni,* 933. Portrait of a man with a book, *906. Count Pietro Secco Suardi (1563); 1628. *Giulio Campi,* Padre Galeazzo Campi; *Paolo Veronese, *899. Annunciation, designed around a perspective device in the centre of the picture. The work is delicately painted in simple colours, in contrast to the rich golden hues of the figure of St Barbara in the *Holy Family with St Barbara (1433.), a work of the artist's maturity.

From the W. Corridor a door (B) gives access to the **Corridoio Vasariano.** This an only be visited by previous appointment at the administrative offices on the third floor near the entrance to the gallery: small groups are conducted c. twice a week. It was built by Vasari in 1565 in 5 months, on the occasion of the marriage of Francesco de' Medici and Joanna of Austria. Its purpose was to connect Palazzo Vecchio viâ the Uffizi and Ponte Vecchio with the new residence of the Medici dukes at Palazzo Pitti (comp. p 98), in the form of a covered passageway. It affords unique views of the city, and is hung with notable paintings including a celebrated collection of self-portraits (begun by Cardinal Leopoldo). A series of rooms (with works by the school of Caravaggio, including *Artemisia Gentileschi, Borgognone,* and *Ann. Carracci*) precede the entrance to the corridor proper. Here, displayed by regional schools, are 17C works: *Guido Reni* Susannah and the Elders), *Guercino* (Sleeping Endymion), *Dom. Feti, Domenichino, Maratta, Pietro da Cortona, Mattia Preti, Salvator Rosa, Carlo Dolci, Sassoferrato, Gius. Maria Crespi,* and *Sustermans.* There follow 18C paintings by *Vanvitelli, Ricci, Tiepolo,* and others.—The **Collection of Self-portraits** begins, appropriately, with one by *Vasari.* Arranged chronologically, they include works by *Agnolo, Taddeo,* and *Gaddo Gaddi, And. del Sarto, Bandinelli, Beccafumi, Bronzino, Pierino del Vaga, Santi di Tito, Cigoli,* etc. Beyond the centre of Ponte Vecchio: *Salimbeni, Fed.* and *Taddeo Zuccari, Bernini, Pietro da Cortona, Batoni, Luca Giordano, Salvator Rosa,* and *Gius. Maria Crespi.* On the Oltrarno the Corridor continues with 16-18C foreign self-portraits including *Pourbus, Rubens, Gerard Dou, Sustermans, Rembrandt, Van Dyck, Zoffany, Velasquez, Callot, Charles le Brun, Lely, Kneller, Hogarth, Romney,* and *Reynolds.* The Corridor descends past a group of sketches to the collection of 19C self-portraits (*David, Delacroix, Corot, Ingres, Fattori, Millais, Benjamin Constant, Latour,* etc.). The corridor ends with a group of 17-18C portraits (mostly of royalty). Visitors are usually asked to leave the corridor by the Boboli Gardens (comp. p 110).

ROOM 35 (TINTORETTO). 969. *Iac. Bassano,* Portrait of an artist, perhaps a Self-portrait; *Fed. Barocci,* Portrait of a girl, 798. Noli me tangere, 1438. Francesco Maria II della Rovere, 751. Madonna del Popolo; *Jac. Tintoretto,* 924. Portrait of a man with red hair, 921. Portrait of an admiral, 914. St Augustine, 957. Portrait of Iac. Sansovino, 935. Portrait of an old man in a fur, *3085. Leda, 966. Portrait of a Gentleman (attrib.); *El Greco,* SS. John the Evangelist and Francis; *Leandro Bassano,* Family concert.—Beyond the stairs down to the exit (C; comp. below), ROOM 41 contains some fine works by RUBENS and VAN DYCK. *Rubens,* The Risen Christ, 729. Henri IV entering Paris, 722. Henri IV at Ivry, two large paintings composing the first part of a cycle depicting the King's history. 792. Philip IV of Spain, 779. *Isabella Brandt. Van Dyck,* 726. Susterman's mother, 777. Margaret of Lorraine, 1439. Equestrian portrait of Emperor Charles V, 1436. John of Montfort. Also, 745. *Sustermans.* Galileo Galilei; 3141. *Jacob Jordaens,* Portrait of an old lady.

The NIOBE ROOM (42) contains statues forming a group of Niobe and her Children, found in a vineyard near the Lateran in 1583, and transferred to Florence in 1775 from the Villa Medici in Rome. These are Roman copies of Greek originals of the school of Skopas (early 4C B.C.); many of the figures are wrongly restored and others do not belong to the group. The Medici Vase in the centre is a neo-Attic work acquired by Lorenzo de' Medici.

ROOMS 43 and 44. *Works by *Caravaggio* (5312. Young Bacchus 1351. Medusa head, painted on a shield, 4659. Sacrifice of Isaac) 9283. *Mattia Preti,* Allegory of Vanity; and works by *Ann. Carracc* (including 799. Man with a monkey, and 1452. Bacchic scene).—*Rembrandt,* *3890. Self-portrait, *8435. Portrait of an old man, and *1871. Self-portrait as an old man. 1096. *Claude Lorraine,* Seascape 1301. *Jan Steen,* Lunch-party; *Jacob Ruysdael,* two fine Landscapes and other Dutch and Flemish works.—ROOM 45 is to display 18C paintings: 8419. *Piazzetta,* Susannah and the Elders; 3139. *G.B. Tiepolo,* Erection of an imperial statue (for a ceiling); works by *Fr. Guardi,* *Canaletto,* and *Aless. Longhi.* Two portraits of children by *Chardin.*

A door at the end of the Corridor (beyond a small Bar) gives on to the roof of the Loggia della Signoria (D) with a splendid view over Piazza della Signoria beyond the buildings of the city to the hills of Fiesole.—A long flight of stairs (comp. above), or a lift, descend from the West Corridor to the exit. On the landing are two beautiful *Portraits of Maria Theresa by *Goya,* and the famous sculptured Boar, a copy of a Hellenistic original, and the model for the 'Porcellino' in the Mercato Nuovo (comp. p 187).

7   GALLERIA DEGLI UFFIZI TO PALAZZO PITTI

This route follows the course of the CORRIDOIO VASARIANO which is described on p 97.

From the river 'façade' of Palazzo degli Uffizi (Pl. 16; 8; see p 88) there is a striking view of Palazzo Vecchio with its tower. The COR RIDOIO VASARIANO, the covered way built by Vasari in 1565 to link Palazzo Vecchio and the Uffizi with the new residence of the Medici Palazzo Pitti, can be seen here as it leaves the Uffizi building, crosses above the busy road, and continues on a raised arcade towards Ponte Vecchio. On the bridge, its line of rectangular windows pass above the little picturesque shops which overhang the river. On this very narrow part of the Lungarno is the fine old *Palazzo Girolami* (No. 6) with a pretty loggia and coat-of-arms.

The fame of **Ponte Vecchio** (Pl. 16; 5, 7; open to pedestrians only) lined with quaint medieval-looking houses, saved it from damage in 1944 (although numerous ancient buildings at either end were blown up instead in order to render it impassable). Near the site of the Roman crossing (which was a little farther upstream) it was the only bridge over the Arno until 1218. The present bridge of three arches was reconstructed after a flood in 1345 probably by *Taddeo Gaddi* (also attrib. to *Neri di Fioravante*). The bridge on this site has been lined by shops since the 13C; the present jewellers' shops have pretty fronts with wood shutters and awnings, and they overhang the river supported on brackets. They were well restored after severe damage in the flood of 1966. The excellent jewellers here continue the traditional skill of Florentine goldsmiths whose work first became famous in the 15C. Many of the greatest Renaissance artists were trained as goldsmiths (including Ghiberti, Brunelleschi, and Donatello). The most famous Florentine goldsmith, Benvenuto Cellini, is aptly recorded with a bust (1900) in the middle of the bridge. Above the shops on the left side can be seen the round windows of the Corridoio Vasariano. From the opening in the centre there is a view of Ponte Santa Trinita (p 165). On the corner of a house here is a sundial and worn inscription of 1345. The Corridoio Vasariano leaves the bridge supported on elegant brackets in order not to disturb the medieval angle tower which defended the bridge (Torre dei Mannelli; restored after the War).

Across Borgo San Jacopo (see p 170) is a fountain reconstructed here in 1958 with a 16C bronze statue of Bacchus and a Roman sarcophagus. Via Guicciardini continues towards Piazza Pitti; on the left opens Piazza Santa Felicita with a granite column of 1381 marking the site of the first Christian cemetery in Florence. Here is **Santa Felìcita** (Pl. 16; 7), probably the oldest church in Florence after San Lorenzo. Syrian Greek merchants came to settle in the suburbs here, near the river and on a busy Roman consular road, in the 2C, and are thought to have introduced Christianity to the city. The paleochristian church, dedicated to the Roman martyr, St Felicity, was last rebuilt in 1736 by *Ferd. Ruggieri* in a 15C style.

In the PORTICO are the tombs of (r.) Card. Luigi Rossi (d. 1518) by *Raff. da Montelupo*, and (l. above) of Barduccio Chiericini (d. 1416).—The fine INTERIOR is chiefly notable for the superb *Works (1525–27) by *Pontormo* in the Cappella Capponi (1st on r.), which include a remarkable altarpiece of the Deposition, in a magnificent contemporary frame, a fresco (recently detached and restored) of the Annunciation, and the tondoes in the cupola of the Evangelists (except St Mark, which is attrib. to *Bronzino*). These are considered among the masterpieces of 16C Florentine painting.—Over the 4th altar on the r. is a striking painting (the Martyrdom of the Maccabei brothers) by *Ant. Ciseri* (1863), and over the 4th altar on the l., St Louis providing a banquet for the poor by *Simone Pignone* (1682). Over the high altar, Nativity, by *Santi di Tito* (temporarily removed for restoration).—The pretty SACRISTY, in the style of Brunelleschi (off the r. transept), has a polyptych of the Madonna and Child with Saints, by *Taddeo Gaddi,* in its original frame; St Felicity and her seven children by *Neri di Bicci* (removed for restoration), a Crucifix attrib. to *Pacino di Buonaguida,* and two detached 14C frescoes of the Nativity and Annunciation, attrib. to *Niccolò di Pietro Gerini*.

At the end of the road (left) No. 15 is *Palazzo Guicciardini,* reconstructed on the site of the residence of Luigi di Piero Guicciardini, Gonfalonier of Justice, which was burnt down during the uprising in 1378 of the Ciompi (cloth-workers). Part of the façade has re-

mains of graffiti decoration. The courtyard and garden, created c
1620, can be seen through the grille. Here is a large stucco relief of
Hercules and Cacus attrib. to Ant. del Pollaiolo. Francesco Guicciardini was born here in 1483. On his retirement from political life in
1530 he wrote his famous 'History of Italy'. Casa Campiglio, nearby,
where Machiavelli lived and died in 1527, has been destroyed. The two
great statesmen and writers, who had served different causes, became
close friends at the end of their careers.

Beyond is Piazza Pitti (p 179) dominated by Palazzo Pitti (Rte 8)

8   PALAZZO PITTI AND THE BÓBOLI GARDENS

*Palazzo Pitti (Pl. 9; 4) was built by the merchant Luca Pitti, an ef-
fective demonstration of his wealth and power to his rivals the Medici.
The majestic golden-coloured palace is built in huge rough-hewn
blocks of stone of different sizes. Its design is attributed to
Brunelleschi although it was begun c. 1457 after his death. *Luca
Fancelli* is known to have been engaged on the building, but it i
generally considered that another architect, whose name is unknown,
was also involved. The palace remained incomplete on the death of
Luca Pitti in 1472; by then it consisted of the central seven bays with
three doorways. Houses were demolished to create the piazza in front
of the palace, and its site was chosen here, on the slope of a hillside, to
make it more imposing. *Bartolomeo Ammannati* took up work on the
building c. 1560 and converted the two side doors of the façade into
elaborate ground-floor windows. These were then copied after 1616
by *Giulio* and *Alfonso Parigi the Younger* when they enlarged the
façade to its present colossal dimensions (possibly following an
original design). The two 'rondòs' or wings were added at the end of
the 18C (on the right), and in the 19C (on the left).

In 1549 the palace was bought by Eleonora di Toledo, wife of Cosimo I. I
became the official seat of the Medici dynasty of grand-dukes after Cosimo
moved here from Palazzo Vecchio (to which he connected the Pitti by means of
the Corridoio Vasariano, comp. p 98). The various ruling families of Florence
continued to occupy the palace, or part of it, until 1919 when Victor Emmanuel
III presented it to the State.

The central door leads into the ATRIUM by *Pasquale Poccianti* (c
1850). The splendid *COURT (1560–70) by *Ammannati* serves as a
garden façade to the palace. It is a masterpiece of Florentine Mannerist architecture, with bold rustication in three orders. Nocturnal
spectacles were held here from the 16C to 18C. The lower fourth side
is formed by a terrace with the 'Fontana del Carciofo' (named from
the bronze artichoke on top), by *Fr. Susini* and *Fr. del Tadda,* beyond
which extend the Bóboli gardens (see below). The grotto beneath the
terrace has another fountain with a porphyry statue of Mose
(Roman, restored in the 16C). Under the portico to the right is the en
trance to the celebrated ****Galleria di Palazzo Pitti** or **Galleria
Palatina,** formed in the 17C, and installed here in the 18C. It was
opened to the public in 1834. The reception rooms on the piano nobile
were decorated in the 17C by *Pietro da Cortona* for the Medici grand
dukes. They contain the masterpieces of the collection, including

numerous famous works by Raphael and Titian. The arrangement of
the pictures (most of them richly framed) still preserves to some extent
the character of a private royal collection of the 17C-18C, the
aesthetic arrangement of the rooms being considered rather than the
chronological placing of the paintings. This produces a remarkable
effect of magnificence even though in some cases the pictures are difficult to see on the crowded walls. Only some of the paintings (all of
which are well labelled) have been mentioned in the description below,
and asterisks have been used sparingly.

Tickets for the Galleria Palatina (which include adm to the Appartamenti
Monumentali and the Museo degli Argenti) are purchased off the courtyard, left
of the stairs up to the gallery. Here there is also a cloakroom and W.C. There is
no lift to the picture galleries.
    All the rooms are named as indicated in the description below; room numbers
on the first floor have been given only to correspond with the Plan on p 103.
    Admission, see p 58. *Galleria Palatina.* The six main rooms of paintings are
numbered 1-6 on the Plan. The other groups of rooms (numbered 7-15 and
16-26) of the picture gallery are sometimes closed for certain periods of the year.
The *Appartamenti Monumentali (ex Reale)* are numbered II-XIV on the plan
and are usually open at the same time as the Galleria Palatina. The remaining
rooms on the first floor (XV-XXII on the plan) are closed except for exhibitions,
etc.—On the SECOND FLOOR, is the *Galleria d'Arte Moderna* (adm see p 58);
tickets are purchased at the entrance on the second floor. On the GROUND
FLOOR, off the left side of the courtyard, is the entrance to the *Museo degli
Argenti* (adm as for the Galleria Palatina). The *Museo delle Carrozze* (coach
musuem) in the right wing of the palace (entered from the piazza) has been closed for restoration. Admission to the *Collezione Contini Bonacossi,* temporarily
exhibited in the Meridiana pavilion, is sometimes granted on special request.

The GRAND STAIRCASE by *Ammannati* ascends past (3rd landing)
the 'Genio mediceo', a bronze statue attrib. to the circle of Tribolo, to
the entrance of the Galleria Palatina. The ANTICAMERA or SALA DEGLI
STAFFIERI (A) contains statues by *Baccio Bandinelli* (Bacchus), and
Pietro Francavilla (Mercury). The GALLERIA DELLE STATUE (B) is
decorated with sculptures and Florentine tapestries by *Pietro Fevère.*
From the windows there is a view of the courtyard and Bóboli gardens
(with the Forte di Belvedere on the skyline).—To the left is the SALA
DELLE NICCHIE (1), a neo-classical room by *Gius. Maria Terreni* and
Gius. Castagnoli (late 18C), where two seascapes by *Van der Velde the
Elder* are temporarily exhibited, and the Triumph of Galatea, by *Luca
Giordano.* To the r. (overlooking Piazza Pitti) is the entrance to the
first of the main rooms of paintings.
    The SALA DI VENERE (1) has the earliest ceiling (1641–2) of the fine
group executed for the following four rooms by *Pietro da Cortona* for
Ferdinand II. His pupil *Ciro Ferri* completed the Sala di Saturno in
1666. The Baroque decoration, including fine stucchi, illustrates the
life of the Medici prince by means of extravagant allegories. The paintings here include: 409. *Seb. del Piombo,* Baccio Valori; *Titian,* *185.
Concert (an early work). The attribution of this famous work has been
much discussed and it appears that more than one hand was involved.
It has also been attrib. to *Giorgione* who may have been responsible
for the figure on the left. The portrait of pope Julius II is a copy by *Titian* of an original by Raphael now in the National Gallery of London
(a replica of which is in the Uffizi, see p 96). On the two end walls, *4,
15. *Salvator Rosa,* Two large seascapes painted for cardinal Gian
Carlo de' Medici.—9. *Rubens,* Ulysses in the Phæcian Isle, a companion to *14. Return from the hayfields, with a superb joyful land-

scape. Above, 8. *Guercino,* Apollo and Marsyas, and other 17C works by the Tuscan artists, *Matteo Rosselli* and *Rutilio Manetti.—*54. *Titian,* Pietro Aretino, one of his most forceful portraits, exquisitely painted. After a quarrel with the artist, Aretino presented the painting to Cosimo I in 1545. 84. *Bonifazio Veronese,* Sacred Conversation; *Titian,* *18. Portrait of a lady ('la bella'), commissioned by the Duke of Urbino in 1536.—In the centre, the *'Venus Italica' sculpted by *Canova,* and presented by Napoleon in exchange for the Medici Venus which he had carried off to Paris.

SALA DI APOLLO (2). 150. *Anthony Van Dyck,* Charles I and Henrietta Maria; (above) 4263. *Rubens,* Isabella Clara Eugenia, dressed in the habit of a nun; 220. *Guido Reni,* Cleopatra; 41. *Crist. Allori,* St Julian; *Cigoli,* Portrait of a man; *81. *And. del Sarto,* Holy family.—116. *Sustermans,* Portrait of Vittoria della Rovere dressed as a Roman vestal; 50. *Guercino,* St Peter healing Tabitha; *237. *Rosso Fiorentino,* Madonna enthroned with Saints, a typical Florentine Mannerist work painted in 1522 for the church of Santo Spirito; 55. *Barocci,* Federigo, prince of Urbino in his cradle; 380. *Dosso Dossi,* St John the Baptist.—131. *Tintoretto,* Vincenzo Zeno (recently restored); *58. *And. del Sarto,* Deposition (1523); *Titian,* *92. Portrait of a Gentleman (c. 1540), once thought to be the Duke of Norfolk. It is justly one of his most famous portraits, revealing the intense character of the unknown sitter. *67. Mary Magdalen, another beautifully painted work by *Titian,* which was frequently copied.

SALA DI MARTE (3). *83. *Tintoretto,* Luigi Cornaro (recently restored); *82. *Anthony Van Dyck,* Card. Guido Bentivoglio, a fine official portrait; 80. *Titian,* Andrea Vesalio.—*201. *Titian,* cardinal Ippolito de' Medici, in Hungarian costume; *86. *Rubens,* Consequences of War, a huge allegory painted in 1638 and sent to his friend and fellow countryman at the Medici court, Sustermans. One of Rubens' most important works, it shows Venus trying to prevent Mars going to war, while both figures are surrounded by its destructive and tragic consequences. 216. *Paolo Veronese,* Portrait of a man, once thought to be Daniele Barbaro; 256. *Fra' Bartolomeo,* Holy Family.—56, 63. Two paintings of the Madonna and Child, typical works by the Spanish painter *Murillo.* 235. *Rubens* (attrib.), Holy Family; *85. *Rubens,* 'The Four Philosophers' (Rubens, his brother Filippo, Justus Lipsius, and Jan van Wouwer), a charming portrait group. Rubens' brother and van Wouwer were both pupils of the great Flemish humanist Lipsius, famous for his studies of Seneca, whose bust is present.

The SALA DI GIOVE (4) was the throne-room of the Medici and has the most refined decoration by *Pietro da Cortona* in this suite of rooms. *110. *Venetian School,* Three Ages of Man. This fine work has had various attributions, the most convincing of which seems to be *Giorgione.* *245. *Raphael,* Portrait of a lady ('la Velata' or 'la Fornarina'), one of the most beautiful of all Raphael's paintings. The grace and dignity of the sitter pervade the work, which is painted with a skill which anticipates the hand of Titian. It was purchased by Cosimo II de'Medici. 112. *Borgognone,* Battle Scene; 139. *Rubens,* Holy Family (an early work).—370. *Piero del Pollaiolo* (attrib.), Head of St Jerome (a small work); *16C Flemish School,* Jacobina Vogekort; *And. del Sarto,* Madonna in glory, Annunciation (an early work);

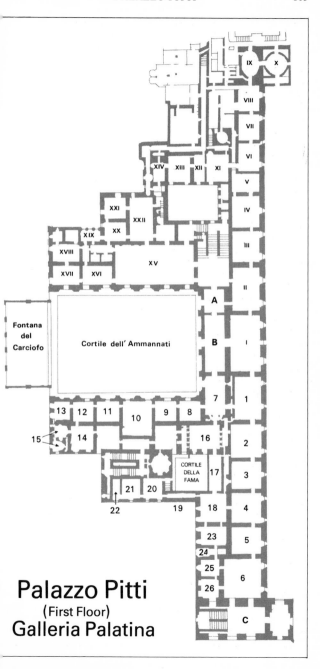

IX
X
VIII
VII
VI
XIV XIII XII XI
V
XXI
XXII
IV
XIX
XX
III
XVIII
XVII XVI
XV
II
A
Fontana
del
Carciofo
Cortile dell' Ammannati
B
I
7
1
13 12 11
10
9 8
15
14
16
2
CORTILE
DELLA
FAMA
17
3
21 20
22
19
18
4
23
5
24
25
6
26
C

Palazzo Pitti
(First Floor)
Galleria Palatina

125. *Fra' Bartolomeo,* St Mark.—149. *Bronzino,* Guidobaldo delle
Rovere; 113. *Fr. Salviati,* The Fates; *64. *Fra' Bartolomeo,* Deposi-
tion, his last and one of his best works; (above) 141. *Rubens,* Nymphs
and satyrs in a fine landscape; *272. *And. del Sarto,* the Young St
John the Baptist (1523; badly restored in the 19C). One of the most
well-known representations of the Baptist, this picture was owned by
Cosimo I and formerly hung in the Tribuna of the Uffizi. 219.
Perugino, Madonna in adoration ('del sacco'); 156. *Guercino,*
Madonna 'of the house-martin'.—In the centre, marble statue of Victory, by *Vinc. Consani.*

SALA DI SATURNO (5). *Raphael,* *151. Madonna 'della Seggiola', a
beautifully composed tondo, among the artist's most mature works (c.
1514–15). It was purchased by the Medici shortly after Raphael's
death, and became one of the most popular paintings of the Madonna. 152. *And. Schiavone,* Samson and the Philistine; 158. *Raphael,*
cardinal Bernardo Dovizi da Bibbiena.—207. *Rid. del Ghirlandaio,*
Portrait of a man (thought to be a goldsmith), showing the influence
of Raphael; 42. *Perugino,* Mary Magdalen (similar to his self-
portraits); 159. *Fra' Bartolomeo,* The Risen Christ appearing to his
Disciples; *164. *Perugino,* Deposition (1495; recently restored);
Raphael, *59. Maddalena Doni, in the pose of Leonardo's Gioconda,
and (61.) Agnolo Doni, her husband. *174. Vision of Ezekiel (a tiny
work); 165. Madonna 'del Baldacchino', a large unfinished altarpiece
of unusual design (1507–08).—*Raphael,* 171. Cardinal Tommaso In-
ghirami; 166. *Ann. Carracci,* Head of a man; 172. *And. del Sarto,*
Disputation on the Trinity; *178. *Raphael,* Madonna 'del Granduca',
an early work (c. 1504–05), showing the influence of Leonardo. It
received its name after its purchase in the 18C by Ferdinand III of
Lorraine; (above the door), 179. *Seb. del Piombo,* Martyrdom of St
Agatha.

SALA DELL'ILIADE (6), with a ceiling by *Sabatelli* of 1819 illustrating
the Iliad. 243. *Velazquez* (attrib.), Equestrian portrait of Philip IV of
Spain; 186. *Paolo Veronese,* Baptism of Christ; 190. *Sustermans*
Count Valdemar Christian of Denmark; 187. *Fr. Pourbus the
Younger,* Eleonora de' Medici; *And. del Sarto,* *191. and (opposite)
225., two large paintings of the Assumption, the former among the
most important late works by this artist; *Artemesia Gentileschi,* 398
Judith, and 142. Mary Magdalen (by one of the few women artist
represented in the gallery).—*Titian,* *200. Philip II of Spain, *215
Diego de Mendoza.—224. *Rid. del Ghirlandaio,* Portrait of a young
woman; *229. *Raphael,* Portrait of a woman expecting a child ('la
Gravida', c. 1506); 391. *Fr. Pourbus the Younger,* Eleonora of Man
tua as a child (daughter of Eleonora de' Medici, see No. 187); 223
Joos van Cleve (attrib.), Portrait of a man.—4273. *16C English
School,* Elizabeth I.—In the centre of the room, Charity, a fine mar
ble group by *Lor. Bartolini.*

The exit from the Gallery in summer (kept locked in winter) is through the
VESTIBULE (C) which contains a fountain attrib. to *Fr. di Simone Ferrucci* (from
the Villa di Castello). The GRAND STAIRCASE, a monumental work by *Luigi de
Moro* (c. 1895–97) descends to the garden.

The other rooms of the Galleria Palatina which contain the smalle
works in the collection may be entered from the Sala di Venere (see

above; Plan 1). The SALA DEL CASTAGNOLI (7) is named after the artist who decorated it. It contains a magnificent mosaic table in pietre dure made in Florence in the 19C with Apollo and the Muses (the bronze base of the four seasons is by *Giov. Duprè*).

A door (sometimes closed) leads into the SALA DELLE ALLEGORIE (Pl. 8) with a statue of the young Michelangelo by *Emilio Zocchi* (1861). The vault is frescoed by Volterrano. The paintings include: 582. *Volterrano*. The Parsons's jest (Pievano Arlotto); 33 dep. *Giov. da San Giovanni*, Portrait of the pievano Arlotto; *Volterrano*, 107. Love sleeping, 105. Mercenary Love; *Sustermans*, Portraits of the Puliciani; 2129. *Artemesia Gentileschi*, Madonna and Child; 2120. *Giov. da San Giovanni*, The Wedding night; 1344. *Crist. Allori*, Mary Magdalen in the desert; 2578. *Volterrano*, Antonio Baldinucci; 1529. *Giov. da San Giovanni*, Angels waiting on Christ.—SALA DELLE BELLE ARTI (9). Paintings by *Cigoli* and *Carlo Dolci*.—The SALONE D'ERCOLE (10) is frescoed with scenes from the life of Hercules by *Pietro Benvenuti* (1828). The huge Sèvres vase dates from 1784.—SALA DELL'AURORA (11). Paintings by *Empoli, Lor. Lippi, Crist. Allori, Jac. Ligozzi,* and *Jac. Vignali.*—The SALA DI BERENICE (12) contains works by *Fr. Furini, Carlo Dolci, Orazio Riminaldi, Giov. Biliverti,* and *Fr. Curradi* (Narcissus).—SALA DI PSICHE (13). Fine works by *Salvator Rosa:* 470. The Wood of the Philosophers, land- and sea-scapes, a battle scene, and sketches on wood.—SALA DELLA FAMA (14). Flemish works (*Willem van Aelst,* etc.).—The Vestibule and Bathroom (15) of Empress Maria Luisa (wife of Napoleon) were designed in neo-classical style by *Giuseppe Cacialli* (c. 1805).

From the Sala del Castagnoli (see above) is the entrance to the neo-classical SALA DELLA MUSICA (16) by Cacialli (1811–21) with drum-shaped commodes. The GALLERIA DEL POCCETTI (17) received its name from the traditional attribution of the frescoes in the vault to *Poccetti;* it is now thought these are by *Matteo Rosselli* and his pupils (c. 1625). The table inlaid in pietre dure is attrib. to *G.B. Foggini* (1716). The paintings include: *Rubens,* 761, 324. Duke and Duchess of Buckingham; 249. *Pontormo,* Francesco da Castiglione; *Gaspare Dughet* (brother-in-law of Poussin), four Landscapes; *Dom. Feti,* two small biblical scenes; *Fr. Furini,* Hylas and the Nymphs; 408. *Peter Lely,* Cromwell; 188. *Niccolò Cassana,* Portrait of an artist (formerly thought to be Salvator Rosa's self-portrait).—Beyond is the SALA DI PROMETEO (18). *Gius. Ribera (Lo Spagnoletto),* St Francis; 379. *Pontormo,* Adoration of the Magi; 167. *Baldassarre Peruzzi,* Dance of Apollo with the Muses (this famous and unusual small work was formerly attrib. to Giulio Romano); 364. *Iac. Sellaio,* Tondo of the Madonna in adoration; 357. *Botticelli (attrib.),* Madonna and Child with the young St John; *1165. *Rubens,* The Three Graces, a small painting in monochrome; 347. *Fr. Botticini,* Tondo of the Madonna in adoration with angels; *Umbrian school (attrib.),* Epiphany; *343. *Filippo Lippi,* Large tondo of the Madonna and Child, a charming composition with scenes from the life of the Virgin in the background. This is one of Lippi's best works, and had a strong influence on his contemporaries. *Guido Reni,* Young Bacchus, a well-known painting; 355. *Luca Signorelli,* Tondo of the Holy Family, in a lovely frame; 348. *School of Botticelli,* Tondo of the Madonna and Child with angels; *Botticelli,* 372. Portrait of a man (a damaged painting), 353. Portrait of a lady in profile (the identification of the sitter, and the author of this interesting work are still much discussed). 354. *Cosimo Rosselli,* Nativity; 604. *Marco Palmezzano,* Caterina Sforza; 359. *Beccafumi,* Tondo of the Holy Family; 182. *Pontormo,* The eleven thousand martyrs; *Il Bachiacca,* Mary Magdalen; 365. *Mariotto*

Albertinelli, Holy Family; *Fr. Salviati,* Portrait of a man.

A door (sometimes closed) leads into the CORRIDOIO DELLE COLONNE (19) hung with small Flemish paintings by *Cornelis van Poelenburgh, Paul Brill, Frans Franken, Jan Breughel* (Orpheus), *David Rychaert* (Temptations of St Anthony), and others.—SALA DELLA GIUSTIZIA (2). 494. *Titian (attrib.),* Portrait of a Gentleman; *Titian,* 228. The Redeemer, an early work, *495. Portrait of a man, once thought to be Vincenzo Mosti; *Tintoretto,* 410, 65. Two portraits; and works by *Bonifazio Veronese.*—SALA DI FLORA (21). 21 dep., *Pontormo,* Portrait of a lady; *Paolo Veronese,* St Catherine; 88, 87. *And. del Sarto,* Story of Joseph, two beautiful small works; and works by *Dom. Puligo.*—SALA DEI PUTTI (22). Dutch works by *Rachele Ruysch, Willem Van Aelst, Ludolf Backhuysen, Jacob Jordaens,* and *Godfried Schalken* (Girl with a candle).

From the Sala di Prometeo (18; see above) is the entrance to the SALA DI ULISSE (23). *16C Florentine School,* Portrait of a man; 70. *Tintoretto,* Andrea Frizier, Grand Chancellor of Venice; *Moroni,* (128. and 121.) two fine portraits; *338. *Filippino Lippi,* Death of Lucrezia, a beautiful small painting (once part of a 'cassone'), showing the influence of Botticelli. *94. *Raphael,* Madonna 'dell'Impannata' (so named from the window in the background), a mature composition, perhaps with the collaboration of his workshop.—Beyond the splendid 'Empire' bathroom (24) by *Cacialli* is the SALA DELL'EDUCAZIONE DI GIOVE (25). *96. *Crist. Allori,* Judith with the head of Holofernes (with portraits of the artist, his mistress, and her mother), one of the most famous Florentine works of the 17C; typical pious works by *Carlo Dolci; Carletto Caliari,* Christ taking leave of his mother; *183. *Caravaggio,* Sleeping Cupid, a late work; *Carletto Caliari;* The Maries at the sepulchre; two tiny Medici portraits by *Bronzino;* Claude of Lorraine, by *Jean Clouet; Ant. Van Dyck,* Portrait of a man; (above) *Tintoretto (or his School),* Deposition.—The *SALA DELLA STUFA (26) is beautifully frescoed by *Pietro da Cortona* (1637–41; the four Ages of the World) and *Matteo Rosselli* (1622; Fames and Virtues, on the ceiling). The restored majolica pavement (Triumph of Bacchus, 1640) is by *Bened. Bocchi.*

The other half of the piano nobile along the façade of the palace is occupied by the **Appartamenti Monumentali (ex Reali)**, entered from the Sala delle Nicchie (B; comp. above). This series of state apartments, most of them lavishly decorated in the 19C by the Dukes of Lorraine, are notable particularly for their numerous portraits of the Medici by Sustermans, the Flemish painter who was appointed to the Medici court in 1619 and remained in their service until his death in 1681, and a fine group of 18C Gobelins tapestries.

The SALA VERDE (II) has a painting (formerly in the ceiling) of the Allegory of Peace between Florence and Fiesole, by *Luca Giordano,* a painting showing the studio of an artist (for long thought to be that of Rubens), by *Cornelis de Baelheur,* and The Risen Christ, an early work by *Rubens.* The inlaid ebony Cabinet was built for Vittoria della Rovere in 1680.—The SALA DEL TRONO (III) and SALA CELESTE (IV), contain portraits by *Sustermans* and his master *Frans Pourbus the Younger.*—The CAPPELLA (V) has a Madonna by *Carlo Dolci* (in a rich frame by *G.B. Foggini*), and a portrait of Card. Carlo de' Medici by *Sustermans.*—SALA DEI PAPPAGALLI (VI). School *of Botticelli,* Tondo of the Madonna and Child with angels; 764. *Titian,* Giulia Verana, duchess of Urbino (?); *Fr. Pourbus the Younger,* Elizabeth of France; *Sustermans,* Vittoria della Rovere, Maria Maddalena d'Austria. The Cabinet in ebony and ivory is by *G.B. Foggini.*—The SALA GIALLA (VII) and the CAMERA DA LETTO DELLA REGINA MARGHERITA (VIII) contain a magnificent series of hunting tapestries showing Louis XV, on cartoons by *J.B. Oudry.*—The oval TOLETTA DELLA REGINA (IX) is decorated in the Chinese style on a design by *Ignazio Pellegrini*. The adjoining circular SALA DI MUSICA DELLA REGINA (X) is usually kept closed. From the Sala dei Pappagalli (VI; above) is the entrance (not always open) to the APPAR-TAMENTI DI UMBERTO I, four rooms (XI-XIV) elaborately decorated, with poor portraits by *Sustermans*.—The remaining series of rooms (XV-XXII) are normally kept closed and used only for exhibitions. The 18C SALA BIANCA (XV) or DEL BALLO is by *Gaspare Maria Paoletti*. The SALA DI BONA (XXII) is frescoed by *Bernardino Poccetti* (1608).

On the floor above the Galleria Palatina is the **Galleria d'Arte Moderna** (for adm see p 58), founded c. 1860 and moved here after 1918. The collection is particularly representative of Tuscan art of the 19C, notably the 'Macchiaioli' school (Giovanni Fattori, Silvestro Lega, Telemaco Signorini, etc.). Many of the rooms on this floor were decorated in the 19C by the last grand-dukes Ferdinand III and Leopold II. In every room there is a detailed catalogue of the works displayed which cover the period from the mid-18C up to the end of the First World War. They are arranged chronologically and by schools. The collection of 20C works (particularly representative of the years between the two Wars), and including paintings by Gino Severini, Ardengo Soffici, De Chirico, and Casorati, among many others, is to be arranged on this floor in rooms to the r. of the stairs.

ROOM 1. Neo-classicism. *Pompeo Batoni*, Hercules at the crossroads (1742), and works by *Stef. Tofanelli* and *Gaspare Landi*.—RR 2-6 (left; not always open) contains works of the Romantic period, including paintings by *Fr. Hayez*.—R. 7. Portraits by *Pietro Benvenuti* and *Vinc. Camuccini*; head of Napoleon I by *Canova* (or a contemporary copy); landscape by *Nicolas Didier Boguet;* (l. wall) *Françoise Xavier Fabre,* Antonio Santarelli (1812).—R. 8. Portraits of the last grand-dukes of Tuscany, and a huge Sèvres vase with a bronze mount by P. Thomire.—R. 9 is devoted to the Demidoff family in Florence, and includes a model by *Lor. Bartolini* for his monument on Lungarno Serristori (comp. p 168).—R. 10. On the end wall, a huge painting by *Gius. Bezzuoli* showing Charles VIII's entry into Florence. Also here: *Amos Cassioli,* Battle of Legnano; *Aristodemo Costoli,* Dying gladiator; *Giov. Duprè,* Cain and Abel, two bronze statues; *Pio Fedi,* St Sebastian.—R. 11 (right) contains paintings by *Stef. Ussi*.—R. 12. *Ant. Ciseri.*—The SALA DA BALLO (1825) has two statues of the young Bacchus, by *Giov. Duprè*.—R. 13. Good portraits by *Giov. Boldoni, Giov. Fattori,* and *Ant. Puccinelli.*—R. 14. Landscapes by *Ant. Fontanesi.*—R. 15. (Cristiano Banti collection). Works by *Cristiano Banti, Fr. Altamura,* and *Giov. Boldini.*—R. 16 (Diego Martelli collection). Works by the 'Macchiaioli', a school of painters founded in Tuscany in the mid-19C whose works were characterized by 'macchie' or spots of colour. Taking their inspiration direct from nature, they could be termed Tuscan Impressionists, and the results they obtained were often of the highest quality. The painters represented here include *Gius. Abbati, Giov. Fattori, Silvestro Lega, Raffaello Sernesi, Telemaco Signorini,* and *Fed. Zandomeneghi.* The collection also includes two landscapes by *Camille Pissarro.*—In R. 17 are genre scenes by *Gius. Abbati, Gius. De Nittis, Dom. Induno,* and *Silvestro Lega,* and sculptures by *Adriano Cecioni.*—R. 18. The Risorgimento. Bust of Mazzini by *Cecioni,* and battle-scenes by *Giov. Fattori* and *Silvestro Lega.*—R. 19. *Ant. Ciseri.*—R. 20. *Stef. Ussi.*—RR. 23 and 24 (the Ambron collection) display more fine works by the Macchiaioli school including *Giov. Fattori, Telemaco Signorini, Vito d'Ancona,* and *Vinc. Cabianca.*—R. 25. Peasant scenes by *Egisto Ferroni, Fattori, Signorini,* and *Enrico Banti.*—R. 26. Works by *Eugenio Cecconi.*—R. 27. *Fil. Palizzi, Gius. de Nittis, Dom. Morelli, Pio Joris, Gaetano Esposito,* etc.—R. 28 German artists working in Florence in the late 19C, including *Arnold Böcklin* and *Adolf Hildebrand.*—R. 29. *Adolfo De Carolis, Lor. Viani, John Singer Sargent,* and sculptures by *Medardo Rosso.*—R. 30 contains works by *Elisabeth Chaplin* and *Armando Spadini,* among others.

The ***Museo degli Argenti** (for opening times, see p 58), arranged in the summer apartments of the grand-dukes, is entered from the left side of the courtyard.

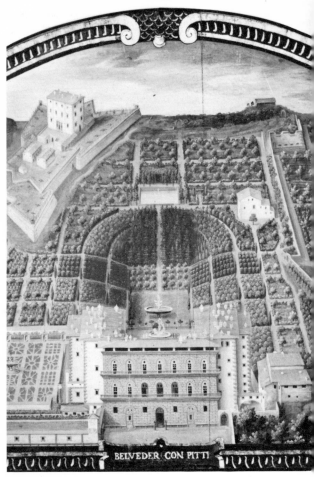

Palazzo Pitti and Forte di Belvedere, from a tempera lunette by Giusto Utens, 1599. (Museo di Firenze com'era)

The entrance hall has tapestries and a portrait of Leopoldo de' Medici (later Cardinal) by *Sustermans*.—SALA DI GIOVANNI DI SAN GIOVANNI. The exuberant and colourful frescoes by *Giov. di San Giovanni* were begun after the marriage of Ferdinando II and Vittoria della Rovere in 1634. They represent the apotheosis of the Medici family. The decoration of the end walls was completed by his pupils *Cecco Bravo, Fr. Furini,* and *Ottavio Vannini*.—In the room to the left, the SALA BUIA, is displayed (central case) the magnificent *Collection of sixteen vases in pietre dure which belonged to Lorenzo il Magnifico, and which bear his monogram 'LAV.R.MED'. Most of them date from the Late Imperial Roman era; others are Byzantine or medieval Venetian works. They were mounted in silver-gilt in the 15C (some by *Giusto da Firenze*) or later in the grand-ducal workshops. In the four smaller cases are Antique cups and dishes in pietre dure and some Byzantine works. Also here are 15C church vestments, and reliquaries

13-15C).—Beyond is the GROTTICINA, with a little fountain and a pretty frescoed ceiling with birds by Florentine artists (1623–34). Here are portraits of five grand-duchesses, including Christine of Lorraine, by *Pulzone*. The exquisitely carved limewood relief by *Grinling Gibbons* was presented to Cosimo III in 1682 by Charles II.—To the r. of the Sala di Giovanni di San Giovanni, beyond the CHAPEL decorated by local craftsmen in 1623–34, are two RECEPTION ROOMS with delightful trompe l'oeil frescoes by the Bolognese painters, *Angelo Michele Colonna* and *Agostino Mitelli* (1635–41). The cabinet, brought to Florence in 1628, was made in Augsburg. Also here are several fine tables in pietre dure (16-17C), a 17C prie-dieu, and a chessboard made in 1619 on a design by *Iac. Ligozzi*.

The rooms towards the Boboli gardens were the living quarters of the grand-dukes. Here, and on the mezzanine floor, are displayed their eclectic collection of personal keepsakes, gifts presented by other ruling families, objets d'art made specially for them, etc. In the room to the r. are vessels in rock crystal and pietre dure including (802.) a lapis lazuli vase (1583, designed by *Buontalenti* with a gold mount by *Jacques Bilivert*), a rock crystal vase (721.) in the form of a bird with a gold enamelled mount), and a lapis lazuli shell (413.) with the handle in enamelled gold in the form of a snake. The so-called 'Coppa di Diana di Poitiers' (540.), in rock crystal with an enamelled gold lid, is thought to have been made for Henry II of France. A fiasca (620.) in rock crystal has an incised scene of Parnassus and a gold ornamental chain.—The ivories in the two rooms to the left include statuettes made for Cardinal Leopoldo by the German *Balthazar Stockamer* in the mid-17C, an elaborate composition of Curtius riding his horse into the abyss, and a series of turned vases, also of German manufacture, particularly remarkable from a technical point of view.—Stairs lead up to the MEZZANINE where the grand-ducal collection of jewellery has always been kept. In the two rooms to the r.: rings with cameos and intaglio; cameo portraits; the Jewellery collection of the last of the Medici, the electress Anna Maria; ex-voto in precious stones of Cosimo II in prayer made in the grand-ducal workshops in 1617–24; relief of Cosimo I and his family in pietre dure by *Giov. Ant. de' Rossi* 1557–62); oval in pietre dure of Piazza Signoria by *Bern. Gaffurri* (1598); Roman head of Hercules.—The first two rooms to the left of the stairs contain gold and silversmiths' work from the Treasury of Ferdinando III brought to Florence in 1814 (mainly from Salzburg), including elaborate nautilus shells, a double chalice made from an ostrich-egg mounted in silver gilt (c. 1370–80), two ornamental cups made from buffalo horns with silver gilt mounts (14C), etc. The series of silver gilt dishes from Salzburg were made by *Paul Hübner*, c. 1590.—Beyond a painted 'loggia' (early 17C) is another frescoed room overlooking the courtyard which contains exotic and rare objects from all over the world. These include an Islamic powder horn, nautilus shells, 17C shell figurines, a mitre with scenes of the Passion depicted in gold thread and birds' feathers (Mexican, c. 1545), etc.—Other rooms contain plaster casts of the silver plates belonging to the last Medici grand-dukes which were melted down in 1799; Chinese and Japanese porcelain, etc.

In the PALAZZINA DELLA MERIDIANA (adm see p 58), which was begun in 1776 by Gaspare Maria Paoletti, the **Collezione Contini-Bonacossi** was arranged in 1974. It includes a fine collection of Italian (and some Spanish) paintings and furniture of the 15-17C, majolica, etc. Some of the most important works include: R. 1. *Agnolo Gaddi*, Madonna and Child with Saints.—R. II. *Paolo Veneziano*, Two scenes from the life of St Nicholas.—R. III. *Bern. Zenale*, St Michael archangel, St Bernard; *Sassetta*, Madonna della Neve (altarpiece); *Defendente Ferrari*, Madonna and Child.—R. IV. *Giov. Bellini*, St Jerome in the desert; *Paolo Veronese*, Count Giuseppe da Porto and his son Adriano; *Vinc. Catena*, Supper at Emmaus; *Gian Lorenzo Bernini*, Martyrdom of St Lawrence (sculpture).—R. V. *Bramantino*, Madonna and Child with Saints; *Giov. Ant. Boltraffio*, Portrait of the poet Casio; *Cima da Conegliano*, St Jerome in the desert.—R. VI. *Fr. Goya*, Bullfighter; *El Greco*, 'The tears of St Peter'; *Diego Velazquez*, The water-carrier.—RR. VII-IX. Della Robbian tondoes, statuettes by *Bambaia*, etc.—R. X. *And. del Castagno*, Madonna and Child with angels and Saints and two children of the Pazzi family (fresco from the castle of Trebbio).—R. XI. *Iac. Tintoretto*, Portrait of a man, Minerva, and Venus.

On the hillside behind Palazzo Pitti lie the magnificent ***Bóboli Gardens,** laid out for Cosimo I by *Tribolo,* and perhaps also *Amman-*

nati, after 1550, and extended in the early 17C. They are thought to
have been opened to the public for the first time in 1766. The normal
entrance is from the piazza through an archway in the left wing of the
palace (they can also be reached from the courtyard of Ammannati
comp. p 100). For adm see p 57. The charming garden in front of the
Museo delle Porcellane (adm see p 58) is only open with the museum
There are three additional exits from the gardens: one at Porta
Romana, one at the Annalena gate on Via Romana, and one at the
Forte di Belvedere (comp. the Plan on p 111). The biggest public park
in the centre of Florence, the gardens are beautifully maintained. They
are always cool even on the hottest days in summer, and are a
delightful place to picnic. Many of the statues which decorate the
walks are restored Roman works, but a considerable number remain
unidentified. Two worn statues in the gardens were recognized as
works by Cellini only just before the last war (they are now in the
Bargello, see p 144).

On the left of the entrance arch is the so-called *'Fontana del Bacco'* (1), really
an amusing statue of Pietro Barbino, the pot-bellied dwarf of Cosimo I, seated
on a turtle, by Valerio Cioli (1560). Here can be seen the last stretch of the Cor
ridoio Vasariano from the Uffizi (comp. p 97). A path descends to the
scenographic *GROTTA DEL BUONTALENTI (2), named after its architect (1583–88)
and restored in 1980. The two statues in the niches on the façade (begun by
Vasari) are by Baccio Bandinelli. The walls of the first chamber are covered with
fantastic figures carved in the limestone by Piero di Tommaso Mati. In the four
corners are casts of Michelangelo's unfinished 'slaves' (the originals, placed here
in 1585, have been removed to the Accademia, see p 113). The charmingly
painted vault is by Bern. Poccetti. Beyond an erotic group of Paris abducting
Helen, by Vinc. de' Rossi, the innermost grotto contains a beautiful statue of
Venus emerging from her bath (c. 1565) by Giambologna, and pretty murals by
Poccetti.

The carriage-way, flanked by two porphyry statues of Dacian prisoners (from
the Villa Medici in Rome, with bas-reliefs of the late-3C on their pedestals)
winds up through the gardens. The ancient square bell-tower of Santa Felicita
can be seen near a rose-garden with a colossal seated figure of Jupiter of
unknown provenance. A narrow path leads to a little grotto, with stalactites and
bizarre goats, begun in 1553. The main path emerges on the terrace behind
Palazzo Pitti, overlooking the courtyard and *Fontana del Carciofo* (3; se
above). From the terrace there is a magnificent view of the Duomo and Cam
panile behind Orsanmichele.

The AMPHITHEATRE (4) was designed by Ammannati in 1599, in imitation of a
Roman circus. Spectacles were held here by the Medici. The huge granite basin
comes from the Baths of Caracalla and the obelisk of Rameses II was taken from
Heliopolis by the Romans in 30 B.C., and found its way to the Villa Medici in th
17C. It was brought here in 1790 from Rome where its companion now adorns
the Dogali Monument.—On the first terrace behind the Amphitheatre are three
Roman statues (5), including a fine Ceres.—On the upper level is a large fish
pond surrounded by terraces planted with trees (above which can be seen the
Forte di Belvedere). Here is the *Neptune Fountain* (8) by Stoldo Lorenzi
(1565–68). A short detour to the left leads through romantic winding alleys over
shadowed by ilexes and a cypress grove, to the rococo *'Kaffehaus'* (6), built in
1776 by Zanobi del Rosso (a cafè here is open in summer). In the garden in front
(with a good view of Florence and Fiesole) is the *Ganymede Fountain* (7)
thought to date from the 17C. Behind the Kaffehaus there is access to the Fort
di Belvedere (see p 181). From the Neptune Fountain steps continue to the top of
the garden and a colossal Statue of *'Abundance'* (9), in a niche of bay and ilex
Begun by Giambologna, it was finished by Pietro Tacca. From here the view em
braces the whole city, beyond the Pitti and the tower of Santo Spirito.

A short double flight of steps (r.) continues to the *Giardino del Cavaliere* (10)
a delightful secluded walled garden on a bastion constructed by Michelangelo in
1529. The fountain has three monkeys attrib. to Giambologna or Tacca, and
cupid attrib. to Pierino da Vinci. The view from the terrace is one of the most
charming in Florence, embracing the rural outskirts of the city. On the extreme

Boboli Gardens

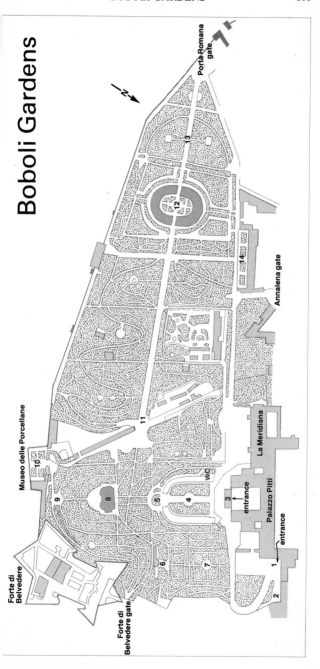

left is the bastion of Forte di Belvedere, then, behind a group of cypresses, San Miniato with its tower. The fields and olive groves are dotted with beautiful old villas. To the r. is the residential area of Bobolino beside a splendid stretch of the city walls. Here, in the Casino del Cavaliere, enlarged in the 18C, the MUSEO DELLE PORCELLANE was opened in 1973 (adm see p 58). It contains a well displayed collection of Italian, German, and French porcelain from the Medici and Lorraine grand-ducal collections. Room 1 displays 18C French porcelain (Tournai, Chantilly, Vincennes, Sèvres, including the delicate 'alzata da ostriche'). In the centre, beneath a Venetian chandelier, the dinner service of Elisa Baciocchi, and a plaque with a portrait of her brother Napoleon in Sèvres porcelain, after Françoise Gérard (1809–10). Also here, 18-19C Doccia and Neapolitan ware.—In the other two rooms, 18-19C works made in the Meissen and Vienna porcelain factories.

At the foot of the double stairs, another flight of steps leads down between seated Muses to the *Prato dell'Uccellare*, with a grove of cedars of Lebanon (view), at the end of a range of garden houses. To the left the magnificent long VIOTTOLONE (11) descends steeply through the gardens. A majestic cypress avenue planted in 1637 by Alfonso Parigi the Younger, it is lined with statues, many of them restored Roman works (and some of them carved in the 16C and 17C). The arboured walks and little gardens to the r. and l., with delightful vistas, provide some of the most beautiful scenery in the park. The paths are laid out between box hedges and laurel avenues. On the l. a path ends at a colossal bust of Jupiter, attrib. as an early work to Giambologna (here a path lined with fountains follows a stretch of the city walls). The statues of the four seasons are by Pietro Francavilla.—At the bottom of the avenue are two groups of statues depicting folk games (17-18C). The statues of animals in this part of the garden are by Fr. del Tadda. The ISOLOTTO (12) was laid out by Alfonso Parigi in 1618. It is a circular moat with fine sculptural decorations surrounding an island with garden and a copy of Giambologna's Fountain of Oceanus (original in the Bargello, p 146), on a huge granite base quarried by Tribolo in Elba. The fanciful groups of statues on the balustrade are by Giulio Parigi. The island recalls the so-called Naval Theatre, Hadrian's retreat at his villa near Tivoli. In the niches in the surrounding hedge are 17C statues of peasants, etc.

Beyond is the *Hemicycle* (13), surrounded by plane-trees, with two neo-classical columns. Some of the colossal busts are Antique. The four statues, generally considered to be 17C works, may include a Roman work, and the statue of Aesculapius has recently been attrib. to Tribolo. The green provides a cool playground for local children in summer, and the traditional football game in 16C costume (see p 56) is sometimes held here. At the end of the garden are marble figures of bird-catchers, and three grotesque figures attrib. to Romolo del Tadda. On top of a Roman sarcophagus is a fountain of a peasant with a barrel by Giov. Fancelli. At the exit from the garden through the walls, beside Porta Romana, is a statue of Perseus attrib. to Vinc. Danti. Just outside the gate (l.), in the former Royal Stables is the *Istituto d'Arte*, with a Museum of Plaster-casts.—Buses from Porta Romana return to the centre of the city; otherwise a path leads back through the gardens following the left wall along Via Romana. Beyond the *Fountain of the Vintage* (1599–1608), by Valerio Cioli, is the *Orangery* (14; 1789), near the Annalena gate, another exit from the garden. Nearby is a small grotto with statues of Adam and Eve by Michele Naccherino. A path continues past more greenhouses to emerge by the Meridiana wing of Palazzo Pitti. The hillside here was used probably since Roman times as a quarry for pietra forte. The nearest exit from the gardens is beneath the Fontana del Carciofo into Ammannati's courtyard.

9   GALLERIA DELL'ACCADEMIA AND SANTISSIMA ANNUNZIATA

From Piazza San Marco (see Rte 10) the straight Via Ricasoli (Pl. 6; 6) leads towards the Duomo (view of the Campanile). Beyond the Accademia di Belle Arti (p 121) is the entrance at No. 60 to the ***Galleria dell'Accademia** (Pl. 6; 6; adm see p 57), visited above all for its famous works by Michelangelo, but also containing an important collection of Florentine paintings. The gallery is being re-arranged and expanded (1980–83).

The collection was formed in 1784 with a group of paintings given, for study purposes, to the Academy by Pietro Leopoldo I. Since 1873 some important sculptures by Michelangelo have been housed here, including the David.

The entrance leads into the first room of the PINACOTECA. *Fra' Bartolomeo,* Isaiah and Job; *Fr. Granacci,* Madonna and Child with Saints; *Mariotto Albertinelli,* Annunciation (1510), Madonna enthroned with Saints; *Filippino Lippi,* St John the Baptist and St Mary Magdalen; *Fr. Botticini,* SS Augustine and Monica; *Perugino,* and *Filippino Lippi,* *Descent from the Cross; *Perugino,* Assumption and Saints; *Rid. Ghirlandaio,* Madonna and Child with SS Francis and Mary Magdalen; *Albertinelli,* The Trinity; *Bart. di Giovanni,* St Jerome; *Fra' Bartolomeo,* *Madonna enthroned with Saints and angels (a painting which may be returned to the Pitti); *Fr. Granacci,* Virgin of the Sacred Girdle.—In the centre, the original plaster model for the Rape of the Sabine (comp p 79), by *Giambolognga.*

The GALLERIA (in course of re-arrangement) contains **Sculptures by *Michelangelo.* The four SLAVES or PRISONERS (c. 1521–23) were begun for the ill-fated tomb of Julius II. In 1585 they were placed in the Grotta del Buontalenti in the Bóboli gardens (comp. p 110). The ST MATTHEW (1504–08), one of the twelve apostles commissioned from the sculptor by the Opera del Duomo, was the only one he ever began. These are all magnificent examples of Michelangelo's unfinished works, some of them barely blocked out, the famous 'non-finito', much discussed by scholars. They evoke Michelangelo's unique concept expressed in his poetry, that the sculpture already exists within the block of stone, and it is the sculptor's job merely to take away what is superfluous. The way in which Michelangelo confronted his task, as Cellini noted, was to begin from a frontal viewpoint, as if carving a high relief, and thus the statue gradually emerged from the marble.—The Pietà from Santa Rosalia in Palestrina is an undocumented work, and is not now usually considered to be by Michelangelo's own hand.

To the right are three more rooms of the PINACOTECA. ROOM 2. (On screen) 004. Madonna and Child by a Florentine master c. 1430; 3160. *And. di Giusto,* Madonna and Child with angels; *8457. Frontal of a 'cassone' or marriage-chest of the Adimari family (15C), showing a wedding scene with elegant guests in period dress in front of the Baptistery; 8508. *Mariotto di Cristofano,* Scenes from the life of Christ and of the Madonna; 171 dep. *'Master of the Castello Nativity,'* Nativity (from the Villa di Castello, comp. p 209); 1562. *Cosimo Rosselli,* Madonna and Child with Saints; 4632. *Filippino Lippi,* Annunciation an early work; a copy from a painting by his father, *Fra' Filippo Lippi*); 3162, 164. *Mariotto di Cristofano,* Resurrection, Marriage of St Catherine; 8624. *Domenico di Michelino,* St Tobias and three archangels.—ROOM 3. *3166. *Botticelli,* Madonna and Child with the young St John and angels (an early work); 381. *Pupil of Paolo Uccello* (attrib.), The Thebaids; *8637. *Aless. Baldovinetti,* Trinity and Saints (much ruined); 8623. *Seb. Mainardi* (attrib.), Pietà.—R. 4. *8661. *Lor. di Credi,* Adoration of the Child; *8456. *Botticelli,* Madonna 'of the Sea'; 8663. *Raffaellino del Garbo,* Resurrection; 8631–33. *Cosimo Rosselli,* God the Father, Moses and Adam, David and Noah; 8627–29. *Bart. di Giovanni,* Deposition, St Francis, and St Jerome; 1621. *Seb. Mainardi,* SS. Stephen, James, and Peter.

The TRIBUNE was specially built in 1873 to exhibit the *DAVID by *Michelangelo* (1501–4) when it was removed from Piazza della Signoria (comp. p 79). It is perhaps the most famous single work of art of western civilisation, and has become all too familiar through endless reproductions, although it is not the work by which Michelangelo is best judged. It was commissioned by the city of

Florence to stand outside Palazzo Vecchio where its huge scale fits its setting. Here it seems out of place in its cold heroic niche. The colossal block of marble, 4.10 metres high, quarried in 1464 for the Opera del Duomo, had been left abandoned in the cathedral workshop. The marble was offered to several other artists, including And. Sansovino and Leonardo da Vinci before it was finally assigned to Michelangelo. The figure of David, uncharacteristic of Michelangelo's works, stands in a classical pose suited to the shallow block of marble. The hero, a young colossus, is shown in the moment before his victory over Goliath. A celebration of the nude, the statue established Michelangelo as the foremost sculptor of his time at the age of 29.—The walls of the Tribune are to be hung with Florentine paintings by Michelangelo's contemporaries, including *Aless. Allori, Bronzino,* and *Santi di Tito.*

To the left are three more rooms of the PINACOTECA displaying early Tuscan works (13-14C). ROOM 5. *3345. Crucifix by the Sienese school; 8459. *Pacino di Buonaguida,* Tree of the Cross (restored); (on screen) Byzantine works; 8466. *'Maestro della Maddalena',* Mary Magdalen with stories from her life.—R. 6. 3469. *And. Orcagna,* Madonna and Child with angels and saints; 8464. *Nardo di Cione,* Triptych with the Trinity and two Saints; works by the *Gaddi,* and by *Bern. Daddi* and his school.—R. 7. *Jac. di Cione,* Coronation of the Virgin; *8467. *Giov. da Milano,* Pietà; 8581–8603. Scenes from the life of Christ and from the life of St Francis by *Taddeo Gaddi* (from the Sacristy of Santa Croce).

The huge room at the end of this wing is to be devoted to 19C works by members of the Accademia di Belle Arti (comp. p 121). Among the most famous Academicians at that time was the sculptor *Lorenzo Bartolini* who is here represented by a remarkable group of original plaster *Models for some of his best works.

From the entrance, stairs lead up to the **First Floor** where several rooms are in the course of arrangement. Here will be displayed Florentine paintings of the 14C and 15C, including works by *Lor. Monaco,* the *'Master of the Madonna Straus',* Lo Starnina, Neri di Bicci, Giov. del Ponte,* and *Rossello di Jac. Franchi.*

At the crossing of Via Ricasoli with Via degli Alfani is a small piazza with the entrance to the *Conservatorio Luigi Cherubini* (Pl. 6; 6), the conservatory of music named after the greatest Florentine musician Luigi Cherubini (1760–1842) who spent most of his career in Paris. The remarkable *MUSEUM OF OLD MUSICAL INSTRUMENTS, a collection begun by the last of the Medici and the grand-dukes of the House of Lorraine, is one of the most interesting in Italy. It still awaits a definitive arrangement here and is at present not on view. It includes the 'Viola Medicea' built by Antonio Stradivari in 1690; violins and 'cellos by Stradivari, Guarneri, Amati, and Ruggeri; a harpsichord by Bart. Cristofori, etc. The library contains autograph compositions. Via degli Alfani continues left (at the end can be seen the green dome of the synagogue) past the entrance (No. 78) to the OPIFICIO DELLE PIETRE DURE (Pl. 6; 6) founded here in 1588 by the grand-duke Ferdinando I.

The craft of working hard or semi-precious stones ('pietre dure') was perfected in Florence. Beautiful mosaics were made to decorate cabinets, table-tops, etc. (many of them are preserved in Palazzo Pitti). The workshop is now dedicated to restoration work (and forms part of the Istituto di Restauro). A *Museum* here (adm see p 58) exhibits some fine works in mosaic, including several tables on the ground floor, and a bust of Vittoria della Rovere in 'pietre dure'. The two rooms at the top of the stairs contain 19C objects, and the work benches and instruments used by the craftsmen. In wall cases are numerous samples of semi-precious stones.

Via degli Alfani continues across Via dei Servi (see below). On the right is an octagonal building, the ROTONDA DI SANTA MARIA DEGLI ANGELI (Pl. 6; 6; called 'Il Castellaccio' from its fortress-like air; no adm). It was begun by Brunelleschi in 1434 as a memorial to the soldier Fil. degli Scolari (d. 1424), and left unfinished in 1437. Modelled on the Temple of Minerva Medica in Rome, it was one of the first centralized buildings of the Renaissance. After a period of use as a church, it was completed in 1959 as a lecture-hall. In the square behind are the buildings of the Faculty of Letters and Philosophy of the University. At No. 48 Via Alfani, *Palazzo Giugni* is a characteristic work by Ammannati (c. 1577) with a fine courtyard.

Via dei Servi (Pl. 6; 6), on the line of an ancient thoroughfare leading N. from the city, is documented as early as the 12C as far as the Porta di Balla (comp. below). It was extended beyond the city gate in the 13C, and used by Brunelleschi in his Renaissance design of Piazza Santissima Annunziata to provide a magnificent view of the cupola of the Duomo. It is now lined by a number of handsome 16C palaces. Going towards the Duomo, on the right, Nos. 15 and 17 were restored in 1959 as government offices. The pretty fountain at No. 17 can be seen from the road. No. 15, *Palazzo Niccolini* was designed by Baccio d'Agnolo in 1548–50. Its beautiful façade is typical of Florentine palaces of this period. The small courtyard has graffiti decoration, and in the garden beyond is an elaborate double loggia, probably by Giov. Ant. Dosio. Opposite, *Palazzo Sforza Alimeni* (No. 12), c. 1510–20, has two good ground-floor windows; the coat-of-arms on the corner has been replaced by a modern copy. The house across Via del Castellaccio is on the site of the studio of Benedetto da Maiano in 1480–98.
The next crossing, the Canto di Balla, is on the site of the old Porta di Balla, a postern gate in the 12C walls. Here is a worn coat-of-arms by Baccio da Montelupo on the corner of *Palazzo dei Pucci*, one of the largest palaces in Florence, which bears the name of one of the oldest families in the city. The central part of the long façade (which stretches as far as Via Ricasoli) dates from the 16C, and is in part attrib. to Ammannati; the wings on either side are 17C extensions. In the little piazza is the church of **San Michele Visdomini** (Pl. 16; 2; or *San Michelino*) of ancient foundation, known to have been enlarged by the Visdomini family in the 11C. It was demolished in 1363 in order to make way for the E. end of the Duomo, and reconstructed on this site a few years later.
INTERIOR. Right side: *Empoli*, Nativity; *Pontormo*, *Holy Family (1518); left side: *Poppi*, Madonna and Saints; *Passignano*, St John the Baptist; *Poppi*, Madonna. In the l. transept, *Poppi*, Resurrection. The 18C vault fresco in the crossing of the Fall of Satan is by *Niccolò Lapi*. In the two chapels flanking the high altar, sinopie and fresco fragments have recently been revealed, attrib. to *Mariotto di Nardo* (lights on r. and l.).
Opposite the church, *Palazzo Incontri* (reconstructed in 1676) was owned by Piero il Gottoso in 1469. Via de' Pucci leads to Via Ricasoli, and on the corner is the *Tabernacolo delle Cinque Lampade*, with a fresco (r.) by Cosimo Rosselli. Via Ricasoli is named after Baron Ricasoli (1809–80), mayor of Florence. He lived at No. 9 which has a courtyard of the late 16C.

Via dei Servi leads N. to *Piazza Santissima Annunziata (Pl. 6; 6), designed by Brunelleschi, and surrounded on three sides by porticoes. It remains the most beautiful square in Florence, despite its use as a car park.

On the right is the Spedale degli Innocenti; in front is the church of the Annunziata and the convent of the Servite order, with remains of five Gothic windows; to the left, the colonnade (modelled on the earlier one opposite) by Antonio da Sangallo and Baccio d'Agnolo (1516–25); at the corner of Via dei Servi, Palazzo Riccardi-Mannelli, formerly Grifoni, is now the seat of the President of the Regional Government of Tuscany. It is thought to have been begun in 1557 by Ammannati probably on a design by Giul. di Baccio d'Agnolo, and then finished by Buontalenti and Giambologna. It has an ornate brick façade with a decorative frieze. In the middle of the square are an equestrian statue of the grand-duke Ferdinando I, by Giambologna (his last work, cast by Tacca in 1608), and two bizarre bronze fountains by Tacca and his pupils (1629).—On the festival of the Annunziata (25 March) a fair is held in the piazza and adjoining streets; home-made sweet 'biscuits' ('brigidini') are sold from the stalls.

The *Spedale degli Innocenti (Pl. 6; 6; properly, *Ospedale degli Innocenti*), opened in 1445 as a foundling hospital, the first institution of its kind in Europe, is still operating as an orphanage. Vincenzo Borghini, prior here from 1552–80, was an outstanding figure of 16C Florence, friend of Vasari, and counsellor to Duke Cosimo on artistic and literary matters. The 'Arte della Seta' commissioned *Brunelleschi* (who had become a member of the Guild in the capacity of goldsmith) to begin work on the building in 1419. The *COLONNADE (1419–26) of nine arches is one of the first masterpieces of Renaissance architecture. It takes inspiration from classical antiquity as well as from local Romanesque buildings. The last bays on the right and left were added in the 19C. In the spandrels are delightful *Medallions, perhaps the best known work of *Andrea della Robbia* (1487), each with a baby in swaddling-clothes against a bright blue ground (the end ones on each side are 19C). Beneath the portico at the left end is the 'rota' constructed in 1660 to receive abandoned babies (walled up in 1875). The fresco under the central vault of the colonnade is by *Bern. Poccetti* (1610), that in the lunette above the door of the church is by *Giov. di Francesco* (1459; very damaged). The CHURCH (open in the early morning only) was remodelled in neo-classical style in 1786 by *Bern. Fallani*. It contains an altarpiece of the Annunciation by *Mariotto Albertinelli* and *Giov. Ant. Sogliani*.

The CONVENT may be visited to see the **Museo dello Spedale degli Innocenti** (adm see p 58). The oldest parts of the convent buildings, around two cloisters, were modified in the 18-19C, but have recently been restored to their original design by *Brunelleschi*. The main 'CHIOSTRO DEGLI UOMINI' (1422–45) was decorated in 1596 with a clock tower, and graffiti (drawn with lime) showing the emblems of the 'Arte della Seta' and the other two hospital foundations (San Gallo and Scala), which were united here in the 15C. Over the side door into the church is a beautiful lunette of the Annunciation by *And. della Robbia*. Children can usually be seen playing in the delightful gardens beyond the passage leading from the courtyard. A door on the r. here leads past offices to the oblong *'CHIOSTRO DELLE DONNE' (1438), another beautiful work by *Brunelleschi*, with 24 slender Ionic columns beneath a low loggia. The charming perspective of the colonnades is reminiscent of the background in some Renaissance paintings. This part of the convent was reserved for the women who worked in the Institute.

From the main cloister stairs lead up to the GALLERY. Here are displayed detached frescoes, many of them from Ognissanti: *16C Florentine School*, Crucifixion; *17C Florentine School*, Adoration of the Shepherds; *Circle of Fra Bartolomeo*, Crucifixion with Mary Magdalen; *Bicci di Lorenzo*, Madonna enthroned between SS George and Leonard (sinopia of 1430 from Porta San Giorgio); series of large frescoes from Ognissanti by *Aless. Allori* (1575); *Dom. Ghirlandaio* (and his workshop), Madonna and Child.—In the small rooms off the cloister: terracotta crib by *Matteo Civitali*, beneath a fresco of St Catherine and the Philosophers by *Bern. Poccetti* (1612). In the room to the l.: *Bicci di Lorenzo*, St Anthony Abbot, Madonna and Child between Saints (both sinopie); *Lor. Monaco*, Crucifixion, Christ in Pietà. The last room has models and plans of the hospital.—The stairs continue to the Long Gallery (formerly the day nursery) which has been arranged as a **Pinacoteca**: *'Master of the Madonna Straus'*, Coronation of the Virgin; *Giov. del Biondo*, Annunciation between Saints; *Cenni di Francesco*, Madonna and Child (detached fresco); *Neri di Bicci*, Coronation of the Virgin; *Botticelli*, Madonna and Child with an angel (an early work copied from Filippo Lippi). Beyond an archway is a little room dominated by the splendid *Adoration of the Magi by *Dom. Ghirlandaio*. The brightly coloured work includes a scene of the Massacre of the Innocents and two child Saints in the foreground. The predella is by *Bart. di Giovanni*. The altarpiece was commissioned for the high altar of the church by the prior, Francesco Tesori

(d. 1497), whose tomb slab has been placed in the floor here. The *Madonna and Child by *Luca della Robbia* (c. 1445–50) is one of his most beautiful works. The Madonna enthroned is by *Piero di Cosimo*. In the long gallery, Bust of Cione Pollini (15C); *Jacopino del Conte* (attrib.), Madonna of the Innocenti; *Giov. di Francesco Toscani,* Triptych of the Madonna and Child with Saints.

The church of the ***Santissima Annunziata** (Pl. 6; 6; closed 12.30–16) was founded by the seven original Florentine members of the Servite Order in 1250, and rebuilt, along with the cloister, by *Michelozzo* and others in 1444–81.

Of the portico the central arch is ascribed to *Ant. da Sangallo,* the rest is by *G.B. Caccini* (1600). The middle door, over which is a lunette with an Annunciation in mosaic by *Dav. Ghirlandaio* admits to the **Atrium** or **Chiostrino dei Voti,** by *Manetti* (1447) from a design by *Michelozzo.* The series of frescoes on the walls are particularly interesting since most of them were painted in the second decade of the 16C by the leading painters of the time. They have suffered from humidity and have been detached and restored. From r. to l.: *Rosso Fiorentino,* Assumption (1), a very early work; *Pontormo,* *Visitation (2; showing the influence of And. del Sarto); *Franciabigio,* Marriage of the Virgin (3; the head of the Virgin was damaged by the painter himself in a fit of anger). Beyond a marble bas-relief of the Madonna and Child by an unknown sculptor (sometimes attrib. to *Michelozzo*), *And. del Sarto,* *Birth of the Virgin (4). The Coming of the Magi (5) contains *And. del Sarto's* self-portrait in the right-hand corner. Here intervenes the great door, in front of which are two bronze stoups by *Ant. Susini* (1615). The colours in the fresco of the *Nativity (6) by *Aless. Baldovinetti* (1460–62) have faded because they were mistakenly prepared by the artist. The landscape is particularly beautiful. The Vocation and Investiture of San Filippo Benizzi (7) by *Cosimo Rosselli* (1476) has recently been returned here, together with the following frescoes, after restoration. The Scenes from the life of San Filippo Benizzi (8-12) are interesting (but damaged) works by *And. del Sarto* (1509–10).

The heavily decorated and dark INTERIOR, with a rich ceiling by *Pietro Giambelli* (1664–69) on a design by *Volterrano,* was otherwise considerably altered in the 17-18C. The nave is being restored. At the W. end the shrine of the Madonna (13), highly venerated by Florentines, is bedecked with ex-votos, hanging lamps, and candles. The huge *Tabernacle (almost hidden by the devotional images), commissioned by Piero il Gottoso (dei Medici), was designed by *Michelozzo* and executed by *Pagno di Lapo Portigiani* (1448–61). It has a bronze grille by *Maso di Bartolomeo,* and an incongruous 17C canopy. It protects a painting (also difficult to see) of the Annunciation, traditionally ascribed to a friar who was miraculously assisted by an angel. The adjoining chapel (14; usually closed) was built as an oratory for the Medici (1453–63). It has five beautiful panels inlaid by the Opificio delle Pietre Dure (comp. p 114) in 1671 with the symbols of the Virgin (the rose, lily, moon, sun, and star). Here also is a small painting by *And. del Sarto* of the Head of the Redeemer (1515).

SOUTH SIDE. 1st chap., Altarpiece of the Madonna by *Empoli,* and vault frescoes by *Matteo Rosselli;* 2nd chap. (15), Crucifix in wood by *Ant. da Sangallo* (1483); 5th chap. (16), Monument to Orlando de' Medici, a delicate work by *Bern. Rossellino* (1456). In the transept chap. (17) a small painted crucifix has recently been restored and attrib. to *Aless. Baldovinetti.* In the next chap. (18), Dead Christ supported by Nicodemus, whose head is a self-portrait of the sculptor *Bandinelli* who is buried here. Behind the monument are the portraits of Bandinelli and his wife in relief. At the end of the aisle is a splendid organ (1521; being restored) by *Dom. di Lor. di Lucca.*

The large circular TRIBUNE (in restoration) at the E. end of the church was begun by *Michelozzo* and completed in 1477 by *Leon Battista Alberti*. It has a very unusual design, a rotonda preceded by a triumphal arch, derived from antique buildings. The huge fresco of the Coronation of the Virgin in the cupola (difficult to see) is by *Volterrano*. The high altar, with a frontal by *G.B. Foggini* (1682) bears a silver ciborium by *Ant. Merlini* (1656) on a design by *Alfonso Parigi*. Behind are the choir stalls and two lecterns of English workmanship (15C). On the left of the great arch, in the pavement beneath a statue of St Peter, is the burial place of And. del Sarto. The *Tomb (19) of Bp Angelo Marzi Medici, with an expressive effigy of the Bishop, charged with the fervour of the Counter Reformation, is signed by *Fr. da Sangallo* (1546).

The nine semicircular chapels which radiate from the Sanctuary have been closed while restoration work is in progress. The entrance is usually on the left. In the chap. to the r. (20), *Aless. Allori,* Birth of Maria, and Miracle of the Blessed Manetti (one of the founders) by his son, *Cristofano*. In the chapels to the l.: Madonna and Saints after *Perugino* (21); Resurrection by *Bronzino* and a wood statue of St Roch by *Veit Stoss* (22). The E. chap. (23) was reconstructed by *Giambologna* as his own tomb, and contains fine bronze reliefs and a bronze Crucifix by him, and other works by his pupils including *Francavilla*. The Madonna is attrib. to *Bern. Daddi*. Behind the altar, above the sarcophagus of Giambologna and Pietro Tacca, is a Pietà by *Ligozzi*.

The SACRISTY (24), with a fine vault, was built by *Pagno di Lapo* from Michelozzo's design. The chapel in the N. transept (25) is also the work of *Michelozzo* (1445–47), covered in the 18C by trompe l'oeil frescoes. It contains a terracotta statue of the Baptist by *Michelozzo* and a Deposition painted by *Ferd. Folchi* (1855). A door here admits to the cloisters (see below).—The 4th chap. on the N. side of the nave (26) contains an Assumption by *Perugino;* 3rd chap. (27), Crucifixion by *Giov. Stradano*. The Last Judgement by *Aless. Allori* is a copy of various figures in Michelangelo's fresco in the Sistine Chapel. 2nd chap. (28) *Holy Trinity with St Jerome, by *And. del Castagno;* the Cappella Feroni (29), with elaborate Baroque decoration by *G.B. Foggini* (1692), contains another fresco by *Castagno,* *St Julian and the Saviour.

The **Chiostro dei Morti,** with its memorial stones, is entered from outside the church, to the left of the portico. At the end of the entrance walk, over a door (30) into the church, is the so-called *Madonna del Sacco (from the sack on which St Joseph is leaning), an original portrayal of the Rest on the Flight into Egypt. It is one of *And. del Sarto's* best works. The other colourful frescoed lunettes (suffering from humidity; some of them removed for restoration) in the cloister are by *A. Mascagni, Bern. Poccetti, Matteo Rosselli,* and *Ventura Salimbeni*. They illustrate the origins of the Servite order and are interesting documents of 17C Florence.—The CAPPELLA DI SAN LUCA (sometimes opened on request) has belonged to the Accademia delle Arti del Disegno (Academy of Design) since 1565 (comp. p 186); a special Mass for artists is held on St Luke's Day. In the vault below are buried Cellini, Pontormo, Franciabigio, Montórsoli, Bartolini, and many other artists. In the vestibule is a Crucifix attrib. to *Fr. da Sangallo* and a 15C sinopia of the Madonna enthroned. The chapel has been well restored after the flood of 1966. The altarpiece of St Luke painting the Madonna is an interesting self-portrait by *Vasari,* a founder member of the Academy. On the left wall is a detached (and damaged) fresco by *Pontormo* of the Madonna with Saints (including St Lucy). On the r. wall is a fresco of the Trinity by *Aless. Allori*. On the W. wall, *Santi di Tito,* Allegory of Architecture. The ceiling fresco of the Vision of St Bernard is by *Luca Giordano*. The clay statues which lean dramatically out of their niches are the work of various Academicians, including *Montórsoli* (who was also a member of the Servite Order). The little

organ (1702) was made by Tommaso Fabbri da Faenza.—In the REFECTORY
traces have recently been found of sketches made in 1358 by *Fr. Talenti* and
Giov. di Lapo Ghini for the columns and capitals in the Duomo.—In the 17C
SAGRESTIA DELLA MADONNA (31), also off the cloister, is an Assumption by *Iac.
Vignali.*—The ORATORIO DI SAN SEBASTIANO (32), entered from the portico (r. of
the Atrium) has a vault fresco by *Poccetti.*

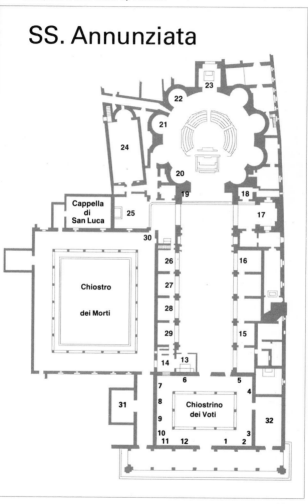

SS. Annunziata

Via della Colonna leads out of Piazza Santissima Annunziata
beneath an archway. The road skirts Palazzo della Crocetta, with its
garden, now the home of the ***Museo Archeologico** (Pl. 7; 5 adm see
p 58). The entrance is at No. 38. Although severely damaged in the
flood of 1966, and still closed on the ground floor, it includes one of
the most important collections of Etruscan antiquities in existence.

The two rooms at the foot of the staircase display recently restored objects from the collections, including the famous **François Vase,* a krater made by Ergotimos and painted by Kleitias in Athens (signed c. 570 B.C.). It is decorated with six rows of paintings of mythological scenes. It was found in an Etruscan tomb at Vulci. FIRST FLOOR. The **Egyptian Museum** is slowly being re-arranged and re-labelled; only the first two rooms have so far been completed. The contents of the other rooms may be moved round when they are modernized. ROOM I Prehistoric objects; two fine polychrome statuettes (restored) maidservant preparing yeast for beer, and maidservant kneading dough (2625–2475 B.C.); material of the XIIth Dynasty (19C B.C.), including part of a granite statue of a Pharaoh.—R. II. Bas-reliefs including one with the plan of a tomb preceded by a courtyard (14C B.C.); one showing craftsmen at work (7-6C B.C.); polychrome relief for the tomb of Seti I, representing the goddess Ma'at and Hathor and the Pharaoh (c. 1292 B.C.); scribes recording objects (fragment; c. 1400 B.C.).—ROOMS III-V. Sarcophagi, mummies, canopic vases, papyri, stelæ, and Coptic fabrics.—R. VI. Statuettes in limestone and wood; portrait of a young woman, from the Flavian period.—R. VII Statuettes of divinities; amulets, scarabs; plant ornaments.—R VIII Very rare Hittite **Chariot* in wood and bone from a Theban tomb of the 14C B.C.; vases, necklaces, sandals, and arms.

The **Etrusco-Greco-Roman Museum** occupies ROOMS IX—XXII of the First Floor and the whole of the Second Floor. FIRST FLOOR. Etruscan sculpture. ROOM IX. Urns with mythological subjects and from the heroic cycles of the Greek world; in the centre, alabaster sarcophagus from Tarquinia (4C B.C.) with tempera paintings of a battle between the Greeks and Amazons.—R X. Sculptured urns, sarcophagi, and statues; urn in the form of an Etruscan house; urn with banqueting and dancing scene; lid of a sarcophagus with an obese Etruscan.

Etruscan, Greek, and Roman bronzes (left). ROOM XI. Etruscan inscribed mirrors and decorative bronzes.—R XII. Small Greek and Roman bronzes; Roman and Christian lamps; urn with the symbolic ship of the Church.—R XIII. The **Idolino,* a remarkable bronze statue of a young athlete offering a libation, probably a Roman copy of a Greek original by Polykleitos of c. 420 B.C. found at Pésaro in 1530; the base is of 16C workmanship. It is justly the most famous work in the collection. Torso of an athlete, a Greek original of the 6-5C B.C. The **Horse's Head* probably came from a Greek quadriga group of the Late Hellenistic period. It is thought that both Verrocchio and Donatello saw it in the garden of the Palazzo Medici Riccardi before executing their equestrian statues.—R XIV, the Long Gallery, contains a bronze Minerva from Arezzo, a copy of a 5C Greek work; the **Chimera,* also from Arezzo (found in the 16C), an Etruscan work of the 5C B.C., a fantastical animal, with the body of a lion, the head of a ram (on its back), and a serpent's tail (restored); and the **Arringatore,* or Orator, dedicated to Aulus Metullus by an Etruscan artist of the 4C or 3C B.C. (found near Perugia in 1566).—R XV. Bronze fittings, arms, and various instruments; inscribed bronzes and seals, among them the well-known Seal of Magliano, which has a double inscription showing names of divinities and ritual prescriptions.

SECOND FLOOR. Here the exhibits are poorly labelled and crowded into old-fashioned showcases. PREHISTORIC COLLECTION. In two rooms to the r.; objects of the Rinaldone culture, and finds from Campiglia d'Orcia, Populonia, and Montemercano.—ITALIC AND MEDITERRANEAN COMPARISONS. R III. Examples of the civilization of Central Italy, including the bronze cap-shaped helmet, chased by Oppeano of Este.—R IV. Cypriot ceramics and sculpture; antiquities from Asia Minor.—R V. Cretan ware bronzes.—Vases and Terracottas. R VI. Vases from Greece and Rhodes, including a huge amphora.—R VII (with an unusual view of the cupola of the Duomo). Decorated ceramics of the various Greek factories under Oriental influence.—R VIII. Primitive Italic and Etruscan vases of impasto and black bucchero ware of the 9-8C B.C.—R IX. Etruscan vases of impasto and bucchero ware (7-6C B.C.).—R X. Etruscan bucchero ware of the 6-5C B.C.

ROOMS XI-XII. GREEK VASES in painted terracotta, with Etruscan imitations, a series largely dating from the finest period of the art, and important for the perfection of the paintings (some of which may be assigned to the school of Polygnotos) and for the light they throw on Greek mythology.—ROOM XII contains two well-known vases from Populonia and various vessels.—R XIII. Etruscan vases in imitation of the Attic, and Faliscan vases from Southern Italy.—R XIV. Late Italic vases (3C-1C B.C.).—R XV. Etruscan and Roman terracottas.

From Room VI is the entrance to RR XVII and XVIII which contain reproductions of tomb frescoes of Etruria, and the Tomb of Larthia Scianti, in polychrome terracotta, with a reclining effigy of the deceased. A room containing a complete gilt bronze armour is normally kept closed.—In the garden are reconstructed Etruscan tombs.

The COIN ROOMS (ancient Greek and Roman coins, Medieval and modern Italian coins, especially from Tuscany) and the COLLECTION OF PRECIOUS STONES are visible only with special permission. The latter includes gems, cameos (head of Alexander the Great and Olympia), vitreous paste (*Unguent box of Torrita), silver (bowl with Bacchus, Pan, Ariadne, and Silenus; shield of Flavius Ardaburius Aspar), a silver situla from Chiusi, the *Mirror of Bomarzo, and the seal-ring of Augustus, in gold and jasper, found in his mausoleum. A precious collection of Greek, Etruscan, and Roman sculpture is also on view to students with special permission.

In the same building is the INSTITUTE OF ETRUSCAN AND ITALIC STUDIES, with an extensive library.

10   SAN MARCO, PALAZZO MEDICI-RICCARDI, AND SAN LORENZO

Piazza San Marco (Pl. 6; 6), one of the liveliest squares in the city with several cafès, is a meeting-place for students of the University and Academy of Art, both of which have their headquarters here. In the garden is a statue of general Manfredo Fanti by Pio Fedi (1873). On one corner is the *Loggia dell'Ospedale di San Matteo,* one of the oldest porticoes in Florence (1384). The seven arches may be inspired Brunelleschi's Loggia degli Innocenti (Rte 9). This is now the seat of the ACCADEMIA DI BELLE ARTI, an art school opened in 1784, but formerly part of the Accademia del Disegno, founded more than two centuries earlier (comp. p 186).

Over the three doors are fine Della Robbian lunettes. The Mannerist courtyard has unusual columns. A tabernacle with the Rest on the Flight into Egypt, one of the best works of *Giovanni di San Giovanni,* is preserved in a classroom (sometimes shown on request). The famous Gallery of the Accademia is in the adjoining building (entrance at No. 60 Via Ricasoli; see Rte 9).

Across Via Cesare Battisti are the administrative offices of the University of Florence, next to which (entrance on Via La Pira) is the *Giardino dei Semplici* (Pl. 6; 4), a botanical garden laid out here in 1545–6 by Tribolo for Cosimo I. Adm see p 57. At No. 4 is the entrance to the Museum of Minerals and the Botanical Museum, both part of the University study collections (adm see p 58).

The N. side of the square is occupied by the Dominican church and convent of San Marco, which contains the ***Museo di San Marco** (or *'dell'Angelico';* Pl. 6; 6; adm see p 58), famous for its works by the 'Blessed' Fra' Angelico. The ground floor is in the course of restoration, so that when completed more rooms and the small cloisters of the monastery will be accessible to the public.

The convent was favoured by Cosimo il Vecchio who ordered *Michelozzo* to enlarge the buildings (1437–52), and who here founded a public library, the first of its kind in Europe. The founding prior, Antonino Pierozzi (1389–1459), was made archbishop of Florence in 1446, and was later canonized. Another famous defender of Republican values, Girolamo Savonarola (1452–98), a native of Ferrara, became prior in 1491. His dramatic preachings ended when he was burnt at the stake in Piazza della Signoria seven years later (comp. p 78). The painters Fra' Angelico and Fra' Bartolomeo were both friars here.

The beautiful **Cloister of St Antonino**, with broad arches and delicate Ionic capitals, was built by *Michelozzo.* In the centre is a venerable cedar of Lebanon. In the lunettes are scenes from the life of St Antonino, by *Bernardino Poccetti* and other painters of the 16-17C (in poor condition, but recently restored). In the corners are frescoes by *Fra' Angelico:* St Thomas Aquinas (1; very worn); Christ as a Pilgrim welcomed by two Dominicans (2); Pietà (3; damaged); *St Dominic at the foot of the Cross (4).

The **Pilgrims' Hospice**, by *Michelozzo,* contains a superb collection of paintings by *Fra' Angelico,* many of them from Florentine churches: *Deposition (from Santa Trinita, c. 1435–40; the cusps are by *Lor. Monaco*); Madonna and Child with St John the Baptist and three Dominican Saints; a predella with the Marriage and Dormition of the Virgin; *Last Judgement (1431; from Santa Maria degli Angioli); Naming of St John the Baptist (c. 1430–32); Panels from the Life of Christ (including the *Flight into Egypt). These served as cupboard doors in the Santissima Annunziata. The Marriage at Cana, Baptism of Christ, and Transfiguration are attrib. to *Alesso Baldovinetti.* *Madonna 'della Stella' (a little tabernacle from Santa Maria Novella); Madonna and Child (possibly from the Certosa of Galluzzo); *Deposition (1436; of the Compagnia del Tempio). *Zanobi Strozzi,* Madonna and Child with Angels (from Santa Maria Nuova).—At the end of the room is the famous *Tabernacle of the Linaioli, with the Madonna enthroned with Saints by *Fra' Angelico,* commissioned by the flax-workers guild in 1433 for their headquarters. The beautiful marble frame was designed by *Ghiberti.*—*Fra' Angelico,* Pala 'del Bosco ai Frati' (c. 1450); two tiny roundels with the Crucifixion and Coronation of the Virgin; Coronation of the Virgin (a tabernacle from Santa Maria Novella); Madonna enthroned with Saints painted for the high altar of the church of San Marco (c. 1438–40), with two scenes from the predella of SS Cosmas and Damian (one showing a leg transplant); Annunciation and Adoration of the Magi (a tabernacle from Santa Maria Novella); Pala 'di Annalena'.

The **Great Refectory** has been restored. In the LAVATORIUM is a lunette of St Peter Martyr enjoining silence (and its sinopia), by *Fra' Angelico* (detached from the cloister), and a Della Robbian tabernacle. The Great Refectory contains 16C and 17C works by *Giov. Ant. Sogliani, Fra' Paolino,* and others. The large detached fresco (very ruined) of the Last Judgement is by *Fra' Bartolomeo.* On the end wall is a fresco of St Dominic and his brethren fed by Angels by *Sogliani* (1536).—A door from the Lavatorium is to be opened and several rooms (5) here will display more works by *Fra' Bartolomeo* (including a large Madonna with St Anne and other Saints, in monochrome, at present in restoration), and other works owned by the convent. From the small cloister (6) beyond there will be access to a MUSEUM (which has been closed for many years) arranged in the cells of the FORESTERIA (7; guest-quarters of the convent, some of them with a lunette over the door by *Fra' Bartolomeo*), and in underground rooms. Here was collected the material salvaged from the demolition at the end of the 19C of the Mercato Vecchio and part of the Ghetto (the central part of this area of the city is now occupied by Piazza della Repubblica; comp. p 75). This includes numerous architectural fragments dating from the medieval and early Renaissance periods. The 19C arrangement has been preserved but the rooms have been restored.

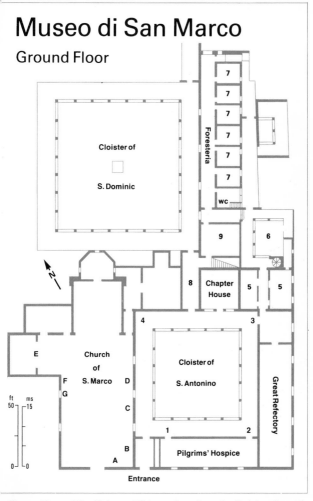

Museo di San Marco

Ground Floor

Cloister of S. Dominic

Foresteria

7
7
7
7
7
7
WC

9   6

8   Chapter House   5   5

4   3

E   Church of S. Marco   D

F
G

Cloister of S. Antonino

Great Refectory

C

1   2

B

A

Pilgrims' Hospice

Entrance

ft ms
50 15

0   0

Chapter House. *Crucifixion and Saints, a large fresco by *Fra' Angelico* and assistants (1441–42). The convent bell is in the style of Donatello.—To the left a door gives access to a corridor (8) with a wood crucifix from the church of San Marco attrib. to *Baccio da Montelupo*. At the end may be seen the CLOISTER OF ST DOMINIC (no adm), also by *Michelozzo*. To the left, at the foot of the stairs up to the Dormitory, is the **Small Refectory** (9) with a charming Last Supper frescoed by *Dom. Ghirlandaio* and his workshop, and Della Robbian terracottas.

FIRST FLOOR. The ***Dormitory** consists of 44 small monastic cells beneath a huge wood roof, each with their own vault and adorned with an intimate fresco by *Fra' Angelico* and his assistants. It is still uncertain how many of the frescoes (all of them recently well restored) are by the hand of the master alone, and how many are by artists (whose names are unknown) employed in his studio. Others are attrib to *Zanobi Strozzi* and *Benozzo Gozzoli*. At the head of the staircase is the *Annunciation, justly one of the most famous works by Angelico. In the cells (beginning to the left): 1. *'Noli me tangere'; 3. *Annunciation; 5. Nativity (perhaps with the help of an assistant); 6 *Transfiguration; 7. Mocking of Christ in the presence of the Madonna and St Dominic (perhaps with the help of an assistant); 8. Maries at the Sepulchre; 9. *Coronation of the Virgin; 10. Presentation in the Temple; 11. Madonna and Child with Saints (probably by an assistant).—At the end of the next corridor are the rooms (12-14; if closed sometimes opened on request) occupied by Savonarola as prior, with some mementoes and his *Portrait (with the attributes of St Peter Martyr; c. 1497), by his supporter and fellow friar, *Fra' Bartolomeo*. The other cells in this corridor have frescoes of Christ on the Cross by followers of Fra' Angelico.—Cells 23-29 are frescoed by assistants while on the wall outside in the corridor is a *Madonna enthroned with Saints attrib. to the master himself.—In the third corridor is the Cell (31; if closed, sometimes opened on request) of St Antonino, with Christ in Limbo by an assistant of Angelico, who also probably painted the scenes in the next four cells (32-35) showing the Sermon on the Mount, Arrest of Christ, Agony in the Garden, and the Institution of the Eucharist. Cell 36 has an unusual scene of Christ being nailed to the Cross. Cells 38 and 39 were occupied by Cosimo il Vecchio in retreat; the Adoration of the Magi, designed by Angelico, was restored in the 19C.—The *LIBRARY, a light and delicate hall, is one of the most pleasing of all *Michelozzo's* works (1441). It contains illuminated choirbooks and psalters (mostly 15-16C), and a missal illuminated by Fra' Angelico as a young man (not always on display).

The church of **San Marco** (Pl. 6; 6), founded in 1299, and rebuilt with the rest of the convent in 1442, received its present form in 1580 on a design by *Giambologna*. The façade dates from 1780.

INTERIOR (see Plan on p 123). On the W. wall, 14C fresco of the Annunciation (A), a version of the famous fresco in the Annunziata (see p 117), and, above the door, a painted Crucifix in the style of Giotto. Right side: Ecce Homo (B), devotional figure in wood of the 16C; 2nd altar (C), *Fra' Bartolomeo*, *Madonna and six Saints (1509; showing the influence of Raphael); 3rd altar (D) *Madonna in prayer, a remarkable 8C mosaic which had to be cut into two pieces for its journey from Constantinople.—The tribune was added in 17C by *Pier Fr. Silvani;* the decoration dates from the early 18C.—The CHAPEL OF S ANTONINO (E; which contains his body) was designed by *Giambologna* and was decorated by his contemporaries: in the vestibule are frescoes by *Passignano;* the bronzes are by *Giambologna* and *Francavilla;* the altarpiece of the Descent into Limbo is by *Aless. Allori;* to the r. is the Calling of St Matthew, by *Batt. Naldini* and to l., Healing of the Leper, by *Fr. Morandini.*—On the 3rd altar on l. side (F) is an altarpiece by *Cigoli.* On the wall are the tomb slabs (G) of the great humanist scholar Pico della Mirandola (1463–94), and of his friend, the poet Politian (Ang. Ambrogini, 1454–94). On the W. wall is an interesting painting of the Transfiguration.

Museo di San Marco

First Floor

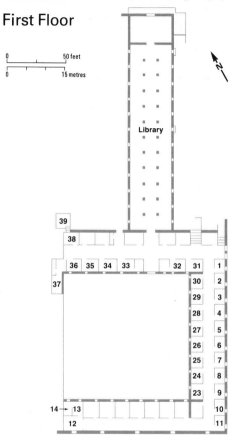

0   50 feet

0   15 metres

N

Library

39
38
36 35 34 33   32 31   1
37   30   2
                  29   3
                  28   4
                  27   5
                  26   6
                  25   7
                  24   8
                  23   9
14 → 13   10
12   11

From the N. side of Piazza San Marco runs VIA CAVOUR (Pl. 6; 6) in which, on the left, is the *Casino Mediceo,* built by Buontalenti (1568–74), and now occupied by the law courts. A worn plaque on the garden wall records the site of the Medici Garden here where Cosimo il Vecchio and Lorenzo il Magnifico collected antique sculpture, and where Bertoldo held a school of art. At No. 69, beyond, is the **Chiostro dello Scalzo** (Pl. 6; 4; the cloister, at present in restoration, should be reopened in 1982), a small arcaded courtyard of the early 16C, with fine *Frescoes in monochrome, by And. del Sarto and Franciabigio 1514–26), depicting the history of St John the Baptist. Via Cavour ends in Piazza Libertà (Rte 22).—From Piazza San Marco Via Cavour leads in the other direction S. towards the Duomo. On the right is the *Biblioteca Marucelliana* (Pl. ; 6), founded by Fr. di Aless. Marucelli (1625–1703) and opened to the public in 752. On the other side of the road are two palaces (Nos 22 & 4) by Gherardo ilvani. Opposite Palazzo Medici-Riccardi (see below), on the bend of the road, is Palazzo del Cardinale Panciatichi, by Ant. Ferri (1696). Set back from the road, at the beginning of Via de' Martelli is the little church of **San Giovannino degli Scolopi** (Pl. 6; 2), begun by Ammannati in 1579. Over the 4th altar on the r., Preaching of St Francis Xavier, the best work of Fr. Curradi. 1st altar on l. Angels, Jacob's Dream, and the Fall of Lucifer, by Iac. Ligozzi. The 2nd chap on l. was designed by Ammannati as his burial place (1592); the altarpiece is b Aless. Allori.

From P.za San Marco Via degli Arazzieri (the site of the Florentin tapestry factory) leads into Via Ventisette Aprile. Here on the left the former convent of **Sant'Apollonia** (Pl. 6; 4; ring for adm, se p 57), founded in 1339 and enlarged in 1445. The vestibule contain works by *Paolo Schiavo*. In the Refectory is a *Last Supper, th masterpiece of *And. del Castagno* (c. 1450; recently restored), set i an unusual painted marble 'loggia'. Above are equally fine frescoe (much ruined) also by him, of the Crucifixion (removed for restora tion), Deposition, and Resurrection. The sinopia is displayed on th opposite wall. Among his other works collected here (in course of re arrangement) are a Pietà, and Crucifixion and Saints (temporaril removed). The fresco of St Eustace (also removed for restoration with charming scenes from his life is attrib. to his school. The larg Crucifix is by *Raffaello da Montelupo*. Also here, a sinopia by *And del Castagno* from SS. Annunziata.

VIA SAN GALLO (Pl. 6; 4) leads towards P.za della Libertà (Rte 22). To the r. the *Loggia dei Tessitori,* part of the weavers' guild-house (c. 1500; the columr have been poorly restored). Farther on is the church of **San Giovannino de Cavalieri** (Pl. 6; 4). In the tribune, surrounded by incongruous frescoes b Gherardini, is a large Crucifixion by Lor. Monaco. At the end of the r. aisle is a Annunciation, a good painting by the 'Master of the Castello Nativity'. In the aisle is a Nativity by Bicci di Lorenzo, and a Coronation of the Virgin by his sor Neri di Bicci.—Beyond is *Palazzo Pandolfini* (No. 74), built as a villa on the out skirts of the town for Bp Giannozzo Pandolfini with a terrace on the first floor and a big garden and orchard. It was designed by Raphael (the most importar architectural work by him to survive), and executed by Giov. Fr. and Aristotil da Sangallo (1516–20). When the 'portone' is open the pretty garden façade ca be seen.

Via San Gallo leads S. from Via Ventisette Aprile. On the left (No 10) is *Palazzo Marucelli,* built by Gherardo Silvani c. 1630. The coat of-arms over the elaborate doorway was set up by its later owner Em Fenzi (1784–1875), a banker who financed the Livorno railway Across Via Guelfa VIA DE' GINORI (Pl. 6; 5,6) continues lined with number of fine palaces on the right. No. 15, *Palazzo Taddei* was buil by Baccio d'Agnolo for the merchant Taddei who commissioned from Michelangelo the tondo which now bears his name and is owned b the Royal Academy, London. Raphael, while staying here as a friend of the family, in 1505 saw and copied the tondo (the plaque is on th wrong house). The tabernacle in Via Taddei has a Crucifixion b Giov. Ant. Sogliani. *Palazzo Ginori* (No. 11; Pl. 6; 5) is also attrib. t Baccio d'Agnolo (c. 1516–20). *Palazzo Montauto* (No. 9) has remain of 15C graffiti and two ground floor windows attrib. to Ammannati Diotisalvi Neroni lived at *Palazzo Neroni* (No. 7; with pronounce rustication) before his exile as an enemy of the Medici in 1466. On th left (No. 14) is the entrance to the BIBLIOTECA RICCARDIANA founde by Riccardo Riccardi and opened to the public in 1718. It contains il luminated MSS. and incunabula. It forms part of the extension o

'alazzo Medici-Riccardi which stands on the corner of Piazza San
.orenzo (see below). Via Gori leads left skirting its imposing flank.

*Palazzo Medici-Riccardi (Pl. 16; 2; entrance on Via Cavour, adm
ee p 58) is now the seat of the Prefect. This town mansion on Via
.arga (renamed Via Cavour) was built for Cosimo il Vecchio by
Michelozzo after 1444, and was the residence of the Medici until 1540
vhen Cosimo I moved into Palazzo Vecchio. Its rusticated façade
erved as a model for other famous Florentine palaces, including those
uilt by the Strozzi and Pitti. Charles VIII of France stayed here in
494 and the emperor Charles V in 1536. It was bought by the Riccardi
n 1659 and before the end of the century was extended towards Via
le' Ginori, and the façade on Via Cavour was lengthened by seven
ays.

The dignified COURTYARD, with composite colonnades, is decorated
vith medallions ascribed to *Bertoldo,* inspired by antique gems. Some
ncient sculptures, mainly Roman, are preserved here and in the pret-
y second court. The first door on the right gives access to the staircase
vhich leads up to the dark little *Chapel, the only unaltered part of
Michelozzo's work, with a beautiful ceiling and marble inlaid floor.
he walls are entirely covered with decorative *Frescoes, the master-
iece of *Benozzo Gózzoli* (1459–60) of the Procession of the Magi to
ethlehem. They are one of the most pleasing, even if not one of the
nost important fresco cycles of the Renaissance. Commissioned by
*iero di Cosimo, they depict some of the participants of the Council
f Florence in 1439 which attempted to heal the Eastern schism.
osimo il Vecchio had been instrumental in having the Council
ransferred to Florence from Ferrara, and so adding prestige to his
ouse and city by the presence in Florence of pope Eugenius IV,
oseph, the Patriarch of Constantinople, and the emperor John VI
*aleologus, with their retinues. It is thought the vividly coloured
rescoes must have been painted before the altar wall was bricked up
n order to make use of the daylight (details of the frescoes are il-
uminated on request by the custodian). The decorative cavalcade is
hown in a charming landscape with hunting scenes. The Oriental
ignitaries are distinguished by their beards and fancy head-dresses,
vhile many of the Florentines wear red hats. The personalities of the
*Medici family are shown with their emblem of the three ostrich
eathers.

The procession is seen approaching along the distant hills on the r.
vall. The figures in the foreground are led by the third King, an
dealized portrait of Lorenzo il Magnifico, on a splendid grey charger.
ehind him, also mounted, is his father Piero di Cosimo, with a servant in Medici livery, and other members of his family. On the ex-
reme left, on a bay horse, Sigismondo Malatesta is depicted next to a
nan thought to represent Gian Galeazzo Sforza. In the crowd behind
an be seen Benozzo Gozzoli's self-portrait, with his signature in gold
ettering on his red beret.—On the wall opposite the altar is the second
ing, in the guise of John Paleologus in splendid Oriental dress.
ehind him on the extreme left are the three daughters of Piero di
osimo on grey horses.—On the last wall, the painting of the first
ing (seated on a mule) was cut in two when the wall was moved to ac-

commodate the staircase in the 17C. He represents the Patriarch of Constantinople. In front of him is a young huntsman with a cheeta (possibly Giuliano, another son of Piero di Cosimo). The processio winds away into the distance.—On either side of the altar are beautif landscapes with angels, recalling those of the painter's master, Fra Angelico. The altarpiece is a copy by Pseudo Pier Francesco Fiore tino of a Madonna by Filippo Lippi.

The next door on the right in the courtyard admits to the stairs up to the firs floor GALLERY (lift), an elaborate Baroque loggia (1670–88) covered by a fresc of the Apotheosis of the second Medici dynasty, by *Luca Giordano* (1683).—Th former private apartments of the Medici, occupied by the MEDICI MUSEUM, wi a collection of portraits and memorials to the Medici family, have been i definitely closed.

The back of Palazzo Medici-Riccardi stands on the corner of PIA: za SAN LORENZO (Pl. 16; 2), filled with a busy street market (open a day exc. Mon in winter and Sat in summer); the stalls have leathe goods, clothing, straw, jewellery, etc. for sale (and they continue th length of Via dell'Ariento, see below). The seated statue of Giovan delle Bande Nere is by Baccio Bandinelli (1540). The long façac (14C-15C) of Palazzo della Stufa (No. 4) overlooks the piazza. Abov the market awnings rises the pretty flank of the church with the larg dome of the Chapel of the Princes, and the smaller cupola of the Ne Sacristy, and the campanile (1740). *San Lorenzo (Pl. 16; 1; close 12-15.30) was intimately connected with the Medici after they commi sioned *Brunelleschi* to rebuild it in 1425–46. It is the burial place of a the principal members of the family from Cosimo il Vecchio t Cosimo III.

A basilica on this site, outside the walls, was consecrated by St Ambrose o Milan in 393, thought to be the earliest church in Florence. The church of : Zenobius the most famous Bp of Florence, it served as cathedral of the ci before the bishop's seat was transferred, probably in the late 7C, to San Reparata (on the site of the present cathedral). Michelangelo spent much time designing a grandiose façade by order of Leo X (his model survives in the Ca Buonarroti, comp. p 161), but only the interior façade was ever built; the e terior remains in rough-hewn brick. On 14 July 1564 a solemn memorial servi was held here in honour of the 'divine' Michelangelo, organized by the A cademia del Disegno.

The grey cruciform INTERIOR, built with pietra serena, with pulvin above the Corinthian columns in pietra forte, is one of the earliest an most harmonious architectural works of the Renaissance. It was com pleted on Brunelleschi's design by *Ant. Manetti* (1447–60) and *Pagn di Lapo Portigiani* (1463). In the r. aisle (2nd chap; 1), *Rosso Fioren tino,* *Marriage of the Virgin (1523); gothic tomb-slab of the organi: Fr. Landini (1398). At the end of this aisle is a *Tabernacle (2) b *Desiderio da Settignano,* of extremely fine workmanship. In the nav are two bronze *Pulpits (3 and 4; raised on columns in the 17C) b *Donatello* (c. 1460). These were his last works and they were finishe by his pupils *Bertoldo* and *Bart. Bellano.*

The beautifully carved panels have a border of classical motifs around the to Many of the scenes are crowded and grim and present a unique iconograph The pulpit on the N. side (3) shows the Agony in the Garden, St John th Evangelist and the Flagellation (these last two both 17C imitations in wood Christ before Pilate and Christ before Caiaphas; the Crucifixion and Lament tion over the Dead Christ; and the Entombment. The pulpit on the S. side (shows the Maries at the Sepulchre; Christ in Limbo, the Resurrection, and Chri

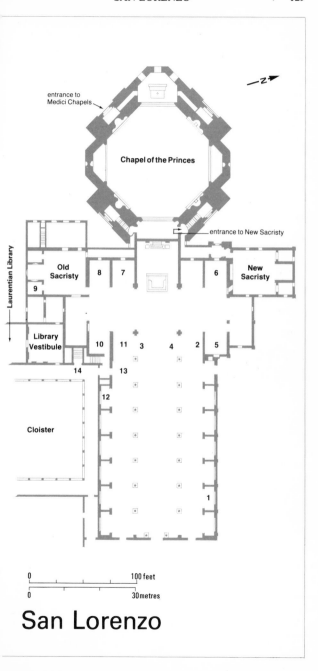

San Lorenzo

appearing to the Apostles; Pentecost; the Martyrdom of St Lawrence, St Luk
and the Mocking of Christ (the last two both 17C imitations in wood).

Beneath the dome three grilles in the pavement and a simple inscrip
tion with the Medici arms mark the grave of Cosimo il Vecchio 'Pate
Patriae' (d. 1464). On the high altar is a crucifix by *Baccio d*
Montelupo.—RIGHT TRANSEPT. 1st chap. (5), 15C painting of th
Madonna and Child with Saints, a Roman sarcophagus, and a fresc
fragment of a female saint (attrib. to *Nardo di Cione*). In the chape
opposite (6) is a monument (left) to the goldsmith Bernardo Cennini
who printed the first book in Florence in 1471.—LEFT TRANSEPT. 1s
chap. (7), Madonna and Child, a charming statue in polychrom
wood attrib. to *Alberto Arnoldi,* and two paintings attrib. to *Raf*
faellino del Garbo or his school. 2nd chap. (8), a good painting by th
School of Ghirlandaio of St Anthony Abbot, St Leonard, and S
Julian.

Inlaid doors gives access to the ***Old Sacristy** (1420–29), the firs
part of the church to be rebuilt. One of the earliest and pures
monuments of the Renaissance by *Brunelleschi,* it was built at the ex
pense of Giovanni Bicci de' Medici. The vault is particularly notewor
thy. The decorative details are mainly by *Donatello:* above the friez
of cherubs' heads, the *Tondoes in the pendentives and lunettes depic
the four Evangelists and scenes from the life of St John the Evangelist
Modelled in terracotta and plaster they are much discoloured an
ruined, but are remarkable for their composition. Over the two littl
doors are large reliefs of SS. Cosmas and Damian and SS. Lawrenc
and Stephen. The bronze *Doors have figures of the Apostles an
Martyrs in animated discussion. The terracotta bust of St Lawrenc
(or St Leonard) has been attrib. to Donatello or Desiderio da Set
tignano. On the altar is a triptych (very worn) by the school of Tadde
Gaddi, below a wood crucifix of the centre of the 15C. The raised seats and presse
are decorated with inlay. In the centre is the sarcophagus of Giovann
di Bicci de' Medici (d. 1429) and Piccarda Bueri, parents of Cosimo i
Vecchio, by *Buggiano* (1434). Set into the wall is the magnificent por
phyry and bronze sarcophagus of Giovanni and Piero de' Medici th
sons of Cosimo il Vecchio. This was commissioned from *Verrocchi*
in 1472 by Lorenzo il Magnifico and his brother Giuliano. In the littl
chapel (9) is a lavabo with fantastic creatures, by the workshop o
Donatello.

In the last chapel in the left transept (10) is a monument (1896) t
Donatello (d. 1466; buried in the vault below) and an *Annunciatio
by *Filippo Lippi.* The marble sarcophagus of Niccolò Martelli is b
the school of Donatello. In the LEFT AISLE (11) is a huge fresco of th
Martyrdom of St Lawrence, by *Bronzino.* The Cantoria is afte
Donatello. In the last chap. in this aisle (12) is a painting of Christ i
the carpenter's workshop by *Pietro Annigoni,* one of the best know
contemporary artists living in Florence.

The CLOISTER, by Manetti (1457–62), entered from the left aisle (13
or from the left of the façade, has graceful arcades in the style o
Brunelleschi. A staircase (14), near a statue of the historian Paol
Giovio, by Fr. da Sangallo (1560) ascends to the ***Biblioteca Lauren**
ziana (or *Laurentian Library;* Pl. 16; 1; adm see p 57). It was begun b
Michelangelo c. 1524 at the order of Clement VII (Giulio de' Medici

o house the collection of MSS. made by Cosimo il Vecchio and Lorenzo il Magnifico. It is a remarkable monument of Mannerist architecture.

The solemn **Vestibule**, filled with an elaborate staircase, was constructed by *Vasari* and *Ammannati* on *Michelangelo's* design in 1559–71. A somewhat disturbing work, it has been interpreted by scholars in numerous different ways. It testifies to Michelangelo's sculptural conception of architecture, with a pronounced use of pietra serena in the tall room.—The peaceful **Reading Room**, a long hall, provides an unexpected contrast. Here the angle at which the architectural decoration can be seen has been carefully calculated, and the inlaid desks, also by Michelangelo, form an intricate part of the design. It is interesting to note that the heavily decorated vestibule is invisible from the aisle (only a blank wall is framed in the doorway). The fine wood ceiling and terracotta floor were added by *Tribolo*.

The collection is famous above all for its Greek and Latin MSS.; it has been augmented over the centuries and now includes 11,000 MSS. and 4000 incunabula. *Exhibitions are held every year, here and in the adjoining rooms (the circular 'tribune' was added in 1841). The oldest codex is a famous 5C Virgil. Other works owned by the library include: Syrian gospels of the 6C; the oldest MS. of Justinian's Pandects (6-7C); the Codex Amiatinus (from Monte Amiata) written in the monastery of Jarrow in England in the 8C; a Choir Book illuminated by Lorenzo Monaco and Attavante; a Book of Hours which belonged to Lorenzo il Magnifico; the Città di Vita of Matteo Palmieri, with illuminations in the style of Pollaiolo and Botticelli; a Treatise on Architecture with MS. notes by Leonardo da Vinci; the MS. of Cellini's autobiography; and a parchment of the Union of Greek and Roman churches recording the abortive effort of the Council of Florence in 1439.

The entrance to the **Medici Chapels** (Pl. 6; 5; adm see p 57) is from outside San Lorenzo, in P.za Madonna degli Aldobrandini. In the Crypt of the Chapel of the Princes, built on a design by *Buontalenti*, are the tomb slabs of numerous members of the Medici family. A staircase leads up to the ***Chapel of the Princes,** the opulent, if gloomy, mausoleum of the Medici grand-dukes, begun by *Matt. Nigetti* (1604) on a plan by Giov. de' Medici, illegitimate son of Cosimo I; its minor details were only completed in this century. It is a high octagon, 28 m in diameter, entirely lined with dark-coloured marbles and semi-precious stones, a tour de force of craftsmanship in pietre dure. The mosaic arms of the 16 towns of Tuscany are especially notable. In the sarcophagi round the walls, from right to left, are buried Ferdinando II, Cosimo II, Ferdinando I, Cosimo I, Francesco, and Cosimo III. The second and third sarcophagi are surmounted by colossal statues in gilded bronze, by *Tacca*. The vault frescoes are by *Pietro Benvenuti* (1828). Behind the altar two treasuries of the Medici popes contain the mitre of Leo X and reliquaries presented by Clement VII.

A passage to the left leads past two trophies attrib. to *Silvio Cosini* intended to decorate a tomb in the New Sacristy. The so-called ***New Sacristy,** built by *Michelangelo* in 1520–24 and 1530–33, was left unfinished when he finally left Florence in 1534 in anger at the political climate in the city. It balances Brunelleschi's Old Sacristy (see above) and drew inspiration from it, but was used from its inception as a funerary chapel for the Medici family. It is built in dark pietra serena and white marble in a severe and idiosyncratic style. It produces a strange, cold atmosphere, in part due to the diffusion of light exclusively from above, and the odd perspective devices on the upper parts of the walls. *Michelangelo* executed only two of the famous ***Medici Tombs,** out of the three or more originally projected. To the left of the entrance is that of LORENZO, DUKE OF URBINO (1492–1519) grandson of Lorenzo il Magnifico. The statue of the Duke shows him seated, absorbed in meditation, and on the sarcophagus below are the reclining figures of Dawn and Dusk. Opposite is the tomb o GIULIANO, DUKE OF NEMOURS (1479–1516), the third son of Lorenzo il Magnifico. Both these comparatively insignificant members of the Medici family are shown through idealized portraits; only their tomb ensured their fame. Beneath are the figures of Day and Night, the last with the symbols of darkness (the moon, the owl, and a mask), is con sidered to be among the finest of all Michelangelo's sculptures.—The entrance wall was intended to have contained the architectural monu ment to Lorenzo il Magnifico and his brother Giuliano; the only par carried out by Michelangelo is the *Madonna and Child. It is his las statue of a Madonna and one of his most beautiful. The figures on either side of St Cosmas and St Damian, the medical saints who wer the patrons of the Medici, are by Montórsoli and Raff. da Montelupo Lorenzo il Magnifico's coffin was transferred here from the Old Sacristy in 1559.

On the walls behind the altar architectural graffiti (explained by a diagram) have recently been uncovered. Some of these are attrib. to *Michelangelo,* and others to his pupils, including *Tribolo.* The door to the left of the altar gives access to a little room where charcoal *Draw ings of great interest were discovered on the walls in 1975. Small groups are conducted c. every ½ hr (by appointment at the ticket of fice). The drawings have aroused much discussion among art historians, most of whom recognise them as works by *Michelangelo.* It is thought that he hid here for a time under the protection of his friend, the prior of San Lorenzo, after the return of the Medici in 1530. They clearly refer to works by Michelangelo, such as his statue of Giuliano in the adjoining chapel. The large figure study for a Resurrection of Christ (on the entrance wall) is particularly remarkable.

At No. 4 in Piazza Madonna, Palazzo Mannelli-Riccardi has a painted façade of the mid-16C (very ruined) and a bust of Ferdinando I by Giov. dell'Opera. The animated VIA DELL'ARIENTO leads away from San Lorenzo. It is lined with numerous market stalls (comp. p 128), and passes the huge *Mercato Centrale* (Pl. 6; 5), the principal food market in the town (open Mon-Sat, 7-13; also 16.30-19.30 on Sa exc. in July and Aug), well worth a visit. The magnificent cast-iron building by Gius. Mengoni (1874) was restored in 1980 when a mez zanine floor was constructed for the sale of fruit and vegetables, and a car park opened in the basement. The market produce is generally of good value; Via Sant' Antonino is another crowded street with popular food shops, and in Via Panicale are more market stalls selling clothes (locally known as 'Shanghai'). Via Chiara was Cellini's bir thplace. Via dell'Ariento ends in VIA NAZIONALE, a busy street typical of the anonymous areas around railway stations. Here is a huge taber nacle attrib. to Giov. della Robbia (1522) above a fountain. In Via Faenza, just to the left, by a tabernacle by Giov. da San Giovanni (1615), is the entrance (No. 42; ring for adm, see p 57) to the so-called **Cenacolo di Foligno** (Pl. 6; 5), a fresco of the *Last Supper by *Perugino* (c. 1493–96; recently restored) painted in the refectory of the ex-convent of Sant'Onofrio (or Foligno). In the background is a love-ly landscape with the Agony in the Garden. There are long-term plans to open a small museum here; it is at present a deposit for restored works of art.—On the next corner (l.) the poet Lamartine, then a diplomatic secretary, lived in 1826–29.

In VIA GUELFA (Pl. 6; 5), which also traverses Via Nazionale, is the church of **San Barnaba**. It preserves a 14C portal with a Della Robbian lunette. Inside, on the l. wall is a painting of the Madonna and Saints by P. F. Toschi, and a frag-ment of a fresco of Saints enthroned attrib. to Spinello Aretino.—Nearby is a big edifice (awaiting restoration) built by Bart. Silvestri on the site of the convent of Sant'Orsola as a tobacco manufactory in 1810. At the N.W. end of Via Guelfa, then on the outskirts of the city, Luca della Robbia and his nephew Andrea pro-bably had their house and kiln (after 1446).

11 SANTA MARIA NOVELLA AND OGNISSANTI

*Santa Maria Novella (Pl. 5; 6; closed 12-15) is the most important Gothic church in Tuscany. The first church, called Santa Maria delle Vigne, was built in 1094 on the site of a chapel (probably 9C). The Dominicans were given the property in 1221, and building was begun in 1246 at the E. end of the present church. The Dominican friars *Sisto* and *Ristoro* are thought to have been the architects of the impressive nave, begun in 1279. The church was completed under the direction of *Fra' Jacopo Talenti* in the mid-14C, when the great Dominican preacher Jacopo Passavanti was Prior.

The lower part of the beautiful marble *FAÇADE, in a typical Tuscan Romanesque style, is attrib. to *Fra' Jacopo Talenti*. In 1456–70 *Leon Battista Alberti* was commissioned by Giov. di Paolo Rucellai to com-plete the upper part of the façade. Its classical lines are in perfect har-mony with the earlier work. He also added the main portal (executed by *Giov. di Bertino*). Exquisite inlaid friezes bear the emblems of the Rucellai (a billowing ship's sail) and of the Medici (a ring with ostrich feathers); in 1461 Giovanni Rucellai's son Bernardo married Nannina, daughter of Piero de' Medici. Below the tympanum an inscription in handsome classical lettering records the name of the benefactor and the date 1470. The use of scrolls to connect the nave roof with the lower aisle roofs was an innovation which was frequently copied in church façades of later centuries. The two astronomical instruments by Egnazio Danti were placed here in 1572. To the right of the façade is a long line of Gothic arcaded recesses, the 'avelli' or family-vaults of Florentine nobles. These extend around the old cemetery, with its cypresses, on the r. side of the church. The painter Domenico Ghirlan-daio (d 1494) was buried here (4th 'avello').—The CAMPANILE, also at-trib. to *Fra' Jacopo Talenti,* was grafted onto an ancient watch tower.

INTERIOR. The spacious nave has remarkably bold stone vaulting, its arches given prominence by bands of dark grey pietra serena. 14C frescoes of Saints on the intrados of the arches have recently been ex-posed. The composite pillars between nave and aisles have classical capitals. The bays decrease in width as they approach the three fine stained glass lancet windows at the E. end. The interior was altered by *Vasari* in 1565 when the rood-screen (which formerly divided the church at the steps in the fourth bay) and the friars' choir were demolished, and side altars were set up in the nave (replaced by the present Gothic tabernacles in the 19C).—On the W. wall (1) is a fresco by the Florentine school (late 14C). The stained glass in the rose window (removed for restoration) is thought to have been designed by *And. di Bonaiuto* (c. 1365). Over the W. door is a good fresco of the Nativity (also being restored), which may be an early work by *Botticelli*. On the l. of the door (2), Annunciation, by *Santi di Tito*.

SOUTH AISLE. 1st altar (3), *Girol. Macchietti*, Martyrdom of St Lawrence; Monument (4) to the Blessed Villana delle Botti (d 1361) by *Bern. Rossellino* (1451), with two pretty angels. 2nd altar (5) *G.B. Naldini*, Nativity; 16C Monument (6) to Giovanni da Salerno, founder of the convent, by *Vinc. Danti*, in imitation of Rossellino's monument nearby. The next two altarpieces (7 and 8) are also by *Naldini*. On the r. of the Deposition is a monument (9) to Ruggero Minerbetti (d 1210), by *Silvio Cosini* (c. 1528) with bizarre Mannerist trophies. Beyond a highly venerated modern statue of the Madonna of the Rosary with St Dominic, the 5th altar (10) has a painting of St Vincent Ferrer by *Jac. del Meglio*.—The 15C CAPPELLA DELLA PURA (or 'Purità'; A) has recently been restored. The 14C fresco of the Madonna and Child with St Catherine, and a donor, was detached from an 'avello' outside the church. The wood Crucifix by *Baccio da Montelupo* over the other altar has been removed for restoration. —On the 6th altar (11), Miracle of St Raymond, by *Jac. Ligozzi*.

SOUTH TRANSEPT. 15C bust of St Antonino in terracotta, and three Gothic tombs (12): Tomb of Bp Aliotti (d 1336), once attrib. to *Tino da Camaino;* (l.) Tomb of Fra' Aldovrando Cavalcanti (d 1279); and, below, tomb of Joseph, Patriarch of Constantinople (who attended the Council of Florence in 1439 and died in the convent in the following year), with a contemporary fresco of him.—The simple classical sarcophagus tomb of Paolo Rucellai preceeds the CAPPELLA RUCELLAI (B; light on left), which used to house Duccio's famous Madonna (removed to the Uffizi, see p 90). It now contains a marble *Statuette of the Madonna and Child signed by *Nino Pisano,* and the bronze tomb slab of the Dominican general Fr. Lionardo Dati, by *Ghiberti* (1425; removed from the nave in front of the high altar). The walls have traces of 14C frescoes: those flanking the closed Gothic window are attrib. to the circle of the 'St Cecilia Master' (c. 1305–10). The large painting of the Martyrdom of St Catherine is an interesting work by *Giul. Bugiardini*. On the wall outside the chapel is the tomb slab of Corrado della Penna, Bp of Fiesole (d 1313).—The CAPPELLA DEI BARDI (C) was formerly used by the Laudesi brotherhood (founded c. 1245 by St Peter Martyr) who commissioned the 'Rucellai' Madonna for this chapel (comp. above) in 1285. The bas relief of Riccardo di Ricco Bardi kneeling before St Gregory dates from the year after his death in 1334 when his heirs took possession of the chapel. Ruined frescoes of the late 14C partially cover earlier fresco fragments; on the side walls the lunettes (with the Madonna enthroned) of c. 1285 have recently been attrib. to *Cimabue*. The altarpiece of the Madonna of the Rosary is by *Vasari*.—The CAPPELLA DI FILIPPO STROZZI (D; light on l.) was acquired by the great Florentine banker in 1486. He commissioned *Filippino Lippi* to decorate it. The exuberant *Frescoes

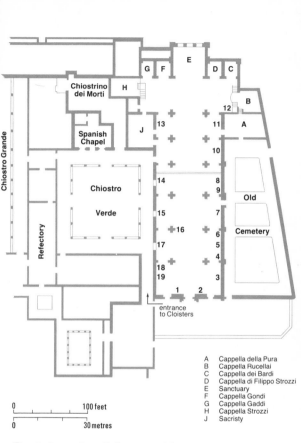

Chiostrino dei Morti

Spanish Chapel

Chiostro Grande

Chiostro Verde

Refectory

Old Cemetery

entrance to Cloisters

A	Cappella della Pura
B	Cappella Rucellai
C	Cappella dei Bardi
D	Cappella di Filippo Strozzi
E	Sanctuary
F	Cappella Gondi
G	Cappella Gaddi
H	Cappella Strozzi
J	Sacristy

0 _____ 100 feet

0 _____ 30 metres

S. Maria Novella

were not finished until after 1502 on the artist's return from Rome. They are full of allusions to Antiquity and are conspicuously different from other fresco cycles in Florence of this period. On the r. wall is the Crucifixion of St Philip the Apostle, and his miracle before the Temple of Mars (the terrible stench of the monster he conjures forth from its steps kills the king's son). On the l. wall is the Martyrdom of St John the Evangelist, and the raising of Drusiana. In the vault, Adam, Noah, Abraham, and Jacob. *Filippino* also designed the beautiful stained glass window and the trompe l'oeil frescoes in grisaille on this wall. Behind the altar, *Tomb of Filippo Strozzi, exquisitely carved by

Benedetto da Maiano (who had also been involved in the building of
Palazzo Strozzi for his patron). Boccaccio in the 'Decameron' takes
this chapel as the meeting-place of a group of young people during the
Plague year of 1348.

On the MAIN ALTAR is a bronze Crucifix by *Giambologna*. In the
SANCTUARY (E; light behind the altar) the stalls are attrib. to *Bacci
d'Agnolo*. The delightful *Frescoes, commissioned by Giovanni Tor
nabuoni, are the masterpiece of *Dom. Ghirlandaio* (assisted by his
brother *Davide*, his brother-in-law, *Seb. Mainardi*, and his pupils, in
cluding perhaps the young Michelangelo).

They replaced a fresco cycle by Orcagna (fragments of which, with heads of
Prophets, have been detached from the vault), and may follow a similar
iconographical design. Many of the figures are portraits of the artist's contem
poraries, and the whole cycle mirrors Florentine life in the late 15C. On the
wall are scenes from the life of St John the Baptist, including (lower register) the
Angel appearing to St Zacharias in the temple (with portraits of the Tornabuoni
and famous humanist scholars), the Visitation, and (above) Birth of St John
(showing ladies of the Tornabuoni family).—On the l. wall, scenes from the life
of the Virgin, including (lower register) the Expulsion of St Joachim from the
Temple (with members of the Tornabuoni family, and, in the group on the r.
the self-portraits of the artists), and the Birth of the Virgin (with portraits of the
Tornabuoni ladies).—On the end wall, Coronation of the Virgin, Miracle of St
Dominic, Death of St Peter Martyr, Annunciation, St John the Baptist in the
desert, and the two kneeling figures of the donors, Giovanni Tornabuoni and his
wife Francesca Pitti.—In the vault, the four Evangelists. The stained glass win
dows (c. 1491) were also designed by Ghirlandaio.

NORTH TRANSEPT. The CAPPELLA GONDI (F) has handsome marble
decoration by *Giul. da Sangallo*. Here is the famous *Crucifix by
Brunelleschi, traditionally thought to have been carved to show
Donatello how the Redeemer should be represented (comp. p 158).
is his only sculpture to survive in wood. It was made to wear a loin
cloth. The damaged vault frescoes of the four Evangelists are thought
to date from the end of the 13C.—The CAPPELLA GADDI (G), by *Gio
Ant. Dosio* (1575–77) has a cupola decorated by *Aless. Allori*, and a
painting of Christ raising the daughter of Jairus by *Bronzino*. The two
bas-reliefs on the walls are by *Giov. Bandini*.—At the end of the
transept the *CAPPELLA STROZZI (H) is a remarkably well-preserved ex
ample of a Tuscan chapel of the mid-14C. It contains celebrated
*Frescoes by *Nardo di Cione*, his most famous work (c. 1357; recently
detached and restored), carefully designed to cover the entire chapel
They represent (in the vault), St Thomas Aquinas and the Virtues; on
the end wall, the Last Judgement; on the l. wall, Paradise, a huge
crowded composition; and on the r. wall, Inferno, a pictorial com
mentary on Dante's 'Inferno'. The splendid frescoed decoration
completed on the intrados of the entrance arch with a frieze of Saints
The stained glass window is designed by *Nardo di Cione* and his
brother *Andrea di Cione (Orcagna)*, who painted the fine *Altarpiece
of the Redeemer giving the Keys to St Peter and the book of wisdom
to St Thomas Aquinas (1357), remarkable also for its unusual
iconography.—On the outside wall of the ancient chapel at the base of
the Campanile (closed, but containing very old frescoes) is a ruined
fresco (in restoration) of the Coronation of the Virgin, traditionally
attrib. to *Buffalmacco*.

The SACRISTY (J) has a fine cross-vault by *Fra' Jac. Talenti* (c.
1350). The stained glass windows date from 1386, and are thought to

have been designed by *Niccolò Gerini* (restored in 1975). On the l. of the door is a Lavabo in terracotta with a charming landscape by *Giov. della Robbia* (1498); the upper part may be by *And. della Robbia*. Above the entrance, *Crucifix, an early work by *Giotto*. The huge cupboard on the opposite wall was designed by *Buontalenti* (1593). On the walls: *Jac. Ligozzi,* Conversion of St Paul; *Giov. Stradano,* Baptism of Christ; *Pietro Dandini,* St Vincent Ferrer; *Vasari,* Crucifixion.

NORTH AISLE. 6th altar (13), *Aless. Allori,* Saints; 4th altar (14), *Vasari,* Resurrection and Saints; (15) *Fresco of the Trinity and the Virgin and St John the Evangelist with donors, above a skeleton on a sarcophagus, a remarkable work by *Masaccio* (c. 1428). It is famous for its perfect composition and accurate perspective which gives it an almost metaphysical atmosphere. The architecture of the shadowy niche owes much to Brunelleschi.—To the l., St Lucy with a donor by *Dav. Ghirlandaio*. The Pulpit (16) from which Caccini denounced Galileo's astronomical theories, was designed by *Brunelleschi* and executed by his adopted son *Buggiano*. On the 2nd altar (17), *Aless. Allori,* Christ at the well; to the l., Annunciation, in the manner of *Bicci di Lorenzo*. The monument (18) to Ant. Strozzi (1524) is by *And. Ferrucci,* with a Madonna by his pupil, *Silvio Cosini*. 1st altar (19), *Santi di Tito,* Resurrection of Lazarus.

To the l. of the church is the entrance to the *CLOISTERS (adm see p 57), now belonging to the Comune of Florence. The Convent of Santa Maria Novella was one of the richest and largest in Florence, and it remains an oasis of calm in this busy part of the city. Eugenius IV transferred the Papal court here in 1434–43. The Romanesque *CHIOSTRO VERDE (c. 1330–50) receives its name from the green tone of its decoration (in the vaults are roundels of Dominican Saints). The damaged *Frescoes by *Paolo Uccello* and assistants, painted in terraverde, have all been returned here after restoration (comp. below). They illustrate stories from Genesis. Four cypresses surround the raised well, and there is a good view of the side of the church, the exterior of the sacristy with its stained glass windows, and of the campanile. Off the cloister opens the **Cappellone degli Spagnuoli,** or *Spanish Chapel*. It received its name in the 16C when it was assigned by Duchess Eleonora di Toledo to the Spanish members of her suite. It was originally the Chapter House, built by *Jac. Talenti* in the mid-14C with a splendid cross-vault and two fine Gothic windows. The walls and vault are entirely covered with colourful *Frescoes by *Andrea di Bonaiuto* (sometimes called *Andrea da Firenze*) and assistants (c. 1365), the most important work by this otherwise little-known artist who was influenced by the Sienese school of painting.

The pictorial decoration, on a monumental scale, is carefully designed to fit the wall space. The subjects are: in the vault, the Resurrection, Ascension, the Navicella, and Descent of the Holy Ghost; altar wall, Via Dolorosa, Crucifixion, Descent into Limbo.—On the right wall, the Mission, Works, and Triumph of the Dominican Order illustrated by various scenes. In front of the elaborate church, the artist's vision of the completed Duomo, is the Church Militant with the Pope and Emperor and Church dignitaries. In the foreground (r.), behind a group of kneeling pilgrims, are the presumed portraits of Cimabue, Giotto, Boccaccio, Petrarch, Dante, etc. The scene on the bottom right shows St Dominic sending forth the hounds of the Lord ('Domini canes'), with St Peter Martyr and St Thomas Aquinas. Above, four seated figures symbolizing the Vices are surrounded by representations of dancing, etc. A dominican friar taking confession shows the way to salvation, and those absolved are sent on towards the Gate of Paradise guarded by St Peter. On the other side of the gate the Blessed look up towards Christ in Judgement surrounded by angels.—The opposite wall shows the Triumph of Catholic doctrine personified in St Thomas Aquinas, who is shown enthroned beneath the winged Virtues. On his right and left are Doctors of the Church. In the Gothic choir-stalls below are 14 female figures symbolizing the Arts and Sciences, with, at their feet, historical personages representing these virtues.—On the entrance wall is the Life of St Peter Martyr (damaged).—On the altar is a Madonna with Saints by *Bern. Daddi* (restored). The apse has been covered while the works by *Aless. Allori* and *Poccetti* are being restored.

On the r. of the Chapel is the entrance to the CHIOSTRINO DEI MORTI (recently reopened after restoration). Here are frescoes ascribed to *Giottino* (scenes from the Life of the Virgin), and a Giottesque figure of St Thomas Aquinas. In the Chapel of St Anne are frescoes of St Luke, St John the Evangelist, and St Thomas Aquinas by a follower of *Nardo di Cione* (c. 1360).

From the left walk of the Chiostro Verde a passage leads towards the imposing GREAT CLOISTER (no adm; in use as a police barracks), which can be seen through a glass door. The frescoes by Cigoli, Bronzino, and Poccetti are gradually being returned here after restoration. The *Cappella dei Papi* (adm only by special permission) has frescoes by Pontormo.—On the left, beyond a chapel with a tomb slab of the Ubriachi family and traces of wall decoration showing their emblem, is the large **Refectory**, with superb cross-vaulting in three bays by *Talenti*. On the entrance wall, a large fresco of the Manna in the desert, by *Aless. Allori* surrounds a good fresco attrib. to a follower of *Agnolo Gaddi,* contemporary with the building, and probably part of a larger composition which covered the entire wall. It shows the Madonna enthroned between St Thomas Aquinas, St Dominic (at whose feet is the Prior of the convent, Fra' Jacopo Passavanti), St John the Baptist, and St Peter Martyr. On the l. wall, *Aless. Allori,* Last Supper (1583); this formerly covered the Madonna enthroned.—At the far end of the hall are interesting *Frescoes (detached from the Chiostro Verde) painted in terraverde on a dull red background, by *Paolo Uccello:* to the l., Creation of Adam, and of the Animals, and the Creation and Temptation of Eve (c. 1430); to the r., the Flood, and the Recession of the Flood (with Noah's ark), and the Sacrifice and Drunkenness of Noah (c. 1446). Although much damaged, they are remarkable for their figure studies and perspective device; the later works are among the most mysterious and disturbing paintings of the Florentine Renaissance.

PIAZZA SANTA MARIA NOVELLA, with its irregular shape, was created by the Dominicans at the end of the 13C. The two obelisks were set up in 1608 (resting on bronze tortoises by Giambologna) as turning posts in the course of the annual chariot race (Palio dei Cocchi) which was first held here in 1563. The *Loggia di San Paolo* was erected on the S.W. side of the square in 1489–96. It is a free copy of Brunelleschi's Loggia degli Innocenti, with terracottas by Giov. della Robbia. The beautiful *Lunette beneath the arcade (r.) of the Meeting of St Francis and St Dominic is by And. della Robbia. The tabernacle on the corner of Via della Scala contains a fresco by Francesco d'Antonio (recently restored). In the house on the corner here Henry James wrote 'Roderick Hudson' in 1872. In Via della Scala (No. 16) is the *Pharmacy* of Santa Maria Novella, with characteristic 17C furnishings.

Off the E. side of the square, the winding Via delle Belle Donne leads shortly to a crossroads in the middle of which stands the *Croce del Trebbio* (from 'trivium'), a granite column reconsecrated in 1338 with a Gothic capital bearing symbols of the Evangelists. Above this is a Cross of the Pisan school, protected by a wooden tabernacle. It is traditionally thought to commemorate a massacre of heretics which took place here in 1244, but the date of its erection is unknown.

Via de' Fossi leads towards the Arno. It takes its name from the ditch outside the city walls built here in 1173–75, and contains a number of well-known antique shops. The church of Ognissanti may be reached from here either by Via de' Fossi and then Borgo Ognissanti, or by Via Palazzuolo (r.) which leads past the bare church façade of

San Paolino (Pl. 5; 7) of 10C foundation, and then (l.) Via del Porcellana.

The church of **Ognissanti** (Pl. 5; 7) was founded in 1256 by the Umiliati, a Benedictine Order particularly skilled in manufacturing wool. This area of the city became one of the main centres of the woollen cloth industry, on which medieval Florence based her economy. Mills on the Arno were used for washing, fulling, and dyeing the cloth. The church was rebuilt in a Baroque style in the 17C. The façade by *Nigetti* (1637) incorporates a glazed terracotta Coronation of the Virgin ascribed to *Bened. Buglioni*.

The INTERIOR has been restored after severe flood damage in 1966. The trompe l'oeil ceiling fresco dates from the 18C. South side, 2nd altar, frescoes of the Pietà and the Madonna della Misericordia, early works by *Dom.* and *Davide Ghirlandaio*. The Madonna protects the Vespucci (Amerigo is supposed to be the young boy whose head appears between the Madonna and the man in the dark cloak). The family tombstone (1471) is in the pavement l. of the altar. The Vespucci, merchants involved in the manufacture of silk, held political office in the 15C as supporters of the Medici. Amerigo (1451–1512), a Medici agent in Seville, gave his name to America having made two voyages in 1499 and 1501–2 following the route charted by his Italian contemporary Columbus.—3rd altar, *Santi di Tito*, Madonna and Saints; 4th altar, *Matteo Rosselli*, Martyrdom of St Andrew. The 17C pulpit has bas-reliefs by a pupil of *Bened. da Rovezzano*.—South transept (1st altar on r.), *Iac. Ligozzi*, San Diego healing the sick. In the adjacent Baroque chapel the round tombstone in the pavement marks the burial place of Filipepi (Botticelli). On the main altar, wood Crucifix by *Viet Stoss*; in the dome above, frescoes by *Giov. da San Giovanni* (1616–17).—From the North Transept a door leads into the Sacristy where decorative wall paintings of the late 13C have recently been uncovered. The Crucifixion (being restored), with its sinopia, is by *Taddeo Gaddi,* and the Resurrection and fragment of the Ascension is attrib. to *Agnolo Gaddi.* The painted Crucifix is by the school of *Giotto*.—North side, 3rd altar, *Maso di San Friano,* Assumption (the angels are by *Santi di Tito*).

On the left of the church is the entrance (No. 42) to the CONVENT (ring for Adm; see p 57). The Cloister, in the style of Michelozzo, incorporates octagonal pilasters which support part of the Gothic church. The old campanile can also be seen here. The 17C frescoes (*Giov. da San Giovanni, Iac. Ligozzi,* etc.) have been detached and restored and will be returned here. The pretty vaulted REFECTORY, with its lavaboes and pulpit in pietra serena contains a *Last Supper, by *Dom. Ghirlandaio* (1480). The delightful background contains plants and birds which are Christian symbols. On the r. wall, *St Augustine's vision of St Jerome, by *Botticelli,* and on the l. wall, *St Jerome by *Dom. Ghirlandaio,* both painted c. 1481 (and removed here from the church). The fresco of the Annunciation dates from 1369. The sinopia belongs to the Last Supper.—A small MUSEUM (usually locked), on the other side of the cloister, has a 15C Madonna and Child in terracotta, and vestments etc. from the sacristy.

Piazza Ognissanti opens onto the Arno. On the r. is *Palazzo Lenzi,* built c. 1470. The graffiti were repainted when the palace was restored in 1885. It is now occupied by the French Institute, founded in Florence by Julien Luchaire for the University of Grenoble in 1907–8. Across the Arno, the domed church of San Frediano in Cestello is prominent.

12   VIA TORNABUONI: SANTA TRINITA AND PALAZZO STROZZI. PALAZZO RUCELLAI

Ponte Santa Trinita (see p 165) crosses the Arno at the beginning of Via Tornabuoni (Pl. 16; 5, 3), the most elegant street in Florence, famous for its fashionable shops (including Ferragamo and Gucci). At the beginning on the r. is the splendid battlemented *PALAZZO SPINI-

FERONI (Pl. 16; 5), one of the best preserved and largest privat
medieval palaces in the city. It was built for Geri degli Spini in 128
possibly by Lapo Tedesco, master of Arnolfo di Cambio (and restore
in the 19C). Opposite is the church of *Santa Trinita (Pl. 9; 2; close
12-16). The Latin pronunciation of its name betrays its ancient foun
dation. A church of the Vallombrosan Order existed on this site a
least by 1077. Probably rebuilt in 1250–60, its present Gothic form
dates from the end of the 14C and is attrib. to *Neri di Fioravante*. Th
FAÇADE (in poor condition) was added by *Buontalenti* in 1593–94. Th
relief of the Trinity and the statue in the niche to the l. are by *Gio
Caccini*. The bell-tower (1396–97) can just be seen behind to the left

The fine INTERIOR has the austerity characteristic of Cistercian churches. O
the entrance wall the interior façade of the Romanesque building survives. Th
church is unusually dark (best light in morning); each chapel has a light: the swi
ches are inconspicuously placed to the left. High up on the outside arches c
many of the chapels are remains of 14-15C frescoes (some restored); the most in
teresting are those by *Giov. del Ponte* outside the choir chapels. SOUTH AISLE. 1
chap., Wood Crucifix and detached fresco and sinopia of the 14C; 3rd chap
altarpiece of the Madonna enthroned with four Saints, by *Neri di Bicci*. On th
walls, detached fresco and sinopia by *Spinello Aretino* (considerably ruined
found beneath a fresco by Lor. Monaco in the adjoining chapel.—The 4th chap
is entirely frescoed (including the entrance arch) by *Lor. Monaco* (1422; damag
ed). The *Altarpiece of the Annunciation is also by him.—5th chap., Pietà
fresco attrib. to *Giov. Toscani*, and a noble altar by *Bened. da Rovezzano*, pa
of a monument to St John Gualberto, founder of the Vallombrosan Orde
(damaged in the siege of Florence, 1530). The painting of Christ resurrected, an
Saints, is by *Maso di San Friano*. In the side entrance porch are six worn 'avelli
or Gothic tombs.—In the SACRISTY is the tomb of Onofrio Strozzi, by *Piero
Niccolò Lamberti* (1421) with painted decoration on the arch by *Gentile d
Fabriano*. Here are displayed detached frescoes of the 14C, including a Pietà an
'Noli me tangere'.
CHOIR CHAPELS. *SASSETTI CHAPEL, with frescoes (light in chapel) of the life c
St Francis by *Dom. Ghirlandaio* commissioned in 1483 by Francesco Sassetti,
merchant and typical figure of Renaissance Florence. The scene in the lunett
above the altar (St Francis receiving the Rule of the Order from Pope Honoriu
takes place in Piazza della Signoria and those present include: (in th
foreground, r.) Lorenzo il Magnifico with Sassetti and his son, and, to his righ
Antonio Pucci. On the stairs are Agnolo Poliziano with Lorenzo il Magnifico
sons, Piero, Giovanni, and Giuliano. In the Miracle of the boy brought back t
life (beneath) is Piazza Santa Trinita (with the Romanesque façade of the churc
and the old Ponte S. Trinita). The altarpiece, the *Adoration of the Shepherd
(1485), also by *Ghirlandaio*, is flanked by the kneeling figures of the donors
Francesco Sassetti and Nera Corsi, his wife. Their tombs, with black porphyr
sarcophagi, are attrib. to *Giul. da Sangallo*. The decoration of the chapel in
cludes numerous references to classical antiquity (the Sibyl announcing the com
ing of Christ to Augustus on the outside arch; the four Sibyls on the vault; th
Roman sarcophagus used as a manger in the Adoration of the Shepherds; an
the carved details on the tombs).—In the chap. to the r. of the main altar, th
painted Crucifix is said to have bowed approvingly to St John Gualberto whe
he pardoned his brother's assassin.—In the Sanctuary, on the wall to the r. c
the 15C classical main altar is a Triptych of the Trinity, by *Mariotto di Nardc
The fine figures in the vault of David, Abraham, Noah, and Moses are almost a
that remains of the fresco decoration of the sanctuary by *Ales.
Baldovinetti*.—The 1st chap. l. of the altar was redecorated in 1635. The bronz
altar frontal of the Martyrdom of St Laurence is by *Tiziano Aspetti*; on the
wall, St Peter receiving the keys, by *Empoli*; the two lunette frescoes are by *Gio
da San Giovanni*.—In the 2nd chap. l. of the altar, *Tomb of Benozz
Federighi, Bp of Fiesole (d 1450), by *Luca della Robbia* (1454–57). This wa
made for San Pancrazio and was moved here in 1896. The beautiful marble e
figy is surrounded by an exquisite frame of enamelled terracotta mosaic on
gold ground. On the walls are detached fresco fragments by *Giov. d
Ponte*.—The little chapel in the N. transept decorated by *Passignano* (1574) cor
tains a reliquary of St John Gualberto.

NORTH AISLE. 5th chap., Mary Magdalen, a fine statue in wood by *Desiderio da Settignano,* finished by *Benedetto da Maiano.*—4th chap., detached fresco of St John Gualberto surrounded by Vallombrosian saints, by *Neri di Bicci,* and on the outside arch) fresco of St John Gualberto pardoning his brother's assassin by *Bicci di Lorenzo.*—3rd chap., 14C frescoes, and an Annunciation by *Neri di Bicci.* The tomb of Giuliano Davanzati (1444) was adapted from a Paleochristian sarcophagus with a relief of the Good Shepherd.—2nd chap., Annunciation and St Jerome, good works by *Ridolfo del Ghirlandaio.*—The vault of the 1st chap. (1603) was painted by *Bernardino Poccetti.* It contains two statues by *Giov. Caccini,* and an altarpiece of the Annunciation by *Empoli.*—The CRYPT (with remains of the Romanesque church) dates from the 11C (approached from the nave, lights on l.; shown by the sacristan on request). It contains a bust of the Saviour in painted terracotta attrib. to *Pietro Torrigiano* c. 1519).

In the little Piazza Santa Trinita stands the *Column of Justice,* a granite monolith from the Baths of Caracalla in Rome, presented by Pius IV to Cosimo I in 1560. The porphyry figure of Justice, by Tadda 1581) has a bronze cloak added subsequently. The three narrow medieval streets leading out of the E. side of the piazza are described in Rte 21. Opposite the impressive curving façade of Palazzo Spini-Feroni is *Palazzo Buondelmonti* (No. 2) with a façade of c. 1530 attrib. to Baccio d'Agnolo. In 1819 the Swiss scholar Gian Pietro Vieusseux here founded a scientific and literary association (comp. below) which became a famous intellectual centre in Italy; it was attended by Manzoni, D'Azeglio, Leopardi, Stendhal, and Dumas, among others. Across Via delle Terme is **Palazzo Bartolini-Salimbeni* (No. 1), perhaps the best work of Baccio d'Agnolo (1520–23), restored in 1961 as the French Consulate. Various types of stone were used in the fine façade, and the unusual courtyard has good graffiti decoration. The Hôtel du Nord was opened here in 1839, and the American writers Ralph Waldo Emerson, James Russell Lowell, and Herman Melville all stayed here.

Beyond Via Porta Rossa (with a good view of Palazzo Davanzati, see p 187) Via Tornabuoni continues, lined with handsome mansions. On the l. *Palazzo Minerbetti* (No. 3) dates from the 14C-15C. *Palazzo Strozzi del Poeta* (No. 5) was reconstructed by Gherardo Silvani in 1626. The *Palazzo del Circolo dell'Unione* (No. 7) may have been designed by Vasari. The pretty doorway is surmounted by a bust of Francesco I by Giambologna. On the r. is *Doney's* a famous cafè (and now also a restaurant) frequented by foreigners in Florence, including Edmond and Jules Goncourt in the mid-19C, and, in this century, D. H. Lawrence, 'Ouida', and the Sitwells. Beyond rises the huge **Palazzo Strozzi** (Pl. 16; 3; the exterior is undergoing a long process of restoration), the last and grandest of the magnificent Renaissance palaces in Florence, built for Filippo Strozzi (d 1491).

It is typical of the 15C town-mansion, half-fortress, half-palace, with all three stories of equal emphasis constructed with large rough blocks of stone. It was begun by *Benedetto da Maiano* in 1489. *Giuliano da Sangallo* executed a model comp. below), but he is not now thought to have been involved in the building. The wrought-iron torch-holders and fantastic lanterns were designed by Benedetto da Maiano and executed by *Caparra.* The side most nearly complete faces Piazza Strozzi; *Cronaca* continued the building and was responsible for the great projecting cornice, suggested by Antique examples, which was left half-finished when money ran out after the death of Filippo Strozzi. *Cronaca* also built the courtyard (finished in 1503). The palace is now the seat of the *Gabinetto Vieusseux,* a lending library (comp. above), and various learned institutes, and is used for exhibitions and lectures. A small *Museum* (adm see p 58) illustrates the history of the palace and preserves the model by Giul. da Sangallo.—In Piazza Strozzi, *Palazzo dello Strozzino,* also built for the Strozzi family, has a façade begun by Michelozzo and completed by Giul. da Maiano.

The crossroads in Via Tornabuoni with Via Strozzi, Via della Vigna Nuova, and Via della Spada, marks the centre of the Roman colony and subsequently the W. gate of the Roman city (comp. Plan on pp 30–1). The palace fitting the awkward site between Via della Vigna Nuova and Via della Spada was the home from 1614 of Sir Robert Dudley (1573–1649), Duke of Northumberland, who, on leaving England, became a naval engineer and took charge of the Arsenal in Livorno for Cosimo II and Ferdinando II (plaque placed in Via della Vigna Nuova in the 19C by his biographer John Temple Leader). In the corner house (l.) George Eliot stayed while gathering material for 'Romola'. Via della Vigna Nuova, on the site of a huge orchard, leads past the narrow old Via dell'Inferno (l.) to a little opening in front of *Palazzo Rucellai (Pl. 5; 8; no adm). This was the town house of Giovanni Rucellai (1403–81), one of the most respected intellectual figures of Renaissance Florence (author of the 'Zibaldone', his memoirs), as well as one of the wealthiest businessmen in Europe. It was almost certainly designed for him by *Leon Battista Alberti* and executed by *Bern. Rossellino* (c. 1446–51).

Its dignified façade with incised decoration is in striking contrast to the heavy rustication of other Florentine palaces of the period. The three stories, with classical pilasters and capitals of the three orders, are divided by delicately carved friezes bearing the Rucellai and Medici emblems. The five bays of the front were later increased on the r. to seven bays. The design of the façade had a lasting influence on Italian architecture.—Facing the palace is the *Loggia dei Rucellai* with three arches also attrib. to Alberti (now an exhibition centre) and a graffit frieze.

Via della Vigna Nuova continues to the Arno; Via dei Palchetti skirts Palazzo Rucellai (r.) and Via de' Federighi (view left of the garden of Palazzo Niccolini above a high wall) continues into Piazza San Pancrazio. Here is the ex-church of SAN PANCRAZIO (Pl. 5; 8), one of the oldest in the city, founded before 1000. Deconsecrated in 1809 it was later used as a tobacco factory, and as a military store. It is at present being restored and converted into a Museum for the sculptural works left to the city by Marino Marini (scheduled to open in 1982). The beautiful classical porch is by Alberti.—In Via della Spada (No 18) is the entrance to the remarkable *Cappella di San Sepolcro* built in 1467 by Alberti for Giovanni Rucellai. It was reopened in 1981 after restoration. It contains a *Model in inlaid marble of the Sanctuary of the Holy Sepulchre. Via della Spada, a local shopping street, returns to Via Tornabuoni (view of Palazzo Strozzi).

At No. 19 Via Tornabuoni, *Palazzo Larderel* (Pl. 16; 3), attrib. to Giov. Ant. Dosio (begun 1580) is a model of High Renaissance architecture. On the r., preceded by a wide flight of steps is the Baroque church of SAN GAETANO (open for services only) by Matt. Nigetti and Gherardo and Pier Fr. Silvani (1604–48). In the huge interior is a painting by Pietro da Cortona (Martyrdom of St Lawrence) and lunettes in the Ardinghelli chapel by Lor. Lippi (17C). In Piazza Antinori is *Palazzo Antinori,* one of the most beautiful smaller Renaissance palaces in Florence. Built in 1461–69, with a pretty courtyard, it is at-

rib. to Giul. da Maiano. It has been owned by the Antinori since
1506.

Via degli Agli and Via Vecchietti (l.) lead to the church of **Santa
Maria Maggiore** (Pl. 16; 3), with a rough exterior in pietra forte. Pro-
ably founded in the 8C, it was rebuilt in its present Gothic Cistercian
orm at the end of the 13C. At the corner of the façade is the
Romanesque bell-tower. In the dark interior the 17C altarpieces are
obscured by candles. On the pilasters and on the W. wall are 13-14C
frescoes, some by *Mariotto di Nardo*. The internal façade was design-
d by *Buontalenti*. In the chap. to the l. of the choir: *Madonna enthroned, a Byzantine relief in painted wood, attrib. to *Coppo di Mar-
ovaldo;* (r.) a column which survives from the tomb of Brunello
Latini (d 1294), Dante's teacher, and (l.) tomb (1272) of Bruno Bec-
uti with the figure of the defunct attrib. to *Tino da Camaino*. The
wo detached frescoes (very ruined) in the sanctuary are attrib. to a
ontemporary of Spinello Aretino.

13   MUSEO NAZIONALE DEL BARGELLO

*Palazzo del Bargello** (Pl. 16; 6; *Palazzo del Podestà*), a massive
attlemented medieval fortress-building in pietra forte stands in Piaz-
a San Firenze. Built in 1250 as the 'Palazzo del Popolo' it is the oldest
eat of government which survives in the city.

It was begun, according to Vasari, on a design by a certain 'Lapo', the master
f Arnolfo di Cambio, and was already partly finished by 1255. Building con-
inued until 1330–50; the splendid upper hall was vaulted by Neri di Fioravante
nd Benci di Cione in 1345. The tower is 57 metres high. Well restored in
857–65, it still preserves its 14C aspect. It was at first the seat of the 'Capitano
el Popolo', who, during his one year term of office, held supreme authority in
he government of the city. From the end of the 13C until 1502 the palace was the
fficial residence of the 'Podestà', the governing magistrate of the city, who was
raditionally a foreigner. In the 16C the building became known as the
'Bargello', when the police headquarters were moved here and prisons were in-
alled (in use until 1858–59). In 1786, when the grand-duke Pietro Leopoldo
bolished the death sentence, instruments of torture were burnt in the courtyard.

The palace now contains the ****Museo Nazionale,** famous for its
uperb collection of Florentine Renaissance sculpture, including
umerous works by Donatello and the Della Robbia family. 16C
lorentine sculpture is well represented by Michelangelo, Cellini, and
Giambologna, among others, and an exquisite collection of small
Mannerist bronzes. In no other museum of the city can the Florentine
Renaissance be better understood. The building also houses a notable
ollection of decorative arts. The entrance is at No. 4 Via del Procon-
olo (adm see p 58).

The museum came into being in 1859 when the collection of sculpture and ap-
ied arts formerly in the Uffizi (comp. p 88) was transferred here. In 1888 the
mportant Carrand Collection was left to the museum, and later acquisitions in-
uded a large group of armour and a collection of fabrics. The whole of the
round floor was submerged to a height of nearly 4 metres in the flood of 1966.
he 16C sculpture and armoury which suffered most damage have since been
eautifully restored. The rooms of sculpture are arranged mostly by period and
chool. Room numbers refer to the numbers on the plans in the text. The collec-
on of decorative arts is in the course of re-arrangement.

Ground Floor. ROOM 1, a fine hall, contains 16C sculpture by

Michelangelo and his Florentine contemporaries. On the wall by th
door is a fresco of the Madonna and Child with Saints attrib. to *Tad
deo Gaddi.* (In wall case) *Rustici,* sculptural group in terracotta o
horsemen engaged in battle (after Leonardo da Vinci); *And. San
sovino,* Madonna and Child (terracotta). In the centre, three super
works by *Michelangelo:* *Bacchus drunk, made on his first visit t
Rome c. 1497 for the banker, Jacopo Galli. It was kept in his garde
for over 50 years and was then purchased by the Medici and brough
to Florence. Michelangelo's first important piece of sculpture, i
shows the influence of classical works. The *Tondo of the Madonn
and Child with the infant St John was made for Bartolomeo Pitti c
1503–05. It is a charming work, and a fine example of the sculptor'
'schiacciato' technique. The *Bust of Brutus is a much later work (c
1539–40), derived from Imperial Roman portrait busts, and is the onl
bust Michelangelo ever sculpted. It was made after the murder o
Duke Alessandro de' Medici and is an exaltation of Republicanism a
against the tyranny of the Medici. It was left unfinished, an
Michelangelo's pupil Tiberio Calcagni added the drapery.—Behin
Michelangelo's tondo there is another tondo of the same subject b
Rustici. Beyond the door, *Jac. Sansovino,* *Bacchus, which takes it
inspiration from Michelangelo's statue. The small figure calle
*Apollo (or David) is another beautiful work by *Michelangelo* in
'contrapposto' position. According to Vasari, it was carved for Bacci
Valori, but later formed part of the Medici collection. The statuettes
models, and replicas (in cases against the wall) by followers o
Michelangelo include works by *Pietro Francavilla, Tribolo, Giam
bologna* (a model for his giant 'Appennino' at Pratolino), *Bart. Am
mannati,* and *Vinc. Danti.* The marble figure of Leda by *Ammanna
(c. 1540–50) is one of the best copies which has survived of the famou
painting by Michelangelo commissioned by Alfonso d'Este and late
destroyed. The marble bust of Cosimo I is a good work by *Bandinell

In the second part of the hall: *De' Rossi,* *Dying Adonis; *Ban
dinelli,* colossal statues of Adam and Eve, which were not considere
suitable for the Duomo. The two statues by *Ammannati* were intende
for the Nari tomb in Santissima Annunziata (1540), but because of th
opposition of Bandinelli they were never set up there. The clay bas
reliefs of the Passion of Christ displayed in wall-cases are by *De' Ros
(formerly attrib. to Donatello). There follow a group of *Works b
Cellini. The Narcissus, carved from a worn block of marble with tw
holes, was damaged in Cellini's studio during an Arno flood
Together with the Apollo and Hyacinth, also displayed here, it late
found its way to the Boboli gardens, and the two statues were onl
reidentified and brought under cover just before the last War. Th
splendid bronzes exhibited here include a scale model of Cellini'
famous statue of Perseus (in the Loggia della Signoria, p 79), and th
relief (Perseus releasing Andromeda) and statuettes (Danae an
Perseus, Mercury, Minerva, and Jove) from the pedestal of thi
statue. *Vinc. Danti's* statue representing Honour overcoming Deceit i
exhibited near *Giambologna's* colossal Virtue repressing Vice (c
Florence victorious over Pisa). The bronze cupboard door was mad
by *Vinc. Danti* for Cosimo I. The colosssal *Bust of Cosimo I was th
first work *Cellini* cast in bronze (1545–48). His talent as a goldsmit

Second Floor

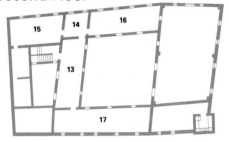

First Floor

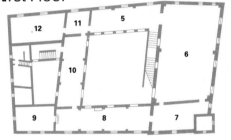

Ground Floor

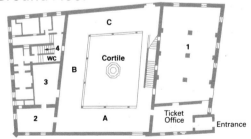

Museo Nazionale
del Bargello

can be seen in the delicate carved details of the armour. Beyond another bronze relief (Moses and the Serpent) by *Danti,* is a portrait bust of Michelangelo by *Daniele da Volterra.*

The Gothic *CORTILE, the finest part of the palace, is adorned with a large number of coats-of-arms of the former Podestà. Here is displayed more 16C sculpture: under the colonnade (A): *Vinc. Danti,* idealized statue of Cosimo I dressed as a Roman; *Niccolò di Pietro Lamberti,* St Luke the Evangelist (formerly in a niche of Orsan michele). The cannon, cast by *Cosimo Cenni* in 1620 shows the planet Jupiter with its four satellites discovered by Galileo in 1610. Against the far wall (B) are six fine statues (including Juno) by *Ammannati* (1556–63) from an allegorical fountain intended for the S. end of the Sala dei Cinquecento in Palazzo Vecchio (p 82). On the last wall (C) *Giambologna,* Oceanus, a colossal statue from the Boboli gardens (see p 112); *Tribolo,* *Fiesole (in pietra serena) from the garden of the Villa di Castello; *Dom. Poggini,* Clio. The Fisherboy (1877) is by the Neapolitan sculptor, *Vinc. Gemito.* The *Cannon of St Paul is a wonderful piece of casting by *Cenni* (1638). It was commissioned by grand-duke Ferdinando II for Livorno castle.—Off the courtyard is the SALA DEL TRECENTO (2) with 14C sculpture. Here are displayed statues from Orsanmichele, capitals from the Badia, and colossal statues of the Madonna and Child and SS Peter and Paul from the Porta Romana, by *Paolo di Giovanni.* The three acolytes are by *Arnolfo di Cambio,* and works by *Tino da Camaino* include a fine Madonna and Child.—The room next door (3) is used for exhibitions.

The **First Floor** may be reached by the staircase (4) or from the open stairway in the courtyard. The LOGGIA (5) provides a charming setting for works by the Flemish born *Giambologna,* perhaps the greatest Mannerist sculptor who worked in Florence, who had a wide influence on his contemporaries. The life-like group of bronze birds was made for a grotto at the Villa di Castello. The female statue in marble represents Architecture. His most successful and influential work was the bronze *Mercury. The statue, which seems almost on the point of flying away, invites the beholder to walk around it.

The SALONE DEL CONSIGLIO GENERALE (6) is a splendid 14C vaulted hall. Here are displayed works by *Donatello,* the greatest sculptor of the Quattrocento, and his contemporaries. In the middle of the room is his Marzocco, the Florentine heraldic lion, in pietra serena. On the end wall is the reconstructed tabernacle from Orsanmichele (comp p 76) which contains *St George, made for the guild of armourers c 1416. By endowing the statue with a sense of movement, Donatello here resolves the difficult problem of placing a figure within a niche but at the same time not letting it appear to be confined. The remarkably well composed statue, at once recognized as a new departure from Gothic forms, shows the Saint as the young Champion of Christendom. The bas-relief is a copy of the original. Other works by *Donatello* include (l.) *David with the head of Goliath (sometimes interpreted as Mercury), in bronze. One of the earliest and most beautiful free-standing nude statues of the Renaissance it was probably made between 1430–40 for the Medici. On their expulsion from Florence it was moved in 1495 to Palazzo della Signoria. The other *David, in marble (between the windows) is an early work by

Ganymede attrib. to *Cellini* or *Tribolo; Bernini,* small model in terracotta for a fountain in Pistoia; *Rustici* (perhaps with the collaboration of *Giov. della Robbia*), large relief in white terracotta (Noli me tangere); statue of the Madonna and Child by the workshop of the Sicilian sculptor *Domenico Gagini; Iac. Sansovino,* Madonna and Child, a large relief in papier mâchè.—Room 14 contains beautiful works in enamelled terracotta by *And. della Robbia:* Bust of a boy; *Madonna 'of the cushion', in a pretty tabernacle; *Madonna of the Stonemasons (1475). The portrait of a lady (a circular relief) has recently been attrib. to Andrea's uncle, *Luca della Robbia.* In the centre are two exquisite models in bronze for the Mercury and Rape of the Sabine by *Giambologna.*

Room 15 displays works by *Verrocchio* and fine Renaissance portrait busts. In the centre: *Ant. del Pollaiolo,* *Hercules and Antaeus, a beautiful small bronze group, also the subject of a painting (now in the Uffizi, comp. p 92) by the same artist. *Verrocchio's* bronze *David was made for the Medici, and then acquired by the Signoria in 1476. It owes much to Donatello's earlier statue of the same subject (see p 146). To the r. of the door are charming marble works by *Mino da Fiesole:* busts of Cosimo il Vecchio's two sons, Giovanni and *Piero il Gottoso (1453; the first dated portrait bust of the Renaissance); two Madonnas; portrait of Rinaldo della Luna; and a tabernacle.—On the window wall: *Bened. da Maiano,* *Pietro Mellini, signed and dated 1474, a remarkable portrait of this rich Florentine merchant as an old man; *15C Florentine School,* Bust of Giuliano di Piero de' Medici, murdered in the Pazzi conspiracy; *Bened. da Maiano,* a large high relief of the Coronation of Ferdinand of Aragon, with six boy musicians (purchased in London in 1970).—On the end wall, the works by *Ant. Rossellino* include a bust of Francesco Sassetti; a painted relief of the Madonna in a tabernacle; a marble tondo of the Nativity; busts of a young boy, and of the young St John the Baptist; and the portrait bust of Matteo Palmieri, Renaissance statesman and scholar (1468). This was on the façade of his Florentine palace until the 19C, which accounts for its weathered surface.—On the wall opposite the windows: *Ant. del Pollaiolo,* *Young cavalier, a bust thought to be a portrait of a member of the Medici family (in terracotta); *Verrocchio* (attrib.), Portrait bust of Piero di Lorenzo de' Medici (in terracotta; also attrib. to Piero del Pollaiolo); Resurrection, a polychrome relief; bas-relief in terracotta of the Madonna and Child from Santa Maria Nuova; *Bust of a lady holding flowers. Formerly part of the Medici collection, this is one of the loveliest of all Renaissance portrait busts, and was once attributed to Verrocchio's pupil, Leonardo da Vinci. *And. del Pollaiolo,* *Portrait of a man, another marble bust; *Verrocchio,* Death of Francesca Tornabuoni-Pitti, a tomb relief; *Matt. Civitali,* Faith, Portrait relief of a lady; *Fr. Laurana* (a Dalmatian artist who worked at the Court of Urbino), *Battista Sforza, duchess of Urbino (a marble bust).

From Room 14 there is access to the Salone del Camino (16), with a superb display of small Renaissance *Bronzes, the most important collection in Italy. The fashion for collecting small bronzes was begun by Lorenzo il Magnifico following a Roman tradition. The statuettes, animals, bizarre figures, plaquettes, candelabrum, bells, etc. were often copies of Antique works, or small replicas of Renaissance statues. They include works by *Tacca, Tribolo, Bandinelli, L'Antico, Briosco (Il Riccio), Caradosso, Giambologna, Leone Leoni,*

Pietro da Barga, Massimo Soldani, and *Roccatagliata.* On the r. of the door, *Jac. Sansovino,* Christ in glory, a bas relief in a tabernacle. The splendid *Chimneypiece is the work of *Benedetto da Rovezzano.* In front, two bronze horses by *Tacca.* By the windows, *Giambologna,* the dwarf Morgante riding a monster, and an Anatomical figure, a famous work made in wax by *Lod. Cigoli* (1598–1600) and fused in bronze by *G.B. Foggini* after 1678.

From R. 13 a door leads into the SALA DELLE ARMI (17) with a magnificent display of *Arms and armour from the Medici, Carrand, and Ressman collections (well labelled). It includes saddles decorated with gold, silver, and ivory, a shield by Gaspare Mola (17C), and numerous sporting guns, dress armour, oriental arms, etc. Also, a fine bust in marble by *Fr. da Sangallo,* an idealized portrait of Giovanni delle Bande Nere. The bronze bust of Ferdinando I is by *Pietro Tacca.*—The MEDAGLIERE MEDICEO has been closed to the public for many years (adm only with special permission). This huge collection of Italian medals was started by Lorenzo il Magnifico. Among the most notable are those designed by *Pisanello.*—The SALA FRANCHETTI may be reopened to be used as an exhibition hall and to display the study collection of materials.

14   FROM THE BADIA FIORENTINA TO SANTA MARIA NUOVA

In **Piazza San Firenze** (Pl. 16; 6), where seven streets converge, a miscellany of buildings are assembled. Opposite the corner of Palazzo Vecchio stands *Palazzo Gondi (No. 2), a beautiful palace built c 1489 by Giul. da Sangallo with a pretty little courtyard. It was completed (and the façade on Via de' Gondi added) with great taste by Gius. Poggi in 1872–84. The square is dominated by SAN FIRENZE, a huge Baroque building, now occupied by the law courts, by Fr Zanobi del Rosso (1772–75). It is flanked by two church façades designed by Ferd. Ruggieri (1715). The church of *San Filippo Neri* (l.) by Gherardo and Pier Fr. Silvani (1633–48) has an unusually tall interior.—At the end of the piazza the slender tower of the Badia rises opposite the battlemented Bargello (see Rte 13). At the beginning of Via del Proconsolo (l.) is a portal by Bened. da Rovezzano (1495) with a Madonna in enamelled terracotta by Bened. Buglioni, which leads into the courtyard of the **Badia Fiorentina** (Pl. 16; 6), the church of a Benedictine abbey founded in 978.

Willa, the widow of Uberto, Margrave of Tuscany, founded the monastery in his memory, richly endowing it with property. Their son Count Ugo, a benefactor of the monastery, is buried in the church. One of the first hospitals in the city was established here in 1031. The tolling of the bell, mentioned by Dante ('Paradiso', XV, 97-98), regulated life in the medieval city. At one time the 'Consiglio del Popolo' met here. The church was rebuilt on a Latin cross plan in 1284–1310 probably by *Arnolfo di Cambio.* This building was radically altered in 1627–31 when *Matteo Segaloni* reconstructed the interior.

The VESTIBULE, with a Corinthian portico, is by *Bened. da Rovezzano.* From here there is a good view of the graceful CAMPANILE, Romanesque below (1307) and Gothic (after 1330) above.—The disappointing 17C INTERIOR preserves fragments of frescoes from the old church on the W. wall. The carved wood ceiling (17C) has been restored. On the l., *Madonna appearing to St Bernard, a large panel of great charm by *Filippino Lippi* (c. 1485). On the r., tomb of Gian nozzo Pandolfini, from the workshop of *Rossellino,* and a sculpted altarpiece of the Madonna and Saints (1464–69) by *Mino da Fiesole.* In the r. transept, tomb of Bernardo Giugni, the Florentine statesman (1396–1466), with a good effigy and statue of Justice, also by *Mino.* A Baroque chapel here has vault frescoes by *Vinc. Meucci.* Above is a fine organ (1558; well restored) by *Onofrio Zeffirini* with paintings by *Fr. Furini* and *Baccio del Bianco.* In the chap. to the l. of the presbytery, Way to Calvary, by *G.B. Naldini.* In the l. transept, *Monument to Ugo (d 1001), Margrave of Tuscany, son of the foundress of the church, an ex quisite work by *Mino da Fiesole* (1469–81). Above is a good painting of the Assumption and two Saints by *Vasari*. In the chapel are displayed four damaged frescoes detached from a wall of the church. They illustrate the Passion of Christ (including the suicide of Judas) and are attrib. to *Nardo di Cione*. The two 19C statuettes are by *Amalia Duprè*.

Interesting fragments of 14C frescoes with scenes from the life of the Virgin (some attrib. to *Giotto*) were detached with their sinopia from the Choir. These have been restored but have not yet been returned here. On the right of the Choir with stalls of 1501), a door gives access to a flight of stairs which lead to the up-per loggia of the **Chiostro degli Aranci**, by *Bern. Rossellino* (c. 1434–36), a peaceful cloister where orange trees were once cultivated. The interesting fresco cycle illustrates scenes from the life of St Benedict (restored in 1973, when the sinopie were also detached). By an unknown master (usually known as the Maestro del Chiostro degli Aranci') working in the decade after the death of Masaccio, they have been attrib. to *Giov. di Consalvo,* a Portuguese artist and follower by Fra' Angelico. One of the lunettes in the N. walk contains an early fresco by *Bronzino*.

In Via del Proconsolo (r.) rises the handsome *Palazzo Pazzi-Quaratesi* (No. 10; no adm) attrib. to *Giul. da Maiano* (1458–69). The Pazzi coat-of-arms (removed from the exterior) is displayed in the vestibule which leads to a pretty courtyard (with good capitals'). The Pazzi, one of the oldest Florentine families, who made their fortune as bankers, organised a notorious conspiracy in 1478 against the Medici (comp. p 33) when Giuliano, brother of Lorenzo il Magnifico, was killed by Francesco de' Pazzi. Francesco, who was wounded, hid here before being seized by the mob and hung from a window of Palazzo Vecchio.—Across Borgo degli Albizi, a street lined with fine palaces described on p 193, is *Palazzo Nonfinito,* begun in 1593 by Buonalenti. The great courtyard is attrib. to Cigoli. The building was continued by Vinc. Scamozzi and others, but was left unfinished. It now houses the **Museo Nazionale di Antropologia ed Etnologia** (Pl. 16; 4), founded in 1869 by Paolo Mantegazza, the first museum of its kind in Italy. It is at present closed for structural repairs (for adm times when it reopens, see p 58).

The collection, displayed in some 35 rooms, is probably the most important ethnological and anthropological museum in Italy. It covers: *Africa* (notably Ethiopia, Eritrea, Somalia, and Libya); *North Pakistan,* (a rare *Collection made in 1955–60 by Paolo Graziosi of material relating to the Kafiri); *South America* (including mummies, etc. from Peru, collected in 1883) and *Mexico; Asia* (Melanesia, the Islands of Sumatra, including the Modigliani collection c. 880, Tibet, and Japan, with the Fosco Maraini collection of Ainu material); and material from the Pacific Ocean probably acquired by Captain Cook on his last voyage in 1776–79.

Via del Proconsolo emerges in Piazza del Duomo (see Rte 2); to the . Via dell'Oriuolo leads to the old *Convento delle Oblate* (No. 24) which now houses the **Museo di Firenze com'era** (Pl. 6; 8; adm see p 58), a topographical historical museum of the city. The maps, paintings, and prints displayed in several rooms of the old convent illustrate the life of the city since the 15C.

Of particular interest are the prospect of the city, a 19C copy in tempera of the Pianta della Catena' an engraving of 1470 now in Berlin, and the first topographical plan of Florence drawn by *Stefano Bonsignori* in 1584 for the grand-duke Francesco I.—In the second room is a charming series of lunettes of the Medici villas by the Flemish painter, *Giusto Utens* (1599) from the Villa di Artimino. The cartographic collection is continued with works by *Valerio Spada* (1650), *F.B. Werner* (1705), and *Fed. Fantozzi* (1843 and 1866). The views of Florence include paintings by *Thomas Patch* and *Gius. Maria Terreni,* and engravings by *Telemaco Signorini* of the Mercato Vecchio in 1874 before its demolition.—At the end of the room are exhibited paintings by *Ottone Rosai*

(1895–1957), a Florentine painter whose works are well-known locally. The collection was left to the city by his family.—In the last hall (in the course of re arrangement) are a fine series of engravings (1754) with views of the city and villas in the environs, by *Giuseppe Zocchi,* and lithographs by *A. Durand* (1863) The elevations and sections of the Duomo, Baptistery, and Campanile publishe by *Sgrilli* in 1755, were drawn by *G.B. Nelli* (1661–1725) who made the firs measured survey of these buildings for the Opera del Duomo. The famou 'Fiera' of Impruneta was engraved by *Jac. Callôt* in 1620. Plans by *Gius. Pogg* architect when Florence was capital of Italy, complete the collection.

Via Folco Portinari leads N. from Via dell'Oriuolo to SANTA MARIA NUOVA (Pl. 6; 8), a hospital founded in 1286 by Folco Portinari believed to be the father of Dante's Beatrice. It is still operating as on of the main hospitals of Florence. The unusual portico (1574–1612) i a good work by Bern. Buontalenti. Beneath it, in the centre, is th church of SANT'EGIDIO (c. 1420) with a cast of a terracotta by Delli Delli (1424) in the lunette above (original see below).

In the Interior, immediately on the r., are the remains of the Portinari tomb The first altarpiece on the r. (Madonna and Child with Saints) is by *Felic Ficherelli* (1654–57). The small marble tabernacle to the l. of the high altar b *Bern. Rossellino* (1450), incorporates a bronze door by *Ghiberti*.—A door to th r. of the church leads into a cloister, the oldest part of the hospital, with a Piet by *Giov. della Robbia*. To the l. of the church, in another old courtyard, is th tomb slab of Monna Tessa, the servant of Portinari who persuaded him to foun the hospital, and a small tabernacle with a fresco of Charity by *Giov. da Sa Giovanni*. The incongruous neo-classical pavilion is a monument to Count Gal Tassi, benefactor of the hospital.—In the offices of the Presidenza, above (adr only by special request), are the original lunette by *Delli* (comp. above), a fresc of the Crucifixion, an early work by *And. del Castagno*, and a Madonna an Child by *And. della Robbia* (formerly in Sant'Egidio). The Salone di Martino (sometimes shown on request) contains detached frescoes (formerly flanking th church doorway) of Martin V consecrating the church, by *Bicci di Lorenzo* (wit its sinopia), and the same pope confirming its privileges, by *And. di Giusto* (re painted). Also a detached fresco of the Resurrection (damaged), recentl discovered, attrib. to *Pietro Gerini*.

At No. 1 Via Bufalini a plaque marks the site of Ghiberti's workshop, wher the Baptistery doors were cast.—In Via Sant'Egidio (No. 21) is the entrance t the **Museo Fiorentino di Preistoria** (Pl. 6; 8; adm see p 58), a museum o prehistory founded in 1946. Exhibited in three large rooms, the material is we labelled and arranged chronologically and geographically. The lower hall dedicated to Italy, and includes a human skull of the Paleolithic era found Olmo near Arezzo in 1865; in the upper hall material from Europe, Africa, an Asia is displayed.—In Via della Pergola is the house (No. 59) where Cellini ca his 'Perseus' (comp. Rte 4), and where he died in 1571. The **Teatro della Pergol** (Pl. 7; 7), on the site of a wooden theatre erected in 1656 by Ferd. Tacca (famou for the comedies performed here), dates in its present form from the 19C. Whe Gordon Craig was director in 1906 'Rosmersholm' was produced with Eleonor Duse. Plays and chamber music concerts are now given here (comp. p 55).

15   SANTA CROCE AND CASA BUONARROTI

PIAZZA SANTA CROCE (Pl. 10; 2), one of the most attractive an spacious squares in the city, has been used since the 14C for tou naments, festivals, and public spectacles, and the traditional footba game was held here for many centuries (comp. p 56). It is the centre c a distinctive district of the city, with numerous narrow old streets c small houses above artisans' workshops. In medieval Florence th area was a centre of the wool industry. One side of the piazza is line with houses whose projecting upper stories rest on brackets. These a the characteristic 'sporti', a familiar architectural feature of th medieval city. The wooden brackets were replaced in the 15C and 16 by stone supports. *Palazzo dell'Antella* (No. 2) was built by Giulio Parigi and its polychrome façade (now very worn) is supposed to have been painted in three weeks in 1619 by Giov. da San Giovanni, Passignano, Matteo Rosselli, Ottavio Vannini, and others.—The unusual palace at the end of the square facing the church is *Palazzo Cocchi* (*Serristori*), built above a 14C house c. 1470–80, and recently attrib. to Giul. da Sangallo. The ungainly monument to Dante, beside the church façade, was erected by Enrico Pazzi (1865).

*Santa Croce (Pl. 11; 1; closed 12.30-15), the Franciscan church of Florence, was rebuilt in 1294 or 1295 possibly by *Arnolfo di Cambio*. The nave was still unfinished in 1375 and it was not consecrated until 1442. Remains of an earlier 13C church were found beneath the nave in 1967. The CAMPANILE was added in 1842 by *Baccani*. The bare stone front was covered with a neo-Gothic FAÇADE in 1853–63 by *Nic. Matas;* its cost was defrayed by an English benefactor, Francis Sloan. Along the left flank of the church a picturesque 14C arcade survives (recently restored). The church is much visited by tourist groups.

The huge wide INTERIOR has an open timber roof. The vista is closed by the polygonal sanctuary and the 14C stained glass in the E. windows. The Gothic church was rearranged by *Vasari* in 1560 when the choir and rood-screen were demolished and the side altars added, with tabernacles by *Fr. da Sangallo*. Fragments of frescoes by Orcagna which formerly decorated the nave have been uncovered, and some are exhibited in the Museum (see below). In the pavement are numerous fine tomb-slabs. For five hundred years it has been the custom to bury or erect monuments to notable citizens of Florence in this church; it is the burial place of Ghiberti, Michelangelo, Machiavelli, and Galileo.—WEST WALL. In the round window the stained glass Deposition was composed from a cartoon attrib. to *Giov. del Ponte*. Monuments here commemorate the 19C patriots Gino Capponi and G.B. Niccolini.

Piazza Santa Croce at the start of the traditional football game, a detail from an engraving by Alexander Cecchini, 1600. (Kunsthistorisches Institut)

SOUTH AISLE. 1st pillar (1) *Madonna 'del Latte', a charming relief by *Ant. Rossellino* (1478), above the tomb of Fr. Nori killed in the Pazzi conspiracy. The Tomb of Michelangelo (2) was designed by *Vasari* and includes a statue of architecture by *Giov. dell'Opera.* Michelangelo died in Rome in 1564 but his body was transported to Florence for an elaborate funeral service (comp. p 128). 2nd altar (3), *Vasari,* Way to Calvary. The cenotaph to Dante (4) is a cold neo-classical work by *Stef. Ricci* (1829). Dante, exiled in 1302 as an opponent of the Guelf faction in the government, never returned to his native city. He died in 1321 in Ravenna where he was buried. 3rd altar (5), *Jac. Coppi di Meglio,* Ecce Homo. On the nave pillar (6), *Pulpit by *Bened. da Maiano* (1472–76), a beautifully composed work decorated with delicately carved scenes from the life of St Francis and four Virtues. The monument (7) to Vittorio Alfieri (d 1803), the poet, by *Ant. Canova* was erected at the expense of the Countess of Albany. 4th altar (8), *Aless. del Barbiere,* Flagellation of Christ, a good work. The monument (9) to Niccolò Machiavelli (d 1527), who is buried here, is by *Inn. Spinazzi* (1787). 5th altar (10) *And. del Minga,* Agony in the Garden, an unusual painting. By the side door (probably moved from another part of the church) is a *Tabernacle (11) with a beautiful high relief in gilded limestone of the Annunciation by *Donatello.* A very unusual work, there is a remarkable bond between the two figures.—On the other side of the door, *Tomb of Leonardo Bruni (12), by *Bern. Rossellino* (c. 1446–47), one of the most harmonious and influential sepulchral monuments of the Renaissance. The architectural setting takes its inspiration from Brunelleschi. Bruni, who died in 1444, was an eminent Florentine humanist, a Greek scholar, a historian of the city, and Chancellor of the Republic. He is shown crowned with a laurel wreath in a beautiful serene effigy. The touching epitaph was composed by Carlo Marsuppini, his successor as Chancellor, who is buried opposite (see below).—The monument (13) to Gioacchino Rossini (1792–1868), the composer, is by *Gius. Cassioli,* a sad imitation of the Bruni tomb, and placed too close to it. 6th altar (14), *Cigoli,* Entry into Jerusalem. The sepulchral statue (15) of Ugo Foscolo, the poet, is by *Ant. Berti* (1936).

SOUTH TRANSEPT. The CASTELLANI CHAPEL (A) contains decorative *Frescoes by *Agnolo Gaddi* and assistants (among them probably *Gherardo Starnina*). They depict (r.) the histories of St Nicholas of Bari and St John the Baptist, and (l.) St Anthony Abbot and St John the Evangelist. On each wall is a white terracotta statue of a saint by the *Della Robbia.* The altar relief of the Maries at the Sepulchre is by a follower of *Nicola Pisano.* Behind is a tabernacle by *Mino da Fiesole* and a painted Crucifix by *Nic. di Pietro Gerini.* Among the monuments is one to the Countess of Albany (d 1824; comp. p 165).—The BARONCELLI CHAPEL (B; light on r. of the altar) has *Frescoes by *Taddeo Gaddi* (father of Agnolo) who worked with Giotto for many years and was his most faithful pupil. These are considered among his best works, executed in 1332–38, and reveal his talent as an innovator within the giottesque school (they include one of the earliest known night scenes in fresco painting). On either side of the entrance arch, Prophets, and tomb (r.) of a member of the Baroncelli family (1327) with a Madonna and Child in the lunette also

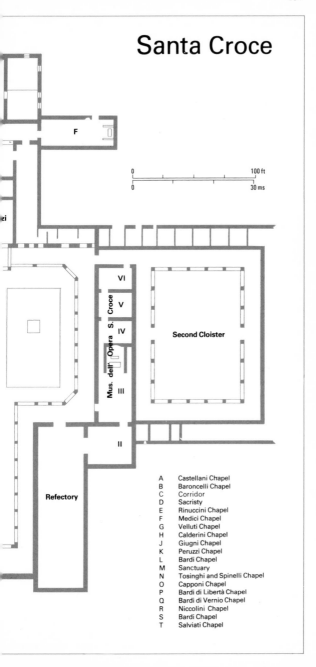

Santa Croce

0   100 ft
0   30 ms

F

VI
V
IV
III
II

Mus. dell' Opera S. Croce

Second Cloister

Refectory

A	Castellani Chapel
B	Baroncelli Chapel
C	Corridor
D	Sacristy
E	Rinuccini Chapel
F	Medici Chapel
G	Velluti Chapel
H	Calderini Chapel
J	Giugni Chapel
K	Peruzzi Chapel
L	Bardi Chapel
M	Sanctuary
N	Tosinghi and Spinelli Chapel
O	Capponi Chapel
P	Bardi di Libertà Chapel
Q	Bardi di Vernio Chapel
R	Niccolini Chapel
S	Bardi Chapel
T	Salviati Chapel

stigmata; in the vault, Poverty, Chastity, Obedience, and the Triump
of St Francis. On the end wall, Franciscan Saints, including S
Catherine. Left wall: the Saint stripping off his garments; the Sain
appearing to St Anthony at Arles; Death of St Francis. Right wall: th
Saint giving the Rule of the Order; the Saint being tried by fire befor
the Sultan (a particularly fine work); and the Saint appearing t
Brother Augustine and Bp Guido of Assisi.—On the altar, St Franc
and scenes from his life by a Florentine artist of the 13C.

The polygonal vaulted SANCTUARY (M) is frescoed by *Agnolo Gadd*
(c. 1380), and has fine stained glass lancet windows also designed b
him. In the vault, Christ, the Evangelists, and St Francis, and (on th
walls) the *Legend of the Cross. Over the altar, a large polyptych o
the Madonna and Saints by *Nic. Gerini,* and four Fathers of th
Church by *Giov. del Biondo* (1368). Above hangs a fine Crucifix b
the *'Master of Figline'*.—The TOSINGHI AND SPINELLI (now SLOA
CHAPEL (N) has an Assumption of the Virgin above the entrance arch
a repainted fresco of the 14C. On the altar, Polyptych by *Giov. a
Biondo* (1372).—The CAPPONI CHAPEL (O) contains sculptures in
cluding a Pietà by the Florentine sculptor *Libero Andreo*
(1926).—The BARDI DI LIBERTÀ CHAPEL (P) contains an altarpiece b
Giov. della Robbia, and frescoes of the Lives of St Lawrence and S
Stephen by *Bern. Daddi.*—The BARDI DI VERNIO CHAPEL (Q) has co
ourful and well preserved *Frescoes of the Life of St Sylvester b
Maso di Banco (after 1367), perhaps the most original follower o
Giotto. The first Gothic tomb contains a Last Judgement with th
figure of Bettino de' Bardi (c. 1367), also attrib. to *Maso di Banco;*
the second niche, Deposition attrib. to *Taddeo Gaddi*. The altarpiec
by *Giov. del Biondo* has been removed for restoration.

NORTH TRANSEPT. The NICCOLINI CHAPEL (R) was designed b
Giov. Ant. Dosio. The dome has good frescoes by *Volterran*
(1652–64). The statues are by *Francavilla* and the paintings by *Ales*
Allori.—The second BARDI CHAPEL (S) contains the celebrate
wooden *Crucifix by *Donatello* (not seen to advantage here). Th
story told by Vasari of Brunelleschi's complaint that it was a me
'peasant on the cross' is now thought to be apocryphal.—In th
SALVIATI CHAPEL (T) is the *Tomb of Princess Sofia Czartoryska
1837), with a Romantic effigy by *Lor. Bartolini.* Outside the chap
(16) is a monument to the composer Luigi Cherubini (d 1842; born
No. 22 Via Fiesolana not far N. of the church).

NORTH AISLE. Monument (17) to Raffaello Morghen (d 1833), th
engraver, by *Ed. Fantacchiotti.* On the nave pillar (18), monument
Leon Battista Alberti (d 1472), an unfinished group by *Lo*
Bartolini.—On the r. of the side door, *Monument to Carlo Marsu
pini (19), the humanist scholar and Chancellor of the Republic
1453), by *Desiderio da Settignano.* It takes its inspiration from th
Bruni monument opposite (see above) and incorporates some e
quisite carved figures. The fine classical sarcophagus may possibly
the work of *Verrocchio.* The organ above the door is by *Nofri da Co
tona* (1579; restored).—Beyond the door (20) monument to Vit
Fossombroni (d 1844) by *Bartolini.* 5th altar (21), Ascension by *Gio
Stradano.* The painting of the Deposition is by *Bronzino.* In the pav
ment between the 5th and 4th altar (22) is the handsome tomb-sla
with niello decoration and the emblem of an eagle which marks th

ourial place of Lorenzo Ghiberti, and his son Vittorio. 4th altar (23), *'asari,* Incredulity of St Thomas. The next two altarpieces (Supper at :maus and the Resurrection; 24 and 25) are good works by *Santi di *ito.*—Galileo Galilei (1564–1642), the great scientist who spent the atter part of his life in Florence, was tried by the Inquisition for his ontention that the earth was not at the centre of the Universe. He was ot allowed Christian burial inside the church until 1737 when a Monument (26) was set up to him by *G.B. Foggini.* In the pavement in ne centre of the nave (27) is the tomb-slab with a relief of his ancestor nd namesake Galileo Galilei, a well known physician in 15C lorence. The remains of frescoes on the wall (28) have been attrib. to *Mariotto di Nardo.* 1st altar (29), *G.B. Naldini,* Deposition. On the all (30) are remains of frescoes of three Saints (15C).

On the right of the church is the entrance to the conventual uildings and the **Museo dell'Opera di Santa Croce** (Pl. 11; 1; adm see 58). Here in 1966 the water of the Arno reached a height of nearly 6 netres (marked by the highest plaque to the left of the Pazzi Chapel); ne buildings and works of art have since been carefully restored. The IRST CLOISTER dates from the 14C; opposite the arcade along the bare othic flank of the church is a portico and loggia. On the green lawn a group of cypresses with acanthus plants (and an incongruous war emorial). The neo-Gothic campanile rises behind the charming ome and lantern of the *****Cappella dei Pazzi,** one of the most famous orks by *Brunelleschi.* It was commissioned as a Chapter House by ndrea de' Pazzi in 1429 or 1430. Most of the work was carried out by runelleschi from 1442 until his death in 1446, but it was not finished ntil the 1470s.

The PORTICO may have been designed by *Giul. da Maiano.* It bears a terracotta ieze of cherubs' heads attrib. to the *Della Robbia* workshop. Beneath the col-nnade is a barrel vault and a shallow cupola lined with a delightful polychrome amelled terracotta decoration by *Luca della Robbia,* with a garland of fruit rrounding the Pazzi arms. Over the door is a medallion with *St Andrew, also *Luca* (c. 1461). The carved wooden door is by the brothers *De Maiano.*—The autiful calm INTERIOR is one of the masterpieces of the early Renaissance. elicately carved pietra serena is used to pronounce the architectural features ainst a plain white ground. The illumination in the chapel is increased by little :uli in the rib-vaulted dome. The twelve *Roundels in enamelled terracotta of e seated Apostles (c. 1442–52) are by *Luca della Robbia.* In the pendentives of e cupola are polychrome roundels of the Evangelists, thought to have been ad-d c. 1460. These may have been designed by *Donatello* and glazed by the *Della obbia.* In the small rectangular sanctuary are decorations by the school of onatello and a stained-glass window attrib. to *Aless. Baldovinetti.*
On the left of the chapel is an exhibition room, and, beyond, a small courtyard etween the Pazzi chapel, the corridor outside the sacristy with windows by lichelozzo, and the exterior of the Baroncelli chapel of the church.—The *SE-OND CLOISTER is reached through a doorway by *Michelozzo.* This is another autiful work by *Brunelleschi,* finished in 1453 after his death. It is one of the ost pleasant spots in the city.
Off the First Cloister is the entrance to the **Museo dell'Opera di Santa Croce** omp. the Plan on p 156). The REFECTORY is a fine Gothic hall with large win-ws. Here is displayed *Cimabue's* great Crucifix which has been restored after it as almost completely destroyed in the flood. It was the greatest single loss of a ork of art in 1966. The end wall is decorated with a huge *Fresco by *Taddeo addi* (detached in one piece and restored) of the Last Supper below the Tree of e Cross and four scenes showing St Louis of Toulouse, St Francis, St Benedict, d Mary Magdalen annointing the feet of Christ in the house of Simon the narisee. On the two long walls (below roundels of Saints) are detached agments of a large fresco by *Orcagna* of the Triumph of Death and Inferno

which used to decorate the nave of the church before Vasari's side altars were s
up. The detached 14C fresco (attrib. to *Giov. del Biondo*) includes one of t
earliest views of the city (including the Baptistery and Duomo). In
reconstructed tabernacle (a cast) is *Donatello's* colossal gilded bronze *St Lou
of Toulouse, commissioned by the Parte Guelfa for a niche in Orsanmichele. C
the entrance wall, Christ carrying the Cross and Crucifixion, two fine detach
frescoes of the early 15C. Above the door into the next room, Coronation of t
Virgin, by *Maso di Banco.*

ROOM II. 14-15C stained glass from the church; a fresco of St Francis by *Ia
Ligozzi;* Madonna and Child (fresco), attrib. by some scholars to *Paolo Uccel
(and by others to a 14C artist); detached fresco showing the young Madonn
sewing, a charming work attrib. to the *'Maestro del Bambino Vispo'.*—T
following rooms have been closed temporarily for structural repairs. ROOM II
formerly the Cappella dei Cerchi, has traces of late-13C painted decoration
Here are displayed enamelled terracottas by *And. della Robbia* and h
workshop, and frescoes by *Nic. di Pietro Gerini.* In the corridor is a fine detac
ed fresco from the tomb of a Cardinal.—ROOM IV (overlooking the secor
cloister). The three large sketches were detached from the walls of the Cappe
dei Pazzi during restoration work in 1966. These interesting studies include tw
colossal heads of Saints. The detached frescoes include: *15C Tuscan Schoo
Martyrdom of St Thomas; 'Maestro della Madonna Straus',* Madonna enthro
ed (a sinopia); *14C Florentine School,* St John the Baptist.—ROOM V contai
sculptural fragments including the reconstructed tomb of Gastone della Torr
by *Tino da Camaino;* a relief of St Martin dividing his cloak with a beggar,
pietra serena, from a demolished rood-screen chapel in the church (15C); and
Madonna annunciate by *Tino da Camaino.*—The last room (VI) displays 1
works including ceiling paintings of two angels by *Matteo Rosselli,* a ciboriur
and the sinopia of the fresco by *Ligozzi* in R II. Other works of art owned by t
convent will be returned here after restoration.—Beneath the colonnade, ju
before the exit from the cloister, is a memorial to Florence Nightingale, nam
after the city where she was born.

To the right of the monastic buildings of Santa Croce is the modern extensi
of the **Biblioteca Nazionale** (Pl. 11; 3), the older buildings of which extend to t
entrance on Piazza dei Cavalleggeri. The main building was erected in 1911–
by Cesare Bazzani. The National Library was formed from the collection b
queathed by Ant. Magliabechi (d 1714) and first opened to the public in 1747. 1
the original collection were joined the Biblioteca Palatina-Medicea (1711) ar
the library of Ferdinando III (1861), together with several monastic collection
It includes an important collection of material relating to Dante and Galileo.
became a copyright library for books published in Italy in 1870. In 1966 nearly
third of the library's holdings was damaged in the flood and a restoration cent
here will be at work salvaging the books for many years to come.

Corso dei Tintori takes it name from the dyers' workshops documented he
as early as 1313.—Nearby is *Borgo Santa Croce,* a handsome street in whi
Palazzo Spinelli (No. 10), built in 1460–70, has good graffiti decoration on t
façade and in the courtyard. No. 8, the *Casa Morra,* belonged to Vasari and co
tains frescoes by him. Palazzo Antinori-Corsini (No. 6) has a beautiful courtya
dating from the end of the 15C.

On the left side of Santa Croce is Via di San Giuseppe, where, in t
house next to the church, the Trollope family lived in 1843–45. The li
tle church of *Santa Maria della Croce al Tempio,* with frescoes by Bi
ci di Lorenzo, is closed for restoration. Farther on, on the l. is t
church of *San Giuseppe* (often closed), by Baccio d'Agnolo (151\
which contains a painted cross by Lor. Monaco, and a good 18
organ (altarpieces by Santi di Tito, Cigoli, and Vignali have be
removed for restoration).—Via delle Pinzóchere leads past a fi
palace (No. 3) to ***Casa Buonarroti** (Pl. 11; 1; adm see p 57), a hou
in Via Ghibellina (No. 70). Three houses on this site were purchased
1508 by Michelangelo. He left the property to his only descendant, h
nephew Leonardo, who united the houses into one building followi
a plan already drawn up by Michelangelo. In turn, his son, call
Michelangelo, an art collector and man of letters, made part of t

house into a gallery in 1612 as a memorial to his great-uncle. The last member of this branch of the Buonarroti family founded the present museum in 1858. In the charming little rooms of the house are displayed some important sculptures by Michelangelo, and facsimiles of his drawings owned by the museum, as well as an interesting small eclectic collection of works of art made by Michelangelo's descendants.

Ground Floor. In the room to the left of the vestibule (with a ceiling fresco of the Dream of Jacob by *Iac. Vignali,* 1621), are displayed two large statues: Venus and two cupids, an undocumented statue thought by some scholars to be an early work by *Michelangelo* (the two unfinished cupids are particularly interesting), although it has also been attrib. to *Vinc. Danti.* The unfinished statue of a slave was identified in 1965 by the director of the Museum and also attrib. to *Michelangelo* as a companion to the other four slaves in the Accademia carved for the tomb of Julius II. The facsimiles of drawings by *Michelangelo* owned by the Museum include studies for a Venus, the Resurrection, Ganymede, and the Fall of Phaeton.—The other rooms on this floor contain the collection of Antiquities and Renaissance works begun by Michelangelo Buonarroti the Younger (1568–1647), and continued by the archaeologist Filippo Buonarroti (1661–1733). Room II. Here is displayed a statue made up from a classical head and a medieval draped toga. The five Etruscan urns include two polychrome terracotta urns from Chiusi (2C B.C.) with battle scenes, and a fragment of an alabaster urn representing Ulysses and the Sirens. The right arm and hand come from a good Roman copy of the Discobolos of Myron.—R III contains Etruscan bronzes of the 5-2C B.C., and Roman fragments in marble and terracotta. The two archaic stelai from Fiesole in pietra serena, one showing a seated satyr playing a lyre (beginning of the 5C B.C.; found in 1720), and the other with a warrior (late 6C B.C.), are among the best preserved Etruscan stelai of this period. Two statues of Florentine magistrates, and a little relief with two goats are Roman works (1C A.D.). The ancient Ionic capital was used as a model by Giul. da Sangallo in the cloister of Santa Maria Maddalena dei Pazzi (see p 163).

Beyond the courtyard, R IV contains a collection of minerals, semi-precious stones, and coins. The portraits here include Buonarroto di Leonardo as an old man, and his brother Michelangelo Buonarroti the Younger, and his three nephews, by *Crist. Allori.*—R V. Wooden casket (c. 1373); *And. Ferrucci & Valerio Cioli,* Cupid (in marble); beautiful head of a child in terracotta attrib. to the school of *Verrocchio* or *Ant. Rossellino;* works attrib. to *And.* and *Giov. della Robbia;* majolica plates, and a 16C carved wooden frieze.—R VI. *Guido Reni* (attrib.), Portrait of an old man; *Titian* (attrib.), Amorous scene, an early work showing the influence of Giorgione; *Giov. di Francesco,* *Predella with scenes from the life of St Nicholas of Bari; *Florentine school* (c. 1420), tiny painting of a man, thought to represent Narcissus at the fountain.—In R VII are displayed numerous portraits of Michelangelo including a fine head by *Daniele da Volterra* (the bust is attrib. to *Giambologna*), and the portrait of the artist in a turban by *Giul. Bugiardini* (a replica).

First Floor. In the vestibule at the top of the stairs, Portrait of Michelangelo attrib. to *Marcello Venusti,* and the sword thought to have belonged to Buonarroto Buonarroti, Captain of the Guelf party in 1392.—The room to the left (VIII) contains small sculptures by *Michelangelo:* The *Madonna of the Steps, a marble bas-relief, is his earliest known work, carved at the age of 15 or 16. The low 'schiacciato' relief shows the influence of Donatello. The *Battle relief is also one of his earliest works, carved just before the death of Lorenzo il Magnifico in 1492, and left unfinished. Modelled on ancient sarcophagi, it represents a mythological battle between Greeks and centaurs. The small models in terracotta by *Michelangelo* include a study for Hercules and Cacus, a statue intended as a pair to David outside Palazzo Vecchio (the commission was given instead to Bandinelli), the torso of a Hermaphrodite, and the fragment of a female allegorical figure, perhaps for a niche in the funerary monument of Giuliano de' Medici. The tiny model in wood (1562) was made for a Crucifix which Michelangelo intended to carve in the last years of his life (comp. the drawing). The relief in stucco of the Deposition was made from a design by Michelangelo. The facsimiles of drawings by *Michelangelo* exhibited here include two early studies from Giotto (comp. p 155) and Masaccio.—R IX (l.) contains the wooden model for the façade of San Lorenzo designed by *Michelangelo.* It was commissioned by Leo X in 1516 but never carried out. Here are displayed

drawings of architectural works commissioned from Michelangelo by the tw
Medici popes, Leo X and Clement VII, and by the grand-duke Cosimo I. The
include studies for the Medici Chapel, the Laurentian Library, the façade of Sa
Lorenzo, and for the church of San Giovanni dei Fiorentini in Rome.

The four rooms on the other side of R VIII were decorated for Michelangel
Buonarroti the Younger c. 1613–37 as a celebration of his famous great-uncl
and his family. The first room, finished in 1620, illustrates Michelangelo's lif
and apotheosis, with paintings by *Crist. Allori, Giov. Biliverti, Empoli, Fr
Furini, Giov. da San Giovanni, Passignano,* and *Matteo Rosselli.* Opposite th
statue of Michelangelo by *Pietro Novelli* is a copy of the cartoon of the so-calle
Epiphany by Michelangelo's pupil, *Ascanio Condivi.*—The next room i
dedicated to the Buonarroti family, with a bust of Michelangelo the Younger b
Giul. Finelli, Bernini's pupil.—The Chapel has a pretty ceiling, and frescoes c
Florentine Saints by *Jac. Vignali.*—The Library is decorated with an engagin
frieze of illustrious Florentines by *Cecco Bravo, Matteo Rosselli,* and *Don
Pugliani.*

In the room (X) off the Vestibule are a series of studies for the fortifications o
Florence made by *Michelangelo* when he was put in charge of the defences of th
city by the last Republican government in an attempt to withstand the siege c
1529–30. Facsimiles are displayed of the original drawings owned by th
museum. The small wax models are early works by *Michelangelo*: a David (c
1501), and a Hercules (for Fontainebleau). The St Jerome is of doubtful attribu
tion.—R XI. *Crucifix in painted poplar wood, found in Santo Spirito in 1963,
documented work thought to have been lost. Its attribution to *Michelangelo* ha
been accepted by most scholars. It shows the slight figure of Christ in an unusu
'contrapposto' position, a design copied by his followers. Here are displaye
more facsimiles of drawings including a Madonna and Child, and studies of th
nude.—R XII. Colossal *Torso by *Michelangelo,* a model in clay and wood for
river god, intended for the Medici Chapel. It was presented by Ammannati to th
Accademia del Disegno in 1583. The drawings include anatomical studies, th
head of 'Leda', and architectural plans of the Medici Chapel.—The last roor
(XIII) contains works derived from Michelangelo. The two paintings of 'Noli m
tangere' are attrib. to *Bronzino* and *Battista Franca.* The copy in bronze of th
Madonna of the Steps was made in 1565 by *Giambologna.* The Crucifixion b
Marcello Venusti is a copy of a drawing made by Michelangelo for Vittoria Co
onna. The collection also includes two anatomical drawings by *Eugène Delacroi
and an etching by *Albrecht Dürer.* The case of models includes two b
Michelangelo (a river god in black wax, and a torso in terracotta).

16   SANT'AMBROGIO AND SANTA MARIA MADDALENA DEI PAZZI

This route, which covers the area to the N. of Santa Croce, is of secondary im
portance apart from the churches, and can be combined with Rte 15.

The church of **Sant'Ambrogio** (Pl. 11; 1) was rebuilt in the late 13C
It has a 19C façade. The interior has pretty Renaissance side altars
and an open timber roof. Badly damaged in the flood of 1966, most o
the works of art have now been returned after restoration.

SOUTH SIDE: Deposition, a fresco by the school of *Nic. Gerini* (its sinopia i
displayed nearby). In the pavement beside the 1st altar is the tomb slab o
Cronaca (d 1508), the architect of a number of fine palaces in the city. 1st altar
Annunciation, a very damaged 14C fresco; 2nd altar, *Madonna enthroned wit
St John the Baptist and St Bartholomew, a beautiful fresco attrib. to the schoc
of Orcagna. Above the 4th altar is an interesting fragment of a mural drawing o
St Onuphrius, recently attrib. to the 'Master of the Fogg Pietà' (14C).—Th
Chapel on the l. of the high altar (CAPPELLA DEL MIRACOLO) contains an exquisit
*Tabernacle by *Mino da Fiesole* (1481), who is buried here (tomb slab in th
pavement at the entrance to the chapel, 1484). The tabernacle contains
miraculous chalice, and the large *Fresco by *Cosimo Rosselli* shows a processio
with the chalice in front of the church. It includes portraits of many of th
artist's contemporaries, and his self portrait (to the left). On the wall nearby
displayed the sinopia.—NORTH SIDE: 4th altar, *Raffaele dei Carli* (attrib.), Saint

and Annunciation. In the pavement is the tomb slab of Verrocchio (d 1488). 3rd altar, *Cosimo Rosselli,* Madonna in glory with Saints. Between the 3rd and 2nd altars, a wooden statuette of St Sebastian by *Leon. Del Tasso* stands in a graceful niche with a tiny painted roundel of the Annunciation, attrib. to the workshop of Filippino Lippi. 2nd altar, *And. Boscoli,* Visitation. On the wall, *Alesso Baldovinetti,* *Angels and Saints surrounding a Nativity by his pupil *Graffione.* On the W. wall is a strange fresco of the Martyrdom of St Sebastian, attrib. to *Agnolo Gaddi.* A triptych by *Bicci di Lorenzo* has been removed for restoration.

Just to the S. of the church (off Via de' Macci) is the *Market of Sant'Ambrogio* (Pl. 11; 1), a cast-iron building opened in 1873. This is the biggest produce market in the town after the central market at San Lorenzo; fruit and vegetables are sold outside.

From Piazza Sant'Ambrogio Via Pietrapiana leads to PIAZZA DEI CIOMPI (Pl. 11; 1), named after the famous revolt of Florentine clothworkers in 1378. The graceful *Loggia del Pesce* designed in 1568 by Vasari for the sale of fish, was reconstructed here after the demolition of the Mercato Vecchio (comp. p 75). It looks somewhat incongruous in these humble surroundings. In the square is the *Mercatino,* a 'junk' and 'antique' market where bargains can sometimes be found. On a house here a damaged inscription records the home of Lorenzo Ghiberti. Cimabue lived in Borgo Allegri, which was given this name, according to Vasari, after his painting of the Madonna left his studio in a joyous procession down the street.

From Piazza Sant'Ambrogio Via dei Pilastri leads towards Borgo Pinti passing (r.) Via Farini with the huge SYNAGOGUE (Pl. 7; 7), an elaborate building in the Spanish-Moresque style with a tall green dome. It was built in 1874–82 when the Ghetto was demolished (comp. p 75). The church is shown on request, and a small museum may be opened. In the garden is a Jewish School. At the end of Via Farini can be seen the large *Piazza d'Azeglio,* planted with plane trees and reminiscent of a London square.—Via dei Pilastri continues to BORGO PINTI (Pl. 7; 7, 5), a long narrow old street leading out of the city. At the beginning (l.) are two 17C palaces, Palazzo Caccini (No. 33) and Palazzo Roffia (No. 13). To the right at No. 56 is the entrance to the ex-Convent of **Santa Maria Maddalena dei Pazzi** (Pl. 7; 7) which has been beautifully restored after severe flood damage. It is named after a Florentine Carmelite nun (1566–1607) who was canonized during the Counter Reformation. It is famous for its fresco by Perugino.

In the *CLOISTER by *Giul. da Sangallo* beautiful large Ionic capitals support a low architrave. Modern bronze panels have been made for the door of the church by the Florentine sculptor, *Marcello Tommasi.* The interior of the Church has pretty lateral chapels with altarpieces by *Raff. del Garbo, Cosimo Rosselli, Carlo Portelli, Dom. Puligo, Santi di Tito,* and *Fr. Curradi,* all of which have not yet been returned here after restoration. The main chapel is decorated by *Pier Fr. Silvani* and contains two paintings by *Luca Giordano.*—The CHAPTER HOUSE (entered from the crypt of the church or from the cloister; adm see 58) contains a beautiful and very well preserved *Fresco of the Crucifixion and Saints by *Perugino* (1493–96), one of his masterpieces. Also here, Christ on the Cross and St Bernard, a detached fresco with its sinopia, by his workshop.

Borgo Pinti continues across Via della Colonna, with the Museo Archeologico (see Rte 9). On the right (No. 68) is *Palazzo Ximenes,* home of the Sangallo brothers (c. 1499). The Borgo next crosses Via Giusti.

In Via Giuseppe Giusti (l.) is the *German Institute* (No. 44) with an excellent art history library. No. 43 is a bizarre little house built by Federico Zuccari, the Roman painter, in 1579.—Via Gino Capponi, beyond, honours Gino Capponi

(1792–1876) the statesman-historian whose grandiose home, *Palazzo Capponi* (No. 26) was built in 1698–1713 by Carlo Fontana. The huge palace has a fine garden and is now the Italian headquarters of Sotheby Parke Bernet, the auctioneers. Here the poet Giuseppe Giusti died suddenly in 1850. No. 22 (plaque) was built by Andrea del Sarto in 1520 on his return from France; he died here ten years later. Nearby is the Oratory of the Confraternità di San Pietro Martire (No. 4), with a charming little courtyard (sometimes open for concerts, etc.). *Palazzo di San Clemente* (No. 15), on the corner of Via Micheli, is an unusual building by Gherardo Silvani. It was bought by Charles Stuart, the Young Pretender in 1777, and from here, in 1780, his wife, the Countess of Albany, fled to the nearby Covento delle Bianchette.

At the end of Borgo Pinti is the once-famous garden of *Palazzo Salviati* (No. 80), which is at present closed. Opposite stands *Palazzo della Gherardesca* (No. 99), with a fine 19C garden. The palace, built by Giul. da Sangallo for Bartolomeo Scala in the 15C (with interesting bas-reliefs in the courtyard), was enlarged in the 18C by Ant. Ferri.—The Borgo ends at Piazza Donatello, with the English cemetery, described on p 198.

17   THE ARNO BETWEEN PONTE ALLA CARRAIA AND PONTE ALLE GRAZIE

This route follows the right and left banks of the Arno between the four bridges in the centre of the city, all of them built for the first time by the 13C (the other bridges, up and down stream, were added after 1836). The roads along the Arno (recorded as early as the 13C) are known as the 'Lungarni' (sing., 'Lungarno'). Lined with handsome palaces and some elegant shops (but very busy with traffic) they provide magnificent views of the city on the river. Since the disastrous flood of 1966 the bed of the river here is being dredged in an attempt to prevent it overflowing its banks.

Ponte alla Carraia (Pl. 9; 1) was the second bridge to be built over the Arno after Ponte Vecchio. Constructed in wood on stone piles in 1218–20 it was known as 'Ponte Nuovo'. It was reconstructed after floods in 1269 and 1333; the 14C bridge may have been designed by Giotto. It was repaired by Ammannati in 1559, enlarged in 1867, and replaced by a new bridge (a copy of the original) after it was blown up in 1944. From the foot of the bridge is a view to the S.E. of the campanile of Santo Spirito, with, on the skyline, the Forte di Belvedere and the bell tower of San Miniato.—At the N. end in the busy *Piazza Goldoni* is a statue of Carlo Goldoni (by Ulisse Cambi, 1873) and *Palazzo Ricasoli* (No. 2, with several coats-of-arms) built c. 1475. A road leads to the church of Ognissanti (described on p 139). Lungarno Vespucci, opened in the 19C, leads away from the centre of the city towards the park of the Cascine past two modern bridges which can be seen downstream, Ponte Vespucci and Ponte della Vittoria. Also downstream on the left bank is the domed church of San Frediano in Cestello.

LUNGARNO CORSINI leads past the huge *Palazzo Corsini* (Pl. 9; 2) built from 1650 to c. 1737 in a grandiose Roman Baroque style. The architects included Alfonso Parigi the Younger and Ferdinando Tacca. It contains the GALLERIA CORSINI, the most important private art collection in Florence (adm by appointment only at 11 Via Parione).

The fine paintings include a series of Apollo and the Muses, painted for the ducal palace at Urbino by *Giov. Santi*, *Tim. Viti*, and others; a cartoon of Julius

*The Lungarno Nuovo (now Vespucci) photographed from
Piazza Goldoni c. 1890, shortly after it was opened.
(Archivio Alinari)*

, attrib. to *Raphael*; Crucifixion, by *Giov. Bellini*, Poetry, by *Carlo Dolci*; and
Madonnas by *Signorelli, Pontormo,* and *Filippo Lippi*.

Farther along the Lungarno is (No. 4) *Palazzo Gianfigliazzi* (1459;
reconstructed). Alessandro Manzoni stayed in a hotel here in 1827
(plaque). Next door the British Consulate now occupies *Palazzo
Masetti (Castelbarco)* where the Countess of Albany, widow of Prince
Charles Edward Stuart lived from 1793 until her death. Her 'salon'
was frequented by Chateaubriand, Shelley, Byron, Foscolo, and Von
Platen. Here in 1803 died the dramatist Alfieri, her second husband,
and here later she was joined by Xavier Fabre, the painter.

The next bridge is ***Ponte a Santa Trìnita** (Pl. 9; 2), first built in
1252 and several times rebuilt after flood damage. The present bridge
is an exact replica (beautifully executed by Riccardo Gizdulich) of the
bridge begun by Ammannati in 1567 and destroyed in 1944. The finest
of all the bridges across the Arno, it was commissioned by Cosimo I
and it is probable that Ammannati submitted his design to
Michelangelo for his approval. The high flat arches which span the
river are perfectly proportioned and provide a magnificent view of the
city. The four statues were set up on the parapet for the marriage of
Cosimo II; Spring (l.), the best work of Pietro Francavilla (1593), was
recovered from the Arno.

At the beginning of Via Tornabuoni (Rte 12; Pl. 16; 5) stands Palazzo Spini-Feroni. LUNGARNO ACCIAIOLI continues with a good view of
Ponte Vecchio. In a group of old houses overhanging the opposite
bank of the river is the little tower and river gate of the church of San
Iacopo sopr'Arno. The Lungarno becomes narrower and an old lane
(signposted) leads to the ancient church of SS Apostoli (see p 191).
The modern buildings on both banks of the river here replace the
medieval houses which were blown up in 1944 in order to render Ponte
Vecchio impassable. **Ponte Vecchio,** the most famous bridge across

the Arno, is described on p 99. At the foot of the bridge is the bus, Por Santa Maria, at the bend of which can be seen the lantern of th Duomo above the top of Orsanmichele. Lungarno Archibusieri described in Rte 7, continues parallel to the raised Corridoi Vasariano. The narrow road skirts the façade of the Uffizi; from th little terrace on the river there is a view of the huge Uffizi buildin with Palazzo Vecchio at the end. In Piazza dei Giudici (with a view o the tower of Palazzo Vecchio) stands *Palazzo Castellani*, a fin medieval palace owned in the 14C by an important Florentine famil whose wealth was based on the cloth trade. It now contains th **Museo di Storia della Scienza** (Pl. 16; 8; adm see p 58), with beautifully displayed and well maintained collection of scientific in struments, many of them restored after severe flood damage in 1966

A large part of the collection was owned by the Medici grand-dukes, and th Museum of Physics and Natural Sciences, directed by Felice Fontana, and open ed in 1775 by the grand-duke Pietro Leopoldo of Lorraine, was moved to thes premises in 1929. On each floor excellent hand lists (also available in English) a lent to visitors. There is a lift.

Ground Floor. The first room contains the desk used by Pietro Leopold grand-duke in 1765–90, for his chemical experiments.—In the second room a alchemist's studio has been reconstructed; human weighing machines are als displayed here.—The clocks in the third room include (wall case to the r.) model for a pendulum clock designed by Galileo and made by his son Vincenzi and Vinc. Viviani, and a pendulum clock made by Fil. Treffler for Ferdinand II. Also here is a curious 'writing machine' constructed in the 18C by Fec Knaus.—Beyond a corridor with more clocks, the last room has a fine display c bicycles (penny-farthings, etc.), showing their development from 1818–70, in cluding a primitive wooden bicycle made by Carl Friedrich Drais in 1817. Th fire extinguisher dates from 1794.—A small room near the stair-well contains a exhibition relating to the Polish scientist, and founder of modern astronomy Copernicus (1473–1543) who studied at Bologna and Padua.

First Floor. Room I (mathematical instruments of the 16C and 17C). In th large central case is a 'Giovilabio', the design of which is attrib. to Galileo (and may have been used by him). Galileo was the first to see the four largest moor of Jupiter. Among the surveying instruments is a quadrant by Tobias Wolkm (c. 1610) and a compass constructed by Crist. Schissler. In the small central cas the 'odometer' was used by Schissler to measure the shape of the earth. Some c the Day and Night clocks were made in the 16C by the Della Volpaia. The com pass belonged to Vinc. Viviani, disciple of Galileo.—In an adjacent room a navigational instruments: quadrants (one of which belonged to Sir Robe Dudley), and sextants, many of which were inventd by Sir Robert, who w made Director of the Arsenal of Livorno by Ferdinando I.—Room I Calculators of the 17C-19C; a compass which may have been used b Michelangelo; and a case of armillary spheres including an Arab globe showin the constellations (c. 1080).—R III. Sundials (by the Della Volpaia family an Stef. Bonsignori) and a fine collection of 17C globes.—R IV. Huge Ptolema sphere built by Ant. Santucci in 1588; barometers, globes, and a case c astrolabes.

Room V contains a precious collection of instruments which belonged Galileo: the lens he used in discovering the four largest moons of Jupiter (crac ed by the scientist himself before he presented it to Ferdinando II), his two woo telescopes, a compass bearing his signature, and his lodestones. The bones of h right middle finger were removed from his tomb when his remains were transfe red to the church of Santa Croce. The astrolabe, traditionally associated wit Galileo, was probably made instead by Egnazio Danti for Cosimo I.—The oth two cases contain material relating to the Accademia del Cimento, an experimen tal academy founded by Cardinal Leopoldo in 1657. This includes elaborate gla and an amusing set of thermometers, one used by the grand-duke Ferdinando to hatch eggs and boil them.—R VI. 17C and 18C telescopes one of whic belonged to Torricelli, disciple of Galileo, and microscopes.—R VII. 18C an 19C microscopes and instruments used in optical experiments.—R VIII. Larg 18C and 19C telescopes, two of them made by G.B. Amici of Modena.—R I contains mechanical instruments made in the 18C by order of the grand-du Pietro Leopoldo I, including models of several inventions by Galileo (an instr ment for measuring the acceleration of gravity, and a water pump).

The **Second Floor**, with a scientific library, was opened in 1975. Room I. 16C and 17C scientific instruments and the books that describe their manufacture or use; gnomons and astrolabes.—R 2. Large burning lens made by Bened. Bregans of Dresden and given by him to Cosimo III (used in the early 19C by Davy and Faraday to experiment with high temperature chemicals).—R 3. Instruments concerning fluids and gases (fountains, pumps, pneumatic machines).—R 4. Electrostatic machines. In a niche on the N. wall, large lodestone (of natural magnetic rock) given by Galileo to Ferdinando II.—In the next two rooms, anatomical models by Gius. Ferrini in wax, for use in obstetrics, and in the last room, the surgical instruments of Aless. Brambilla (1728–1800).—In the corridor, one of the first cylinder phonographs built in 1890 by Edison; acoustic horn designed by Vinc. Viviani; and the speaking trumpet of Ferdinando II.

Lungarno Gen. Diaz continues past the heavy neo-classical colonnade of the Camera di Commercio and P.za Mentana (monument to those who fell at Mentana in 1867). Just before the bridge is the garden of Pal. Malenchini. Via de' Benci leads away from the Arno towards Santa Croce, lined with a number of fine palaces described on p 195. *Palazzo Corsi*, at No. 6, formerly thought to be the work of Giul. da Sangallo, is now generally attrib. to Cronaca. It is an attractive small palace open to the public as the **Museo Horne** (Pl. 10; 4; adm see p 58). The interesting collection of 14C-16C paintings, sculpture, and decorative arts (notable furniture and majolica) was presented to the nation, along with his house, by the English art historian Herbert Percy Horne (1864–1916). Many of the contents have been restored after damage in the 1966 flood. The important collection of 17-18C drawings (Italian and English schools) is now housed in the Uffizi.

The courtyard has interesting capitals. The **Ground Floor** has not yet been reopened to the public. It contains bronzes and medals, a stone bas-relief of the Madonna and Child by *Iac. Sansovino*, and a Madonna and two angels by *Neri di Bicci*, which illustrates the extent to which a painting can be ruined by water.

First Floor. In each room there is a printed list of the contents. Room I. *Dosso Dossi*, Allegory of Music; (wall case) *Masaccio* (attrib.), Story of Julian (a tiny work, unfortunately very ruined).—Bozzetti by *Gian Lor. Bernini*, *Ammannati*, *Giambologna*, and *G. Fr. Rustici*.—Above a 'cassone' by Ammannati, *Pietro Lorenzetti*, SS John Gualberto, Catherine of Alexandria, and Margaret (a fragment of a polyptych).—*Bern. Daddi*, Madonna enthroned and Crucifixion (a diptych); *Simone Martini* (attrib.), Portable diptych of the Madonna and Child and Pietà; *Benozzo Gozzoli*, Deposition, a crowded composition left unfinished at the death of the painter (the colours have darkened with time); *Bart. di Giovanni*, Mythological scene.—R II. Paintings by *Fr. Furini*; *Benozzo Gozzoli* (attrib.), Ecce Homo; *Dom. Beccafumi*, Mythological scene; *Jac. del Casentino*, Madonna and Child; *15C Emilian School*, Madonna and Child with two angels; *Giotto*, *St Stephen (part of a polyptych), the most precious piece in the collection; *Filippino Lippi*, Scene from the Story of Esther (panel of a marriage-chest); *School of Lor. di Credi*, Tondo of the Nativity.—R III. *Nic. di Tommaso*, SS John the Evangelist and Paul; frontal of a 15C 'cassone' with a battle scene; *Maestro della Croce dei Da Filicaia'*, Madonna enthroned with Saints. Over the fireplace, *Desiderio da Settignano*, Relief of the head of the young St John the Baptist (replica of a work in the Bargello).—*13C Tuscan School*, Madonna and Child with a donor; *Beccafumi*, *Tondo of the Holy Family, with a beautiful contemporary frame. The statue of St Paul is by *Vecchietta*.

Second Floor. Room I contains several fine pieces of 15C furniture. *Ercole Roberti* (attrib.), St Sebastian; *Bart. della Gatta*, St Roch (restored); (in case) *Fil. Lippi*, Pietà (a pax); *Filippino Lippi*, Crucifix (a late work, much faded, once used as a processional standard); *Ant. Rossellino*, Madonna and Child, a relief in polychrome terracotta; *School of Sodoma*, Scene from the Battle of Anghiari (of historical interest as a contemporary copy of Leonardo's lost fresco in Palazzo Vecchio); *'Master of the Horne Triptych'* (14C Florentine), Madonna and Saints; *Lor. Monaco* (or his School), Portable Crucifix.—R II. *Neri di Bicci*, Archangel Raphael, Tobias, and St Jerome; *Beccafumi* (attrib.), Drunkenness of

Noah.—The Loggia on the top floor will be opened to the public after restoration.

Ponte alle Grazie (Pl. 10; 4) was first built in 1237 and called 'Ponte Rubaconte'. Its present name is taken from an oratory of Santa Maria delle Grazie which formerly stood on the bridge. Destroyed in 1944, it was replaced by a bridge of modern design. From here the view embraces Lungarno delle Grazie with the monumental entrance and two square towers of the Biblioteca Nazionale and the tall spire of Santa Croce; in the distance upstream can be seen the rural banks of the Arno; and across the river the tall Porta San Niccolò is conspicuous beyond the garden of Palazzo Demidoff (and above, on the skyline, stands San Miniato). At the S. end of the bridge is Piazza dei Mozzi.

Lungarno Serristori leads away from the Oltrarno district past a little public garden with a pavilion and a good monument (recently restored) to Niccolò Demidoff by Lor. Bartolini. *Palazzo Serristori* (1515; with a river front of 1873) was the home of the traitor Baglioni.

At No. 1 P.za dei Mozzi stands the large *Palazzo Bardini* built by the famous antiquarian and collector Stefano Bardini in 1883 to house his huge collection of works of art bequeathed to the city in 1923 as the **Museo Bardini** (Pl. 10; 4; adm see p 58). His eclectic collection includes architectural fragments, sculpture, paintings, the decorative arts, furniture, ceramics, carpets, arms and armour, musical instruments, etc. Many of the rooms were built specially to contain the

fine doorways, staircases, and ceilings from demolished buildings. The rooms are crowded with a miscellany of works (labelled systematically only on the first floor).

Ground Floor. From the vestibule is the entrance (r.) to Room 1 with numerous medieval and Renaissance architectural fragments. The bust of St John the Baptist is by *And. Sansovino*.—Beyond is R 2 with interesting classical sculpture including a sarcophagus with Medusa's head, used again in the Middle Ages.—RR 3-5 are closed for structural repairs.—Beyond R 6 with a well-head and more architectural fragments is a large room (7) formerly a courtyard, covered by a coffered ceiling with glass inserted in the panels. The medieval sculpture here includes a fine arch on the end wall between two good sarcophagi, and *Charity, a remarkable statue ascribed to *Tino da Camaino*. The Romanesque pulpit is decorated with mosaic.—In the small adjacent room (8) is a well-head of red Veronese marble, and the tomb of Riccardo Gattula (1417).—R 9 (off the vestibule) is approached through a fine doorway. Here are two chimneypieces (one from the bottega of Desiderio da Settignano, and the other, with the Este coat-of-arms, a Lombard work). The amusing putto was made for a fountain.—Stairs lead to R 10, a large vaulted room built in the form of a crypt to display tomb slabs and altar tombs. Here is an *Altarpiece attrib. to *And. della Robbia* and a relief after Donatello.

First Floor. A fine staircase leads up from R 9 to RR 11-13 which have been closed for restoration for a number of years. They contain tournament-shields and parade-armour, as well as battle-armour; also a rare battle-lantern such as those depicted in the frescoes in the Sala dei Cinquecento in Pal. Vecchio.—R 14, facing the stair-head, contains plaster and other reliefs, including a polychrome Madonna ascribed to *Donatello* (removed for restoration), and a

The Arno from outside Porta S. Niccolò, an engraving by Gius. Zocchi, 1754. (Museo di Firenze com'era)

painted tondo attrib. to *Ambr. Lorenzetti.*—R 15 (r.; beyond R 16), the Salone, is notable for its 17C carpets and portraits (including works by *Fr. Salviati*), and its furniture. Among the busts is one, at the end, of a girl with gilded hair. The central cases contain bronze medals, plaques, and statuettes. Also here, detached frescoes (from Pal. Pucci) by *Giov. da San Giovanni*, and two tondoes by *Volterrano.*—R 16, a hall furnished like a sacristy, with a fine chimneypiece and ceiling, contains a large Crucifix attrib. to a follower of Bernardo Daddi; *Michele Giambono*, St John the Baptist; *Giul. Bugiardini* (?), Madonna and Child; painted and gilded reliefs and statuettes.—R 17 continues the collection of furniture and coloured statuettes, and in R 18 is the delightful *Virgin Annunciate, perhaps the loveliest object in the collection, a terracotta figure of a young girl in a flowered robe (Sienese, 15C); here also are other painted figures including St Catherine of Siena (Sienese, beginning of 15C), and St John (13C). The painting of St Michael is by *Ant. Pollaiolo.*—R 19 displays old musical instruments (including a spinet made in Rome in 1577).—On the upper floor the GALLERIA CORSI (adm only with special permission) contains the large artistic bequests of Alice and Arnaldo Corsi (1939).—From R 18 a small staircase descends to R 20, the Sala del Crocifisso, named from a large realistic Crucifix (1387); here also are fine inlaid stalls (15C); 15-16C furniture, and a 17C wood model of Pisa Baptistery. The wood ceiling is notable.

At the end of P.za dei Mozzi, on Via de' Bardi, the three 13C palaces of the Mozzi family, owned by Ugo Bardini, son of Stefano, also an art collector, and left to the state in 1965, are described in Rte 19. LUNGARNO TORRIGIANI (Pl. 10; 4) follows the S. bank of the Arno back towards Ponte Vecchio. Next to the 16C *Palazzo Torrigiani* is a little public garden with the quaint Lutheran church (1899). Across the Arno can be seen the cupola of the Duomo with (r.) the towers of the Badia and the Bargello, and (l.) the campanile and tower of Pal. Vecchio. Beyond the garden of Pal. Canigiani the lungarno merges with Via de' Bardi (comp. Rte 19) at a road fork. The old Costa dei Magnoli runs uphill beneath an arch of Palazzo Tempi to Costa San Giorgio (p 181) also reached by steps at the end of Vicolo del Canneto. Via de' Bardi continues the foot of Ponte Vecchio, passing beneath the Corridoio Vasariano. Via Guicciardini, which leads l. to P.za Pitti, and the bronze fountain on the corner are described on p 99. Here the houses front the Arno; **Borgo San Jacopo** (Pl. 9; 2), busy with traffic, continues parallel to the river. The Borgo, an ancient road leading out of the city, is mentioned as early as 1182. By a modern hotel a terrace opens onto the river opposite the campanile of SS Apostoli, with a good view l. and r. of Ponte Santa Trinita and Ponte Vecchio. Amongst the buildings here rebuilt after the war some restored medieval towers survive. On the corner of the pretty Via Toscanella *Torre Marsili di Borgo* (No. 17) is a fine towerhouse awaiting restoration. Above the door is an Annunciation from the Della Robbia workshop and two damaged angels. On the r. of the road is the church of SAN JACOPO SOPR'ARNO (Pl. 9; 2), with an 11C portico of three arches transported here in 1529 from the demolished church of San Donato a Scopeto. In the Baroque interior the romanesque columns were revealed (with questionable taste) during restoration work. The church (which had a river gate) is used by a cultural organization for concerts and exhibitions. The Borgo ends in the busy Piazza Frescobaldi with a pretty corner fountain. Via Maggio, described in Rte 19, leads inland.

The Arno is regained at the end of Ponte Santa Trinita. The elaborate *Palazzo Frescobaldi* (r.) was reconstructed in the 17C. LUNGARNO GUICCIARDINI (Pl. 9; 1, 2) provides a splendid view of the opposite bank of the river (with the imposing Pal. Corsini) as far as the park of the Cascine. Beyond the red façade of Pal. Capponi (No. 1) is Via dei Coverelli with a palace with restored graffiti. The famous garden (no adm) of the yellow-coloured *Palazzo Guicciardini* (No. 7) includes a magnolia tree planted in 1787. *Palazzo Lanfredini* (No. 9), by Baccio d'Agnolo, has bright graffiti decoration (restored). Beyond the Presbyterian church (No. 19), Ponte alla Carraia is regained.

Lungarno Soderini (Pl. 9; 1) continues beyond the bridge past a little pavilion-house, with a view of the huge church of San Frediano in Cestello and the Seminary. The diagonal stone dike in the river, the Pescaia di Santa Rosa, was built at the same time as the water mills on the Arno. In P.za del Cestello is the rough-hewn façade of the church of San Frediano (p 177) and the *Granaio di Cosimo III* (1695) a good building by G.B. Foggini (now used as a barracks). From the piazza is a view across the river of Ognissanti and its bell tower, with the campanile of S.M. Novella behind. Beyond the modern Ponte Vespucci is the wall of Porta San Frediano (see Rte 19).

18   THE OLTRARNO: SANTO SPIRITO AND SANTA MARIA DEL CARMINE

In the characteristic district on the S. bank of the Arno known as the 'Oltrarno', the two most important churches are Santo Spirito and Santa Maria del Carmine, and around them focuses the life of this part of the city. From the S. end of Ponte Santa Trinita Via di Santo Spirito and Via del Presto (l.) lead shortly to the church of ***Santo Spirito** (Pl. 9; 1; closed 12-15.30). Its modest 18C façade fronts a pretty square. On the left is the rough stone wall of the convent Refectory, and behind rises Baccio d'Agnolo's slender campanile (1503).

The Augustinian foundation dates from 1250 and the first church was begun in 1292. The convent became a centre of intellectual life in the city at the end of the 14C. In 1428 *Brunelleschi* was commissioned to design a new church, the project for which he had completed by 1434-35. However building was not begun until 1444 just two years before the great architect's death. Construction continued for most of the 15C, first under the direction of his collaborator *Ant. Manetti*, and then by *Giov. da Gaiole*, *Giul. Sandrini*, and *Giov. di Mariano*. *Salvi d'Andrea* completed the cupola in 1481.—A crucifix found in the convent in 1963 has been identified by most scholars as the one known to have been made by Michelangelo for the Augustinians. It is now displayed in the Casa Buonarroti.

The *INTERIOR was designed by *Brunelleschi* but mostly executed after his death and modified in the late 15C. While it remains a superb creation of the Renaissance, remarkable for its harmonious proportions, its solemn colour, and the perspective of the colonnades and vaulted aisles, it also points the way forward to the more elaborate and less delicate 16C style of architecture. The plan is a Latin cross, with a dome over the crossing. The colonnade, whose 35 columns in pietra forte (including the four piers of the dome) have fine Corinthian capitals with imposts above, is carried round the transepts and E. end forming an unbroken arcade. Around the walls is a continuous line of 38 chapels formed by semi-circular niches. Although in itself an admirable Baroque work, the elaborate HIGH ALTAR, with a ciborium in pietre dure beneath a high baldacchino, disturbs the harmony of the architecture. It was begun in the early 17C by *Giov. Caccini*. The church was restored in 1976–81.

The handsome interior façade was designed by *Salvi d'Andrea* (1483–87). The stained glass oculus is from a cartoon by *Perugino*. The side chapels contain interesting works of art which are, however, very poorly lit (difficult to see on a dark day or late in the afternoon). Coin-operated lights have been installed in some chapels.—SOUTH AISLE CHAPELS. 1st altar (1), *Pier Fr. di Jac. Foschi*, Immaculate Conception; 2. Pietà, a free copy of Michelangelo's famous sculpture in St Peter's, by *Nanni di Baccio Bigio*; 3. St Nicholas of Tolentino, a polychrome wood statue by *Nanni Unghero* (on a design by *Iac. Sansovino*), and two angels painted by *Franciabigio*; 4. *Giov. Stradano*, Christ expelling the money-changers from the Temple; 5. *Aless. Gherardini*, Coronation of the Virgin and Saints. Beyond the side door, 6. *Passignano*, Martyrdom of St Stephen, a good work; 7. Tobias and the Archangel, a large altarpiece in stucco and marble by *Giov. Baratta*.

SOUTH TRANSEPT CHAPELS. 8. *Fr. Curradi*, Crucifixion; 9. *Pier Fr. di Jac. Foschi*, Transfiguration; 10. Madonna del Soccorso, a painting of the early 15C, recently attrib. to that *'Master of the Johnson Nativity'*. Above a polychrome marble altar (11) by *Buontalenti* is a 14C wood crucifix from the earlier church; 12. *Filippino Lippi*, *Madonna and Child, with the young St John, Saints, and Tanai and Nanna dei Nerli, the donors. In the background is a view of Palazzo dei Nerli near Porta San Frediano. This is one of Filippino's best and most mature works. The Vision of St Bernard by Perugino (now in Munich) has been replaced by a beautiful (and almost indistinguishable) copy (13) by *Felice Ficherelli*; 14. *Giov. Camillo Sagrestani*, Marriage of the Virgin (1713), his best work. The sarcophagus of Neri Capponi is by *Bern. Rossellino* (1458).

CHAPELS AT THE EAST END. 15. Madonna and Saints, a good painting in the style of *Lor. di Credi*; 16. *Maso di Banco*, Madonna and Child with Saints (a polyptych); 17. *Aurelio Lomi*, Epiphany; 18. *Aless. Allori*, Martyred Saints (1574), with a predella including an interesting view of Palazzo Pitti before it was enlarged; 19. *Aless. Allori*, *Christ and the adulteress, a beautiful painting foreshadowing the 17C; 20. *Jac. Vignali*, Mystical Communion of the Blessed Clara of Montefalco; 21. *15C Florentine School*, Annunciation (showing the influence of the German and Flemish schools); 22. *Florentine Master of the late-15C*, Nativity.

NORTH TRANSEPT CHAPELS. 23. *'Maestro di Santo Spirito'* (late 15C), Madonna enthroned between SS John the Evangelist and Bartholomew; 24. *St Monica and Augustinian nuns in black habits, traditionally attrib. to *Botticini*, but now thought by many scholars to be the work of *Verrocchio*. It is a very unusual and beautifully composed painting. 25. *Cosimo Rosselli*, Madonna enthroned between Saints; the Cappella Corbinelli (26) has sumptuous marble decoration and an *Altarpiece sculpted by *And. Sansovino*. 27. *Trinity with SS Mary Magdalen and Catherine, a good painting of the late 15C, attrib. to the *'Maestro di Santo Spirito'*; 28. *Raff. dei Carli*, *Madonna enthroned with Saints; 29. Way to Calvary, copy by *Mich. Ghirlandaio* of a painting by Ridolfo del Ghirlandaio, and a stained glass window showing the Incredulity of St Thomas.

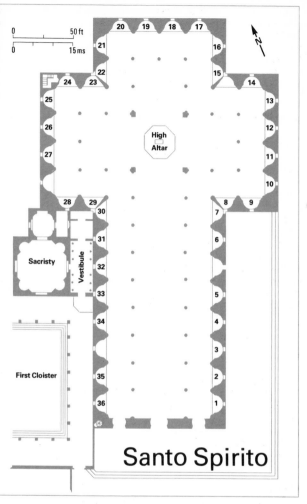

Santo Spirito

NORTH AISLE CHAPELS. 30. *School of Fra' Bartolomeo*, Madonna
nthroned and Saints. The marble bust of Tom. Cavalcanti by
Iontòrsoli has been recently restored. 31. Copy by *Fr. Petrucci*
f an important altarpiece of the Madonna enthroned with Saints by
.osso Fiorentino, removed to the Pitti (p 102).—A door (32) beneath
ιe organ, leads into a grandiose *VESTIBULE* with 12 Corinthian col-
ιmns supporting a barrel vault elaborately coffered, built by *Cronaca*
ι 1491. The adjoining *SACRISTY* is an octagonal chamber inspired by
ιe architectural works of Brunelleschi, with Corinthian pilasters,
esigned by *Giul. da Sangallo* (1489), with a lantern and dome ex-
:uted on a model of *Ant. del Pollaiolo* and *Salvi d'Andrea* (1495).

Off the vestibule is the FIRST CLOISTER by *Alfonso* and *Giulio Parig* (early 17C).—In the remaining chapels in the N. aisle: 33. *Rid. d Ghirlandaio* (attrib.), Madonna with St Anne and other Saints; 34 *Rutilio Manetti*, St Thomas of Villanova; 35. Copy by *Taddeo Lar dini* (1579) of a statue of the risen Christ by Michelangelo in th church of the Minerva in Rome; 36. *Pier Fr. di Jac. Foschi*, Resurree tion.

The SECOND CLOISTER, was built by *Ammannati* c. 1565. It is now part of military barracks (no adm). Off the cloister is the CAPPELLA CORSINI (also close to the public) with the Gothic tombs of Tom. Corsini (d 1366) and of Neri Co sini, Bp of Fiesole (d 1377) and a contemporary fresco of the Resurrection ar two Saints.

To the left of the church, at No. 29, is the entrance to the REFECTORY (adm se p 57), the only part of the 14C convent to survive. Above a fresco of the La Supper (almost totally ruined) is a huge *Crucifixion (also damaged), both them painted c. 1360–65. They are attrib. to *And. Orcagna* and his bottega, pre bably including his brother *Nardo di Cione*. A partial restoration after years neglect revealed one of the most dramatic scenes of the Crucifixion in 14 Florentine painting. Here is displayed the **Fondazione Salvatore Romano**, left the city in 1946, with an interesting collection of sculpture (including mar works from the Romanesque period). Beneath the fresco, two sea lions (3 Romanesque works from Campania, flank a polychrome high relief (5) of th Madonna of the Misericordia (15C Sienese school).—Against the far wa Madonna and Child (8), large polychrome relief attrib. to *Jac. della Querci* and a fountain (15) attrib. to *Ammannati*.—On the end wall the two damage fragments of bas reliefs (21) found in Padua are thought to be works Donatello from the church of the Santo. The stone portal is signed by *Natale Ragusa* (1471).—In the centre of the room: Angel (44) and Virtue (38), both fir statuettes by *Tino da Camaino*; numerous 11C sculptural fragments an primitive stone reliefs; and a marble font (45) from Torcello (6C).

Palazzo Guadagni in Piazza Santo Spirito, from a lithograph by A. Durand, 1863. (Museo di Firenze com'era)

PIAZZA SANTO SPIRITO is one of the most attractive small squares in ie city, planted with a few trees, and the scene of a little daily market. is the centre of a distinctive district with numerous medieval houses nd artisans' workshops. The most handsome house in the piazza is *Palazzo Guadagni* (No. 10), probably built by Cronaca c. 1505. Its leasing, well-proportioned façade with a top floor loggia became the model for many 16C Florentine mansions.

Borgo Tegolaio which leads out of one corner of the piazza is a medieval street hich takes its name from the brick factories which were once here. In *Via delle aldaie* the wool-dyers had their workshops.

Via Sant'Agostino, a local shopping street, leads from Piazza Santo pirito across Via de' Serragli (Rte 19) into Via Santa Monaca. On the orner is a tabernacle with the Madonna enthroned and Saints by Lor. Bicci (1427). In Via dell'Ardiglione (l.) a plaque on a little house ist beyond the arch across the road records the birthplace of Filippo ippi in 1406. Via Santa Monica ends in Piazza del Carmine, a large quare used as a car park. Here is the interesting rough stone façade of ie church of **Santa Maria del Carmine** (Pl. 9; 1; closed 12-15.30), amous for its frescoes by Masaccio in the Cappella Brancacci. A 'armelite convent was founded here in 1250 and the first church egun in 1268. This was almost completely ruined by fire in 1771 when ie sacristy and two chapels alone escaped destruction. The huge main iterior was rebuilt in an undistinguished late Baroque style (1782). he interest of the church lies almost exclusively in the small **BRAN-ACCI CHAPEL at the end of the r. transept. The frescoes, illustrating ie life of St Peter, were commissioned by Felice Brancacci, a rich lorentine merchant and statesman, c. 1424, from *Masolino* and *Masaccio*.

Restoration of the chapel and frescoes, begun in 1981, is expected to take c. 2 s. Meanwhile, visitors are not allowed in the chapel, but some frescoes can still e seen through the scaffolding.

The design of the whole fresco cycle may be due to *Masolino* who probably orked on the frescoes in 1425 and again in 1427 together with his pupil *Masac-o* who seems to have taken over full responsibility for them after Masolino's eparture for Rome in 1428. Later that year Masaccio himself broke off work oruptly on the frescoes for an unknown reason, and left for Rome, where, by ie end of the year, he had died at the early age of 27. Brancacci was exiled from lorence in 1436 as an enemy of the Medici and the cycle was only completed ome 50 years later by *Filippino Lippi* (c. 1480–85) who carefully integrated his yle with that of Masaccio, possibly following an earlier design. In 1690 the iapel was saved from demolition through the efforts of the Accademia del isegno and Vittoria della Rovere, wife of Cosimo III. In the 18C the lunettes id vault of the chapel, probably frescoed by Masolino, were destroyed.

The frescoes by *Masaccio* were at once recognized as a masterpiece id profoundly influenced the Florentine Renaissance. All the major 'tists of the 15C came here to study the frescoes which combine a erfect application of the new rules of perspective with a remarkable se of chiaroscuro. 'Masaccio...like Giotto a century earlier—himself ie Giotto of an artistically more propitious world—was, as an artist, great master of the significant, and, as a painter, endowed to the ighest degree with a sense of tactile values, and with a skill in render-g them. In a career of but a few years he gave to Florentine painting ie direction it pursued to the end.' (Bernard Berenson, 'The Italian ainters of the Renaissance'.)

The frescoes are arranged in two registers. UPPER ROW: (r. to l.) On the entrance arch, *Masolino*, Temptation of Adam and Eve.—*Masolino*, St Peter, accompanied by St John, brings Tabitha to life, and heals a lame man (with a charming view of Florence in the background). The figures on the extreme left and some details in the background may be by the hand of *Masaccio*.—On the r. of the altar, *Masaccio*, *St Peter Baptising; (l. of the altar): *Masolino*, St Peter preaching.—*Masaccio*, *The Tribute money, perhaps the painter's masterpiece. Three episodes are depicted in the same scene: in the centre, Christ, surrounded by the Apostles, outside the gates of the city is asked by an official (with his back to us) to pay the tribute money owing to the city. Christ indicates to St Peter a lake, and (on the l.) Peter is shown extracting the money from the mouth of a fish at the side of lake. The scene on the r. shows Peter handing over the tribute money to the official. The head of Christ has been attrib. by some scholars to *Masolino*.—On the entrance arch: *Masaccio*, *Expulsion from Paradise, one of the most moving works of the Renaissance.—LOWER Row: (r. to l.). On the entrance arch, *Filippino Lippi*, *Release of St Peter from prison.—*Filippino Lippi*, SS Peter and Paul before the proconsul, and Crucifixion of St Peter.—On r. of the altar, *Masaccio*, SS Peter and John distributing alms; (l. of the altar) *Masaccio*, *St Peter, followed by St John, healing the sick with his shadow.—*Masaccio*, *St Peter enthroned with portraits of friars, his last work; the next half of this panel was begun by *Masaccio* and finished by *Filippino*. shows Peter bringing to life the Emperor's nephew (the faces executed by Masaccio are more strongly illuminated; Filippino's figures are, in contrast, flatter and stand as if in shadow).—On the entrance arch *Filippino Lippi*, St Peter in prison visited by St Paul (on a design by *Masaccio*).—The altarpiece, the Madonna del Carmine, is a Tuscan Byzantine work (mid-13C).

In the APSE of the church is a fine monument to Piero Soderini (d 1522) by *Bened. da Rovezzano*. At the end of the left transept is the sumptuous *CHAPEL OF SANT'ANDREA CORSINI (d 1373) by *Gherardo Silvani* (1675–83), with a ceiling by *Luca Giordano* and marble reliefs by *G.B. Foggini*.—The Gothic SACRISTY (with a 15C statuette of the Madonna over the door) contains a choir chapel frescoed with scenes from the life of St Cecilia by a master influenced by Bicci di Lorenzo. Among the paintings and frescoes here is a polyptych (entrance wall) attrib. to And. da Firenze.—The CLOISTER (early 17C; not always open in the afternoon) surrounds a well and four tall trees. The rooms off the cloister display frescoes detached from the cloister buildings. In the first room, once part of the Refectory: *Aless. Allori*, Last Supper and monochrome frescoes. In the 2nd room, detached fresco fragments from the Cappella di San Girolamo, by *Starnina*; *Fil. Lippi*, the *Rule of the Order (partly destroyed); Crucifixion, beautiful work by an unknown hand; *Giov. da Milano*, Madonna enthroned with Saints. In the 3rd room (where concerts of the Musicus Concentus are held) detached frescoes from the Cappella della Passione attrib. to *Lippo Fiorentino*. On the end wall, remains of a Last Supper by *Fr. Vanni*.

19   THE OLTRARNO: PORTA SAN FREDIANO TO PORTA SAN NICCOLÒ

Porta San Frediano (Pl. 8; 2), and the adjoining stretch of wall with crenellations which runs to the Torrino di Santa Rosa on the banks of the Arno, is the best preserved part of the last circle of walls built by

he Commune in 1284–1333 (comp. the Plan on p 30). The Gate, built
n 1324 (perhaps by And. Pisano), with its high tower, protected the
oad for Pisa. It preserves interesting ironwork, and its huge wooden
doors, decorated with nail heads, with their old locks. High up on the
ower is the emblem of the city in stone. By the Torrino di S. Rosa a
arge 19C tabernacle protects a fresco of the Pietà (16C; very difficult
o see).

BORGO SAN FREDIANO (Pl. 8; 2) gives its name to a characteristic
district with numerous artisans' houses and workshops. Among the
ocal shops are a number of simple antique shops in the side streets.
On the corner of Via S. Giovanni is a tabernacle with the Madonna
and Child with angels (15C). Farther on (l.) is the bare stone exterior
of the large church of SAN FREDIANO IN CESTELLO (Pl. 9; 1), with its
main entrance on the Arno. The church was rebuilt in 1680–89 by Ant.

*he Oltrarno c. 1472, a detail from the 'Pianta della
'atena'*

Maria Ferri. Its fine dome is a conspicuous feature of this part of the city. It contains (r. transept), Virgin in Glory with Saints by *Fr. Currradi*, and (l. transept), *Jac. del Sellaio*, Crucifixion and Martyrdom of St Lawrence. N. side, 1st altar, *Lor. Lippi*, Martyrdom of St Andrew (1639), 3rd altar, Madonna and Child in polychrome wood by the 14C Pisan-Florentine School.—Next to the church is the huge Seminary, and, on the r., opens Piazza del Carmine with the fine bare stone façade of its church (described on p 175). The Borgo ends near the foot of Ponte alla Carraia.

Via de' Serragli (Pl. 9; 1), a long straight road, first laid out in the 13C, leads away from the Arno past a number of handsome 17-18C palaces. Beyond the crossroads with Via S. Monica (which leads r. to S.M. del Carmine, p 175) and Via S. Agostino (which leads l. to Santo Spirito, p 171), Via de' Serragli continues, now lined with simple low medieval houses, through a local shopping area. Farther on, Via del Campuccio diverges r. skirting the garden wall of *Palazzo Torrigiani*. This is the biggest private garden in Florence (no adm) created by Pietro Torrigiani (1773–1848). The fantastic neo-Gothic tower was built by Gaetano Baccani in 1821 as an astronomical observatory. Via del Campuccio ends in Piazza Tasso (Pl. 8; 4) where, on fine days, old furniture etc. is sometimes sold from lorries by dealers who drive up from the S. of Italy. Here in a ramshackle mews between the Torrigiani garden wall and the defensive wall built by Cosimo I, horses and carriages are stabled when not serving as horse cabs for tourists.

From Piazza N. Sauro at the S. end of Ponte alla Carraia VIA SANTO SPIRITO (Pl. 9; 1) continues parallel to the Arno. Here on the r. a school now occupies the 17C Pal. Rinuccini and *Palazzo Manetti* (No 23), with a 15C façade. This was the home of Sir Horace Mann in 1740–86 while serving as English envoy to the Tuscan court. His famous correspondence with Horace Walpole provides a remarkable picture of 18C Florence. Lord and Lady Holland lived in the neighbouring Palazzo Feroni, with G.F. Watts as their guest in 1844–47. *Palazzo Frescobaldi* (No. 11-13) has a very long façade (recently well restored) with several interior courtyards and a garden (view of Santo Spirito), and one flank supported on 'sporti' in Via de Coverelli. Via S. Spirito ends at a busy intersection of narrow streets near the foot of Ponte Santa Trinita.

Via Maggio (Pl. 9; 2, 4) leads away from the Arno. Its name (from 'Maggiore') is a reminder of its origin as the principal and widest street of the Oltrarno. It was opened soon after Ponte Santa Trinita was built in 1252, and it became a fashionable residential street after the grand-dukes moved to Palazzo Pitti in the 16C. It now has a number of antique shops. On the l., *Palazzo Ricasoli* (No. 7), the largest palace on Via Maggio, was built at the end of the 15C or beginning of the 16C with a fine courtyard. On the r. is *Palazzo di Bianca Cappello* (No. 26) with good graffiti decoration attrib. to Bernardino Poccetti (c. 1579). The house was built by the grand-duke Francesco for the beautiful Venetian girl Bianca Cappello who was first his mistress and afterwards his wife. Opposite, *Palazzo Ridolfi* (No. 13) built in the late 16C (attrib. to Santi di Tito), stands next to *Palazzo di Cosimo Ridolfi*, a small palace built at the beginning of the 15C. The numerous narrow old streets on the left of the road lead to Piazza Pitti (see below). Farther on is the worn façade of *Palazzo Commenda di Firenze* (No. 42), built in the late 14C, and reconstructed in the 16C.

Via Maggio ends in Piazza San Felice. No. 8, is the 15C CAS. GUIDI, where Robert and Elizabeth Barrett Browning rented a flat of

the first floor and lived after their secret marriage in 1846 until
Elizabeth's death in 1861 (inscription; shown to visitors Tues-Fri
16-19). Here both poets wrote many of their most important works
and were visited by W.S. Landor, Anthony Trollope, Bulwer-Lytton,
Nathaniel Hawthorne and 'Father Prout' (F.S. Mahony), the Roman
correspondent for Dickens' 'Daily News'. Their son 'Pen' who was
born here in 1849 purchased the house after their death. The apart-
ment has been owned by the Browning Institute since 1971. It contains
a few mementoes of the Brownings. The collection is to be augmented
and the rooms furnished, and a study centre opened. **San Felice** (Pl. 9;
3) is a Gothic church with a Renaissance façade by *Michelozzo* (1457).

INTERIOR. The first half of the nave contains a closed gallery supported by
eight columns and a pretty vault. SOUTH SIDE: 1st altar, remains of a fresco of the
Pietà, attrib. to *Nic. Gerini* (interesting for its iconography); above the side
door, large *Crucifix from the workshop of *Giotto*; 5th altar, Pietà, terracotta
group attrib. to *Cieco da Gambassi*; 6th altar, Madonna and Saints by *Rid.* and
Mich. Ghirlandaio; 7th altar, lunette fresco of the Virgin of the Sacred Girdle
(late 14C Florentine).—In the presbytery the altarpiece has a 15C Madonna and
Child and two Saints of the 16C.—NORTH SIDE: 7th altar, fresco by *Giov. da San
Giovanni* (the angels are by *Volterrano*); 6th altar, triptych by *Neri di Bicci*
beneath a frescoed lunette of the 14C; 1st altar, triptych by a follower of *Botticelli*.
   Via Romana (Pl. 9; 3), one of the most important thoroughfares of the Oltrarno, continues S.W. to *Porta Romana,* a well preserved gate built in 1327 on a
design by And. Orcagna. Just out of P.za S. Felice, at No. 17 (l.) *Palazzo Torrigiani* was built in 1775 by Gaspare M. Paoletti as a natural history museum. It
is known as 'LA SPECOLA' from the astronomical Observatory founded here by
the grand-duke Pietro Leopoldo. Here, in 1814 Sir Humphry Davy and Michael
Faraday used Galileo's 'great burning glass' to explode the diamond. It is now
the seat of a ZOOLOGICAL MUSEUM (adm see p 58) with a comprehensive natural
history display, and a remarkable collection of anatomical models in wax, many
of them by Clemente Susini in 1775–1814.

To the left is Piazza Pitti dominated by the huge Pal. Pitti described
in Rte 8. The pretty row of houses facing the palace includes No. 16,
the home of Paolo dal Pozzo Toscanelli (1397–1482), the famous
scientist and greatest geographer of his time. While staying at No. 21
in 1868 Dostoievsky wrote 'The Idiot'. Via Guicciardini described in
Rte 7 leads past the church of Santa Felìcita (p 99) to Ponte Vecchio.
Here begins ***Via de' Bardi** (Pl. 10; 1), named from the palaces on the
street which were the residence of the Bardi, one of the richest mercan-
tile families in medieval Florence, who, however, were bankrupt by
1340. Among the old houses at the end of the bridge destroyed in 1944
was the Casa Ambrogi, guest house of Horace Mann, where Gray and
Walpole stayed in 1740. At the fork with Lungarno Torrigiani can be
seen the tall Porta San Niccolò (see below). Via de' Bardi continues on
a winding course past a series of noble town houses. On the l. is the
rough stone façade of *Palazzo Capponi delle Rovinate* (No. 36) with a
remarkable courtyard. The palace was built for Niccolò da Uzzano in
the early 15C. *Palazzo Canigiani* (No. 30), with its garden across the
road, has a courtyard (in need of repair) attrib. to Michelozzo. At No.
24 is the little church of *Santa Lucia dei Magnoli* (open only for even-
song), with a terracotta by Buglioni over the door, and inside (1st altar
l.), St Lucy by Pietro Lorenzetti, with an Annunciation at the sides,
ascribed to Iac. del Sellaio. A photographic reproduction of the
famous altarpiece painted for this church by *Dom. Veneziano* (now in
the Uffizi) has been placed here.—Opposite, the pretty old Costa

Scarpuccia climbs up the hill between gardens to Costa San Giorgio. Via de' Bardi ends in Piazza dei Mozzi. On the bend are the fine old PALAZZI DEI MOZZI (Pl. 10; 4) built in the 13-14C and among the most noble private houses of medieval Florence. The severe façades in pietra forte have arches on the ground floor. The Mozzi were one of the richest Florentine families in the 13C, but, like the Bardi, they too lost most of their wealth in the 14C. Gregory X was their guest here in 1273 when he came to Florence to arrange a peace between the Guelfs and Ghibellines. The huge garden up to the walls was acquired by the Mozzi in the 16C. The building, garden, and Villa Bardini were left indirectly to the State in 1965, together with a vast collection of decorative arts (including 16C and 17C furniture), and marble architectural fragments recovered during the demolition of the old centre of the city, by Ugo Bardini. There are long-term plans to open a museum here. The piazza opens out onto the Arno with, at No. 1, the Museo Bardini, left to the Commune by Ugo's father Stefano, described on p 168.

*VIA DI SAN NICCOLÒ, another narrow street of medieval houses, continues beyond Piazza de' Mozzi. On the l. *Palazzo Alemanni* (No. 68) was built in the 14C and 15C and reconstructed later. It is decorated with a row of little demons, copies from Giambologna. Beyond, at a bend in the road with local shops, is the church of **San Niccolò sopr' Arno** (Pl. 10; 4), founded in the 11C and rebuilt at the end of the 14C.

In the tall INTERIOR, with an open timber roof, several interesting frescoes were found beneath the 16C altars during restoration work after 1966. On the W. wall, *School of Neri di Bicci*, St James the Apostle. SOUTH SIDE: 1st altar, St Anthony Abbot (15C); 3rd altar, Pope St Gregory (15C).—In the SACRISTY (off the S. side), *Madonna della Cintola, a beautiful fresco of the late 15C Florentine school (attrib. to Baldovinetti), within a tabernacle in pietra serena by the bottega of Michelozzo. The Trinity and Saints by *Neri di Bicci* and the Madonna and Saints by *Bicci di Lorenzo* have been removed for restoration. Also here, *Poppi*, two small paintings of St Michael and St Gabriel Archangel.—In the chap. to the l. of the high altar, *Empoli*, St John the Baptist.—NORTH SIDE: 3rd altar, *Fr. Curradi*, Miracle of St Nicholas; 2nd altar, Sinopia for the fresco of *St Ansano, attrib. to *Fr. d'Antonio* on the 1st altar. An altarpiece of the Martyrdom of St Catherine by *Aless. Allori* has been removed for restoration.

At the end of Via S. Miniato (r.) can be seen the pretty 14C *Porta San Miniato* in the walls. Via San Niccolò continues past simple houses with workshops on the ground floor, to the massive **Porta San Niccolò** (Pl. 11; 3), whose high tower remains intact. Built c. 1340, it was restored in 1979 (the staircase which leads to the top is sometimes accessible with special permission). From here a ramp leads up the hill towards San Miniato (see Rte 20).

20 FORTE DI BELVEDERE AND THE BASILICA OF SAN MINIATO

San Miniato can be reached directly from the Station or P.za del Duomo by Bus No. 13 (red) which traverses Viale dei Colli (Viale Machiavelli, Viale Galileo, and Viale Michelangelo). The church can also be reached on foot by the steps from Porta San Niccolò (Pl. 11; 3). However, for those with time, the following route on foot is highly recommended (and Bus 13 can be taken from San Miniato to return to the centre of the city).

From the little piazza adjoining Piazza Santa Felìcita (see p 99) the narrow Costa San Giorgio (Pl. 10; 3) winds up the hill towards Forte di Belvedere. At the fork with Costa Scarpuccia (a beautiful road which leads downhill to Via de' Bardi, comp. Rte 19) is the church of San Giorgio sulla Costa (or *Spirito Santo*; Pl. 10; 3; being restored).

The Baroque Interior by *G.B. Foggini* (1705) is one of the best in Florence. The altarpieces are by *Tom. Redi, Jac. Vignali*, and *Passignano*, and on the ceiling the Glory of St George is by *Aless. Gherardini*. On the r. of the altar an early work by *Giotto* (*Madonna and Child with two angels) has not yet been returned here since its restoration.

Farther up the street is the house (No. 19; with a portrait on the façade) purchased by Galileo for his son Vincenzio. Here the great scientist was visited in 1620 by Ferdinando II, under whose protection Galileo was able to live in Florence from 1610 until his death. On the l. is the Villa Bardini with a fine park recently left to the State (comp. p 179). The pretty Costa San Giorgio continues between the high walls of rural villas to (left) Porta San Giorgio (Pl. 10; 5), with a fresco by Bicci di Lorenzo, and, on the outer face, the copy of a stone relief of St George (1284; original in Pal. Vecchio). Dating from 1260 it is part of the walls built to protect the Oltrarno in 1258 (comp. the Plan on p 30), and is the oldest gate to have survived in the city. Here is the entrance to ***Forte di Belvedere** (or *di S. Giorgio*; Pl. 10; 5), a huge fortress designed by Buontalenti (probably using plans drawn up by Don Giovanni de' Medici) in the shape of a six-pointed star.

It was built by order of Ferdinando I in 1590, ostensibly for the defence of the city, but in reality to dominate the supposedly republican citizens. Entered from the Bòboli Gardens by a secret door, guarded day and night until 1850 by a sentry, it remained inaccessible to the public until 1958. It can now also be visited from the Bòboli Gardens (comp. p 110). From the ramparts (adm 9-20) there is a splendid *View in every direction. The Palazzetto at the centre of the fortress has a loggia and two façades, one facing the city and one facing south. The interior is only opened for large exhibitions which are held periodically in this magnificent setting.

Here begins *Via di San Leonardo (Pl. 10; 5) one of the most beautiful and best-preserved roads on the outskirts of Florence. It leads through countryside past villas and their gardens between olive groves behind high walls. A short way along on the left is the church of San Leonardo in Arcetri (Pl. 10; 5; open only for services; at other times ring at No. 25), founded in the 11C.

The church contains a celebrated *Pulpit of the early 13C removed from the church of San Pier Scheraggio, with beautiful bas-reliefs. Over the high altar, *Lor. di Niccolò*, Triptych of the Madonna and Child with Saints. Other paintings include the Madonna of the Sacred Girdle with Saints, and an Annunciation with angels and Saints, both by *Neri di Bicci*, and Tobias and the angel, by the *'Maestro di San Miniato'*.

After c. 600 metres Via S. Leonardo crosses Viale Galileo (part of Viale dei Colli, see below) just after a house (No. 64) on the r. where a plaque records the stay of Tchaikovsky in 1878. Beyond Viale Galileo Via San Leonardo continues; at a fork Via Viviani branches left and ascends past the *Observatory* at Arcetri (students are sometimes admitted) and the imposing 14C *Torre del Gallo* to reach the long village of **Pian de' Giullari** (c. 2 km from Forte di Belvedere). *Villa il Gioiello* (No. 42) was the house where the aged Galileo lived, practically as a prisoner, from 1631 until his death in 1642. Here he wrote some of his most important tracts and was visited by Evangelista Torricelli, Vinc. Viviani, Thomas

Hobbes, and possibly also Milton. The house and farm, with lovely gardens, are owned by the State and there are long-term plans to open them to the public.

From Forte di Belvedere *VIA DI BELVEDERE (Pl. 10; 6), a pictures-que country lane with olive trees, follows the straight line of the city walls built in 1258, reinforced in 1299–1333, and again in the 16C. Even though greatly reduced in height they are the best stretch of for-tifications to survive in Florence. The path descends steeply with a fine view of the defensive towers and the tall Porta San Niccolò beyond. At the bottom by *Porta San Miniato*, a simple 14C arch in the walls, Via del Monte alle Croci returns uphill (view back of the walls). This road (or the stepped Via di San Salvatore al Monte) continues up to the busy Viale Galileo, across which a monumental flight of steps or a winding road lead up past a cemetery (1839) to *San Miniato al Monte (Pl. 11; 7; closed in winter 12-14, in summer 13-15). The finest of all Tuscan Romanesque basilicas, with a famous façade, it is one of the most beautiful churches in Italy. Together with the Baptistery and San Lorenzo it was the most important church in 11C Florence. Its posi-tion on a green hill above the city is incomparable.

The deacon Minias was a member of the early Christian community from the East who settled in Florence. A legend even suggests he was an oriental prince, the son of the King of Armenia. He is thought to have been martyred c. 250 dur-ing the persecutions of the emperor Decius, and buried on this hillside. The pre-sent church, built in 1013 by Bishop Hildebrand, is on the site of a shrine protec-ting the tomb of St Minias. A Benedictine Cluniac monastery, founded here at the same time by the emperor Henry II, was one of the first important religious houses in Tuscany.

The *FAÇADE, begun c. 1090, is built of white and dark greenish marble in a beautiful geometrical design reminiscent of the Baptistery. Above the exquisite little window in the form of an aedicule is a 13C mosaic (restored) of Christ between the Virgin and St Minias, the warrior-martyr. In the tympanum, supported by two small figures in relief, the marble inlay is repeated in the motifs of the pavement in-side. It is crowned by an eagle holding a bale of cloth, emblem of the 'Arte di Calimala' who looked after the fabric of the building.

The very fine *INTERIOR built in 1018–63 is practically in its original state. Its design is unique in Florentine church architecture, with a raised choir above a large hall crypt. (The Sacristan will switch on lights on request). Many of the capitals of the columns come from Roman temples in the city. In the PAVEMENT are tomb slabs, and, in the centre of the nave, seven superb marble intarsia *Panels (1207) with signs of the zodiac and animal motifs. The decoration on the in-side of the nave walls, in imitation of the façade, was carried out at the end of the last century. The open timber roof, with polychrome decoration, was also restored at that time. At the end of the nave is the *CAPPELLA DEL CROCIFISSO (1), an exquisite tabernacle commissioned by Piero il Gottoso from *Michelozzo* in 1448. It is superbly carved and beautifully designed to fit its setting built some four hundred years earlier. It was made to house the Crucifix which spoke to St John Gualberto (later removed to Santa Trìnita); the painted panels of the doors of the cupboard which protected the miraculous crucifix are by *Agnolo Gaddi* (1394–96). The enamelled terracotta roof and ceiling are the work of *Luca della Robbia*. The inlaid coloured marble frieze bears the emblem of Piero de' Medici (whose arms also appear on the

The façade of San Miniato al Monte. (Archivio Alinari)

back of the tabernacle). The copper eagles on the roof, emblems of the 'Arte di Calimala', are by *Maso di Bartolomeo*.—On the outer stone walls of the aisles are a number of frescoes. In the S. aisle: (2) *Paolo Schiavo*, Madonna enthroned with six Saints (1436) and a huge figure of St Christopher (3) dating from the 14C or earlier. Most of the other frescoes on this wall are by 15C artists. In the N. aisle are two detached frescoes (Madonna and Child with Saints, and a Crucifixion with seven Saints) by *Mariotto di Nardo*. By the steps up to the choir is a fresco (4) of the Virgin Annunciate and a fragment of a Nativity scene (restored) dating from the late 13C.

Built onto the N. wall of the church is the *CHAPEL OF THE CAR-DINAL OF PORTUGAL, the funerary chapel of Cardinal Iac. di Lusitania who died in Florence at the age of 25. It was begun by *Ant. Manetti*, Brunelleschi's pupil, in 1460 (and finished, after his death in the same year, probably under the direction of *Ant. Rossellino*). It incorporates some of the best workmanship of the Florentine Renaissance. The exquisitely carved *Tomb of the Cardinal is by *Ant. Rossellino* (1461–66). The ceiling has five *Medallions (1461) by *Luca della Robbia* representing the Cardinal Virtues and the Holy Ghost, against a background of tiles decorated with classical cubes in yellow, green, and purple, among the masterpieces of Luca's enamelled terracotta work. The altarpiece of Three Saints, by *Ant.* and *Piero del Pollaiolo* (1466–67) has been replaced by a copy (original in the Uffizi). The frescoed decoration of this wall, including two angels, is by the same artists. Above the marble Bishop's throne on the W. wall is a painting of the *Annunciation by *Aless. Baldovinetti* (1466–73), who also frescoed the Evangelists and Fathers of the Church in the lunettes beside the windows, and in the spandrels.

Steps lead up to the raised CHOIR with a beautiful marble *Transenna (5) dating from 1207, and *Pulpit (6), also faced with marble. The lectern is supported by an eagle above a carved figure standing on a lion's head. The low columns in the choir have huge antique capitals. The APSE (7) has a blind arcade with six small Roman columns between opaque windows. The large apse mosaic representing Christ between the Virgin and St Minias with symbols of the Evangelists (1297) was first restored in 1491 by Aless. Baldovinetti. The Crucifix above the simple Renaissance altar is attrib. to the Della Robbia. The carved and inlaid stalls by *Giov. di Dom. da Gaiole* and *Fr. di Domenico (Il Monciatto)* date from 1466–70. On the S. side is the SACRISTY (1387), entirely frescoed by *Spinello Aretino*; in the vault are the Evangelists and in the lunettes the *Life of St Benedict, one of his best works (restored in 1840). Here also are two Della Robbia statuettes and stalls like those in the choir. In the lunette above the little door is a pietà by Baldovinetti.—Among the frescoes on the walls of the choir are some very early panels of Saints (8; 13C).

The 11C CRYPT beneath the choir has beautiful slender columns, many of them with antique capitals. The original 11C altar contains the relics of St Minias. The little vaults are decorated with frescoes of Saints and Prophets against a blue ground (light to r. of the altar) by *Taddeo Gaddi*.—A small museum may be opened in an adjoining room beneath the refectory of the monastery.

The **Cloister** (adm only by special request), on the r. side of the church, was begun c. 1425. On the upper walk fragments of frescoes in terraverde by *Paolo Uccello*, illustrating scenes from monastic legends, were revealed, during restoration work, and a sinopia attrib. to *And. del Castagno*.

The massive stone CAMPANILE (which replaces one that fell in 1499) was begun after 1523 from a design by Baccio d'Agnolo, but never finished. During the siege of Florence (1530) Michelangelo mounted two cannon here, and protected the bell-tower from hostile artillery by a screen of mattresses.—The battlemented *Bishop's Palace*, with well-designed twin windows, dates from 1295 when it was used as a summer residence. It was enlarged in 1320 and again by Bp Agnolo Ricasoli. In later centuries it was used as a barracks and hospital, and was restored in this century.—The *Fortezza* which now encloses a cemetery (entrance on the l. side of the church) originated in a hastily improvised defence-work planned by Michelangelo during the months preceding the siege. In 1553 Cosimo I converted it into a real fortress with the help of Fr. da Sangallo, Tribolo and others.—The splendid view from the terrace in front of the church includes the walls climbing the hillside to Forte di Belvedere, and beyond the Lungarno across the river, the Duomo, Campanile, and white roof of the Baptistery, the dome of the Chapel of the Princes beside San Lorenzo, the tower of Pal. Vecchio (and, in front, the towers of the Badia and Bargello).

Near San Miniato, in a grove of cypresses on the side of the hill, is the church of **San Salvatore al Monte** (Pl. 11; 5), a building of gracious simplicity by *Cronaca*, called by Michelangelo his 'bella villanella'—his pretty country maid. It is in the course of restoration.

The INTERIOR has an open timber roof. On the W. wall is a bust of Marcello Adriani (d 1521) by *And. Ferrucci.* In the 2nd N. chap., Deposition, a large ter-racotta group (restored) attrib. to *Giov. della Robbia.* In the 5th S. Chap., Pietà attrib. to *Neri di Bicci.*

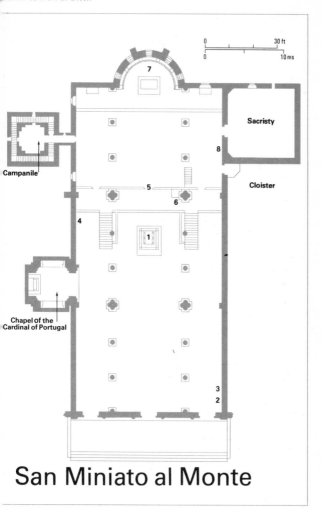

San Miniato al Monte

Steps lead down behind the *Palazzina del Caffè* (now a restaurant), built in 1873 by Gius. Poggi, to **Piazzale Michelangelo** (Pl. 11; 5), a celebrated viewpoint, much visited by tourists. From the balustrade on the huge terrace is a remarkable panorama of the city, its surrounding hills, and beyond (on a clear day) the plain as far as Pistoia and the peaks of the Apennines.

From the parapet the view includes (on the extreme left), the olive fields on the hillside below Forte di Belvedere, from which the city walls descend to Porta San Niccolò. The view down the Arno takes in Ponte Vecchio. On the other side of the river can be seen Pal. Vecchio, the dome of the Chapel of the Princes (San Lorenzo), the campanile and cupola of the Duomo, with the stone towers of the Badia and Bargello in front. Nearer at hand is the huge church of Santa Croce and the green dome of the synagogue.—The monument to Michelangelo (1875) on the terrace is made up of reproductions in bronze of some of the sculptor's famous marble statues in the city.—An *Iris Garden* is open here in May (entrance on the r. of the balustrade).

VIALE DEI COLLI (Pl. 9, 10 and 11; Viale Machiavelli, Viale Galileo, and Viale Michelangelo), a fine roadway 6 km long, was laid out by Gius. Poggi in 1865–70. It is one of the most panoramic drives near Florence, following a winding course from Porta San Niccolò viâ San Miniato and Piazzale Michelangelo to Porta Romana. It is traversed by Bus No. 13 (red) which can be taken from Piazzale Michelangelo back to the centre of the city.

21 MEDIEVAL FLORENCE

This route follows an itinerary through many of the oldest streets in the city N. of the Arno. Important monuments are indicated but described in full in other routes; it has been the intention here to describe as many as possible of the medieval palaces and towers which survive in the city. Towers were first built in the 12C by wealthy Florentines next to their houses, as refuges in times of trouble, as well as status symbols. The towers had to be lowered after 1250 by order of the regime of the 'primo popolo'. Later in the 14C many of them were adapted as houses. The medieval streets often lie on the courses of their Roman predecessors. Destruction of much of the old city took place at the end of the 19C when Piazza della Repubblica and its surrounding thoroughfares were laid out, and during the last War when the old towers and houses in Via Por Santa Maria and at either end of Ponte Vecchio were destroyed. The old streets of the Oltrarno are described in Rte 19.

Orsanmichele (Pl. 16; 6), one of the most significant medieval monuments in the city, is described on p 75. Next to it is PALAZZO DELL' ARTE DELLA LANA, built in 1308 by the Guild of Wool Merchants, but arbitrarily restored in 1905. The 'Arte della Lana' represented the most important Florentine industry which was responsible for the city's economic growth in the 13C (it has been estimated that a third of the population was employed in the woollen cloth industry in the 13-14C). Among the 'stemme' on the building is that of the Guild, the Agnus Dei. At the base of the tower is the little oratory of *Santa Maria della Tromba* (late 14C), one of the largest of the many tabernacles in the city. It was moved here from the Mercato Vecchio, nearby, the commercial centre of the city until the 19C, which was destroyed to make way for Piazza della Repubblica. Behind the grille is a painting of the Madonna enthroned, by Jac. del Casentino. On Via Calimala the 13C Torre Compiobbesi is incorporated in the building. In a shop here are remains of frescoes, including a Madonna and Child and two Saints. On the first floor (adm sometimes granted by the Società Dantesca) are 14C frescoes.—In Via Orsanmichele (No. 4) is *Palazzo dell'Arte dei Beccai*, headquarters of the Butchers' Guild until 1534; their 'stemma' (a goat) can be seen high up on the façade.

The palace (c. 1415–20) has recently been restored as the seat of the *Accademia del Disegno*, the first of all Art Academies, founded in 1563 by members of the Compagnia di San Luca which already existed by 1339. The founders included Vasari, Bronzino, Fr. di Giul. da Sangallo, Ammannati, Vinc. de' Rossi, and Montòrsoli. Cosimo I and Michelangelo were elected the first Academicians.—Adm to the interior is sometimes granted on request (ring). It houses some interesting works of art including a frescoed Crucifix from a Florentine tabernacle, and a painting of the Madonna and Saints, both by *Pontormo*; a bronze bust of Michelangelo by *Daniele da Volterra*; a fresco of the Madonna and Child with Saints by *Mariotto di Nardo*.

Via dell'Arte della Lana crosses Via Lamberti. On the corner here was the site of the first headquarters of the Medici bank, set up in 1397 by Giovanni di Bicci, father of Cosimo il Vecchio. At the next intersection, Via Porta Rossa (so-named since at least the beginning of the 13C) leads (r.) past the **Mercato Nuovo** (Pl. 16; 5), the Florentine straw-market (open daily in summer; closed Mon & Sun in winter). It has been the site of a market since the beginning of the 11C. The loggia was erected by Cosimo I in 1547–51 on a design by G.B. del Tasso for the sale of silk and gold. It is now a market-place for cheap lace, straw work, leather goods, and souvenirs. It is known to Florentines as 'Il Porcellino' from a popular statue on the far side of the loggia. The bronze boar was copied by Tacca from the antique statue in the Uffizi; the delightful base is a copy of the original by Tacca. Coins thrown into the fountain are given to charity. The medieval buildings in Via Por Santa Maria which leads to Ponte Vecchio (p 98) were all destroyed in 1944. Via Porta Rossa continues to **Palazzo Davanzati** (Pl. 16; 5; adm see p 58), now the MUSEO DELLA CASA FIORENTINA ANTICA, and the best surviving example of a medieval nobleman's house in Florence (despite numerous restorations). It is particularly interesting as an illustration of Florentine life in the Middle Ages.

The palace was built in the mid-14C by the Davizzi family and became the property of Bernardo Davanzati, the successful merchant and scholar, in 1578. It remained in his family until the end of the 19C. In 1904 the palace was bought by the antiquarian Elia Volpi who restored it and turned it into a private museum of antiques, which were later sold to various museums all over the world. The Italian State purchased the house in 1951. Interesting graffiti and drawings referring to contemporary events (1441–1516) have been found on many of the walls.

The typical 14C FAÇADE consists of three stories above large arches on the ground floor. The proportions have been altered by the loggia at the top which was added in the 16C and probably replaced battlements. The ironwork is interesting and includes brackets which carry diagonal poles across the windows. These were used to hang out the washing, to suspend birdcages, etc., or for the hangings which decorated the façade on special occasions. The huge Davanzati coat-of-arms dates from the 16C; it was brought from another family house. The palace is separated from the smaller medieval house on the r. by a narrow alley spanned by stone girders.

The INTERIOR, of great interest for its architecture and contemporary wall paintings (rare survivals of a decorative form typical of 14C houses), has been beautifully arranged with the furnishings of a Florentine house of 15C-17C (including tapestries, lacework, ceramics, sculpture, paintings, decorative arts, domestic objects, etc.). The 16-17C furniture is a special feature of the house. The spacious vaulted ENTRANCE HALL runs the whole width of the building and was used as a loggia, for family ceremonies, and later as shops.—The INTERIOR COURTYARD could be entirely cut off from the street in times of trouble. The storerooms here were replenished directly from the alley-ways at the back and side of the building. The well served all five floors of the house. The corner pilaster bears carved heads traditionally supposed to be portraits of the Davizzi family. A detached fresco of a hunting scene (15C Florentine) has been placed

Over: *'Civitas Florentie', the earliest known view of the medieval city, showing the Baptistery, and the incomplete Duomo and Campanile (detail from the fresco of the Madonna della Misericordia, dated 1342, in the Museo del Bigallo).*

VNITAS·

FLORENTIE

here.—The staircase ascends to the upper floors; the lower steps are in stone, th
higher in wood. Beyond a detached fresco of the Madonna enthroned by th
Umbrian school (13-14C), on the **First Floor** landing, is a faded fresco of S
Christopher (14-15C). To the r. is the SALA MADORNALE which runs the width o
the building and was used for family gatherings. It has a painted wood ceilin
(14-15C). Wall hangings were attached to the hooks at the top of the walls t
decorate the room for special occasions. Four holes in the floor were used fo
defence against intruders in the entrace hall below. The fine table of Florentin
workmanship dates from the late 16C, and the painted wood cupboard (16C
stored the family arms. Here are exhibited a series of small coffers (probably us
ed as jewel cases) in decorated wood (15C), a Madonna of the Annunciation i
polychrome terracotta (Florentine, early 15C), and the bust of a boy by *An
Rossellino*. A painted tondo shows a Florentine street scene (by the 'Master o
the Adimari Marriage-chest').—Two small rooms were opened in 1981 with
charming display of *Lace (examples of Flemish, French, and Italian work fro
the end of the 16C to the present day). A conservation centre for lace has bee
set up here.—The SALA DEI PAPPAGALLI, or Dining Room has delightful wa
paintings. The lower part of the walls imitate wall hangings with a motif of par
rots, while above is a painted terrace with trees and flowering shrubs. Th
fireplace, which bears the arms of the Davizzi and Alberti, was probably instal
ed at the end of the 14C. Here the furniture has been used to display collectio
of pottery, including 14C household ceramics contemporary with the building o
the house.—The SALA PICCOLA, probably a child's bedroom, nearby, contain
an elaborate 16C safe, a desk, a 'cassone' by the school of Vasari, and 17
Montelupo ceramics. Also, *And. del Sarto* (attrib.), Daedalus and Icarus, an
Fr. Granacci, *Joseph led to prison.—Off this room is one of several W.C.s i
the house.—The last room on this floor is the CAMERA NUZIALE, or 'dei pavoni
the bedroom. The fine wall paintings bear the coats-of-arms of families relate
to the Davizzi between a delightful frieze of birds. The rare linen *Bed cover,
Sicilian work of the end of the 14C, is decorated with stories of Tristan.

Second Floor. To the r. is the second SALONE, decorated with a pretty series o
small Flemish tapestries illustrating biblical scenes (15C; very well preserved
The interesting portrait of Giovanni di Bicci de' Medici (father of Cosimo il Ve
chio) is attrib. to *Zanobi Strozzi*. The ceramics include a tile with two figur
made in central Italy at the end of the 14C, a charming series of hand-warmers i
the form of shoes (18C), and two fine pharmacy jars.—In the DINING ROOM ar
more ceramics including a series of salt cellars in enamelled terracotta (17-18C
and an inlaid 'cassone' (end of the 16C). The paintings include: *Pier Fr. Fosch
Temple of Hercules, and three stories of Perseus by the *'Maestro di Serumid
chio* (beginning of the 16C), formerly attrib. to Piero di Cosimo—The SALA PICCOL
contains a remarkable collection of 'cassone' which were made to contain
bride's dowry of household linen. One of them illustrates the story of Par
(beginning of the 15C), and two reconstructed chests bear four panels of th
Triumphs of Petrarch, by *Giov. di Ser Giovanni* (*Lo Scheggia*). The 14C pai
tings hung here include: *Rossello di Jac. Franchi*, Madonna del Parto, an
Spinello Aretino, St Stephen and the Crucifixion—A corridor leads into th
Bedroom known as the CAMERA DELLA CASTELLANA DI VERGI, from the charmin
painted *Frieze illustrating a medieval French romance.—On the **Third Floor**
the KITCHEN (normally situated on the top floor in medieval houses). Here, th
warmest place in the house, the women would spend most of their day, passin
their time spinning and weaving, etc. around the big fireplace. Variou
household utensils are displayed here. There is a view from the window of th
dome ('San Frediano in Cestello, the tower of Santa Trinita, and a massive 13
tower ('La Rognosa') rising above a 15C palace nearby.

Next to Pal. Davanzati is a smaller medieval house (No. 15), an
opposite, in the piazza, the old Casa Torre Foresi. Farther along th
street can be seen (l.) the old *Albergo Porta Rossa* with a projectin
upper story supported on stone 'sporti' and wrought-iron lantern
The palace was built by the Bartolini-Salimbeni in the early 16C (the
heraldic emblems decorate the façade), and the hotel opened here i
the mid-19C.—It is now necessary to return along Via Porta Rossa t
Via Pellicceria, at the end of which (r.) is a little piazza surrounded b
an interesting group of old buildings. On the r. is *Palazzo Giandonat*
dating from the 14C, with two arches on the ground floor. Next to it
the 15C *Palazzo Canacci* (No. 3) with grisaille decoration and a fir

ggia (heavily restored at the beginning of this century). At the end is
ALAZZO DI PARTE GUELFA (Pl. 16; 5; adm only with special permis-
on, or when exhibitions are being held), built as the official residence
f the Captains of the Guelf party in the 13C.

The 'Parte Guelfa' was a political and military organization which supported
e Pope and virtually controlled the government of the city from c. 1267 until
76. The famous feud between the Guelfs and Ghibellines (on the side of the
mperor) coloured much of the history of the city during the Middle Ages.—The
utside stair was modified by Vasari. Beneath the crenellations is a row of
emme' and a tall Gothic window. In the 15C the palace was enlarged (see
elow) by Brunelleschi who built a hall (since restored).

On the third side of the square is the rough façade of the ex-church
f Santa Maria Sovraporta. Vicolo della Seta leads down by the side
f the church to the Mercato Nuovo (see above) and Via di Capaccio
.). Here is *Palazzo dell'Arte della Seta* (No. 3), the headquarters of
e Guild of the silk-cloth industry established here at the end of the
4C. It still bears its beautiful 'stemma' encircled by cherubs in the
yle of Donatello. Next to it, extending to Via delle Terme, is the
andsome extension by Brunelleschi to Palazzo di Parte Guelfa (the
tle loggia on the corner was added by Vasari).

Via delle Terme (Pl. 16; 5), a pretty medieval street, takes its name
om the Roman baths which were in this area. At the beginning (r.),
y Chiasso Manetti, is the Casa Torre Buondelmonte (Guidi) which
ces the back of the medieval portion of Pal. di Parte Guelfa (comp.
ove). On the corner of Chiasso di Misure is another interesting
alace (No. 9) with a Renaissance courtyard, and (No. 13 red) a
edieval tower. Opposite is Pal. Canacci (comp. above). Beyond
hiasso Cornino is a small house (No. 17), one story high, above two
ide arches. The road skirts the side of the fine Pal. Bartolini-
alimbeni (see p 141), a 14C building reconstructed in the 16C, with
one benches on the pavement, before emerging in Piazza Santa
rinita in front of the tall Roman column crowned by a statue of
ustice. Here is the grandiose Palazzo Spini-Feroni built in 1289, and
e largest of Florentine medieval private palaces, which, together
ith the other monuments in the piazza, is described in Rte 12.

Borgo Santi Apostoli (Pl. 16; 5), parallel to Via delle Terme and the
rno, leads back out of the square. This was a Roman road which led
om outside the south gate of the city to the Cassia. It had received its
esent name at least by the beginning of the 13C. On the corner of
ia delle Bombarde is *Palazzo Altoviti* with its tower (13C or 14C). In
e attractive little Piazza del Limbo is the romanesque stone façade
f the church of **Santi Apostoli** (Pl. 16; 5; open 8-10, 16-19), one of
e oldest churches in the city (mentioned as early as 1075). The
uilding is considerably lower than the pavement of the Borgo.

According to legend the church was founded by Charlemagne in 786, but it is
ow thought to date from the 10C when it was built partly on the remains of a
oman building. It was restored in 1938. The 16C doorway is ascribed to *Bened.*
Rovezzano.—The basilican INTERIOR has fine green marble columns and
pitals (the first two are from Roman baths). In the 1st chap. in the N. aisle is
e *Sinopia of the fresco of the Madonna and Child formerly on the façade by
olo Schiavo. At the end of the aisle, *Tomb of Prior Oddo Altoviti, by *Bened.*
Rovezzano (1507; the sarcophagus is derived from classical models), and a
1e *Tabernacle by *And. della Robbia* (and assistants), with two sculpted panels
low from the tomb of Donato Acciaioli (1333). On the altar is a painting by the
hool of Orcagna (in restoration). The altarpieces from the S. aisle, by *Vasari,*
omarancio,* and others, have been in restoration since 1966.

In the piazza, *Palazzo di Oddo Altoviti* (No. 1) is the work of Ben
ed. da Rovezzano (c. 1512; altered). On the other side of the church i
Palazzo Rosselli del Turco (No. 19) with various inscriptions and
relief of the Madonna by Bened. da Maiano. The main façade in th
Borgo is by Baccio d'Agnolo (1517). Beyond the characteristi
Chiasso Cornino are the *Palazzi Acciaioli* (No. 8; 14C) with a tower
bearing the emblem of the Certosa del Galluzzo, which was founde
by Niccolò Acciaioli (1340–65). Opposite (No. 27 red) is a building wi
13C portions. At No. 19 (red) is the remains of the 13C fabric of th
Palazzo Usimbardi (*Acciaioli*) whose main 16C façade on the Arn
was destroyed in the war. In the 19C when it was the Grand Hote
Royal, Ruskin, Dickens, Swinburne, Longfellow, and Henry Jame
all stayed here. The original fabric of the *Buondelmonti* palaces nex
door has been destroyed except for a 14C rusticated ground floor an
a few stone arches; No. 6 is the oldest residence of this Florentin
family to have survived. The remainder of the street was badly damag
ed in the last war; on the corner of Via Por Santa Maria the 13
Baldovinetti tower has been restored.—Across Por Santa Maria (se
above) is a secluded little piazza around the church of **Santo Stefano a
Ponte** (Pl. 16; 5; temporarily closed, but normally open for services
another very old church, first built in 969.

The handsome Romanesque decoration on the façade dates from 1233. Th
interior was altered by *Ferd. Tacca* in 1649. It contains altarpieces by *Santi*
Tito, Matteo Rosselli, and others, a painting by *Jac. di Cione*, and a bronze alt
frontal of the Stoning of St Stephen by *Ferd. Tacca*. At the elaborate E. end th
altar steps (removed from Santa Trinita) are a remarkable Mannerist work b
Buontalenti (1574). The rectangular choir behind has a 17C wood ceiling ar
stalls. Beneath is a large crypt. There are plans to open a Diocesan Museum her

To the r. of the church an alley leads past the *Casa dell'Orafo*,
rambling edifice which is honey-combed with the workshops c
numerous Florentine goldsmiths. To the left, the dark Volta de
Girolami is spanned by a series of low arches; at the end, Via d
Georgofili leads l. to Via Lambertesca (with a glimpse r. of the Uffizi
In this street several guilds had their headquarters. A short way to th
left, Chiasso dei Baroncelli, a narrow medieval lane, with the 14C Pa
Benini Formichi, continues. It emerges in Piazza Signoria, dominate
by Palazzo Vecchio, begun in 1298 (described in Rte 5). Vi
Calimaruzza, another road leading into the piazza (l.) was the sea
from the late 14C of the 'Arte di Calimala' (the wholesale cloth im
porters). Their 'stemma' (an eagle holding a bale of cloth in its talon
survives at No. 2a.

Via de' Calzaioli leads out of the N. side of the Piazza and Via Co
dotta soon diverges right. On the corner of the characteristic o
Vicolo dei Cerchi is the well preserved *Palazzo Cerchi* (No. 52 red
dating from the 13C. Beyond, Via delle Farine (r.) has a good view
Pal. Vecchio with its tower. The shop windows in Via Condotta a
framed by a series of medieval arches. On the corner of Via dei Ce
chi, a local shopping street, is the medieval *Palazzo Giug*
(reconstructed) with pretty iron lamp brackets and arcading. Via d
Cerchi leads N. On the corner of Via del Canto alla Quarconia is t
Torre Cerchi (1292–98), and on Via dei Tavolini stands *Torre Gre*
(Galigai) of the 12-13C. Via dei Cimatori (with a view left of Orsa
michele, and r. of the towers of the Bargello and the Badia) continu
r. from Via dei Cerchi. In Via dei Magazzini is the large conve

building (with a fine courtyard) of the Badia (comp. Rte 14), now occupied by the law courts, the entrance to which is (l.) in the little PIAZZA SAN MARTINO. Here is the splendid 13C *Torre della Castagna*, one of the best preserved medieval towers in the city. This was the residence of the 'priori' in 1282 before they moved to Pal. Vecchio. This area is traditionally associated with the great Florentine poet Dante Alighieri. The little chapel of **San Martino del Vescovo** (Pl. 16; 4; open 10-12, 15-17; Sat 15-16; closed Sun & fest.) is on the site of the parish church (986) of the Alighieri and Donati families.

It was rebuilt in 1479 when it became the seat of a charitable institution founded in 1442 by St Antonino, and decorated with charming frescoes by the workshop of *Ghirlandaio* (recently attrib. to *Fr. d'Ant. del Chierico*). They illustrate the life of St Martin and works of charity, and are of great interest for their portrayal of contemporary Florentine life. Here, too, are two notable paintings of the Madonna, one Byzantine and the other attrib. to Perugino (or Nic. Soggi). In an adjoining room are two terracotta angels by the school of Verrocchio and a 14C tabernacle.

On a trattoria (No. 4) in the piazza a terracotta roundel of Mariotto Albertinelli records the Florentine painter who here opened a restaurant. Across Via Dante Alighieri (in which is the entrance to the Badia, see Rte 14), among a group of houses (restored in 13C style in 1911) is the *Casa di Dante,* where the poet is said to have been born (although it is more probable his birthplace was on the present Via Alighieri). It contains a collection of material (little of it original) relating to the poet (adm see p 57). Via Santa Margherita continues past the little church of SANTA MARGHERITA DE' CERCHI, of 12C foundation, where Dante is supposed to have married Gemma Donati. The 14C porch bears the arms of the Cerchi, Adimari, and Donati who lived in the parish. In the interior is a lovely altarpiece of the Madonna enthroned with four female Saints by Neri di Bicci.—An archway leads out onto the **Corso** (Pl. 16; 4), a Roman road. The church (l.) of SANTA MARGHERITA IN SANTA MARIA DE' RICCI (1508) is preceded by a portico by Gherardo Silvani (1611). The interior (reopened after restoration in 1981) was reconstructed by Zanobi del Rosso in 1769. Opposite is the 13C Torre dei Donati.

Some way along the Corso (l.) are several 12C towers on the corner of *Via Sant'Elisabetta.* The ancient Torre La Pagliazza in P.za S. Elisabetta was used as a prison in the 13-14C. Via S. Elisabetta leads to *Via delle Oche* with the 14C Palazzo Visdomini and its tower. On the corner of *Via dello Studio* (r.) is the 13C Palazzo Tedaldini. Via del Canonica, to the N., is another pretty old street. Via dello Studio slopes gently downhill from the Duomo (good view of the cupola) back to the Corso. The ground floor arches betray the medieval origins of the street.

The Corso leads E. past *Palazzo Salviati* (now a bank), built for Maria Salviati, wife of Giovanni delle Bande Nere (and mother of Cosimo I), and altered in the 16C and 17C. In the banking hall is a 14C fresco of the Madonna and Child. The Corso ends at the Canto de' Pazzi, on the site of the E. gate of the Roman city; across Via del Proconsolo (Rte 14) ***Borgo degli Albizi** (Pl. 6; 8) follows the line of the Roman Cassia. The Borgo is named after one of the wealthiest families in Florence in the 14C and 15C who owned numerous palaces in the street. It is one of the most handsome streets in the city. The magnificent palaces at its entrance (Palazzo Pazzi and Palazzo Nonnito) are described on p 151. Next to Pal. Pazzi (r.) a palace with 15C rustication on the ground floor has been converted into a cinema.

Opposite, *Palazzo Vitali* (No. 28) is a beautiful building attrib. to
Bart. Ammannati (late 16C; being restored), with a handsome coat
of-arms. Next to it (No. 26) *Palazzo Matteucci Ramirez di Montalvo*
is a severe work also by Ammannati (1568). The graffiti decoration is
attrib. to Bernardino Poccetti. The owner set up the arms of his friend
Cosimo I on the façade. On the corner of Via de' Giraldi is a 14C
tabernacle with the Madonna enthroned with Saints. Farther on, by
Volta dei Cerchi is a house (No. 22) with medieval fragments next to
the huge *Palazzo Altoviti* (or 'dei Visacci'; No. 18), which dates from
the early 15C. It was enlarged in the 16C when the marble portraits of
celebrated Florentine citizens were placed on the façade (which give
the palace its alternative name). Facing a piazzetta is a little 14C house
(No. 14). Beyond is the grandiose *Palazzo degli Albizi* (No. 12), the
principal residence of the Albizi, a famous Florentine family (see
above). The façade is in two parts: the 14C fabric survives on the l.
and the nine bays on the r. were reconstructed by Silvani in the 17C.
Opposite, a pretty palace (being restored) stands next to the large
Palazzo degli Alessandri (No. 15), the best preserved palace on the
street. A cornice divides the two stories of its fine 14C façade in pietra
forte. Here Canova had has studio. On the left No. 10 has a bust of
Vincenzo Filicaia (1642–1707), who was born here. On the r. is a 16C
house (No. 11) with a marble bust of Cosimo II, out of the top of
which rises a medieval tower, which belonged to the Donati.

The lively little PIAZZA SAN PIER MAGGIORE (Pl. 6; 8) is the centre of
a local shopping area with a few colourful market stalls. The 17C portico by Nigetti is all that survives of the church which gave the square
its name. The little *Palazzo Corbizzi* (No. 1) dates from the 13C. Opposite, next to a pretty house with a projecting upper story rises the
splendid 13C *Torre Donati (Cocchi)*. Just out of the piazzetta, beyond
the Volta di San Piero, an archway with shops, is the 14-15C *Palazzo
Albizi* (enlarged in the 16C and restored).—Via Matteo Palmieri (with
a worn terracotta Madonna and Child on the corner) leads out of the
piazza. In Via Pandolfini (r.) the palace at No. 14 was built for Bacci
Valori who led the siege of Florence in 1530 and was hanged in Piazza
Signoria in 1537 by order of Cosimo I. On the corner of Via
Ghibellina stands the 14C *Palazzo Salviati Quaratesi* (covered for
restoration). The ground floor provided room for stores and shops.
The large tabernacle in Via Ghibellina protects a fresco by Giovanni
da San Giovanni (c. 1616; to be returned here after its restoration).

In Via Ghibellina (No. 110) is the huge *Palazzo Borghese*, with a neo-classical
façade by Gaetano Baccani (1822). It was built in less than a year by Camillo
Borghese, husband of Pauline Bonaparte (sister of Napoleon I) for a party to
celebrate the marriage of Ferdinando III. The elaborate period rooms are now
used by a club.—At the end of the street can be seen the towers of the Bargello
and the Badia.

Via delle Stinche continues across Via Ghibellina past *Palazzo di
Cintoia (Salviati)*, one of the most interesting medieval palaces to survive in the city. It dates from the 14C, and its façade in pietra forte has
picturesque 'sporti'. In Via della Vigna Vecchia is the 14C *Palazzo
Covoni* (No. 7-9). In the little piazza is the church of **San Simone** (Pl.
10; 2; open for services only), founded in 1192–93. The fine doorway
is in the style of Bened. da Rovezzano.

The INTERIOR is a good work by *Gherardo Silvani* (1630). Over the last altar on the S. side, *Jac. Vignali*, Christ showing his wounds to St Bernard (1623). At the end of the N. side is a charming Gothic tabernacle (1363) with the bust of a man, surrounded by enamelled terracotta decoration with cherubs by the *Della Robbia*. Other altarpieces will be returned here after restoration.

Opposite is one of the best known ice-cream shops in the city. Beyond Via della Burella (r.) with another medieval house, the streets follow the shape of the Roman amphitheatre which was built here in the 2-3C A.D. It is estimated that it was big enough to hold c. 15,000 spectators. Via dei Bentaccordi follows the curve across Via Anguillara (with a view l. of the Pazzi Chapel in Santa Croce) and Borgo dei Greci into *Piazza Peruzzi*, named after the famous Florentine family of bankers who reached their greatest prosperity at the end of the 13C. The medieval buildings here include the reconstructed Palazzo Peruzzi (13-14C). An archway leads out into the busy VIA DEI BENCI (Pl. 10; 2) with its old rusticated houses. The view to the left is closed by the tower of the Duomo of Fiesole; to the r., across the river, the green hills of the Oltrarno provide a background to the medieval buildings in Piazza dei Mozzi. On the corner of Borgo Santa Croce is the polygonal 13C *Torre degli Alberti*, with a cafè in the 15C loggia below. The interesting palaces in the Borgo are described on p 160. On Corso dei Tintori is *Palazzo Alberti* (late 14C or early 15C) with a good courtyard. Opposite the 15C *Palazzo Corsi* (No. 6; described, with the Museo Horne, on p 167) are several handsome palaces. *Palazzo Bardi alle Grazie (Serzelli*; No. 5) is an early Renaissance palace attrib. to Brunelleschi (c. 1430) with a fine courtyard. Here the famous 'Camerata fiorentina di Casa Bardi' introduced operatic melodrama. No. 1, *Palazzo Malenchini*, was reconstructed in the 19C on the site of a 14C palace, the residence of the Alberti, an influential merchant family who were exiled in 1387 for political reasons. The great architect Leon Battista Alberti (who had been born while the family were in exile in Genoa) died here in 1472 (plaque).

VIA DEI NERI (Pl. 10; 2), named after the confraternity who comforted criminals on their way from the Bargello to execution, leads out of Via dei Benci back towards Palazzo Vecchio (which can be seen at the end of the street). At the beginning on the r. Via delle Brache has medieval houses with 'sporti'. On Via de' Rustici *Palazzo Rustici (Neri)* dates from the end of the 14C. The road bends at its junction with Via Mosca following the shape of the Roman port of Florence. Here, at No. 23 is the 14C *Palazzo Soldani*. A road (r.) with tablets showing the water levels of the Arno in the floods of 1333 and 1966, leads to the church of **San Remigio** (Pl. 10; 2) founded in the 11C, with an exterior in pietra forte.

The fine Gothic INTERIOR (restored) contains fresco fragments by the school of Giotto and worn roundels of Saints in the vaults (14C). The beautiful panel painting of the *Madonna and Child in the left aisle is by a follower of Cimabue known as the *'Master of San Remigio'*. The painting of the Immaculate Conception by *Empoli* dates from 1591. In a little room below the campanile (adm on request) are early monochrome frescoes with hunting scenes, etc.

In Via dei Neri (corner of Via del Guanto) is the 14C Palazzo Fagni (No. 35) next to the *Loggia del Grano* (Pl. 16; 6), a market erected at the time of Cosimo II by Giulio Parigi and his son Alfonso, and now part of a cinema.—Via della Ninna skirts the side of Palazzo Vecchio to emerge in Piazza della Signoria (Rte 4).

22   THE VIALI

This route follows the wide avenues (or 'viali') laid out in 1865–69
by Giuseppe Poggi after he had demolished the last circle of walls built
around the N. part of the city in 1284–1333. The architect left some of
the medieval gates as isolated monuments in the course of this ring-
road, now busy with traffic. None of the places mentioned are worth
visiting on foot; buses are indicated in the text.—At the foot of Ponte
della Vittoria begins VIALE FRATELLI ROSSELLI (Pl. 4; 5, 6), named
after two brothers, famous leaders of the anti-Fascist movement
murdered in France by order of Mussolini before the last War. The
equestrian statue of Vittorio Emanuele II (removed from Piazza della
Repubblica) is by Emilio Zocchi (1890), and opposite is a small fountain commemorating the diamond jubilee of Queen Victoria. Here is
the entrance to the **Cascine** (Pl. 4; 5; bus 17c from the Duomo and the
Station), a huge public park which skirts the Arno for 3½ kilometres
It is traversed by an avenue open to cars.

The lands of a dairy-farm ('cascina') were acquired by Duke Alessandro de'
Medici and the park enlarged by Cosimo I. It was used as a ducal chase in the
17C, and public spectacles and festivals were held here under the grand-duke
Pietro Leopoldo in the 18C. The grounds were planned as a huge park by Elisa
Baciocchi Bonaparte and first opened regularly to the public c. 1811. In these
gardens the 'Ode to the West Wind' was 'conceived and chiefly written' by
Shelley in 1819, and on the Narcissus fountain here a tablet (1954) com-
memorates its composition. The long park (only a little more than a hundred
metres wide), with fine woods, is not as well maintained as it might be. During
the day it is used as a recreation ground by numerous Florentines, old and
young, and huge public concerts and festivals are held here in summer. It is not
enclosed and it is not advisable to visit the park at night. The *Festa del Grillo* is
held here on Ascension Day. It contains two racecourses, various sport
grounds, tennis courts, a swimming-pool, and a tiny zoo. In the central *Piazzale
delle Cascine* is the Institute of Agriculture and Forestry. At the far end is the
Monumento dell'Indiano, a monument to the Maharajah of Kolhapur who died
in Florence in 1870. From here the view is dominated by a modern suspension
bridge (1978) over the Arno.

Near Piazza Vittorio Veneto (in Corso Italia) is the *Teatro Comunale* (Pl. 4; 6), the most important concert hall in the city. The disappointing interior was rebuilt in 1961. Nearby, on Lungarno Vespucci
is the American Consulate in a building by Gius. Poggi (1860).—Viale
Fratelli Rosselli continues to *Porta al Prato* (Pl. 4; 6), an isolated
gateway (1284) of the city walls. Here Il Prato leads r. to *Palazzo Corsini sul Prato*, built in 1591–94 by Buontalenti with a fine garden
where Prince Charles Stuart stayed as a guest in 1774–77.

Via della Scala diverges r. from the Viale. Near No. 62 is a lunette by Giov.
della Robbia in the façade of a former church. Here is the neo-Gothic American
Episcopalian church (*St James's*; entrance at No. 13 Via B. Rucellai). On the r.
(No. 85) is the 17C *Palazzo Ginori-Venturi* adjoining which are the *Orti
Oricellari* (no adm), a famous Renaissance 'selva'. In these gardens Bernardo
Rucellai (in Latin, 'Oricellari'), who had married Nannina de' Medici in 1466
(sister of Lorenzo il Magnifico), collected the sculptures stolen after the exile of
the Medici in 1494, and refounded the Platonic Academy of Careggi. The villa
was sold to Bianca Cappello in 1573.

The Viale continues to an underpass beneath the railway. The
Railway Station (Pl. 5; 5, 6; *Stazione di Santa Maria Novella*), a short
distance r., is a pleasant functional building built in 1935 by a group
of brilliant young Tuscan architects including Giov. Michelucci and
Piero Berardi. Viale Filippo Strozzi continues round the huge **Fortezza**

za da Basso (Pl. 5; 4; adm only when exhibitions are in progress), a building which has always been something of a white elephant. A massive fortress on a grand scale designed by Antonio da Sangallo the Younger it is of the first importance in the history of military architecture. The exterior wall is still intact.

It was erected by order of Alessandro de' Medici in 1534 to strengthen his position in the city as first Duke of Florence, and as a refuge in times of trouble. It became a symbol of Medici tyranny, and Alessandro was assassinated here by his cousin Lorenzino in 1537. It was very soon obsolete as the grand-dukes had little need to defend themselves. In later centuries it was used as a prison, arsenal, and barracks. After years of neglect and discussion about its future, part of it has been used since the flood as a restoration centre, and a huge prefabricated steel building covered with aluminium was built inside the walls in 1978 as an international exhibition centre. Here the 'Mostra dell'Artigianato' and the prestigious *Pitti' fashion shows are held annually. Public gardens have been laid out on the glacis.

Opposite the Fortezza, across Viale Filippo Strozzi, is *Palazzo dei Congressi*, a modern international conference centre. At No. 14 Viale Strozzi is the *Istituto Geografico Militare*, the most important cartographical institute in Italy. Maps are sold to the public here (the headquarters, with the library and collection of old maps, is in Via Cesare Battisti). A short way to the S.E. (reached by Via Ridolfi) is PIAZZA DELL'INDIPENDENZA (Pl. 5; 4) laid out in 1869 as the first of the 19C squares in Florence. Here are statues of Bettino Ricasoli and Ubaldino Peruzzi, mayor of Florence in 1870. At the N. corner stands the *Villino Trollope*, home of the Trollope family in 1848–66, where the visiting Anthony wrote 'Doctor Thorne' in 1857. Later, when a pensione, it sheltered Thomas Hardy (1887).

From the Fortezza da Basso Bus No. 1 (from the Duomo and Station) runs N.E. to Via Vittorio Emanuele II for the Museo Stibbert (an uninteresting walk of c. 2 km). Situated on the *Colle di Montughi* (now a built-up residential area), with many other villas including the *Villa Fabbricotti* (No. 48; it is now the seat of the Università per gli Stranieri, and the park is open to the public) where Queen Victoria stayed in 1894, the **Villa Stibbert** was inherited from his Italian mother by Frederick Stibbert (1838–1906). A Garibaldian hero, he began a collection c. 1860 which he bequeathed with the villa to the British Government. The bequest was not taken up and the villa eventually passed to the city of Florence. The villa consists of a 14C house and one of the 15C joined together in 1884 by Stibbert by means of the great hall. The balcony here was a favourite seat of Queen Victoria who took pleasure in watching the work of alteration. The eclectic MUSEUM (adm see p 58) has a remarkably bizarre atmosphere with 54 rooms crammed with an extraordinary variety of objects. Groups are conducted every hour through the heavily decorated rooms. The most important part of the collections is the display of arms and armour, both ancient (Etruscan, Roman, Lombard, etc.) and medieval. Specially notable are the five rooms of *Asiatic armour, the equestrian figure of a Condottiere, with 15C armour, and a cavalcade of 28 fully armed horses and knights of the 16C (in the great hall). Some of the most important paintings in the museum stolen in 1977 have since been recovered.—The *Park* is open daily.

Viale Lavagnini continues towards Piazza della Libertà. In Via Leone X (l.) is the *Russian Church* (Pl. 6; 1) built with funds raised from the large Russian colony in Florence (including the Demidoff) and consecrated in 1904. Throughout most of the 19C Florence was a fashionable place to spend the winter for many aristocratic Russian families. The architects of the fine building came from Russia, and the pretty majolica decoration on the exterior was carried out by the Ulisse Cantagalli workshop. It is now a national monument owned by the Russian Orthodox community of Florence and open for services (sung mass) on the 3rd Sun of the month and on major church

festivals.—PIAZZA DELLA LIBERTÀ (Pl. 7; 1) is a handsome arcade
piazza where many streets converge. In the centre is the isolated *Port*
San Gallo, another old city gate, and a *Triumphal Arch* hurriedl
erected in 1739 to commemorate the solemn entry into the city of th
grand-duke Francis II of Lorraine, and his wife Maria Teresa, heir t
the Imperial throne.

The future of the *Parterre,* a modern building on the square, formerly an ex
hibition centre, is under discussion. From the junction just N. of the piazza a
Ponte Rosso (Pl. 7; 1) is the beginning of **Via Bolognese**, the pretty old roa
from Florence to Bologna. Here is the *Horticultural Garden* with an elabora
greenhouse (1879; by Giac. Roster). Via Bolognese (Bus No. 25) continues uphi
out of the city past a number of villas, including (1½ km) *La Pietra* (No. 120)
This is the residence of the historian Sir Harold Acton. It contains one of th
most interesting private collections of works of art in Florence (formed by A
thur Acton) including a notable group of early Tuscan paintings (adm to scholar
sometimes courteously granted by previous appointment).

Viale Giacomo Matteotti leads back towards the river. In the centr
of PIAZZA DONATELLO (Pl. 7; 6) is the disused *English Cemetery,* on
mound shaded by cypresses (adm 9–12, 15–17 or 18; ring). Here (t
the left of the central path) is buried Elizabeth Barrett Brownin
(1809–61). The tomb was designed by Robert Browning and sculpte
by Lord Leighton (finished by Giovannozzi). Nearby is the Pre
Raphaelite sarcophagus of Holman Hunt's wife Fanny who died i
Fiesole at the age of 33. Also buried here: Isa Blagden (d 1873), A
thur Hugh Clough (1819–61), Walter Savage Landor (1775–1864)
Frances Trollope (1780–1863), Theodore Parker of Lexingto
(1810–60), Robert Davidsohn (1853–1937), the German historian o
Florence, and Gian Pietro Vieussyux (1779–1863), the Swis
bibliophile.

Viale Gramsci continues to PIAZZA BECCARIA (Pl. 7; 8), wit
another old city gate. Nearby in Via Scipione Ammirato are two A
Nuoveau houses (Nos. 99 & 101). On the S. side of Piazza Beccaria
huge new building is under construction to house the *Archivio di Stat*
(comp. p 88). It is not expected to be completed until after 1985. Vi
Vincenzo Gioberti leads E. from the piazza to P.za Alberti. The EX
CONVENT OF *SAN* SALVI, just N. of the railway line (c. 1½ km from
Piazza Beccaria) is reached by Bus No. 10 from the Station (and No.
from Via Tornabuoni, and No. 20 from P.za San Marco).

The Vallombrosan abbey of San Salvi has a 14-16C church. In the refector
(entrance at No. 16 Via S. Salvi) is the celebrated ***Cenacolo di San Salvi** by *An*
drea del Sarto (c. 1520-25), a masterpiece of Florentine fresco, remarkable fo
its colouring. This is perhaps the most famous fresco of the Last Supper in Italy
after that by Leonardo da Vinci in Milan. It has been restored since 1966 and
soon to be reopened to the public. A small museum in the conventual building
will display other works by And. del Sarto including a fresco of Christ in Piet
(from SS Annunziata), and 16C altarpieces from suppressed convents. The up
per floor, with the convent cells (now a restoration office) may also b
opened.—Nearby is the sports ground of Campo di Marte with the *Stadio Com*
unale, a remarkable building (1932) by Pier Luigi Nervi. It is capable of holdin
66,000 spectators.

Viale Giovine Italia ends at the Arno by another defensive towe
near PONTE SAN NICCOLÒ (Pl. 11; 4). Across the river begins Viale de
Colli (described in Rte 20), also laid out by Poggi which encircles th
hills of the Oltrarno as far as Porta Romana.

ENVIRONS OF FLORENCE

The most attractive and interesting place in the neighbourhood of Florence, and the most frequently visited, is *Fièsole,* which should on no account be missed even on the most hurried visit to the city. Not only is the little town interesting in itself (particularly for its Roman Theatre and Etruscan remains), but also, from its hill, there is a superb birds'-eye view of Florence. Charming walks and drives may be taken in the vicinity. Other places of interest within easy reach of the city (and all within its Province) are described in the routes below. A plan of the immediate environs of Florence is given on Atlas p 14-15.

Visitors with a little more time at their disposal (and preferably with their own transport), and who wish to see something of the magnificent countryside around Florence, should visit the following districts all described in the 'Blue Guide Northern Italy'). Country bus services from Florence are run by SITA (Via Santa Caterina da Siena), Lazzi (Piazza Stazione), CAP (13 Via Nazionale), and COPIT (P.za S.M. Novella). *Vallombrosa* (SITA bus in 1½ hr), a summer resort on the wooded slopes of the Pratomagno hills, is reached viâ Pontassieve. In its famous monastery, founded by St John Gualberto in 1040, Milton was a guest.—The upper valley of the Arno, beyond Vallombrosa, known as the *Casentino* contains several castles, and the little towns of Poppi and Bibbiena, all rich in Florentine history.—The *Chianti* countryside to the S. of Florence, where the famous Tuscan wine is grown, is traversed by a beautiful road known as the 'Chiantigiana' (N 222) which runs to Siena viâ Greve (SITA bus in hr).—The *Mugello,* N. of Florence at the foot of the Appenines, is an attractive valley, intensely cultivated with numerous summer resorts. It can be reached viâ Fièsole or Pontassieve (SITA bus to Borgo San Lorenzo in 1 hr).

The town of greatest importance near Florence is *Prato,* now an industrial town, but with a number of interesting Renaissance monuments in the old centre, including the church of S.M. delle Carceri by Giuliano da Sangallo, and the Duomo with a pulpit by Donatello and Michelozzo, and important frescoes in the choir by Filippo Lippi. Described in full in the 'Blue Guide Northern Italy', it can be reached by a frequent train service from Florence in c. 20 min, or by bus c. every 20 min in 30 min (viâ the motorway; services run by Lazzi and CAP).

Other famous Tuscan cities, farther afield, and meriting a prolonged visit (see the 'Blue Guide Northern Italy') include *Siena, San Gimignano, Volterra, Pistoia, Lucca, Pisa,* and *Arezzo.* Across the Appenines in Emilia is *Bologna,* also one of the most important and interesting towns in Italy. The best way of reaching these cities is given below.

Siena. Frequent bus services (SITA) in 1¼ hrs (viâ the 'superstrada'), or 2 hrs viâ the old road, N 2). The train service (in 1½-2 hrs, with a change sometimes necessary at Empoli), although passing through pretty country on a secondary line, is less convenient since the railway station of Siena is outside the town.
San Gimignano. Frequent bus services (SITA) viâ Poggibonsi in 1 hr 40 min.
Volterra. SITA bus services in 2 hrs.

Lucca is on a direct railway line from Florence viâ Prato and *Pistoia* with frequent (but slow) services (to Lucca in 1½-2 hrs; to Pistoia in c. ¾ hr). Bus services (Lazzi) to Lucca in 1 hr 20 min; to Pistoia in 50 min.

Pisa is reached by rail viâ Empoli; frequent service in 1¼-1½ hrs. Bus service run by Lazzi in 1 hr 30 min.

Arezzo is on the main railway line between Florence and Rome; most express trains stop here and there is a frequent service (in c. 1¼ hrs).

Bologna, on the main railway line to the N., can be reached by fast train in c. 1½ hrs.

23 FIÈSOLE AND SAN DOMENICO

BUS No. 7 from the Station, Duomo, and P.za San Marco. Frequent service (ev. 10–20 min) taking 30 min from the station, viâ San Domenico. For those with time, it is a beautiful walk (c. 2 hrs from Piazza del Duomo); otherwise the bus can be taken up to Fièsole, and then the descent down to Florence made on foot.

The main road to Fièsole, Viale Alessandro Volta (Pl. 7; 2) begins at Piazza delle Cure. Beyond P.za Edison, Via di San Domenico continues to ascend the hillside with a beautiful view of Fièsole and its villas. A double curve precedes San Domenico.

Walkers may reach San Domenico from Piazza delle Cure, either by taking Viale Aless. Volta and diverging left after c. 500 m. up Via delle Forbici, or by Via Giovanni Boccaccio, just N. of the Piazza which runs along the bank of the Mugnone. This passes (r.) *Villa Palmieri,* the garden of which was the scene of one of the episodes in Boccaccio's 'Decameron'. The villa was bought in 1454 by Marco Palmieri. The present garden was laid out after 1697.—On the bend of the road further up is Villa Schifanoia, now a graduate school of fine arts.

6½ km **San Domenico di Fièsole** (comp. Atlas p 12) is a little hamlet within the commune of Fièsole, with several beautiful private villas. The church of SAN DOMENICO dates from 1406–35; the portico (1635) and campanile (1611–13) were added by Matteo Nigetti.

INTERIOR. The side chapels have fine Renaissance arches in pietra serena and some of the altarpieces have handsome Mannerist frames. SOUTH SIDE, 1st chap. Crucifixion, an interesting painting attrib. to the school of Botticelli; 2nd chap. *Lor. di Credi,* Baptism of Christ (a composition borrowed from the painting by Verrocchio in the Uffizi), and an old copy of a painting of the Madonna and Child with SS John the Baptist and Sebastian by Perugino.—NORTH SIDE, 1s chap., *Fra' Angelico,* *Madonna with angels and Saints (c. 1430; recently restored; light on r.); the architectural background was added by Lor. di Credi in 1501, when the frame was redesigned (the paintings of Saints are by a follower of Lor. Monaco). The panels of the predella are copies; the originals are in the National Gallery, London. While living in the convent Fra' Angelico also painted an Annunciation (now in the Prado) and a Coronation of the Virgin (now in the Louvre), photographs of which are displayed here. 2nd chap., *Giov. Ant Sogliani* (completed by *Santi di Tito*), Epiphany; 3rd chap.; *Jac. da Empoli,* Annunciation (1615). On the high altar is a gilded wood tabernacle of 1613 (*Andrea Balatri*).

In the **Convent of San Domenico** St Antoninus (Antonino Pierozzi 1389–1459) and Fra' Angelico (Guido di Pietro or Fra' Giov. da Fièsole 1387–1455) first assumed the religious habit; they moved down to the convent of San Marco after 1437. The little CHAPTER HOUSE (ring at No. 4, r. of the church contains a beautiful fresco of the Crucifixion by *Fra' Angelico* (c. 1430) and a detached fresco (with its sinopia) of the Madonna and Child, also by him.

The pretty Via delle Fontanelle leads from Piazza San Domenico, passing *La Torraccia,* a large villa with a 14C loggia, now owned by the Comune di Fièsole and used by various societies and as a Music School. This was the residence of Walter Savage Landor from 1829 until 1835 when he left his family here. Emerson, Monckton Milnes and N.P. Willis were among his visitors. The 'Valley of Ladies' described in the 'Decameron' lies within the grounds, which include a fine park and a charming little Italianate garden.

The façade of the Badia Fiesolana. (Archivio Alinari)

Via della Badia dei Roccettini, descending to the left from San Domenico, leads (5 min on foot) to the ***Badia Fiesolana** (see Atlas p 12), the cathedral of Fièsole until 1028. In a beautiful isolated position, it was probably built on the site of the martyrium of St Romulus. Bp Donato of Fièsole (died c. 876), thought to have been an Irishman, was elected to the bishop's see when he stopped here on his journey back from Rome. It was later a Benedictine and Lateranensian house. The church was rebuilt in the 15C under the direction of Cosimo il Vecchio who here founded a library with Vespasiano da Bisticci as his librarian.—In the conventual buildings (undergoing alterations) the *European University Institute* was established in 1976.—The rough stone front incorporates the charming ***FAÇADE** of the smaller Romanesque church with inlaid marble decoration.

The simple cruciform ***INTERIOR** is open only for a service at 11 on Sun; at other times adm is sometimes granted to visitors who ring at the door on the r. The interesting plan of the small church has been attrib. to *Brunelleschi,* or to a close follower. The side chapels have handsome round arches in pietra serena, and five steps precede the E. end, also decorated with pietra serena, and with an elegant inscription to Cosimo de' Medici. Over the 1st l. altar is a 15C Florentine painting of the Pietà.

From the charming terrace in front of the church the view extends beyond cypresses and olives to Florence. On a clear day, to the l. of the Duomo and campanile, can be seen the towers of Palazzo Vecchio, the Bargello, and the Badia, with Forte di Belvedere beyond, and further l., on the skyline, San Miniato. To the r. of the Duomo is the dome of the Chapel of the Princes of San Lorenzo. On the hill opposite the Badia, beyond Via Faentina which follows the floor of the Mugnone valley, is the handsome yellow-coloured Villa Salviati with its cypress avenue. Behind the church rises the hill of Fièsole.

From San Domenico the ascent to Fièsole may be made either by the main road or by the shorter and prettier old road (Via Vecchia Fiesolana, very narrow and steep; comp. p 205); both are lined with fine villas and beautiful trees and provide splendid views of Florence.

8 km **FIÈSOLE** (295 m) is a little town (14,700 inhab.) in a magnificent position on a thickly wooded hill overlooking the valleys of the Arno and the Mugnone. It has always been a fashionable residential district, once much favoured by the English, and its beautiful hillside is enhanced by fine villas and gardens, and stately cypress groves (some of them now threatened by disease). An Etruscan city, its foundation precedes that of Florence by many centuries, and, with its own local government, it is still proudly independent of the larger city. It is crowded with Florentines and visitors in summer when its position makes it one of the coolest places in the neighbourhood of the city. **Plan on Atlas p 12–13.**

Recent excavations suggest that the hill was inhabited in the Bronze Age. The site of *Faesulae,* on a hilltop above a river valley, was typical of Etruscan settlements. Probably founded in the 6C or 5C B.C. from Arezzo, it became one of the chief cities of the Etruscan confederacy. It is first mentioned in 283 B.C., when its people, in alliance with other Etruscans, were defeated by the Romans at Lake Vadimone. With the Roman occupation it became the most important town in Etruria, but the barbarian invasions led to the decay of the city. In 854 the county of Fièsole was merged with that of Florence. After a decisive battle in 1125 in which only the Cathedral and the Bishop's Palace escaped destruction, the ascendancy of Florence over the older city was finally assured.

The bus stops in PIAZZA MINO DA FIÈSOLE, the spacious main square of the town, called after the Renaissance sculptor (c. 1430–84; born at Poppi in the Casentino) who made Fièsole his home. The **Cathedral** (closed 12–15) was founded in 1028, and enlarged in the 13C and 14C. It was over-restored in 1878–83. The tall battlemented bell-tower of 1213 is visible from Florence and the surrounding hills.

The bare stone INTERIOR, with a raised choir above a hall crypt, is similar in plan to San Miniato al Monte. The massive columns have fine capitals (some of them Roman). Lights in the choir (coin-operated) illuminate the church. Above the W. door is a statue of St Romulus, Bp of Fièsole, in a garlanded niche, by *Giov. della Robbia* (1521). Stairs lead up to the CHOIR. On the r. is the CAPPELLA SALUTATI with frescoes in the vault of the Evangelists by *Cosimo Rosselli* and two of *Mino da Fièsole's* best works: the *Tomb of Bp Leonardo Salutati (1465) with a fine portrait bust, and an *Altar-frontal. To the r. of the apse, *School of Cosimo Rosselli,* Coronation of the Virgin, a crowded composition in bad condition, with a contemporary frame. Over the high altar is a large rich *Altarpiece by *Bicci di Lorenzo* (c. 1440); the apse is frescoed by *Nicodemo Ferrucci* (late 16C). On the l. of the apse, *Giov. del Biondo,* Coronation of the Virgin (1372). In a nearby chapel is a marble altarpiece by *And. Ferrucci* (1493). The SACRISTY contains a precious mitre (rarely shown).—The columns in the CRYPT (light; coin-operated) have interesting primitive capitals. The granite font is the work of *Fr. del Tadda* (1569). Behind the grille, surrounding the altar of St Romulus, are four marble columns with charming antique Ionic capitals.

The piazza slopes up to the old *Palazzo Pretorio,* now the town hall, with a loggia decorated with the coats-of-arms of many podestà. Next to it stands the church of *Santa Maria Primerana,* rebuilt in the 16-17C, with a quaint porch. The interior contains a 14C painted Crucifix, a bas-relief with the self-portrait in profile of Fr. da Sangallo executed as a thank-offering in 1542, and a Della Robbian Crucifix with the Madonna and Saints. In the sanctuary is a 13C painting of the Madonna in a Gothic tabernacle, and damaged frescoes attrib. to the school of Taddeo Gaddi.—The unusual equestrian monument (1906) in the piazza celebrates the meeting between Victor Emmanuel II and Garibaldi at Teano. The lower end of the square is occupied by the *Seminary* (1697) and the *Bishop's Palace* (1675), both with fragments of the Etruscan acropolis wall in their garden. Between them Via San Francesco, a very steep paved lane, climbs up the hill, passing (r.) a public park (comp. below). Higher up is a terrace with a *View of Florence dominated by the cupola of the Duomo. Here are two war memorials. Above, beside another viewpoint, is the church of Sant'Alessandro, recently restored (if closed, ask at the Curia Vescovile).

On the site of an Etruscan and Roman temple, it is thought to have been founded in the 6C. The Romanesque church was altered in the 16C and 18C. The bare basilican interior is remarkable for its cipollino marble *Columns with Ionic capitals and bases from a Roman building. An oratory off the l. aisle (light on r.) contains an altarpiece of the Assumption by Gerino da Pistoia (showing the influence of Perugino) and 16C Mannerist frescoes of the Life of the Virgin.

Beyond (l.) the church of Santa Cecilia is the top of the hill (345 m), the site of the Etruscan and later Roman acropolis. Here are the convent buildings of **San Francesco** (closed 12–15). The church of c. 1330 has an attractive little rose-window. The interior was restored in neo-Gothic style in 1905–07. The choir arch is attrib. to *Bened. da Maiano.* All the paintings have been removed for restoration; they include an *Annunciation by *Raff. Del Garbo,* a Crucifixion by *Neri di Bicci,* and an Immaculate Conception by *Piero di Cosimo.* In the Franciscan friary are several charming little cloisters, some remains of the acropolis, and a small missionary MUSEUM of Eastern objets d'art (notable Chinese and Egyptian collections) haphazardly arranged in old-fashioned show-cases.—A gate admits to a public park with an ilex wood, through which shady paths lead back downhill to the main square.

From Piazza Mino the street behind the apse of the cathedral leads to the entrance to the ***Roman Theatre, Archaeological Excavations, and Museum** (adm see p 57).

From the terrace there is a good comprehensive view of the excavations in a plantation of olive trees, backed by the Mugnone valley and the dark cypresses of the hill of San Francesco. The ROMAN THEATRE, built at the end of the 1C B.C., was enlarged by Claudius and Septimius Severus. The *cavea,* excavated in the hillside, is 34 m across and held 3000 spectators. Some of the seats are intact; others have been restored with smaller blocks of stone. Plays and concerts are performed here during a festival held every summer (the 'Estate Fiesolana'; comp p 55).—On the right of the theatre are the ROMAN BATHS, probably built in the 1C A.D. and enlarged by Hadrian. In front are three rectangular swimming baths. The chambers near the three arches (reconstructed at the end of the 19C) consist of the *hypocausis,* with circular ovens, where the water was heated, the *calidarium* with its hypocaust, and the *tepidarium.* In front of the arches is the *palestra,* and behind them the *frigidarium.*—A small terrace here provides a fine view of a long stretch of ETRUSCAN WALLS (reinforced in the Roman and medieval periods), with a gateway, which enclosed the city.—On the other side of the theatre (to the N.W.) is a ROMAN TEMPLE (1C B.C.), with its basement intact, and, on a lower level, remains of an ETRUSCAN TEMPLE (3C B.C.), both of them approached by steps. Nearby, are copies of the two original altars from the temples (the larger one is Roman).

The MUSEUM was built in 1912–14; the exterior is an idealized reconstruction of the Roman temple. Reopened in 1981, it has been modernized and the collections beautifully rearranged. The material is being re-evaluated in the light of new excavations, etc. Under the portico is a fragment from the frieze of the Roman temple. The first five rooms contain the topographical collection from Fièsole and its territory. ROOM I. Etruscan-Roman finds from Fièsole, including the so-called 'She-wolf' in bronze (in fact the torso of a lioness), found on the probable site of the Capitol of Faesulae. In Case 1 is displayed Bronze Age material recently found on the hill of San Francesco and in the Temple area (the first signs of a prehistoric settlement in Fièsole). Also here, Etruscan stelai, and a case of bronzes.—ROOM II. Etruscan urns in pietra serena from the necropolis of Bargellino; cylindrical lead cinerary urn decorated with Roman reliefs; inscribed stelai in pietra serena (2C A.D.); small bronzes; Bucchero ware.—ROOMS III & IV contain material found in the area of the Roman Theatre and Temples, including terracotta antefixes and other architectural fragments (the finds from the Etruscan Temple were made in excavations since 1955); and a marble frieze from the Theatre (which probably decorated the 'pulpitum'). Also displayed here is a head of Claudius.—Stairs lead up to R V which contains medieval finds.—The remaining rooms form the Antiquarium. RR VI & VII contain the well-preserved 'Stele Fiesolana' (5C B.C.), showing a funerary banquet, and dancing and hunting scenes, and an Etruscan collection including urns from Chiusi, Bucchero vases, bronzes, mirrors, etc.—Among the sculpture displayed in R VIII is a torso of Dionysius.

In Via Duprè (No. 1), just to the r. of the entrance to the Roman Theatre, is the small **Museo Bandini** (adm see p 58), a collection of Florentine art begun in 1795 by Angiolo Maria Bandini, and left by him to the Diocese of Fièsole.

The paintings are exhibited in two rooms on the FIRST FLOOR. Hand-lists (available in English) are lent to visitors. ROOM I. *Bernardo Daddi,* St John the Evangelist; *Fra' Angelico* (attrib.), Madonna and Child with angels; *13C Florentine School,* Madonna and Child; *Neri di Bicci,* Madonna in Adoration and Saints; *Taddeo Gaddi,* Annunciation; *Lor. Monaco,* Crucifixion; *Bicci di Lorenzo,* Celestial gerarchy; works by *Jac. di Cione,* and *Nic. di Buonaccorso;* and a small case of Byzantine ivories.—Room II. *15C Florentine School* (Filippino Lippi?), Madonna and Child with an angel; *Jac. del Sellaio,* *Three Triumphs of Petrarch (Divinity, Love and Chastity, and Time); Saints by *Lor. di Bicci, Giov. da Ponte,* and others.—On the GROUND FLOOR a room displays sculptural fragments from the Baptistery of Florence, and Della Robbian works.

A road diverges l. from Via Duprè for the *Cemetery,* where the sculptor Giovanni Duprè (1817–82) is buried (his tomb bears a copy of his Pietà). Against the hill of San Francesco may be seen a large section of the Etruscan wall.—Another stretch of the *Etruscan Wall* can be seen by following Via Santa Maria from Piazza Mino. Via Sant'Apollinare or (r.) Via Belvedere, with superb views, continue up hill to Via Adriano Mari which skirts the wall along the E. limit of the Etruscan city. From here Via Montecéceri (also with magnificent views) leads across to the beautiful woods of *Montecéceri* (public footpaths), with remarkable disused quarries of pietra serena.—In Via del Bargellino (comp. the Plan) are two Etruscan tombs (3C B.C.).

WALKS IN THE VICINITY OF FIÈSOLE

The walks described below follow many beautiful old roads. Even though most of them are very narrow, they are still used by cars, and those on foot should take great care of the traffic.

A. From P.za Mino the narrow ***Via Vecchia Fiesolana*** descends steeply past the hospital of Fièsole and the convent of *San Girolamo* (15-17C; which includes pensione). On the left is the *Villa Medici* (no adm), built by Michelozzo in 1458–61 for Cosimo il Vecchio. Its beautiful garden, one of the earliest of the Renaissance, is built on the steep hillside with a superb view of Florence. It was a favourite retreat of Lorenzo il Magnifico and members of the Platonic Academy.—The road continues downhill (or a path, Via degli Angeli, may be followed); below the villa after two sharp bends, there is a breathtaking view of Florence from the road, here lined with venerable cypresses. At the intersection with Via Duprè Via Vecchia Fiesolana continues down to San Domenico (see p 200), passing several beautiful villas. Via Duprè leads r. to a fork with Via Fontelucente, an even narrower old road which descends l. to the church of *Fontelucente*, built over a spring, in a beautiful isolated spot above the Mugnone valley. It contains a triptych by Mariotto di Nardo. Via Duprè continues with a view across the valley to Via Bolognese, where the hillside was disfigured by modern houses in the 1950s. *Villa Duprè* was the home of the sculptor. The road curves to the r. round the hill, and from the hamlet of San Martino, with the campanile of the cathedral of Fièsole prominent ahead, it is a short way back to Piazza Mino.

B. The pretty Via Benedetto da Maiano diverges from the main Florence road below Fièsole (comp. the Plan; the bus may be taken downhill from Piazza Mino to the request stop here). It passes the entrance to the *Pensione Bencistà*, formerly Villa Goerike where the painter Arnold Böcklin (1827–1901) lived and died.—At a crossroads (2½ km) is the little group of houses called **Maiano**, the home of the brothers Benedetto and Giuliano da Maiano (1442–92 and 1432–90). In the restored church (if closed ring at No. 6), of ancient foundation, the choir is decorated with pietra serena and there are several 16C paintings by G.B. Naldini. A farm now occupies the Benedictine monastery (with a 14C fresco of the Madonna della Misericordia). A road continues uphill for a few hundred metres past a well-known trattoria, and quarries of pietra serena, with fine views of the wooded hills. The road which runs from the crossroads down to Florence passes *Villa Il Salviatino*, the 16C home of Alamanno Salviati. Via Benedetto da Maiano continues with charming views of the hills of Settignano; just after Villa Sant'Ignazio Via Poggio Gherardo diverges left for San Martino a Mensola, Villa I Tatti, and Settignano (comp. Rte 24).

C. From P.za Mino Via Antonio Gramsci, the main street of Fièsole leads uphill through the town into Via Giacomo Matteotti just above the two Etruscan tombs in Via del Bargellino (comp. above). Beyond the locality of Borgunto (where a road leads uphill to Via Adriano Mari and remains of part of the Etruscan walls, comp. above), Via Francesco Ferrucci continues out of the town with increasingly beautiful views of the wide Mugnone valley. Some way along the main road, a by-road (signposted, Montebeni, Vincigliata, and Settignano) diverges right. This runs along a ridge round the N. shoulder of Monte Céceri through magnificent woods. Just beyond *Villa di Bosco* with a restored tower and Italianate garden, there is a superb view of Florence. The road climbs to a fork; on the l. a road leads to Montebeni and Settignano; and to the r. the road continues past *Castel di Poggio* (restored in the 19C; used in summer for performances of the 'Estate Fiesolana'), and then descends, lined with magnificent cypresses, past (5 km) the *Castello di Vincigliata*. The castle was built in 1031, and restored in 1855 by John Temple Leader, who was here visited by Gladstone and Queen Victoria. Further down the hill the road passes Villa I Tatti, before it comes to the main road for Settignano at Ponte a Mensola (see Rte 24).

Longer excursions may be taken to the N. of Fièsole. Beyond Piazza Mino, the main street (described above) continues uphill through the town. Beyond Borgunto it is continued as the 'Strada dei Bosconi' which runs above the beautiful valley of the Mugnone, with superb views, as far as (9 km) *Olmo*. Here it joins Via Faenza (N. 302) which continues N. to Borgo San Lorenzo and the Mugello valley (see the 'Blue Guide Northern Italy').—In the other direction,

Via Faenza returns to Florence along the Mugnone through the village of *L. Caldine,* just outside of which (7½ km from Florence) is the little **Convento della Maddalena,** a hospice of the Dominican convent of San Marco, now run by three friars. Here Fra' Bartolomeo lived and painted several frescoes.

From the entrance gate, protected by some ancient cypresses, the drive passes a little chapel in the orchard with a 'Noli me tangere' (seen through the door) by *Fra' Bartolomeo.* Visitors ring at the convent (preferably 10–12, 16–18) and are conducted by a friar. The CHURCH, with fine pietra serena decoration (including the arms of the founders, the Cresci) was built in 1480. It has been attrib. to a follower of *Michelozzo* or *Giul. da Maiano.* Over the high altar is a painting of the *Madonna in Maestà attrib. to the workshop of *Taddeo Gaddi* (early 14C). Over a 17C side altar is a fresco by *Fra' Bartolomeo* of the *Annunciation above a presepio with terracotta figures from the workshop of Della Robbia against a painted background. The charming portico outside the W. door looks out over the Mugnone valley. The little cloister is also noteworthy.—Bus No. 12 from Florence (P.za delle Cure; Pl. 7; 2) follows Via Faentina as far as Querciola (request stop at the gate of the convent). The old railway which follows the road is being repaired and may be put back into operation.

From Olmo (see above) a road (5 km) leads to *Pratolino* (12½ km from Florence) on the Via Bolognese. The huge park of *Villa Demidoff* (over 150 hectares) has recently been acquired by the Province and will be opened to the public. A remarkable garden was created here in 1569 for Francesco I de' Medici by Buontalenti; only Giambologna's colossal statue of *Appennino survives. In the villa (later demolished) Galileo stayed in 1605–06 as tutor to Cosimo, eldest son of Ferdinando I.—8 km N., on top of a hill (815 m) is the *Convent o, Montesenario* set in woods full of grottoes and cells. Here seven Florentine merchants became hermits and established the Servite Order of mendicant friars in 1233.—Via Bolognese returns to Florence viâ the cemetery of *Trespiano* (near which a by-road leads r. to the pretty romanesque church of Cercina in lovely countryside N. of Careggi, comp. p 208). Via Bolognese enters Florence at Ponte Rosso and P.za della Libertà (Pl. 7; 1).—Bus No. 25 follows Via Bolognese as far as *Trespiano;* No. 46 continues to *Pratolino.*

24   SETTIGNANO

Bus No. 10 from the Station, viâ the Duomo and P.za S. Marco every 10–20 min in ½ hr.

The main road for Settignano diverges left from Lungarno del Tempio near Ponte San Niccolò (Pl. 11; 4). The long straight Via del Campofiore and its continuation Via Lungo l'Affrico run N.E. After c 1 km Via Gabriele d'Annunzio, signposted for Settignano, diverges right. Beyond Coverciano, the locality of **Ponte a Mensola,** at the foot of the hill of Settignano, is reached. Here Via Poggio Gherardo (for Maiano, comp. p 205) branches left from the main road past the entrance to *Villa di Poggio Gherardo,* traditionally thought to be the setting for the earliest episodes in Boccaccio's 'Decameron'. A small road (r.) leads shortly to *SAN MARTINO A MENSOLA, a Benedictine church of the 9C, founded by St Andrew, thought to have been a Scotsman and archdeacon to the bishop of Fièsole, Donato, who was probably from Ireland. It is preceded by a 17C loggia. The 15C campanile was damaged by lightning in 1867. Visitors ring at the door on the right.

The graceful 15C INTERIOR replaced the romanesque church (remains of which have been found beneath the nave). It was altered in the 19C and has recently been restored. Over the altar in the S. aisle is a damaged fresco of the Crucifixion, and a painting of the Madonna enthroned with SS Andrew and Sebastian attrib. to *Cosimo Rosselli.* At the end of the aisle, is a *Triptych (altered) of the Madonna enthroned with two female Saints, by *Taddeo Gaddi.* The Sanctuary is preceded by a beautifully carved arch in pietra serena with two pretty little tabernacles. On the high altar is a triptych of the Madonna and Child with the donor Amerigo Zati, and Saints, by a follower of Orcagna (1391), known as the

Master of San Martino a Mensola'. At the end of the N. aisle, *Annunciation, by a follower of Fra' Angelico. In the pavement a stone marks the burial place of St Andrew. Over the other altar in this aisle is a worn fresco lunette of St Francis receiving the stigmata, and an altarpiece of the *Madonna and four Saints by *Neri di Bicci.*—A tiny room off the sanctuary (l.) contains a MUSEUM. Here is a wooden *Casket, decorated with good paintings by the school of Agnolo Gaddi, which formerly contained the body of St Andrew, first abbot of the priory. The reliquary bust in wood of St Andrew dates from the end of the 14C. The intarsia cupboard in the little sacristy (opposite) is attrib. to *Benedetto da Maiano.*

The little by-road leads from the church to a group of houses by the garden entrance to **Villa I Tatti** (the main entrance is on Via Vincigliata which begins at Ponte a Mensola, and skirts the garden up to the house). The unusual name is probably derived from the Zati family who lived here. It was the home of Bernard Berenson (1865–1959), the art historian and collector, and was left by him to Harvard University as a Centre of Italian Renaissance Studies. A beautiful Italianate garden surrounds the villa which contains Berenson's library (open to post doctorate scholars) and *Collection of Italian paintings (not open to the public).—The pretty by-road continues up the hill through woods past the castles of Vincigliata and Poggio to (6 km) Fièsole (see p 205).

In Via Vincigliata at the bottom of the hill are two plaques recording the writers and artists who lived and worked in the neighbourhood. Via di Corbignano leads to *Villa Boccaccio* (rebuilt), once owned by the father of Giovanni Boccaccio who probably spent his youth here.

From Ponte a Mensola the road continues up to Settignano winding across the old road; both have fine views of the magnificent trees on the skyline of the surrounding hills.—7½ km **Settignano** (178 m), a cheerful village on a pleasant hill, is known for its school of sculptors, most famous of whom were Desiderio (1428–64) and the brothers Rossellino (Antonio Gamberelli, 1427–79, and Bernardo Gamberelli, 1409–64). In the main square is the church of *Santa Maria,* built in 1518, reconstructed at the end of the 18C, and restored in 1976. It contains a charming group of the *Madonna and Child and two angels in white enamelled terracotta attrib. to the workshop of And. della Robbia (in the sanctuary). The 16C organ was reconstructed in 1908 and has been restored. The pulpit was designed by Bern. Buontalenti. On the 1st N. altar is a Resurrection by Maso di San Friano.—In the piazza is a statue of Nic. Tommaseo, the patriotic writer, who died here in 1874.—In the lower Piazza Desiderio, with a monument to the sculptor, there is a superb view of Florence, including the Duomo.

At the *Villa Michelangelo Buonarroti* (no adm) Michelangelo passed his youth a charcoal drawing attrib. to him of a triton or satyr, found on the kitchen wall, was detached and restored in 1979). Mark Twain wrote 'Pudd'nhead Wilson' in *Villa Viviani.*—The 15C *Villa Gamberaia* (no adm), c. 1 km S.E., was once owned by the Gamberelli family of stone-masons, architects and sculptors. It has a splendid *Garden.

A branch road (sign-posted to Montebeni) from Settignano joins a pretty road to Fièsole (comp. above) at Vincigliata. Fièsole may also be reached across the hills from Settignano viâ Maiano.

25   THE MEDICI VILLAS OF CAREGGI, LA PETRAIA, AND CASTELLO. SESTO FIORENTINO

Bus No. 14C from the Station or Duomo to *Careggi* (the penultimate request stop before the terminal).—Bus No. 28 from the Station for *La Petraia, Castello,* and *Sesto.* A bus is recommended to traverse the uninteresting N. suburbs of Florence, but pretty country walks may be taken in the hills behind Careggi and La Petraia.

From the Fortezza da Basso Via del Romito (Pl. 5; 1) and its continuation, Via F. Corridoni, lead N., followed by bus 28 and 14 as far as (3 km) Piazza Dalmazia, in the suburbs of *Rifredi*. Here bus 14C diverges right along the broad Viale Morgagni for *Careggi*, the main hospital of Florence. At the top of the hill, beyond the main buildings of the hospital (request-stop), in a well-wooded park, is the **Villa Medicea di Careggi**, now used as a nurses' home (adm only with special permission from the administration of Santa Maria Nuova).

The 14C castellated farmhouse was acquired by the Medici in 1417. Cosimo i Vecchio returned here after his exile in Venice in 1434, and engaged Michelozzo to enlarge the villa and add a loggia. It became the literary and artistic centre of the Medicean court, the meeting place of the famous Platonic Academy which saw the birth of the humanist movement of the Renaissance. Among its members, who met in the gardens here, were Marsilio Ficino, Angelo Poliziano, Pico della Mirandola, and Greek scholars, including Gemisthos Plethon and Argyropoulos, who came to Florence after the fall of Constantinople. In the villa, Cosimo il Vecchio, Piero di Cosimo, and Lorenzo il Magnifico all died. It was burnt after the expulsion of the Medici at the end of the 15C, but renovated by Cosimo I. In the 19C it was restored by Francis Sloan.

Several pretty walks may be taken in the hills behind Careggi at the foot of Monte Morello. A road follows the Terzolle stream through the hamlet of Serpiolle towards CÈRCINA (c. 1 hr on foot) where the fine romanesque church (*Sant'Andrea*) has an ancient campanile and Renaissance porch. It contains a polychrome wood statue of the Madonna enthroned (13C) and early frescoes attrib. to Dom. Ghirlandaio. The 15C cloister has frescoes with charming country scenes. An unusual festival is held here on the feast of St Anthony Abbot, with a mounted procession and the blessing of animals.

Another walk (½ hr) follows the road (l.) beyond the villa which leads down across the Terzolle towards *Villa La Quiete*, owned since 1650 by the sisters of the Convent of Le Montalve, who here run a school. Its collection of paintings include a Coronation of the Virgin with Saints, by the workshop of Botticelli and a painted Crucifix of the 13C. Via di Boldrone continues to the Villa della Petraia (see below).

From Piazza Dalmazia Bus 28 continues viâ Via Santo Stefano in Pane (10-11C church with Della Robbian decoration) along the busy Via Reginaldo Giuliano. Just beyond (5 km) the locality known as Il Sodo (request-stop), a narrow road on the r. leads up to **Villa della Petraia** (adm see p 59).

Originally a castle of the Brunelleschi, the villa was rebuilt in 1575 for the grand-duke Ferdinando I de' Medici by *Buontalenti*. In 1864–70 it was a favourite residence of Victor Emmanuel II, and in 1919 it was presented to the State by Victor Emmanuel III.—A pretty GARDEN and moat precede the villa which still preserves a tower of the old castle. On the upper terrace of the garden (view) with orange and lemon trees, is a fountain by *Tribolo* with a bronze statue of *Venus (or 'Florence wringing water from her hair'; removed for restoration since 1980) by *Giambologna*, transferred here from the Villa di Castello in 1785. The huge ilex (400 years old) lower down was a favourite tree of Victor Emmanuel II (who built the tree house). A magnificent Park, with ancient cypresses, extends behind the villa to the E. The park and gardens are beautifully maintained.

The VILLA is shown on a guided tour to small groups (ring bell; comp. p 59). The Courtyard was covered with a glass roof and used as a ball-room by Victor Emmanuel II. The decorative Baroque *Frescoes beneath the two side loggias, illustrating the history of the Medici family, are by *Volterrano* (1636–46); those on the other two walls are attrib. to *Giovanni da San Giovanni*. The ground floor rooms were furnished as state apartments in the 19C; they are hung with 17C tapestries. In the Chapel is a painting of the Madonna and Child by *Pier Fr Fiorentino,* and an altarpiece of the Holy Family by the school of *Andrea de Sarto.*—On the first floor the private apartments, decorated in neo-classical style, contain a Chinese painting of the Port of Canton, pastels by *Rosalba Carriera,* and paintings by the school of *Mattia Rosselli.* The gaming room is remarkable 'period piece'.

*Villa di Castello, from a tempera lunette by Giusto Utens,
1599. (Museo di Firenze com'era)*

At the bottom of Via della Petraia, in front of the interesting Baroque façade of *Villa Corsini* (being restored since its acquisition by the
State), Via di Castello leads shortly to **Villa di Castello** (adm to the
gardens only, as for La Petraia). It is now the seat of the Accademia
della Crusca, founded in 1582 for the study of the Italian language.
The first edition of the institute's dictionary dates from 1612.

The villa was acquired by Giovanni and Lorenzo di Pierfrancesco de' Medici,
Lorenzo il Magnifico's younger cousins, around 1477. Here they hung

Botticelli's famous 'Birth of Venus'. Botticelli's 'Primavera' and 'Pallas and th
Centaur' were also later brought here (and all the pictures remained in the hous
until 1761). The villa, inherited by Giovanni delle Bande Nere, was sacked durin
the siege of 1530, but restored under Giovanni's son, Cosimo I by Bronzino an
Pontormo. Like La Petraia it was presented to the State in 1919.

The typical Tuscan GARDEN, described by numerous travellers in the 16C an
17C, was laid out by *Tribolo* for Cosimo I c. 1537. The *Fountain by *Tribol
(with the help of *Pierino da Vinci*) is crowned by bronze figures of Hercules an
Antenaeus by *Ammannati* (1559–60; removed for restoration in 1980). Beneat
the terrace is an elaborate grotto (c. 1570) full of weird animals and encruste
with shell mosaics and stalactites. Giambologna's bronze birds, now in th
Bargello, were removed from here. In the floor are water spouts so that visitor
could be surprised by a thorough drenching from their hosts. From the uppe
terrace, backed by woods, there is a good view. Here is a colossus representin
Appennino rising out of a pool and feeling the cold, by *Ammannati*. The hug
Orangery should not be missed. The garden was admired by Montaigne in 158C

A narrow rural road (parallel to the main road lower down the hill) continue
beyond Villa di Castello towards Sesto (see below) viâ the hamlet of *Quinto*
Here, in Via Fratelli Rosselli is an ETRUSCAN *TOMB known as 'La Montagnola
(ring at No. 95), a tumulus containing a remarkable domed tholos buria
chamber (discovered in 1959).

The bus route ends at (9 km) **Sesto Fiorentino**, a small town (43,70
inhab.). At the entrance on the left is *Villa Corsi Salviati,* where ex
hibitions are held, with an 18C garden. The Post Office occupies th
15C Palazzo Pretorio, and the church has slight Romanesque remains
The MUSEO DELLE PORCELLANE DI DOCCIA (adm see p 58) contains
fine collection of porcelain made in the famous Doccia factory found
ed by Marchese Carlo Ginori in 1737. It includes some of the earlies
porcelain painted by J. K. W. Anreiter von Zirnfeld of Vienna, an
the first models by Gaspero Bruschi and Massimiliano Soldani. Th
firm, known as Richard-Ginori since 1896, continues t
flourish.—Pietro Bernini, father of the famous sculptor Gian Loren
zo, was born in Sesto in 1562.

From Sesto a road leads inland viâ Colonnata to the 'Strada panoramica d
Colli Alti' which skirts the wooded slopes of *Monte Morello* (934 m), wit
magnificent views, as far as Via Bolognese (see p 206).

26 THE CERTOSA DEL GALLUZZO
AND IMPRUNETA

Buses 37 and 36 from P.za Santa Maria Novella to the *Certosa of Galluzz*
No. 37 continues to Tavarnuzze. CAP bus from 13–15 Via Nazionale c. ever
hour to *Impruneta* in 40 min.

Outside Porta Romana begins the long Viale del Poggio Imperial
(Pl. 9; 7), lined with handsome villas and their gardens, and bordere
by a splendid avenue of trees. At the top is the huge villa of *Poggi*
Imperiale (adm see p 59), recently restored.

After its confiscation by Cosimo I in 1565 from the Salviati family, the villa r
mained the property of the grand-dukes of Florence and takes its name from th
grand-duchess Maria Maddalena. The Audience Chamber (1523–25) is decorate
by Rutilio Mannetti, Matteo Rosselli, and Fr. Curradi. The Salone, where occ
sional concerts are held, was designed by Gaspare Maria Paoletti. It is now
girls' school, and Princess Marie José of Belgium (later Queen of Italy) was
pupil here during the First World War.

To the r. the Siena road continues through Gelsomino, passing (r
the thick cypresses of the *Cimitero Evangelico degli Allori,* formerly
cemetery only for Orthodox Greeks. A turn of the road reveals th

picturesque hill of the Certosa.—5 km *Galluzzo,* beside the Ema. Just past the village, immediately to the right of the road on the *Colle di Montaguto* (110 m), stands the **Certosa del Galluzzo** (or *di Val d'Ema;* adm see p 57). There is a view of the monks' cells, the church, and the Gothic Palazzo degli Studi on the edge of the hill.

A road ascends to the car park. Visitors are conducted by a monk. The monastery was founded in 1342 by the Florentine Niccolò Acciaioli, High Steward of the Kingdom of Naples. In 1958 the Carthusians were replaced by Cistercians, their first reappearance in the area since their expulsion by the Grand Duke of Tuscany 176 years earlier. The spacious courtyard dates from 1545. The CHURCH with 17C frescoes by Orazio Fidani, and fine 16C stalls in the *Monk's Choir,* has recently been restored. Beneath the *Lay Brethren's Choir* is a chapel (at present closed for restoration) with the magnificent *Tomb-slab of Card. Agnolo II Acciaioli, formerly attrib. to Donatello and now thought to be the work of Fr. da Sangallo. Also here are three other pavement tombs of the Acciaioli family, and the Gothic monument to the founder, Niccolò Acciaioli (d 1365).—The extensive conventual buildings include two fine cloisters, the *'Colloquio',* with interesting 16C stained glass, and the *Chapter House,* with another expressive tomb slab by Fr. da Sangallo (of Leonardo Buonafede; 1550) and a good fresco of the Crucifixion by Mariotto Albertinelli. The secluded *GREAT CLOISTER is decorated with 66 majolica tondoes of Saints and Prophets, by And. and Giov. della Robbia. One of the monks' cells may be visited; they each have three rooms, a loggia, and a little garden.

The PALAZZO DEGLI STUDI, a fine Gothic hall designed by Fra' Jacopo Passavanti, was begun by Niccolò Acciaioli as a meeting place for young Florentines to study the liberal arts (and completed after his death). It is sometimes used for concerts and houses a PICTURE GALLERY, dominated by five frescoed *Lunettes of the Passion cycle, by *Pontormo* (1522–25), detached from the Great Cloister. These were painted when he came to live in the monastery in order to escape the plague in Florence in 1522. Also exhibited in the main hall: *Mariotto di Nardo,* Coronation of the Madonna with Saints; *Rid. Ghirlandaio,* SS Peter Martyr and George; *School of Orcagna,* Tondo of the Madonna and Child; *Jacopo del Casentino,* Madonna and Child (much ruined); and several other paintings by Florentine masters of the 14C and 15C. A Madonna and Child with St John, by *Lucas Cranach,* stolen in 1973, has since been recovered but is still not on display.—An adjoining room displays 16-17C works.

From (7½ km) *Le Rose* a long but pleasant walk ascends to Impruneta.—The road continues beneath the motorway to a road junction at the entrance to the motorway and the 'superstrada' for Siena. Here a secondary road (N 2) for Siena (signposted for Impruneta) continues to (9 km) *Tavarnuzze.*

From the Siena road beyond Tavarnuzze, a by-road soon diverges r. for (3 km) *Sant'Andrea in Percussina.* Here in the 'Albergaccio' (plaque) Niccolò Machiavelli lived and worked on 'The Prince'. The 'Osteria' in front of the villa is the successor to one frequented by the great statesman and historian.

A by-road ascends from Tavarnuzze to (14 km) **Impruneta** (correctly, *L'Impruneta;* 275 m), a large village (13,700 inhab.), on a plateau, where the great cattle fair of St Luke is still celebrated (mid-October), although it has now become a general fair. The clay in the soil has been used for centuries to produce terracotta for which the locality is famous. The kilns here still sell beautiful pottery (flower pots, floor tiles, etc.). In the large central piazza (where the fair is held) is the COLLEGIATA (*Santa Maria dell'Impruneta*), with a high 13C tower, and an elegant portico by Gherardo Silvani (1634).

The INTERIOR was restored, after severe bomb damage in 1944, to its Renaissance aspect which it acquired in the mid-15C under the Piovano Antonio degli Agli. South side, 1st altar, *Cristofano Allori,* Martyrdom of St Lawrence; 2nd altar, *Passignano,* Birth of the Virgin. In the nave chapel, bronze Crucifix attrib. to *Giambologna.*—At the entrance to the presbytery are two CHAPELS (c.

1452) by *Michelozzo,* with beautiful *Decoration in enamelled terracotta by *Luca della Robbia.* They were reconstructed and restored after bomb damage. The Chapel on the r. was built to protect a piece of the True Cross given to the church by Pippo Spano in 1426. It contains an enamelled terracotta ceiling, and an exquisite relief of the Crucifixion with the Virgin and St John in a tabernacle, flanked by the figures of St John the Baptist and a Bishop Saint. Beneath is a charming predella of adoring angels.—The Chapel on the l. protects a miraculous painting of the Virgin attrib. to St Luke which was ploughed up by a team of oxen in a field near Impruneta. It was taken to Florence to help the city in times of trouble. The beautiful ceiling is similar to the one in the other chapel. The frieze of fruit incorporates two reliefs of the Madonna and Child. The figures of SS Luke and Paul flank a tabernacle which contains the image of the Madonna and Child (usually covered by a painting of Saints). The silver altar frontal designed by G.B. Foggini replaces a marble schiacciato relief attrib. to a follower of Donatello, showing the discovery of the painting, which has been removed to the adjacent chapel.—The large high altarpiece (1375) was partially recomposed after it was shattered in the War. It is the work of *Tommaso de Mazza* and *Pietro Nelli.*—On the N. side of the nave are 16C inlaid stalls and a 15C cantoria. In the Baptistery a painting by the school of Orcagna has been removed for years for restoration.—A door beneath the portico on the r. leads into two Cloisters; off the second (l.) is the little Crypt (11C), with sculptural fragments.

From Impruneta the return by car to Florence may be made by continuing through the town to join (4 km) the 'Chiantigiana' (N 222), just N. of Strada. This beautiful road runs from Florence to Siena through the countryside where the famous Chianti wine is made. On the way back to Florence, beyond the golf course of Ugolino, it passes through the village of *Grássina* which is noted for it. Good Friday Passion play.—The road continues beneath the motorway; a by road diverges r. for *Ponte a Ema,* from which it is a short way (1 km; signposted) to **Santa Caterina dell'Antella,** in pretty countryside. This little chapel was built by the Alberti family in 1387 and frescoed by Spinello Aretino with the *Story o St Catherine (ring for the key at the kennels next door; closed on Sun).—The main road continues into Florence through *Badia a Rípoli.* Here, beside the ancient church of San Pietro, is the Abbazia, founded in 790 with a church (16C portico) and convent (frescoes by Bernardino Poccetti).

27   MONTEOLIVETO AND BELLOSGUARDO. BADIA A SETTIMO AND LASTRA A SIGNA

Bus No. 13 (red) from the Station to Viale Raffaello Sanzio (for *Monteoliveto* and P.za Torquato Tasso (for *Bellosguardo*).—Frequent country bus service (Lazzi) to *Lastra a Signa.*

On the S. bank of the Arno, near Ponte della Vittoria (Pl. 4; 7) is the thickly wooded hill of **Monteoliveto,** with some beautiful private villas and a military hospital. It is reached viâ Viale Raffaello Sanzio and (r.) Via di Monteoliveto (Pl. 8; 1). The hospital occupies the convent of the church of *San Bartolomeo* (for adm ring at No. 72A), with a worn Renaissance portal.

INTERIOR. At the entrance are two unusual stoups in the form of Vestal Virgins (16C and 17C). The W. wall and triumphal arch bear good frescoes by *Bern Poccetti.* In the nave has been placed an interesting fresco fragment (with its sinopia) of the Last Supper by *Sodoma* (very damaged), detached from the convent refectory. At the high altar, Entry of Christ into Jerusalem, by *Santi a Tito.*
Villa Strozzi, on the W. side of the hill, has been owned since 1974 by the Comune of Florence. The park is open to the public.

The adjoining hill to the S. is aptly called **Bellosguardo.** It is best reached from Piazza San Francesco di Paolo (Pl. 8; 4), by Via d Bellosguardo, which winds up the hill (keeping to the left). There is a superb view of Florence just before Piazza di Bellosguardo, with a charming group of houses. The hill, with its villas, was described by Elizabeth Barrett Browning. In *La Torricella* Ugo Foscolo lay sick in 1812 (bust). The short Via Roti Michelozzi (view of Florence) leads up to the *Villa dell'Ombrellino* (*di Bellosguardo;* no adm), with a tower and marble group of Charity attrib. to Francavilla over the door, and a fine garden. It was rented by Galileo in 1617–31, and was also once the home of the tenor Caruso. It has a famous view of Florence.

Beyond Monteoliveto the Pisa road leads out of Florence past a number of suburban villages on the plain where many factories have been built in the last few years.—5 km *San Quirico* has a pretty Renaissance church, served by Fra' Filippo Lippi in 1442. The suburb of *Scandicci,* where much new building has taken place since the War, lies to the S. Here in Villa Mirenda, D. H. Lawrence stayed while completing 'Lady Chatterley's Lover'.—8 km *Casellina.* Just beyond a power station, a by-road (signposted) leads to the church of *San Martino alla Palma* (c. 4 km S.W.), in a magnificent position in low rolling hills (seen from the main road). It was founded in the 10C, and contains a charming Madonna by a follower of Bernardo Daddi.—About 1 km beyond (9 km) *Piscetto,* and 5 min to the right of the road, is the church of *SS Giuliano e Settimo,* an 8C building, altered in subsequent centuries.—About 2 km N.W. of (11 km) *Fornaci* is the **Badia di San Salvatore a Settimo,** a 10C abbey, rebuilt for Cistercians in 1236–37, walled and fortified in 1371, and restored since 1944.

The church has an old campanile and a Romanesque façade with a round 15C window. For adm ring the (inconspicuous) bell by the gate to the l. of the façade. South side, 1st altar, Christ at the sepulchre, an unusual 15C painting; 2nd altar, *Lod. Buti,* Martyrdom of St Lawrence (1574). Behind the high altar in pietre dure is the Choir with a Della Robbian enamelled terracotta frieze of cherubims and the Agnus Dei, and two frescoed tondoes of the Annunciation by the school of Ghirlandaio. On the l. of the high altar is a little marble *Tabernacle, beautifully carved and attrib. to Giul. da Sangallo. The chapel on the l. of the high altar has good *Frescoes (in pooor condition) by *Giovanni da San Giovanni* (1629). N. side, 2nd altar, *School of Ghirlandaio,* Adoration of the Magi, and a wall tomb of 1096.—The interesting remains of the MONASTERY (ring at the Cloister) include much of the old fortifications, and the Chapter House and Lay Brothers Hall.

13 km **Lastra a Signa,** a large village near the confluence of the Vingone and the Arno, has long been famous for the production of straw hats. The old centre (r. of the main road) preserves its walls of 1380, with three gates. Here is the *Loggia di Sant'Antonio* (covered with scaffolding awaiting restoration), formerly a Hospital erected at the expense of the Arte della Seta in 1411. The portico of six arches (the seventh is walled up) has been attrib. as an early work to Brunelleschi. Nearby is the *Palazzo Pretorio,* a small building (also in need of restoration), with the escutcheons of many podestà.

Just beyond the town, off the main road (signposted), is the church of *San Martino a Gangalandi.* The Chapel at the W. end has frescoes by Bicci di Lorenzo and his school (1432; in very poor condition), and a font sculpted by a follower of Ghiberti. Over the first S. altar is a painting of five female Saints by the school of Bronzino. The fine semi-circular apse was decorated in pietra serena by Leon Battista Alberti. On the N. wall is a large detached fresco of St Chistopher, and fragments of 14C frescoes over the 2nd altar.

In the hills to the S.W. is the castle of *Malmantile* (1424), an outpost of Castracani against the Florentines, celebrated in a poem by Lorenzo Lippi.

28   POGGIO A CAIANO

Bus (COPIT) from P.za S.M. Novella every ½ hr in c. ½ hr to *Poggio a Caiano*.—Bus No. 29 from the Station to *Perétola*.

Outside Porta al Prato the long Via del Ponte alle Mosse (Pl. 4; 4) runs towards Pistoia.—6 km **Perétola,** was the home of the Vespucci family before they moved to Florence. The church of *Santa Maria* contains a *Tabernacle by Luca della Robbia (1441; moved here from Sant'Egidio in Florence). The beautiful marble sculptures of two classical angels and the Pietà are framed by decoration in colourful enamelled terracotta, Luca's first documented work in this medium.—At the small airport of Perétola (used by light aircraft and some domestic flights), the motorway from Florence to the coast diverges to the right. On the motorway, a few kilometres N. is the church of San Giovanni Battista, built in the 1960s by the Tuscan architect Giovanni Michelucci.—9 km *Brozzi,* a suburb of Florence severely damaged in the flood of 1966. The church contains an interesting font and ciborium. The church of *Sant'Andrea a Brozzi* (15C), farther on, contains frescoes by Dom. Ghirlandaio and pupils, and a Crucifix by Giov.di Francesco.—18 km **Poggio a Caiano,** at the foot of Monte Albano, is famous for its royal *VILLA. Although the house has been closed for restoration for many years, there are plans to reopen it as a museum of the Medici villas. Meanwhile, only the gardens are open (see p 58). It was acquired in 1480 by Lorenzo il Magnifico who commissioned Giul. da Sangallo to rebuild it. It became Lorenzo's favourite country villa.

The Villa, beyond the Ombrone, is a rectangular building on a broad terrace (fine view) supported by a colonnade. It contains numerous decorated apartments, the most remarkable of which is the *SALONE, with charming frescoes by *Franciabigio, And. del Sarto,* and *Aless. Allori* of incidents in Roman history paralleled in the history of Cosimo il Vecchio and Lorenzo. The colourful, gay *Lunettes (c. 1520), are perhaps the most famous works of *Pontormo.* The polychrome terracotta *Frieze, a classical representation of a Platonic myth, by *And. Sansovino* and *Giul. da Sangallo* was detached from the façade in 1967, and replaced by a copy. The original is to be exhibited in a room of the villa.—The pleasant gardens and park are open to the public daily. Distinguished guests were received at the villa before they entered the city, among them Montaigne in 1581.

To the S.W. of Poggio a Caiano a by-road leads to (5 km) *Carmignano* where the church of San Michele contains a remarkable altarpiece of the *Visitation by *Pontormo* (c. 1530).—The road continues to (20 km) *Vinci,* where Leonardo was born. In the 11C castle a small museum contains models of machines and apparatus invented by Leonardo (see the 'Blue Guide Northern Italy').

Another by-road S. of Poggio a Caiano leads to the Medici *Villa of Artimino (no adm) designed by Bern. Buontalenti (1594) for Ferdinando I. In a delightful position, this is one of the finest of the Medici villas. Galileo was a guest here in 1608. There is a restaurant in the farm buildings.—Just outside the village is the fine romanesque church of San Leonardo. Nearby, at *Comeana,* is the Etruscan *Tomb of Montefortini.

INDEX OF THE
PRINCIPAL ITALIAN ARTISTS

whose works are referred to in the text, with their birthplaces or the schools to which they belonged.—Abbreviations: A. = architect, engr. = engraver, G. = goldsmith, illum. = illuminator, min. = miniaturist, mos. = mosaicist, P. = painter, S. = sculptor, stuc. = stuccoist, W. = woodworker, Flor. = Florence.

ABBREVIATIONS OF CHRISTIAN NAMES

Agost.	= Agostino	Des.	= Desiderio	Ipp.	= Ippolito
Aless.	= Alessandro	Dom.	= Domenico	Laz.	= Lazzaro
Alf.	= Alfonso	Elis.	= Elisabetta	Leon.	= Leonardo
Ambr.	= Ambrogio	Fed.	= Federigo	Lod.	= Lodovico
And.	= Andrea	Fel.	= Felice	Lor.	= Lorenzo
Ang.	= Angelo	Ferd.	= Ferdinando	Mart.	= Martino
Ann.	= Annibale	Fil.	= Filippo	Matt.	= Matteo
Ant.	= Antonio	Fr.	= Francesco	Mich.	= Michele
Baldas.	= Baldassare	G. B.	= Giambattista	Nic.	= Nicola
Bart.	= Bartolomeo	Gasp.	= Gaspare	Pell.	= Pellegrino
Batt.	= Battista	Gaud.	= Gaudenzio	Raff.	= Raffaele
Bened.	= Benedetto	Giac.	= Giacomo	Rid.	= Ridolfo
Benv.	= Benvenuto	Giov.	= Giovanni	Seb.	= Sebastiano
Bern.	= Bernardino	Girol.	= Girolamo	Sim.	= Simone
Cam.	= Camillo	Giul.	= Giuliano	Stef.	= Stefano
Ces.	= Cesare	Gius.	= Giuseppe	Tim.	= Timoteo
Crist.	= Cristoforo	Greg.	= Gregorio	Tom.	= Tommaso
Dan.	= Daniele	Gugl.	= Guglielmo	Vinc.	= Vincenzo
Dav.	= Davide	Iac.	= Iacopo	Vitt.	= Vittorio
Def.	= Defendente	Inn.	= Innocenzo		

ABBATI, GIUS. (c. 1830-68), P. Venice. —107

AGOSTINO DI DUCCIO (1418-81), S. Flor. sch.—20, 147

AGOSTINO DI JACOPO (14C), S. Flor. sch.—63

ALBERTI, LEON BATTISTA (1404-72), A. Flor.—22, 37, 118, 133, 142, 158, 195, 213

ALBERTINELLI, MARIOTTO (1474-1515), P. Flor. sch.—76, 96, 105-6, 113, 116, 193, 211

ALLORI, ALESS. (1535-1607), P. Flor.—84, 94, 97, 114, 116, 118, 124, 126, 136-8, 155, 158, 172, 180, 214

ALLORI, CRISTOFANO (son of Aless.; 1577-1621), P. Flor.—105, 106, 118, 161-2, 211

AMBROGIO DI BALDESE (1352-1429), P. Flor.—71, 76

AMMANNATI, BARTOLOMEO (1511-92), A. & S. Settignano.—26, 79, 84, 85, 100, 101, 109-10, 115, 126, 131, 144, 146, 162, 164, 165, 167, 174, 187, 194, 210

ANDREA DI BONAIUTO (or Andrea da Firenze; fl. 1343-77), P. Flor.—15, 134, 137, 176

ANDREA DEL CASTAGNO see Castagno

ANDREA DA FIRENZE see Andrea di Bonaiuto

ANDREA DI GIUSTO (fl. 1427), P. Flor.—113, 152

ANDREA DEL SARTO (Andrea d'Agnolo; 1486-1530), P. Flor.—26, 94, 96, 97, 102, 104, 106, 117, 118, 125, 164, 190, 198, 208, 214

ANDREOTTI, LIBERO (1875-1933), S. Pescia.—158

ANTICO, L' (Pier Jac. Alari Bonacolsi; 1460-1528), S. & medallist, Mantua.—147, 148, 150

ARNOLDI, ALBERTO (d. 1377), S. & A. Flor (?).—64, 71, 74, 130

ARNOLFO DI CAMBIO (c. 1245-1302), A. & S. Colle Val d'Elsa.—12, 64, 72, 75, 80, 87, 143, 146, 150, 153

ASPETTI, TIZIANO (1565-1607), S. Padua.—140

ATTAVANTE DEGLI ATTAVANTI (1452-c. 1517), illum. Castelfiorentino.—131

BACCANI, GAETANO (1792-1867), A. Flor.—153, 178, 194

BACCIO D'AGNOLO (Bart. Baglioni; 1462-1543), A. Flor.—66, 87, 115, 126, 136, 141, 160, 171, 184, 192

BACCIO DEL BIANCO (c. 1604-56), P. & A. Flor.—150

BACCIO DA MONTELUPO (1469-1535), A. & S. Lucca (?).—76, 115, 123, 130, 134

BACHIACCA, IL (Ant. Ubertini; 1494-1557), P. Flor.—89, 105, 190

BALATRI, AND. (17C), W. Flor (?).—200

BALDOVINETTI, ALESSO (1425–99), P. Flor.—70, 92, 113, 117, 122, 140, 159, 163, 180, 184

BALDUCCIO, GIOV. DI (or Balducci; c. 1317–50), S. Pisa.—74, 155

BAMBAIA, IL (Agost. Busti; 1483–1548), S. Lombardy.—109

BANCO see Maso di Banco, and Nanni di Banco.

BANDINELLI, BACCIO (1493–1560), S. Flor.—26, 69, 72, 79, 82, 83, 95, 97, 101, 110, 117, 128, 144, 148, 150

BANDINI, GIOV. (Giov. dell'Opera; 1540–99), S. Flor.—69, 72, 80, 84, 88, 132, 136, 154

BANTI, CRISTIANO (1824–1904), P. S. Croce sull'Aro.—107

BARATTA, GIOV. (1670–1747), S. Flor.—172

BAROCCI, FED. (Il Baroccio; 1526–1612), P. Urbino.—97, 102

BARTOLINI, LOR. (1777–1850), S. Flor.—104, 107, 114, 118, 155, 158, 168

BARTOLOMEO DI GIOVANNI (fl. 1488), P. Perugia.—113, 167

BASSANO (Jac. da Ponte; 1517/18–92), P. Bassano.—97

BASSANO (Leandro da Ponte; 1557–1622), P. Bassano.—97

BATONI, POMPEO (1708–87), P. Lucca.—97, 107

BAZZANI, CESARE (1873–1939), A. Rome.—160

BEATO ANGELICO see Fra' Angelico

BECCAFUMI, DOM. (1485–1551), P. Siena.—97, 105, 167

BELLANO, BART. (c. 1500), S. Padua.—128

BELLINI, GIOV. (c. 1435–1516), P. Venice.—94, 95, 109, 165

BENEDETTO DA MAIANO (1442–97), S. Maiano.—20, 67, 69–70, 72, 80, 84, 87, 115, 136, 141, 149, 154, 192, 203, 205, 207

BENVENUTI, PIETRO (degli Ordini; fl. 1458), A. Ferrara.—105, 107, 131

BERNARDO DADDI see Daddi

BERNINI, GIAN LORENZO (1598–1680), A., P. & S. Naples.—97, 109, 148–9, 167, 210

BERTOLDO, GIOVANNI DI (1410–91), S. Flor.—125, 127–8, 147

BETTO DI FRANCESCO (fl. 1450–75), S. Flor.—74

BEZZUOLI, GIUS. (1784–1855), P. Flor.—107

BICCI DI LORENZO (1373–1452), P. Flor.—67, 69, 73, 116, 126, 137, 141, 152, 160, 163, 176, 180–1, 202, 204, 213

BICCI see Neri di Bicci

BILIVERTI, GIOV. (1576–1644), P. Flemish (Flor. sch.).—105, 155, 162

BIONDO see Giov. del Biondo

BOLTRAFFIO, GIOV. ANT. (1467–1516), P. Milan.—95, 109

BONACCORSI, NICCOLÒ (c. 1348–88), P. Siena.—90

BONACOLSI see Antico

BONAIUTO see Andrea di Bonaiuto

BONIFAZIO VERONESE (or de' Pitati; 1487–1553), P. Verona.—102, 106

BORDONE, PARIS (1500–71), P. Treviso.—97

BORGOGNONE (Guglielmo Courtois; c. 1678), P. St Hippolyte.—97, 102

BOSCOLI, AND. (c. 1550–1606), P. Flor.—163

BOSCOLI, TOMMASO (1503–74), S. Fièsole.—84

BOTTICELLI (Sandro Filipepi; 1444–1510), P. Flor.—23, 89, 92, 93, 105, 113, 116, 131, 134, 139, 179, 200, 210

BOTTICINI, FR. (1446–98), P. Flor.—93, 105, 113, 172

BRAMANTINO (Bart. Suardi; c. 1455–1536) A. & P., sch. of Bramante.—109

BRIOSCO see Riccio da Padova

BRONZINO (Agnolo di Cosimo Tori; 1503–72), P. Flor. sch.—27, 84–5, 87, 94, 96–7, 99, 104, 106, 114, 118, 130, 136, 138, 151, 158, 162, 187, 210

BRUNELLESCHI, FIL. (1377–1446), A. & S. Flor.—17, 62, 64, 67–8, 70, 73, 100, 115–6, 128, 130, 136–7, 147, 158–9, 171, 191, 195, 213

BRUSCHI, GASPERO (fl. 1740), S. Flor.—210

BUFFALMACCO (Bonamico di Cristofano; 1262–1340), P. Flor.—136

BUGGIANO (And. Cavalcanti, Brunelleschi adopted son; 1412–62), A. & S. Pistoia.—67, 70, 130, 137

BUGIARDINI, GIUL. (1476–1555), P. Flor.—96, 134, 161, 170

BUGLIONI, BENED. (1461–1521), S. Flor.—74, 139, 150, 179

BUONAGUIDA see Pacino di Buonaguida

BUONARROTI see Michelangelo

BUONTALENTI, BERN. (delle Girandole; 1531–1608), A. & P. Flor.—73, 81–2, 88–9, 94, 109–10, 115, 125, 131, 137, 140, 143, 151, 152, 172, 181, 192, 196, 206–8, 214

BUTI, LOD. (c. 1560–1603), P. Flor.—213

BUTTERI, GIOV. MARIA (c. 1540–1606), P. Flor.—84

CABIANCA, VINC. (1827–1902), P. Rome.—107

CACCINI, G.B. (1559/62–1613), A. & S. Flor.—83, 117, 140–1, 148, 171

CACIALLI, GIUS. (1770–1828), A. Flor.—105–6

CALCAGNI, TIBERIO (1532–65), S. & A. Flor.—144

CALIARI, CARLETTO (1570–96), P. Venice.—106

CAMAINO see Tino da Camaino

CAMBI, ULISSE (1807–95), S. Flor.—164

CAMBIASO, LUCA (1527–85), P. Genoese sch.—96

CAMBIO see Arnolfo di Cambio

CAMPI, GIULO (c. 1502–72), P. Cremona.—97

CAMPIGLI, MASSIMO (1895–1971), P. & S. Flor.—80

CAMUCCINI, VINC. (1771–1844), P. Rome.—107

CANALETTO (Ant. Canal; 1697–1768), P. Venice.—98

CANOVA, ANT. (1757–1822), S. Possagno.—102, 107, 154, 194

CAPARRA (Nic. Grosso; 15–16C), ironworker, Flor.—141

CARADOSSO (Crist. Foppa; c. 1452–1527), medallist, Lombardy.—150

CARAVAGGIO (Michelangelo Amerighi da; c. 1569–1609), P. Lombardy.—97–8, 106

CARLI see Raffaellino del Garbo

CARPACCIO, VITTORE (c. 1455–1526), P. Venice.—94

CARRÀ, CARLO (1881–1966), P. Alessandria.—80

CARRACCI, ANN. (1560–1609), P. Bologna.—97–8, 104

CARRIERA, ROSALBA (1675–1757), P. Chioggia.—208

CASENTINO see Jacopo del Casentino

CASORATI, FELICE (1886–1963), P. Piedmont.—80, 107

CASSANA, NICCOLÒ (1659–1713), P. Venice.—105

CASSIOLI, AMOS (1832–91), P. Asciano. —107

CASSIOLI, GIUS. (1865–1942), P. & S. Flor.—154

CASTAGNO, AND. DEL (1423–57), P. Flor.—21, 68–9, 89, 109, 118, 126, 152, 184

CASTAGNOLI, GIUS. (1754–1832), P. Prato.—101

CATENA, VINC. (c. 1470–1531), P. Treviso.—109

CAVALCANTI see Buggiano

CECCO BRAVO (Fr. Montelatici; d. 1661), P. Flor.—108, 162

CECIONI, ADRIANO (1836–86), S. & P. Fontebuona.—107

CELLINI, BENVENUTO (1500–71), G. & S. Flor.—26, 79, 99, 110, 118, 131–2, 144, 148–9, 152

CENNI, COSIMO (early 17C), S. Flor.—146

CENNI DI FRANCESCO DI SER CENNI (fl. 1395–1415), P. Flor.—116

CENNINI, BERNARDO (1415–c. 1498), G. Flor.—74

CIECO DA GAMBASSI (Giov. Fr. Gonnelli; 1603–42), S. Gambassi.—179

CIGOLI (Lod. Cardi; 1559–1613), A. Castelvecchio di Cigoli.—83, 97, 102, 105, 124, 138, 150–1, 154, 160

CIMA DA CONEGLIANO (c. 1459–1517), P. Conegliano.—95, 109

CIMABUE (?Cenno dei Pepi; fl. 1272–1302), P. Flor.—11, 64, 89, 134, 155, 159, 163, 195

CIOLI, VALERIO (1529–99), S. Sett.—110, 112, 148, 161

CIONE, AND. DI see Orcagna

CIONE, BENCI DI (1337–1404), A. Flor.—75, 78, 143

CIONE, JAC. DI (brother of Orcagna; fl. c. 1360–98), P. A. & S. Flor.—15, 90, 114, 192, 204

CIONE, NARDO DI (brother of Orcagna; d. 1365), P. Flor.—15, 71, 90, 114, 130, 136, 138, 151, 174

CISERI, ANT. (1821–91), P. Canton Ticino.—99, 107

CIUFFAGNI, BERN. (1385–1450), S. Flor.—67, 69, 72

CIVITALI, MATTEO (c. 1435–1501), A. & S. Lucca.—116, 149

COLLONA, ANGELO MICHELE (c. 1600–87), P. Como.—109

CONDIVI, ASCANIO (c. 1525–74), P. & S. Ascoli Piceno.—162

CONSANI, VINC. (1818–87), S. Lucca.—104

COPPO DI MARCOVALDO (fl. 1261–75), P. Flor.—63, 143

CORREGGIO (Ant. Allegri; 1489–1534), P. Emilian sch.—95

COSINI, SILVIO (1502–47), S. Pisa.—131, 134, 137

COSTA, LOR. (1460–1535), P. Ferr. sch.—94

COSTOLI, ARISTODEMO (1803–71), S. & P. Flor.—107

CREDI see Lor. di Credi

CRESPI, GIUS. MARIA (Il Cerano; 1557–1633), P. Milanese sch.—97

CRONACA (Sim. del Pollaiuolo; 1454–1508), A. Flor.—66, 81–2, 141, 162, 167, 173, 175, 184

CURRADI, FR. (1570–1661), P. & W. Flor.—105, 126, 163, 172, 178, 180, 210

DADDI, BERN. (c. 1312–48), P. Flor.—14, 67, 71, 73, 78, 90, 114, 118, 138, 158, 167, 170, 204, 213

D'AGNOLO see Baccio d'Agnolo

D'ANCONA, VITO (1825–84), P. Pèsaro.—107

DANDINI, PIETRO (1646–1712), P. Flor.—137

DANIELE DA VOLTERRA (Ricciarelli; 1509–66), A. S. & P. Flor. sch.—146, 161, 187

DANTI, FRA' EGNAZIO (1536–86), A. P. & cartographer, Perugia.—87, 133, 166

DANTI, VINC. (1530–76), P. Perugia.—26, 62–3, 84, 112, 134, 144, 146, 155, 161

DE CHIRICO, GIORGIO (1888–1978), P. Volo (Greece).—80, 107

DEI, MATTEO DI GIOV. (c. 1435–95), P. Siena.—148

DELLA ROBBIA, AND. (1435–1525; nephew of Luca), S. Flor.—72–3, 116, 133, 138, 147, 149, 152, 155, 160–1, 169, 191, 207, 211

DELLA ROBBIA, GIOV. (1469–1529; son of And.), S. Flor.—132, 137–8, 148–9, 152, 155, 158, 161, 185, 196, 202, 211

DELLA ROBBIA, LUCA (1399 or 1400–82), S. Flor.—19, 69–70, 73–4, 76, 117, 133, 140, 147–9, 159, 182–3, 212, 214

DELLA ROBBIA FAMILY.—109, 122, 124, 154, 159, 170, 184, 195, 203-4, 206, 208, 213

DELLI, DELLO (early 15C), A. & S. Tuscany.—152

DE NITTIS, GIUS. (1846-84), P. Barletta.—107

DE PISIS, FIL. (1896-1956), P. Ferrara.—80

DE' ROSSI, VINC. (1525-87), S. Fièsole.—26, 69, 82-4, 110, 144, 187

DESIDERIO DA SETTIGNANO (1428-64), S. Flor.—20, 71, 128, 130, 141, 147, 158, 167, 169, 207

DOLCI, CARLO (1616-86), P. Flor.—97, 105-6, 165

DOMENICHINO (Dom. Zampieri; 1581-1641), P. Bologna.—97

DOMENICO DI MICHELINO (15C), P. Flor.—69, 71, 113

DONATELLO (Donato de' Bardi; fl. 1386-1466), S. Flor.—18, 63, 66, 68-70, 72-4, 76, 79, 87, 128, 130, 136, 146-7, 154, 158-60, 169, 174, 211-12

DOSIO, GIOV. ANT. (1533-1609), A. Flor.—115, 136, 142, 158

DOSSI, DOSSO (Giov. Luteri; 1480-1542), P. Ferrara.—97, 102, 167

DUCCIO DI BONINSEGNA (1260-1319), P. Siena.—11, 90, 134

DUCCIO, AGOSTINO DI see Agostino di Duccio

DUPRÈ, AMALIA (1845-1928), S. Flor.—151

DUPRÈ, GIOV. (1817-82), S. Siena.—105, 107, 204

EMPOLI (Iac. Chimenti; 1551-1640), P. Empoli.—105, 115, 117, 140-1, 162, 180, 195, 200

FABRE, FRANCOISE XAVIER (1766-1837), P. Montpellier.—107, 165

FABRIS, EMILIO DE (1808-83), A. & P. Flor.—66

FALLANI, BERN. (fl. 1771-78), A. Flor. (?).—116

FANCELLI, GIOV. (d. 1586), S. & G. Flor.—112

FANCELLI, LUCA (1430-95), A. Settignano.—100

FANTACCHIOTTI, ED. (1809-77), S. Rome.—158

FATTORI, GIOV. (1825/28-1908), P. Flor.—97, 107

FEDI, PIO (1816-92), S. Viterbo.—79, 107, 121

FERRARI, DEFENDENTE (fl. 1518-35), P. Pied. sch.—109

FERRETTI, GIOV. DOM. (1692-c. 1750), P. Flor.—75

FERRI, ANT. MARIA (fl. 1668-1716), A. Flor (?).—126, 164, 178

FERRI, CIRO (1634-89), P. & A. Rome.—101

FERRONI, EGISTO (1835-1912), P. Signa.—107

FERRUCCI, AND. (1465-1526), S. Fièsole.—67, 69, 137, 161, 185, 202

FERRUCCI, FR. DI SIMONE (1437-93), S. & W. Fièsole.—104

FERRUCCI, NICODEMO (1574-1650), P. Flor.—202

FERRUCCI, SIMONE (1402-69), S. Fièsole.—76

FETI, DOM. (or Bastiano Fetti; 1589-1624) P. Mantua.—97, 105

FICHERELLI, FELICE (1605-69), P. S. Gimignano.—152, 172

FIDANI, ORAZIO (c. 1610-56), P. Flor.—2

FILIPEPI see Botticelli

FINELLI, GIUL. c. 1602-57), S. Carrara.—162

FINIGUERRA, TOMMASO (1426-64), G. Flor.—148

FIORAVANTE see Neri di Fioravante

FOGGINI, G.B. (1652-1735), S. Flor.—105-6, 118, 150, 159, 171, 176, 181, 21 212

FOLFI, MARIOTTO DI ZANOBI (L'Ammogliato; 1521-1600), A. Flor.—80

FONTANA, CARLO (1634-1714), A. Mendrisio, Como.—164

FONTANA, LUCIO (1899-1968), S. & P. Argentina.—80

FONTANESI, ANT. (1818-82), P. Reggio Emilia.—107

FOSCHI, PIER FR. (fl. 1535), P. Flor. sch.—190

FRA' ANGELICO (Giov. da Fièsole or Bea Angelico; 1387-1455), P. Vicchio (Flor.).—20, 90, 122-4, 204, 207

FRA' BARTOLOMEO (Bart. di Paolo del Fattorino or Baccio della Porta; 1475-1517), P. Flor.—26, 96, 102, 104 113, 122-4, 173, 206

FRA' MARIANO DA PESCIA (early 16C), P. Pescia.—86-7

FRA' PAOLINO (c. 1490-1547), P. Pistoia.—122

FRA' RISTORO (d. 1284), A. Campi Bisenzio.—133

FRA' SISTO (d. 1290), A. Flor.—133

FRANCAVILLA, PIETRO (Pierre Franquevill 1548-1615), S. Flor. (born at Cambrai).—101, 112, 118, 124, 144, 158, 165, 213

FRANCESCHINI, BALD. see Volterrano

FRANCESCO D'ANTONIO (15C), P. Pisa.—138, 180

FRANCESCO DI DOMENICO (Il Monciatto; 15C), W. & A. Flor.—184

FRANCHI, ROSSELLO DI JAC. (c. 1376-1457 P. Flor.—67, 114, 190

FRANCIA (Fr. Raibolini; c. 1450-1517), P. Bologna.—94

FRANCIABIGIO (Fr. di Crist. Bigi; 1482-1525), P. Flor.—94, 96, 117-18, 125, 172, 214

FRANCIONE (Fr. di Giov. di Matteo; 1428-95), A. & W. Flor.—87

FURINI, FR. (1603-46), P. Flor.—105, 10 150, 162, 167

GADDI, AGNOLO (or Angelo; son of Taddeo; c. 1333–96), P. Flor.—15, 67, 69, 90, 109, 138–9, 148, 154, 158, 163, 182, 207

GADDI, GADDO (di Zanobi; c. 1260–1332), P. Flor.—66, 97

GADDI, TADDEO (fl. 1332–63), P. Flor.—14, 97, 99, 114, 130, 139, 144, 154, 155, 158–9, 184, 203–4, 206

GAGINI, DOM. (c. 1420–92), S. Sicily (b. in the Ticino).—149

GARBO see Raffaellino del Garbo

GARÒFALO, IL (Benv. Tisi; 1481–1559), P. Ferr.—96

GATTA, BART. DELLA (1448–1502/3), A. & P. Flor.—167

GEMITO, VINC. (1852–1929), S. Naples.—146

GENGA, GIROL. (1476-c. 1563), P. A. & S. Urbino.—94

GENTILE DA FABRIANO (c. 1370–1427), P. Fabriano.—17, 90, 140

GENTILESCHI, ARTEMESIA (Lomi; 1590–1642), P. Pisa.—97, 104-5

GERINI, NICCOLÒ DI PIETRO (fl. 1368–1415), P. Flor.—71, 76, 78, 99, 137, 152, 155, 158, 160, 162, 179

GERINO DA PISTOIA (1480-after 1529), P. Pistoia.—203

GHERARDI, CRIST. (Doceno; 1508–56), P. Sansepolcro.—85

GHERARDINI, ALESS. (1655–1723), P. Flor.—126, 172, 181

GHIBERTI LOR. (1378–1455), A. S. & P. Flor.—61–2, 64, 66, 68–9, 76, 122, 134, 147, 152-3, 159, 163

GHIBERTI, VITTORIO (son of Lor.; 1419–96), S. & G. Flor.—62, 159

GHINI, GIOV. DI LAPO (fl. 1355–71), A. Flor.—64, 119

GHIRLANDAIO, DAVIDE (1451–1525; brother of Dom.), P. & mosaicist, Flor.—66, 117, 136-7, 139

GHIRLANDAIO, DOM. (Dom. di Tom. Bigordi; 1449–94), P. Flor.—23, 66, 80, 87, 92, 116, 124, 130, 133, 136, 139-40, 193, 208, 214

GHIRLANDAIO, MICH. DI RIDOLFO (Michele Tosini; 1503–77), P. Flor. 172, 179

GHIRLANDAIO, RID. DEL (1483–1561; son of Dom.), P. Flor.—71, 85-6, 94, 104, 113, 141, 174, 211

GIAMBELLI, PIETRO (fl. 1664–69), W. Pisa.—117

GIAMBOLOGNA (Jean Boulogne or Giov. Bologna; 1529–1608), S. Flor. sch. (a native of Douai).—26, 73, 76, 79, 84-5, 89, 110, 112-3, 115, 118, 124, 136, 138, 141, 144, 146, 148-50, 161-2, 167, 180, 206, 208, 210-11

GIAMBONO, MICHELE (1420-62), P. Ven.—170

GIORDANO, LUCA ('Luca fa presto'; 1632–1705), P. Naples.—97, 101, 106, 118, 128, 163, 176

GIORGIONE (c. 1478–1510), P. Castelfranco Veneto.—95, 101, 102

GIOTTINO (Giotto di Stefano; c. 1320/30–after 1369), P. Flor.—90, 138, 148

GIOTTO DI BONDONE (1266/7–1337, P. Flor. (perhaps a native of Vespignano in the Mugello).—11, 74, 70, 90, 137, 139, 148, 151, 155, 161, 164, 167, 179, 181, 195

GIOVANNI D'AMBROGIO (fl. 1384–1418), S. & A. Flor.—64, 66

GIOVANNI DI BERTOLDO see Bertoldo

GIOVANNI DEL BIONDO (fl. 1356–92), P. Flor.—15, 69, 74, 116, 155, 158, 160, 202

GIOVANNI DI DOM. DA GAIOLE (1403–79), A. & W. Gaiole in Chianti.—171, 184

GIOVANNI DI FRANCESCO (fl. 1459–70), P. Rimini.—116, 148, 161, 214

GIOVANNI DI MICHELE (fl. c. 1440–50), W. Flor.—155

GIOVANNI DA MILANO (fl. 1350–69), P. at Flor.—15, 90, 114, 155, 176

GIOVANNI DELL'OPERA see Bandini, Giov.

GIOVANNI DAL PONTE (c. 1385–1437), P. Flor.—76, 89, 114, 140, 153, 204

GIOVANNI DA S. GIOV. (Giov. Mannozzi; 1592–1636), P. S. Giovanni Valdarno.—105, 108, 122, 132, 139-40, 152-3, 155, 162, 170, 179, 194, 208, 213

GIROLAMO DA CARPI (1501–56), P. Ferrara.—96

GIULIANO DI BACCIO D'AGNOLO (Giul. Baglioni; 1491–1555), A. & W. Flor.—115

GIULIANO DA MAIANO (1432–90), A. & S. Maiano.—21, 69–70, 80, 84, 87, 142-3, 151, 159, 205, 206

GOZZOLI, BENOZZO (1420–97), P. Flor. sch.—22, 62, 124, 127, 167

GRAFFIONE (Giov. di Michele Scheggini; 1455-c. 1527), P. Pistoia.—163

GRANACCI, FR. (1469/70–1541), P. Flor.—96, 113, 190

GUARDI, FR. (1712–92), P. Ven.—98

GUARDI, IAC. DI PIERO (fl. 1379–1408), S. & A. Flor.—66

GUERCINO (Giov. Fr. Barbieri; 1591–1666), P. Bologna sch.—97, 102, 104

GUIDI, VIRGILIO (c. 1892), P. Rome.—80

GUTTUSO, RENATO (b. 1912), P. Bagheria (Sicily).—80

HAYEZ, FR. (1791–1882), P. Venice.—107

INDUNO, DOM. (1815–78), P. Milan.—107

JACOPINO DEL CONTE (1510-c. 1598), P. Flor.—117

JACOPO DEL CASENTINO (Landini; c. 1300–49), P. Arezzo.—74, 76, 167, 186, 211

JACOPO DA EMPOLI see Empoli

JACOPO DEL SELLAIO (1446–93), P. Flor.—179

LAMBERTI, NICCOLÒ DI PIERO (c. 1370–1451), S. Flor.—66, 72, 76, 146

LAMBERTI, PIERO DI NICCOLÒ (c. 1393–1434), S. Flor.—140

LANDI, GASPARE (1756–1830), P. Piacenza.—107

LANDINI, TADDEO (c. 1550–96), S. & A. Flor.—174

LAPI, NICCOLÒ (d. 1732), P. Flor.—115

LAURANA, FR. (fl. 1458–1502), S. Zara. —149

LEGA, SILVESTRO (1826–95), P. Flor.—107

LEONARDO DA VINCI (1452–1519), A. P. & S. Flor. sch. (born near Empoli).—24, 37, 62, 82, 85, 93, 114, 131, 167, 214

LEONI, LEONE (Il Cavaliere Aretino; 1510–92), S. Lomb.—150

LEVI, CARLO (1912–75), P. Turin.—80

LIGOZZI, JAC. (1547–1627), P. Verona.—83, 105, 109, 118, 126, 134, 137, 139, 160

LIPPI, FILIPPINO (son of Filippo; 1457–1504), P. Flor. sch.—23, 92–3, 106, 113, 134, 150, 163, 165, 167, 172, 175–6

LIPPI, FRA' FILIPPO (c. 1406–69), P. Flor.—20, 92, 105, 113, 130, 175–6, 213

LIPPI, LOR. (1606–65), P. Flor.—105, 142, 178

LIPPO FIORENTINO (c. 1354–1410), P. Flor.—176

LOMI, AURELIO (1556–1622), P. Pisa.—172

LONGHI, ALESS. (son of Pietro; 1733–1813), P. Venice.—98

LORENZETTI, AMBR. (brother of Pietro; d. c. 1348), P. Siena.—90, 170

LORENZETTI, PIETRO (brother of Ambr.; c. 1280–1348), P. Siena.—90, 167, 179

LORENZI, STOLDO (1534–83), S. Settignano.—110

LORENZO DI BICCI (c. 1350–1427), P. & A. Flor.—175, 204

LORENZO DI CREDI (1439–1537), P. Flor.—76, 92–3, 113, 172, 200

LORENZO DI GIOV. D'AMBROGIO (fl. 1396–1402), S. Flor.—66

LORENZO DI NICCOLÒ (Gerini; fl. 1392–1411), P. Flor.—181

LOTTO, LOR. (1480–1556), P. Venice.—96–7

LUINI, BERN. (c. 1475–1532), P. Lombardy.—95

MACCHIETTI, GIROL. (1535–92), P. Flor.—134

MAFAI, MARIO (1902–65), P. Rome.—80

MAIANO see Giuliano, Benedetto & Giov. da Maiano

MAINARDI, SEB. (d. 1513), P. San Gimignano.—113, 136, 148, 155

MAINIERI, GIOV. FR. (fl. 1489–1504), P. Parma.—95

MANETTI, ANT. (1423–97), P. Flor.—128, 171, 183

MANETTI, RUTILIO (1571–1639), P. Siena.—102, 130, 174, 210

MANTEGNA, AND. (1431–1506), P. Padua.—94

MANZÙ, GIAC. (Manzoni; b. 1908), S. Bergamo.—80

MARATTA, CARLO (1625–1713), P. Ancona.—97

MARCO DA FAENZA (Marchetti; d. 1588), P. Faenza.—84

MARCOVALDO, see Coppo di Marcovaldo

MARINI, MARINO (1901–66), S. & P. Pistoia.—80, 142

MARIOTTO DI CRISTOFANO (1393–1457), P. San Giovanni Valdarno.—113

MARIOTTO DI NARDO (c. 1373–1424), P. Flor.—115, 140, 143, 159, 183, 187, 205 211

MARTINI, ARTURO (1889–1947), S. & P. Treviso.—80

MARTINI, SIMONE (c. 1283–1344), P. Siena.—17, 90, 167

MASACCIO (Tom. Guido or Tom. di Ser Giov.; 1401–c. 1428), P. San Giovanni Valdarno.—19, 85, 90, 137, 161, 167, 175-6

MASCAGNI, DONATO (Fra' Arsenio; 1579–1636), P. Flor.—118

MASO DI BANCO (fl. 1341–46), P. Flor.—14, 158, 160, 172

MASO DI BARTOLOMEO (1406–56), S. Arezzo.—69, 117, 183

MASO DI SAN FRIANO (Tom. Manzuoli; 1531–71), P. Flor.—84, 139-40, 207

MASOLINO DA PANICALE (Tom. Fini; maste of Masaccio; 1383–c. 1440), P. Flor.—19, 90, 175-6

MATAS, NIC. (1798–c. 1872), A. Flor.—153

MAZZA, TOMMASO DEL (fl. 1375–91), P. Flor. sch.—212

MAZZOLINO, LOD. (c. 1480–1528/30), P. Ferrara.—96

'MASTER OF THE ADIMARI MARRIAGE-CHEST' (Giov. di Ser Giov. or 'Master o Fucecchio'; fl. c. 1435–60), P. Flor. sch.—190

'MASTER OF THE BIGALLO' (fl. mid-13C), P Flor.—71, 74

'MASTER OF THE BIMBO VISPO' (fl. 1410–25), P. Flor. sch.—160

'MASTER OF THE CASTELLO NATIVITY' (15C), P. Flor. sch.—113, 126

'MASTER OF THE CHIOSTRO DEGLI ARANCI' (15C), P. Flor.—151

'MASTER OF FIGLINE' (or 'Master of the Fogg Pietà'; fl. c. 1320–60), P. Flor. sch.—158, 162

'MASTER OF THE MADDALENA' (fl. late 13C), P. Flor. sch.—64, 90, 114

'MASTER OF S. CECILIA' (fl. c. 1300–20), P Tuscan sch.—134

'MASTER OF THE ST GEORGE CODEX' (earl 14C), P. & illum. Siena or France.—14

'MASTER OF S. MARTINO ALLA PALMA' (fl. c. 1330–50), P. Tuscany.—89

'MASTER OF S. MINIATO' (late 15C), P. Flor. sch.—71, 181

'MASTER OF S. REMIGIO' (fl. c. 1360), P. Tuscany.—195

'MASTER OF THE STRAUS MADONNA' (fl. c 1390–1420), P. Tuscany.—114, 116, 16C

MEDICI, DON GIOV. DE' (1566–1621), A. Flor.—73

Meglio, Jac. Coppi di (1523–91), P. Perètola.—134, 154

Melozzo da Forlì (son of Giul. di Melozzo degli Ambrogi; 1438–94), P. Forlì.—94

Memmi, Lippo (fl. 1317–47), P. Siena.—90

Mengoni, Gius. (1829–77), A. Bologna.—132

Merlini, Ant. (fl. 1656), G. Bergamo or Bologna.—118

Meucci, Vinc. (1699–1766), P. Flor.—150

Michelangelo Buonarroti (1475–1564), A. S. & P. Flor. (b. at Caprese near Arezzo)., —24, 37, 73, 79, 82–3, 95, 110, 113, 128, 130-2, 136, 144, 153–5, 160-1, 165, 171, 184, 187, 207

Michelozzo (Michelozzo di Bart. Michelozzi; c. 1396–1472), A. & S. Flor.—19, 62–3, 66, 69, 74–5, 80, 82, 117–18, 122–4, 127, 142, 147, 155, 159, 179-80, 182, 205–6, 208, 212

Minga, And. del (c. 1540–96), P. Flor.—154

Mino da Fièsole (1431–84), S. Flor. sch. (b. at Poppi).—20, 149-50, 154, 162, 202

Miteli, Agostino (1609–60), P. & engr. Bologna.—109

Mola, Gaspare (1610-66), metalworker, Como or Lugano.—150

Monaco, Lor. (Fra' Lor. degli Angioli; c. 1370–1425), P. Flor. sch.—20, 76, 90, 114, 116, 122, 126, 131, 140, 167, 200, 204

Monte di Giovanni di Miniato (Monte del Fora; 1448–1529), P. illum. & mos. Flor.—74

Montelatici see Cecco Bravo

Montelupo see Baccio da & Raff. da Montelupo

Montórsoli, Giov. Ang. (1507–63), S. W. & A. Montórsoli (Flor).—118, 132, 173, 187

Morandi, Giorgio (1890–1964), P. & engr. Bol.—80

Morelli, Dom. (1823–1901), P. Naples.—107

Moro, Luigi del (1845–97), A. Livorno.—104

Moroni, G.B. (c. 1525–78), P. Bergamo.—97, 106

Naccherino, Michele (1550–1622), S. Flor.—112

Naldini, G.B. (1537–91), P. Flor.—82, 84, 124, 134, 150, 159, 205

Nanni di Baccio Bigio (Giov. Lippi; d. c. 1568), A. & S. Flor.—172

Nanni di Banco (Giov. di Ant. di Banco; c. 1384–1421), S. Flor.—17, 66–7, 72, 74, 76

Nanni di Bartolo (early 15C), S. Flor.—73

Nardo di Cione see Cione

Nardo, Mariotto di see Mariotto di Nardo

Nelli, G.B. (1661–1725), A. Flor.—152

Nelli, Pietro (fl. 1375), P. Flor.—212

Neri di Bicci (1418–91), P. Flor.—99, 114, 126, 140-1, 167, 179-81, 185, 190, 193, 203-4, 207

Neri di Fioravante (fl. 1340–84), A. & S. Flor.—64, 75, 99, 140, 143

Niccolò di Tommaso (fl. c. 1350–80), P. Flor.—167

Nigetti, Dionigi di Matteo (fl. 1565–70), W. Flor.—87

Nigetti, Matteo (1560–1649), A. & S. Flor.—131, 139, 142, 194, 200

Noferi di Antonio (Ant. Carota; 1485–1568), W. Flor.—71

Novelli, Pietro (1603-47), P. Sicily.—162

Orcagna, And. (di Cione; fl. 1344-68), P. & S. Flor.—14, 64, 71, 76, 78, 90, 114, 136, 153, 159, 162, 174, 179, 191, 207, 211–12

Pacino di Buonaguida (fl. c. 1310–30), P. Flor.—99, 114

Palizzi, Fil. (1818–99), P. Chieti.—107

Palma Vecchio (Giac. Negretti; c. 1480–1528), P. Bergamo.—96

Palmezzano, Marco (1456–1539), P. Forlì.—105

Paoletti, Gasp. Maria (1727–1813), A. Flor.—107, 109, 179, 210

Paolo di Giovanni (c. 1403–82), P. & illum. Siena.—146

Paolo Schiavo (1397–1478), P. Flor.—69, 126, 155, 183, 191

Paolo Uccello (Doni; 1397–1475), P. Flor.—20, 66, 68–9, 92, 113, 137-8, 160, 184

Parigi, Alf. the Elder (c. 1590; father of Giulio), A. Flor.—88

Parigi, Alf. the Younger (d. 1656; son of Giulio), A. Flor.—100, 112, 118, 164, 174, 195

Parigi, Giulio (d. 1635), A. & P. Flor.—100, 112, 153, 174, 195

Parmigianino (Fr. Mazola; 1503–40), P. Parma sch.—96

Passignano, Dom. (Cresti; 1560–1638), P. Flor. sch.—83, 115, 124, 140, 153, 162, 172, 181, 211

Pazzi, Enrico (1819-99), S. Ravenna.—153

Perugino (Pietro Vannucci; 1446–1523), P. Umbria.—23, 93–4, 104, 113, 118, 132, 163, 172, 193, 200

Peruzzi, Baldass. (1481–1537), A. & P. Siena.—105

Pesellino, Fr. di Stef. (1422–57), P. Flor. sch.—92

Petrucci, Fr. (14C), metalworker, Siena.—173

Piazzetta, G.B. (1683–1754), P. Venice.—98

Pier Fr. Fiorentino (fl. 1474-97), P. Flor.—208

Pierino da Vinci (nephew of Leonardo; c. 1531–54), S. Flor.—82, 110, 210

PIERO DI COSIMO (pupil of Cosimo Rosselli; 1462–1521), P. Flor.—23, 93, 117, 203

PIERO DELLA FRANCESCA (1416–92), P. Sansepolcro.—90

PIETRO DA BARGA (fl. 1574/88), S. Lucca.—150

PIETRO DA CORTONA (Berrettini; 1596–1669), P. & A. Cortona.—97, 100-2, 106, 142

PIGNONE, SIMONE (c. 1611–98), P. Flor.—99

PISANELLO (Ant. Pisano; 1377–1455), P. & medallist, Lombardy.—150

PISANO, AND. (c. 1270–1348/49), A. & S. Pontedera.—14, 62, 70, 73-4, 177

PISANO, NICOLA (c. 1200–after 1278), A. & S. Apulia.—154

PISANO, NINO (son of And.; d. 1368), S. Pisa.—134

POCCETTI, BERNARDINO (Barbatelli; 1548–1612), P. Flor.—72, 105, 107, 110, 116, 118–19, 122, 138, 141, 178, 194, 212

POCCIANTI, PASQUALE (1774–1858), A. Bibbiena.—100

POGGI, GIUS. (1811–1901), A. Flor.—150, 185-6, 196

POGGINI, DOM. (1520–90), S. Flor.—146, 148

POLLAIOLO, AND. DEL (1433–98), S. & P. Flor. sch.—22, 74, 92, 100, 131, 149, 170, 173, 183

POLLAIOLO, PIERO DEL (brother of Ant.; 1443–96), P. & A. Flor. sch.—92, 102, 149, 183

POMARANCIO (Crist. Roncalli da Pomarance; 1552–1626), P. Tuscany.—191

PONTE see Giov. dal Ponte

PONTORMO (Iac. Carrucci; 1494–1556), P. Flor. sch.—26, 84, 94, 96, 99, 105-6, 115, 117–18, 138, 165, 187, 210-11, 214

POPPI, Il (Fr. Morandini; 1544-97), P. Poppi.—76, 84, 115, 180

PORTELLI, Carlo (d. 1574), P. Arezzo.—71, 163

PORTIGIANI, PAGNO DI LAPO (1406–70), A. Fièsole.—74, 117, 128

PRETI, MATTIA (Il Cavalier Calabrese; 1613–99), P. Naples.—97-8

PSEUDO PIER FR. FIORENTINO (15C), P. Flor.—128

PUCCINELLI, ANT. (1822–97), P. Pisa.—107

PUGLIANO, DOM. (d. 1658), P. Flor.—162

PULIGO, DOM. (Ubaldini; 1492–1527), P. Flor.—106, 163

QUERCIA, JAC. DELLA (1371–1438), S. Siena.—62, 74, 174

RAFFAELLINO DEL GARBO (c. 1466–1524), P. Flor.—113, 130, 162-3, 172, 203

RAFFAELLO DA MONTELUPO (c. 1505–76), S. Flor. sch.—99, 126, 132

RAPHAEL (Raffaello Sanzio; 1483–1520), P. Urbino.—26, 94-6, 102, 104, 106, 165

REDI, TOM. (1665–1726), P. Flor.—181

RENI, GUIDO (1577–1642), P. Bologna.—97, 102, 105, 161

RENZO, AMBR. DI (fl. 1353-58), A. Flor.—71

RICCI, SEB. (1659–1734), P. Belluno.—85, 97

RICCI, STEF. (1765–1837), S. Flor.—154

RICCIARELLI, LEONARDO (16C), stuc. Volterra.—84

RICCIO DA PADOVA (And. Briosco; 1470–1532), A. & P. Padua.—148, 150

RIMINALDI, ORAZIO (1586–1630), P. Pisa.—105

ROBBIA, see Della Robbia

ROBERTI, ERCOLE DE' (c. 1456-96), P. Ferrara sch.—167

ROCCATAGLIATA, NICCOLÒ (fl. 1593–1636), S. Genoa.—150

ROMANINO (Girol. Romani; 1485–1566), P. Brescia.—99

ROMANO, GIULIO (Pippi; c. 1492–1546), A. & P. Rome.—105

ROSA, SALVATOR (1615–73), P. Naples.—97, 101, 105

ROSAI, OTTONE (1895–1957), P. Flor.—80, 151

ROSSELLI, COSIMO (1439–1507), P. Flor.—105, 113, 115, 117, 162-3, 172, 202, 206

ROSSELLI, MATTEO (1578–1650), P. Flor.—102, 105-6, 117–8, 139, 153, 160, 162, 192, 208, 210

ROSSELLINO, ANT. (Gamberelli; 1427–79), S. Settignano.—20, 149, 154, 161, 167, 183, 190, 207

ROSSELLINO, BERN. (Gamberelli; 1409-64), S. Settignano.—20, 117, 134, 142, 151-154, 207, 172

ROSSI see De' Rossi

ROSSO FIORENTINO (G.B. de' Rossi; 1494–1541), P. Flor.—26, 94, 96, 102, 117, 128, 173

ROSSO, MEDARDO (1858–1928), S. Turin.—107

ROSSO, ZANOBI DEL (1724-98), A. Flor.—110, 150, 193

ROVEZZANO, BENED. DA (1474-c. 1554), S. Flor.—69, 139-40, 150, 176, 191

RUGGIERI, FERD. (c. 1691–1741), A. Flor.—99, 150

RUSTICI, G. FR. (1475–1554), S. & P. Flor.—62, 144, 149, 167

SABATELLI, LUIGI (1772–1850), P. Milan.—104

SAGRESTANI, GIOV. CAMILLO (1660–1731), P. Flor.—172

SALIMBENI, VENTURA (1567/68–1613), P. & engr. Siena.—97, 118

SALVI D' ANDREA (fl. 1457-83), S. & A. Flor.—171-3

SALVIATI, FR. (De Rossi; 1510-63), P. Flor.—84-5, 87, 104, 106, 170

SANGALLO, ANT. DA (the Elder; Giambert. 1455–1537), A. & S. Flor.—115, 117

SANGALO, ANT. DA (the Younger; Cordini; 1483–1546), A. Flor.—197

SANGALLO, ARISTOTILE DA (nephew of Ant. Giamberti; 1481–1551), A. & P. Flor.—126

SANGALLO, FR. DA (son of Giul.; 1494–1576), S. & A. Flor.—66, 78, 118, 130, 150, 153, 184, 187, 203, 211

SANGALLO, GIOV. FR. DA (1482–1530), A. Flor.—126

SANGALLO, GIUL. DA (1443/45–1516), A. & engr. Flor.—24, 66, 136, 140–42, 150, 153, 161, 163–4, 167, 173, 213–14

SANSOVINO, AND. (And. Contucci; c. 1470–1529), S. & A. Monte S. Savino.—63, 114, 144, 169, 172, 214

SANSOVINO, JAC. (Tatti; pupil of And.; 1486–1570), A. & S. Flor.—69, 144, 149–50, 167, 172

SANTI, GIOV. (d. 1494), P. Pèsaro.—164

SANTI DI TITO (1538–1603), A. & P. Sansepolcro.—66, 84, 87, 97, 99, 114, 118, 134, 137, 139, 159–60, 163, 178, 192, 200, 212

SARTO see And. del Sarto

SASSETTA (Stef. di Giov.; c. 1392–1451), P. Siena (?).—109

SCAMOZZI, VINC. (1552–1616), A. Vicenza.—151

SCARSELLINO, LO (Ippolito Scarsella; c. 1550–1621), P. illum. & engr. Ferrara (?).—96

SCHIAVO see Paolo Schiavo

SCHIAVONE (And. Meldolla; c. 1520–63), P. & engr. Zara (?).—104

SCIPIONE (Gino Bonichi; 1904–33), P. Macerata.—80

SEBASTIANO DEL PIOMBO (Luciani; c. 1485–1547), P. Venice.—96–7, 101, 104

SEGALONI, MATTEO (fl. 1627), A. Flor.—150

SELLAIO, JAC. DEL (1446–93), P. Flor.—71, 105, 204

SERNESI, RAFF. (1838–66), P. Flor.—107

SEVERINI, GINO (1883–1966), P. Cortona.—80, 107

SIGNORELLI, LUCA (c. 1441–1523), P. Cortona.—93–4, 105, 165

SILVANI, GHERARDO (1579–c. 1675), A. & S., Flor.—125–6, 141–2, 150, 155, 164, 176, 193–5, 211

SILVANI, PIER FR. (son of Gherardo; 1620–85), A. Flor.—124, 142, 150, 163

SIMONE DE' CROCIFISSI (fl. 1355–99), P. Bologna.—90

SIGNORINI, TELEMACO (1835–1901), P. Flor.—107, 151

SIRONI, MARIO (1885–1961), P. Sassari.—80

SMERALDO DI GIOVANNI (1366–1444), P. Flor.—76

SODOMA (Giov. Ant. dei Bazzi; 1477–1549), P. Vercelli.—95, 212

SOFFICI, ARDENGO (1879–1964), P. Flor.—107

SOGGI, NICCOLÒ (c. 1480–1552), P. Arezzo (?).—193

SOGLIANI, GIOV. ANT. (1491–1544), P. Flor.—76, 116, 122, 126, 200

SOLDANI, MASSIMILIANO (1658–1740), S. Flor.—150, 210

SPADA, VALERIO (1613–88), P. Colle Val d'Elsa.—151

SPADINI, ARMANDO (1883–1925), P. Flor.—107

SPAGNOLETTO, LO (Gius. Ribera; 1588–1652), P. (b. in Spain).—105

SPINAZZI, INN. (d. 1798), S. Piacenza.—63, 154

SPINELLO ARETINO (fl. 1373–1410), P. Arezzo.—16, 133, 140, 143, 155, 184, 190, 212

STARNINA, GHERARDO (fl. c. 1390–1410), P. Flor.—90, 114, 154, 176

STRADANO, GIOV. (1523–1605), P. born in Bruges.—82, 84–6, 118, 137, 158, 172

STROZZI, ZANOBI (1412–68), P. Flor.—122, 124, 190

SUSINI, ANT. (d. 1624), S. Flor.—117

SUSINI, FR. (d. 1646), S. Flor.—100

SUSTERMANS, JUSTUS (1597–1681), P. Flor. sch. (b. in Antwerp).—97–8, 102, 104–8

TACCA, FERD. (son of Pietro; 1616/19–86), S. & A. Carrara.—131, 149, 152, 164, 192

TACCA, PIETRO (1577–1640), S. Carrara.—110, 115, 118, 131, 150, 187

TADDA, FR. DEL (Fr. Ferrucci; 1497–1585), S. Fièsole (?).—100, 112, 141, 202

TADDA, ROMOLO DEL (Ferrucci; d. 1621), S. Fièsole.—112

TALENTI, FR. (14C), A. Flor.—16, 64, 70, 75, 119

TALENTI, FRA' JAC. (d. 1362), A. at Flor.—133, 136–8

TALENTI, SIMONE (14C), A. & S. Flor.—75–6, 78

TASSO, DOM. DEL (late 15C), W. Flor.—96

TASSO, G.B. DEL (16C), A. Flor.—81, 187

TASSO, GIUL. DEL (15C), W. Flor.—84

TASSO, LEON DEL (15C), W. Flor.—163

TEDESCO, PIERO DI GIOV. (fl. 1386–1402), S. Flor.—66, 72, 76

TERRENI, GIUS. MARIA (1739–1811), P. & engr. Livorno.—101, 151

TICCIATI, GIROL. (1676–1740), S. A. P. & engr. Flor.—72

TIEPOLO, G.B. (1696–1770), P. Venice.—97–8

TINO DI CAMAINO (c. 1285–1338), S. Siena.—66, 74, 134, 143, 146, 160, 169, 174

TINTORETTO, JAC. (Robusti; 1518–94), P. Venice.—85, 97, 102, 106, 109

TITIAN (Tiziano Vecellio; c. 1485–1576), P. Pieve di Cadore.—96–7, 101–2, 104, 106, 161

TOFANELLI, STEF. (1752–1812), P. Lucca.—107

TOSCANI, GIOV. DI FR. (c. 1370–1430), P. Arezzo or Flor.—117, 140

TOSCHI, PIER FR. (d. 1567), P. Flor. (?).—133

Tosi, Arturo (1871–1956), P.
Varese.—80

Tribolo, Nic. (Pericoli; 1500–50), S.
Flor.—101, 109, 112, 122, 131, 132, 144,
146, 148–9, 184, 208, 210

Tura, Cosmè (1429–95), P. Ferrara.—95

Uccello see Paolo Uccello

Unghero, Nanni (c. 1490–1546), A. & W.
Flor.—172

Urbano da Cortona (c. 1426–1504), S.
Siena.—67, 72

Ussi, Stef. (1822–1901), P. Flor.—107

Utens, Giusto (d. 1609), P. Flemish born
(Carrara).—151

Vaga, Pierino del (Pietro Buonaccorsi;
1500–47), P. Flor.—97

Vanni, Fr. (1563–1610), P. Siena.—176

Vannini, Ottavio (1585–1643), P.
Flor.—108, 153

Vasari, Giorgio (1511/12–74), A. P. & art
historian, Arezzo.—26, 68–9, 81–2, 84–5,
88, 94, 96–8, 110, 118, 131, 133–4, 137,
141, 151, 153–4, 159–60, 163, 187, 191

Vecchietta (Lor. di Pietro; 1410–80), S. &
P. Siena.—147, 167

Veneziano, Dom. (1404–61), P. Flor.
sch.—20, 90

Veneziano, Paolo (fl. 1356–72), P.
Venice.—109

Venusti, Marcello (c. 1512–79), P.
Como.—161–2

Veronese, Paolo (Caliari; 1528–88), P.
Verona.—85, 97, 102, 104, 106, 109

Verrocchio, And. del (1435–88), S. & P.
Flor.—22, 66, 74, 76, 82, 87, 93, 130,
149, 158, 161, 163, 172, 193

Viani, Lor. (1882–1936), P. Viareggio.
—107

Vignali, Jac. (1592–1664), P.
Arezzo.—105, 119, 160–2, 172, 181, 195

Viti, Timoteo (1467–1524), P. Urbino
(Raphael's master).—164

Vivarini, Bart. (fl. 1450–91), P.
Murano.—94–5

Volterrano (Baldass. Franceschini;
1611–89), P. Volterra.—105, 117–18,
158, 170, 179, 208

Zandomeneghi, Fed. (1841–1917), P.
Venice.—107

Zenale, Bern. (1436–1526), P.
Bergamo.—109

Zocchi, Emilio (1835–1913), S. Flor.—105
196

Zocchi, Gius. (1711–67), P. Flor.—152

Zuccari, Fed. (1542–1609), P.
Pésaro.—68–9, 97, 163

Zuccari, Taddeo (1529–66), P.
Pésaro.—97

Zucchi, Jac. (1541–c. 1590), P. Flor.—82,
84, 93

INDEX

Topographical names are printed in **bold** type, names of eminent persons in *italics,* other entries in Roman type.

Accademia d Belle Arti 121
Accademia d. Crusca 209
Accademia d. Disegno 121, 186
Acciaioli, Cardinal Agnolo II 211
Acciaioli, Donato 191
Acciaioli, Niccolò 192, 211
Acton, Sir Harold 198
Agli, Ant. degli 211
Airport 43
Albany, Countess of 37, 154, 164, 165
Albergo Porta Rossa 190
Alberti, Bened. degli 32
Alberti family 212
Albizi, Rinaldo degli 33
Albizi family 193, 194
Alfieri, Vitt. 154, 165
Aliotti, Bp 134
Altoviti, Oddo 191
American church 196
Arcetri 181
Archivio dello Stato 88, 198
Argyropoulos, Joannes 208

Baciocchi, Elisa Bonaparte 36, 112, 196
Badia Fiesolana 201
Badia Fiorentina 150
Badia a Ripoli 212
Badia di S. Salvatore e Settimo 213
Bandini, Ang. Maria 204
Bardi family 32, 134, 158, 179
Bardini, Stef. 168
Bardini, Ugo 170, 180
Bargello, Il 143
Beccuti, Bruno 143
Bellosguardo 212
Berenson, Bernard 207
Biblioteca Laurenziana 130
Biblioteca Marucelliana 125
Biblioteca Nazionale 160
Biblioteca Riccardiana 126
Bigallo, Il 71
Bisticci, Vespasiano da 201
Blagden, Isa 198
Bóboli Gardens 109
Boccaccio, Giov. 37, 136, 200, 206, 207
Böcklin, Arnold 205
Bonaparte, Charlotte 155
Bonaparte, Pauline 194
Borghese, Camillo 194

Borghini, Vinc. 82, 84, 116
Borgo d. Albizi 193
Borgo Allegri 163
Borgo Pinti 163
Borgo SS. Apostoli 191
Borgo S. Croce 160
Borgo S. Frediano 177
Borgo S. Jacopo 170
Borgo Tegolaio 175
Borgunto 205
Botti, Villana delle 134
Bracciolini, Poggio 33, 69
Brancacci, Felice 175
Brienne, Walter de (Duke of Athens) 32
British Institute 54
Browning, Elizabeth Barrett and Robert 37, 178, 198, 213
Brozzi 214
Bruni, Leonardo 33, 154
Bueri, Piccarda 130
Buonafede, Leonardo 211
Buses 52
Byron, Lord 165

'Calcio in costume' 56, 112, 152
Caldine, Le 206
Camera di Commercio 167
Campanile del Duomo 70
Camping 46
Canto de' Pazzi 193
Capello, Bianca 85, 178, 196
Cappella Brancacci 175
Cappella dei Pazzi 159
Cappella di S. Sepolcro 142
Cappelle Medicee 131
Cappellone degli Spagnoli 137
Capponi, Gino 163
Capponi, Neri 172
Capponi, Niccolò 34
Careggi 208
Carmignano 214
Carmine, Il (S.M. del Carmine) 175
Carrand, Louis 148
Casa Buonarroti 160
Casa di Dante 193
Casa Guidi 178
Casa Morra 160
Casa dell'Opera di S. Giovanni 75
Casa dell'Orafo 192
Casa Torre Buondelmonte 191
Casa Torre Foresi 190

Cascine, Le 196
Casellina 213
Casino Mediceo 125
Castel di Poggio 205
Castello di Vincigliata 205
Cavalcanti, Fra' Aldovrando 134
Cavalcanti, Guido 37
Cavalcanti, Tom. 173
Cenacolo di Foligno 132
Cenacolo di Ognissanti 139
Cenacolo di S. Apollonia 126
Cenacolo di S. Salvi 198
Cenacolo di S. Spirito 174
Cennini, Bernardo 130
Cercìna 206, **208**
Certosa del Galluzzo 211
Certosa di Val d'Ema 211
Chapel of the Princes 131
Charlemagne 29, 191
Charles V, Emp. 127
Charles VIII of France 127
Charles Stuart (the Young Pretender) 37, 164, 196
Chateaubriand 165
Cherubini, Luigi 37, 114, 158
'Chiantigiana', La 212
Chiasso dei Baroncelli 192
Chiostri monumentali di S.M. Novella 137
Chiostro dello Scalzo 125
Churches 54
Cimitero Evangelico degli Allori 210
Clement VII 130, 131, 162
Clough, Arthur Hugh 198
Colle di Montughi 197
Collezione Contini Bonacossi 109
Collezione Della Ragione 80
Collezione Loeser 87
Colonna dell'Abbondanza 75
Comeana 214
Conservatorio 114
Convento della Maddalena 206
Convento delle Oblate 151
Corridoio Vasariano 97, 98
Corsi, Alice & Arnaldo 170
Corsini, Neri 174
Corsini, Tom. 174
Corso, Il 193
Corso dei Tintori 160
Costa S. Giorgio 181
Costa Scarpuccia 180, 181

225

Craig, Gordon 152
Cristofori, Bart. 37, 114
Croce del Trebbio 138
Czartoryska, Princess Sofia 158

Dante Alighieri 32, 37, 150, 152, 154, 160, 161, 193
Dati, Fr. Lionardo 134
Davanzati, Bern. 37, 187
Davanzati, Giul. 141
Davidsohn, Robert 198
Davizzi family 187
Davy, Sir Humphry 167, 179
Della Rovere, Vittoria 175
Demidoff family 107, 168, 197
Dickens, Charles 192
Donato, Bp. 201, 206
'Doney's' Cafè 141
Dostoievsky, F. 179
Dudley, Sir Robert 142, 166
Duomo 64
Dutch Institute 54

Eleonora di Toledo 100, 137
Eliot, George 142
Emerson, Ralph Waldo 141, 200
English Cemetery 198
Eugenius IV 64, 127, 137
European University Institute 201

Faraday, Michael 167, 179
Federighi, Benozzo 140
Fenzi, Em. 126
Ficino, Marsilio 33, 67, 208
Fièsole 202
Filicaia, Vinc. 194
Fondazione Salvatore Romano 174
Fontana, Felice 166
Fontelucente 205
Forte di Belvedere 181
Forte di S. Giorgio 181
Fortezza da Basso 196-7
Foscolo, Ugo 154, 165, 213
Fossombroni, Vitt. 158

Gabinetto Vieusseux 141
Galilei, Galileo 37, 98, 137, 146, 153, 159, 160, 166, 167, 179, 181, 206, 213, 214
Galleria dell'Accademia 112
Galleria d'Arte Moderna 107
Galleria Corsi 170
Galleria Corsini 164
Galleria Palatina 100

Galleria di Palazzo Pitti 100
Galleria degli Uffizi 88
Galli, Jac. 144
Galluzzo 211
Gattula, Riccardo 169
Ghetto 75, 163
Ghibellines 29, 191
Giardino dei Semplici 122
Ginori, Carlo 210
Giovanni da Salerno 134
Giovanni da Velletri 63
Giugni, Bern. 150
Giusti, Gius. 164
Goldoni, Carlo 164
Granaio di Cosimo III 171
Gràssina 212
Gregory X 180
Guelfs 29, 190
'Giubbe Rosse' Cafè 75
Guicciardini, Fr. 37, 100

Hardy, Thomas 197
Harvard Center for Renaissance Studies 54
Hawkwood, Sir John 69
Hawthorne, Nathaniel 179
Hobbes, Thomas 181
Holidays 60
Holland, Lord and Lady 178
Horne, Herbert Percy 167
Horticultural Garden 198
Hunt, Holman 198
Hunt, Leigh 37

Iac. di Lusitania, Cardinal 183
Impruneta 211
Institut Français 54, 139
Istituto d'Arte 112
Istituto Geografico Militare 54, 197

James, Henry 138, 192
John XXIII (antipope) 63
John Paleologus, Emp. 127
Joseph, Patriarch of Constantinople 127, 134
Julius Caesar 29

Kunsthistorisches Institut 54, 163

Lamartine, A. de 133
Lando, Michele di 32
Landor, Walter Savage 37, 179, 198, 200
Lastra a Signa 213
Latini, Brunetto 37, 143
Laurentian Library 130
Lawrence, D. H. 141, 213
Leader, John Temple 142, 205
Leighton, Lord 198
Leo X 131, 161
L'Impruneta 211

Le Montalve, Convent of 208
Loggia del Bigallo 71
Loggia del Grano 195
Loggia dei Lanzi 78
Loggia dell'Orcagna 78
Loggia dell'Ospedale di S. Matteo 121
Loggia del Pesce 163
Loggia dei Rucellai 142
Loggia di S. Paolo 138
Loggia della Signoria 78
Loggia dei Tessitori 126
Lowell, James Russell 141
Luchaire, Julien 139
Lully, Jean-Baptiste 37
Lungarno Acciaioli 165
Lungarno Corsini 164
Lungarno Generale Diaz 167
Lungarno Guicciardini 170
Lungarno Serristori 168
Lungarno Soderini 171
Lungarno Torrigiani 170
Lungarno Vespucci 164
Lutheran church 170

Machiavelli, Niccolò 37, 87, 100, 153, 154, 211
Maddalena, Convento della 206
Magliabechi, Ant. 160
Maharajah of Kolhapur 196
Maiano 205
Malmantile 213
Mann, Sir Horace 178, 179
Mantegazza, Paolo 151
Manzoni, Aless. 141, 165
Markets: 'Il Porcellino' 187
  S. Ambrogio 163
  S. Lorenzo 132
Marsuppini, Carlo 33, 154, 158
Marucelli, Fr. di Aless. 125
Mary of Teck 37
Matilda, Countess of Tuscany 29
Medici, Alessandro de' 35, 38-9, 196, 197
Medici, Anna Maria Lodovica de' 35, 38-9, 88, 109
Medici, Cosimo de' (Cosimo il Vecchio) 33, 38-9, 80, 122, 124, 125, 127, 130, 131, 201, 205, 208
Medici, Cosimo I de' 35, 38-9, 81, 82, 84, 87, 88, 100, 109, 122, 131, 162, 165, 166, 184, 187, 196, 208, 210
Medici, Cosimo II de' 38-9, 131
Medici, Cosimo III de'

38-9, 131
Medici, Ferdinando I de'
38-9, 88, 114, 131, 166,
181, 206, 208, 214
Medici, Ferdinando II de'
35, 38-9, 88, 101, 131,
166, 167, 181
Medici, Francesco I de'
38-9, 84, 85, 87, 88, 89,
131, 151, 178, 206
Medici, Giovanni de' (see
also Leo X) 38-9, 130,
131, 149, 181, 209
Medici, Giovanni de'
('delle Bande Nere')
38-9, 210
Medici, Giovanni di Bicci
de' 33, 38-9, 130, 187,
190
Medici, Giuliano de'
(Duke of Nemours)
38-9, 69, 132, 151
Medici, Leopoldo de'
(Cardinal) 35, 38-9, 88,
97, 109, 166
Medici, Lorenzino de'
('Lorenzaccio') 35, 38-9,
197
Medici, Lorenzo de' (Duke
of Urbino) 38-9, 132
Medici, Lorenzo de'
(Lorenzo il Magnifico)
33, 38-9, 69, 108, 125,
131, 132, 149, 150, 205,
208, 214
Medici, Lorenzo di
Pierfrancesco de' 38-9,
92, 93, 209
Medici, Piero di Cosimo
de' (Piero il Gottoso)
33, 34, 38-9, 115, 117,
127, 130, 149, 182, 208
Medici, Piero di Lorenzo
de' 149
Medici Chapels 131
Medici Museum 128
Mellini, Pietro 149
Melville, Herman 141
'Mercatino' 163
Mercato Centrale 132
Mercato Nuovo 187
Mercato Vecchio 75
Milnes, Monckton 200
Milton, John 181, 199
Minerbetti, Ruggero 134
Misericordia, The 71
'Montagnola, La' 210
Montaigne, Michel de 210,
214
Montecéceri 204, 205
Montefortini, Tomb of 214
Monte Morello 208, 210
Monteoliveto 212
Montesenario, Convent of
206
Morghen, Raffaello 158
Mozzi family 32, 180
Mugnone, R. 205

Museo dell'Angelico 122
Museo Archeologico 119
Museo degli Argenti 107
Museo Bandini (Fièsole)
204
Museo Bardini 168
Museo del Bigallo 71
Museo Botanico 122
Museo Fiorentino di
Preistoria 152
Museo della Casa
Fiorentina Antica 187
Museo di Firenze com'era
151
Museo Horne 167
Museo di Mineralogia 122
Museo Nazionale 143
Museo Nazionale di
Antropologia ed
Etnologia 151
Museo dell'Opera del
Duomo 72
Museo dell'Opera di S.
Croce 159
Museo delle Porcellane
(Bòboli) 112
Museo delle Porcellane di
Doccia (Sesto
Fiorentino) 210
Museo di S. Marco 122
Museo dello Spedale degli
Innocenti 116
Museo Stibbert 197
Museo di Storia della
Scienza 166
Museo di Strumenti
Musicali 114
Museo Zoologico 'La
Specola' 179
Museums 56

Neroni, Diotisalvi 126
Niccolò da Tolentino 69
Niccolò da Uzzano 147,
179
Nightingale, Florence 37,
160
Nori, Fr. 154
Novello, Count Guido 32

Observatory (Arcetri) 181
Ognissanti 139
Olmo 205
Oltrarno 171
Opera del Duomo 72
Opificio delle Pietre Dure
114
Oratory of the
Confraternità di S.
Pietro Martire 164
Orsanmichele 75
Orso, Antonio d' 66
Orti Oricellari 196
Ospedale degli Innocenti
116

Palazzina del Caffè 185
Palazzo Acciaioli 192

Palazzo Alberti 195
Palazzo d. Albizi 194
Palazzo Alemanni 180
Palazzo d. Alessandri 194
Palazzo Altoviti 191
Palazzo Altoviti ('dei
Visacci') 194
Palazzo d. Antella 153
Palazzo Antinori 142
Palazzo Antinori-Corsini
160
Palazzo Arcivescovile 75
Palazzo d. Arte dei Beccai
186
Palazzo d. Arte della Lana
186
Palazzo d. Arte della Seta
191
Palazzo Bardi alle Grazie
195
Palazzo Bardini 168
Palazzo d. Bargello 143
Palazzo Bartolini-
Salimbeni 141
Palazzo Benini Formichi
192
Palazzo d. Bianca Capello
178
Palazzo Borghese 194
Palazzo Buondelmonti 192
Palazzo Caccini 163
Palazzo Canacci 190
Palazzo Canigiani 170, 179
Palazzo d. Canonici 72
Palazzo Capponi 164
Palazzo Capponi delle
Rovinate 179
Palazzo d. Cardinale
Panciatichi 126
Palazzo Castellani 166
Palazzo Cerchi 192
Palazzo d. Cintoia 194
Palazzo d. Circolo
dell'Unione 141
Palazzo Cocchi 153
Palazzo Commenda di
Firenze 178
Palazzo d. Congressi 197
Palazzo Corbizi 194
Palazzo Corsi 167
Palazzo Corsini 164
Palazzo Corsini sul Prato
196
Palazzo d. Cosimo Ridolfi
178
Palazzo Covoni 194
Palazzo Davanzati 187
Palazzo Fagni 195
Palazzo Frescobaldi 170
Palazzo Frescobaldi (Via
S. Spirito) 178
Palazzo d. Gherardesca
164
Palazzo Giandonati 190
Palazzo Gianfigliazzi 165
Palazzo Ginori 126
Palazzo Ginori-Venturi 196
Palazzo Girolami 98

Palazzo Giugni 192
Palazzo Giugni (Via Alfani) 115
Palazzo Gondi 150
Palazzo Guadagni 175
Palazzo Guadagni-Riccardi 72
Palazzo Guicciardini 171
Palazzo Guicciardini (Via Guicciardini) 99
Palazzo Incontri 115
Palazzo Lanfredini 171
Palazzo Lenzi 139
Palazzo Malenchini 167, 195
Palazzo Manetti 178
Palazzo Mannelli-Riccardi 132
Palazzo Marucelli 126
Palazzo Masetti 165
Palazzo Matteucci Ramirez di Montalvo 194
Palazzo Medici-Riccardi 127
Palazzo Minerbetti 141
Palazzo Montauto 126
Palazzo d. Mozzi 180
Palazzo Neroni 126
Palazzo Niccolini 115
Palazzo Nonfinito 151
Palazzo d. Oddo Altoviti 191
Palazzo Pandolfini 126
Palazzo d. Parte Guelfa 190
Palazzo Pazzi-Quaratesi 151
Palazzo Peruzzi 195
Palazzo Pitti 100
  Appartamenti Monumentali 106
  Collezione Contini-Bonacossi 109
  Galleria d'Arte Moderna 107
  Museo degli Argenti 107
Palazzo d. Podestà 143
Palazzo d. Pucci 115
Palazzo Ricasoli 164
Palazzo Ricasoli (Via Maggio) 178
Palazzo Riccardi-Mannelli 115
Palazzo Ridolfi 178
Palazzo Rinuccini 178
Palazzo Roffia 163
Palazzo Rosselli del Turco 192
Palazzo Rucellai 142
Palazzo Rustici 195
Palazzo Salviati (Borgo Pinti) 164
Palazzo Salviati (Corso) 193
Palazzo Salviati-Quaratesi 194
Palazzo di S. Clemente 164

Palazzo Serristori 168
Palazzo Sforza Alimeni 115
Palazzo della Signoria 80
Palazzo Soldani 195
Palazzo Spinelli 160
Palazzo Spini-Feroni 139-40
Palazzo Strozzi 141
Palazzo Strozzi-Niccolini 74
Palazzo Strozzi del Poeta 141
Palazzo dello Strozzino 142
Palazzo della Stufa 128
Palazzo Taddei 126
Palazzo Tedaldini 193
Palazzo Tempi 170
Palazzo Torrigiani 178
Palazzo Torrigiani ('La Specola') 179
Palazzo Torrigiani (Lungarno Torrigiani) 170
Palazzo degli Uffizi 88
Palazzo Uguccioni 79
Palazzo Usimbardi 192
Palazzo Vecchio 80
Palazzo 'dei Visacci' 194
Palazzo Visdomini 193
Palazzo Vitali, 194
Palazzo Ximenes 163
Palazzo della Zecca 88
Palmieri, Marco 200
Palmieri, Matteo 131, 149
Pandolfini, Giannozzo 126, 150
Parker, Theodore 198
Passavanti, Fra' Jac. 133, 211
Pazzi, And. de' 159
Pazzi Chapel 159
Pazzi Conspiracy 151, 154
Pazzi family 33, 69
Penna, Corrado della 134
Peretola 214
Peretola airport 44, 214
Peri, Iac. 37
Peruzzi family 32, 195, 197
Pescaia di S. Rosa 171
Petrarch 37
Pharmacy of S.M. Novella 138
Pian de' Giullari 181
Piazza d'Azeglio 163
Piazza Beccaria 198
Piazza del Carmine 175
Piazza dei Ciompi 163
Piazza S. Croce 152
Piazza Donatello 198
Piazza dell'Indipendenza 197
Piazza della Libertà 198
Piazza del Limbo 191
Piazza dei Mozzi 168
Piazza Peruzzi 195
Piazza della Repubblica 75

Piazza SS. Annunziata 115
Piazza S. Firenze 150
Piazza S. Lorenzo 128
Piazza S. Marco 121
Piazza S.M. Novella 138
Piazza S. Martino 193
Piazza S. Pier Maggiore 194
Piazza della Signoria 78
Piazza S. Spirito 175
Piazza Tasso 178
Piazzale Michelangelo 185
Pico della Mirandola 33, 124, 208
Pierozzi, Ant. 122
Pietro Leopoldo, Grand-duke 36, 113, 143, 166, 179
Pillar of St Zenobius 74
'Pippo Spano' (Fil. Scolari) 212
Pisa airport 43
Pitti, Bart. 144
Pitti, Luca 100
Plethon, Gemisthos 208
Poggio a Caiano 214
Poggio Imperiale 210
Poliziano, Angelo 33, 67, 69, 92, 93, 127, 208
Ponte alla Carraia 164
Ponte a Ema 212
Ponte alle Grazie 168
Ponte a Mensola 206
Ponte Rosso 198
Ponte S. Niccolò 198
Ponte a S. Trinita 165
Ponte Vecchio 98
'Porcellino, Il' 187
Porta al Prato 196
Porta Romana 179
Porta S. Frediano 176
Porta S. Gallo 198
Porta S. Giorgio 181
Porta S. Miniato 180, 182
Porta S. Niccolò 180
Portinari, Folco 152
Portinari, Tommaso 93
Post Office 53, 75
Pratolino 206
Presbyterian church 171

Quinto 210

Railway Station 44, 196
Restaurants 46
Ricasoli, Baron 115
Ricasoli, Bettino 197
Riccardi, Riccardo 126
Rossini, Gioacchino 154
Rucellai, Bern. 196
Rucellai, Giov. 37, 133, 142
Ruskin, John 192
Russian church 197

St Ambrose 128
St Andrew 206, 207
St Antoninus 193, 200

St James's church 196
St John Gualberto 140, 182, 199
St Minias 182, 184
St Reparata 64
St Romulus 201, 202
St Zenobius 74, 128
Salutati, Bp Leonardo 202
Salutati, Coluccio 33
Salviati, Alamanno 205
Salviati, Maria 193
Salviati family 210
S. Ambrogio 162
S. Andrea in Percussina 211
SS. Annunziata 117
S. Apollonia 126
SS. Apostoli 191
S. Barnaba 133
S. Bartolomeo 212
S. Carlo dei Lombardi 78
S. Caterina dell'Antella 212
S. Croce 153
S. Domenico 200
S. Domenico di Fiesole 200
S. Felice 179
S. Felicita 99
S. Filippo Neri 150
S. Firenze 160
S. Frediano in Cestello 177
S. Gaetano 142
S. Giorgio sulla Costa 181
S. Giovanni 61
S. Giovanni Battista 214
S. Giovannino dei Cavalieri 126
S. Giovannino degli Scolopi 126
SS. Giuliano e Settimo 213
S. Giuseppe 160
S. Jacopo sopr'Arno 170
S. Leonardo in Arcetri 181
S. Lorenzo 128
S. Lucia dei Magnoli 179
S. Marco 124
S. Margherita de' Cerchi 193
S. Margherita in S. Maria de' Ricci 193
S. Maria degli Angeli 115
S. Maria del Carmine 175
S. Maria d. Croce al Tempio 160
S. Maria del Fiore 64
S. Maria Maddalena dei Pazzi 163
S. Maria Maggiore 143
S. Maria Novella 133
S. Maria Nuova 133
S. Maria Sovraporta 191
S. Maria delia Tromba 186
S. Martino a Gangalandi 213
S. Martino a Mensola 206
S. Martino alla Palma 213
S. Martino al Vescovo 193
S. Michele Visdomini 115

S. Michelino 115
S. Miniato al Monte 182
S. Niccolò sopr'Arno 180
S. Orsola 133
S. Pancrazio 142
S. Paolino 139
S. Pier Scheraggio 89
S. Quirico 213
S. Remigio 195
S. Reparata 67
S. Salvatore al Monte 184
S. Salvatore al Vescovo 75
S. Salvi 198
S. Simone 194
S. Spirito 171
S. Stefano in Pane 208
S. Stefano al Ponte 192
S. Trinita 140
Sargent, John Singer 37
Sassetti, Fr. 140, 149
Savonarola, Girolamo 34, 78, 79, 81, 82, 122, 124
Scala, Bart. 164
Scandicci 213
'Scoppio del Carro' 55
Sesto Fiorentino 210
Settignano 207
Shelley, P. B. 165, 196
Sloan, Francis 153, 208
Soderini, Piero 34, 176
Sozzino, Mariano 147
Spanish Chapel 137
'Specola, La' 179
Spedale degli Innocenti 116
Spini, Geri degli 140
Spirito Santo 181
Squarcialupi, Ant. 69
Stazione di Campo di Marte 44
Stazione di S. Maria Novella 44, 196
Stibbert, Frederick 197
'Strada dei Bosconi' 205
Strozzi, Ant. 137
Strozzi, Fil. 35, 134, 135, 141
Strozzi, Onofrio 140
Synagogue 163

Tabernacolo delle Cinque Lampade 115
Taddei family 126
Tavarnuzze 211
Tchaikovsky, P. 181
Teatro Comunale 196
Teatro della Pergola 152
Tesori, Fr. 117
Tessa, Monna 152
Theatres 55
Tommaseo, Nic. 207
Tornabuoni, Giov. 136
Torraccia, La 200
Torre, Gastone della 160
Torre d. Alberti 195
Torre Baldovinetti 192
Torre d. Castagna 193
Torre Cerchi 192
Torre Compiobbesi 186

Torre d. Donati 193
Torre Donati (Cocchi) 194
Torre d. Gallo 181
Torre Greci (Galigai) 192
Torre La Pagliazza 193
Torre d. Mannelli 99
Torre Marsili di Borgo 170
Torricella, La 213
Torricelli, Evangelista 166, 181
Torrigiani, Pietro 178
Torrino di S. Rosa 176
Toscanelli, Paolo dal Pozzo 70, 179
Trespiano 206
Tribunale di Mercanzia 79
Trollope, Anthony 179, 197
Trollope, Frances 198
Trollope family 160
Twain, Mark 37, 207

Uffizi Gallery 88
Ugo, Margrave of Tuscany 150
University 115, 121, 122
Uberti, Farinata degli 32

Valori, Baccio 144, 194
Vespucci, Amerigo 37, 139, 214
Via d. Ariento 132
Via d. Badia dei Roccettini 201
Via d. Bardi 199
Via d. Belvedere 182
Via d. Benci 195
Via Benedetto da Maiano 205
Via Bolognese 198, 206
Via d. Caldaie 175
Via Calimaruzza 192
Via d. Calzaioli 75
Via d. Campanile 72
Via d. Canonica 193
Via Cavour 125
Via Condotta 192
Via Dante Alighieri 193
Via Faenza 132, 205
Via d. Fontanelle 200
Via d. Forbici 200
Via d. Fossi 138
Via Ghibellina 194
Via d. Ginori 126
Via Giovanni Boccaccio 200
Via Giuseppe Giusti 163
Via Guelfa 133
Via Guicciardini 99
Via Lambertesca 192
Via Maggio 178
Via Nazionale 132
Via d. Neri 195
Via d. Oche 193
Via Pandolfini 194
Via Panicale 132
Via Porta Rossa 187
Via d. Proconsolo 151

Via Ricasoli 112
Via Romana 179
Via d. S. Antonino 132
Via d. S. Domenico 200
Via S. Elisabetta 193
Via S. Gallo 126
Via d. S. Leonardo 181
Via d. S. Niccolò 180
Via S. Spirito 178
Via Scipione Ammirato 198
Via d. Serragli 178
Via d. Servi 115
Via d. Studio 193
Via d. Terme 191
Via Tornabuoni 139
Via Vecchia Fiesolana 205
Via d. Vigna Nuova 142
Viale Alessandro Volta 200
Viale d. Colli 185
Viale Fratelli Rosselli 196
Viale d. Poggio Imperiale 210
Victor Emmanuel II 196, 203, 208
Victor Emmanuel III 100, 208

Victoria, Queen 196, 197, 205
Vieusseux, Gian Pietro 141, 198
Villa d. Artimino 214
Villa Bardini 181
Villa d. Bellosguardo 213
Villa Boccaccio 207
Villa d. Bosco 205
Villa d. Careggi 208
Villa d. Castello 209
Villa Corsi-Salviati 210
Villa Corsini 209
Villa Demidoff 206
Villa Fabbricotti 197
Villa Gamberaia 207
Villa Il Gioiello 181
Villa I Tatti 207
Villa La Pietra 198
Villa La Quiete 208
Villa Medicea di Careggi 208
Villa Medici 205
Villa Michelangelo Buonarroti 207
Villa d. Ombrellino 213
Villa Palmieri 200

Villa d. Petraia 208
Villa d. Poggio a Caiano 214
Villa d. Poggio Gherardo 206
Villa Salviati 202
Villa Il Salviatino 205
Villa Schifanoia 200
Villa Stibbert 197
Villa Strozzi 212
Villa Viviani 207
Villino Trollope 197
Vinci 214
Viviani, Vincenzio 37, 166, 167, 181
Volpi, Elio 187
Volta dei Girolami 192
Volta di S. Piero 194

Walpole, Horace 178, 179
Watts, G. F. 178
Willis, N. P. 200
Wolf, Gerhard 36

Zati, Amerigo 206, 207
Zoological Museum 179

Typeset by Cold Composition Ltd, Tonbridge
Printed in Great Britain by Fletcher & Son Ltd, Norwich

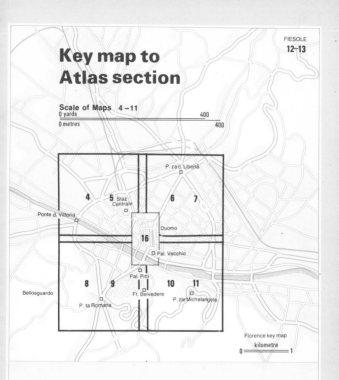

Key map to Atlas section

FIESOLE
12-13

Scale of Maps 4–11

0 yards | 400
0 metres | 400

P. za d. Libertà

4 | 5 Staz Centrale | 6 | 7

Ponte d. Vittoria

Duomo

16

Pal. Vecchio

Pal. Pitti

8 | 9 | 10 | 11

Bellosguardo

Ft. Belvedere

P. ta Romana | P. zle Michelangelo

Florence key map
kilometre
0 ——— 1

ATLAS CONTENTS

Routes   2-3
Florence   4-11
Fièsole   12-13
Environs of Florence   14-15
Centre of Florence   16

Plan of Routes

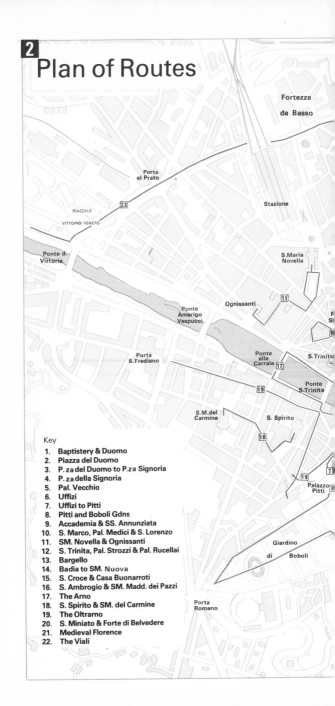

Fortezza da Basso

Porta al Prato

PIAZZALE
VITTORIO VENETO

22

Stazione

Ponte d. Vittoria

S.Maria Novella

Ponte Amerigo Vespucci

Ognissanti

11

Porta S.Frediano

Ponte alla Carraia 17

S.Trinita

19

Ponte S.Trinita

Porta S.Frediano

S.M.del Carmine

S. Spirito

18

19

7

Palazzo Pitti

Giardino di Boboli

Porta Romano

Key
1. **Baptistery & Duomo**
2. **Piazza del Duomo**
3. **P. za del Duomo to P.za Signoria**
4. **P. za della Signoria**
5. **Pal. Vecchio**
6. **Uffizi**
7. **Uffizi to Pitti**
8. **Pitti and Boboli Gdns**
9. **Accademia & SS. Annunziata**
10. **S. Marco, Pal. Medici & S. Lorenzo**
11. **SM. Novella & Ognissanti**
12. **S. Trinita, Pal. Strozzi & Pal. Rucellai**
13. **Bargello**
14. **Badia to SM. Nuova**
15. **S. Croce & Casa Buonarroti**
16. **S. Ambrogio & SM. Madd. dei Pazzi**
17. **The Arno**
18. **S. Spirito & SM. del Carmine**
19. **The Oltrarno**
20. **S. Miniato & Forte di Belvedere**
21. **Medieval Florence**
22. **The Viali**

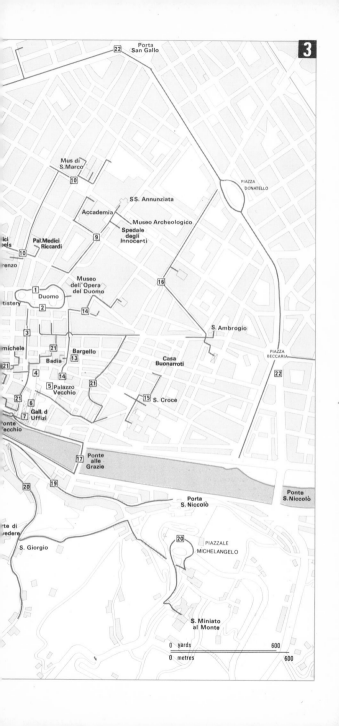

3

Porta
San Gallo
22

Mus di
S.Marco
10

PIAZZA
DONATELLO

SS. Annunziata

Accademia

Museo Archeologico

Spedale
degli
Innocenti

Pal.Medici
Riccardi
10

9

16

ici
els

renzo

Museo
dell'Opera
del Duomo

1
Duomo

2

tistery

14

S. Ambrogio

3

PIAZZA
BECCARIA

michele
21

Bargello

21

Badia
13

Casa
Buonarroti

21

22

4

14

5 Palazzo
Vecchio

21

6

15 S. Croce

Gall. d
7 Uffizi

onte
echio

Ponte alle
Grazie
17

20
19

Ponte
S.Niccolò

Porta
S. Niccolò

rte di
edere

20

PIAZZALE
MICHELANGELO

S. Giorgio

S. Miniato
al Monte

0   yards   600

0   metres   600

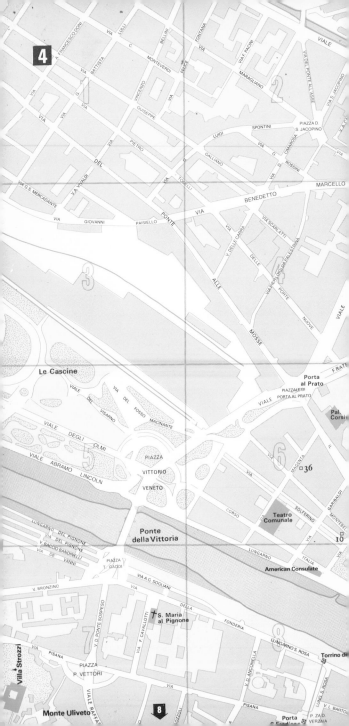

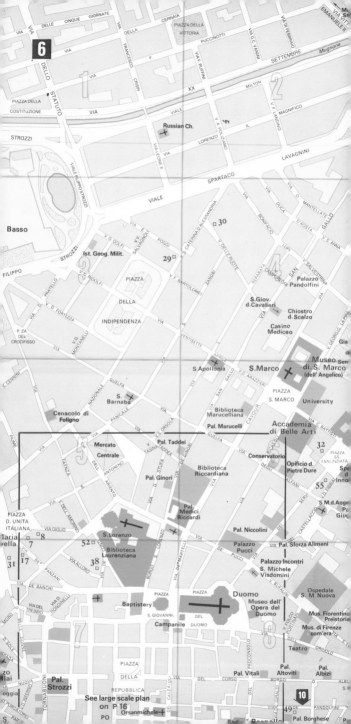

PO

PIETRAPIANA

Loggia del Pesce

S. Ambrogio

BORGO LA CROCE

PIAZZA

VIA A. SOL

VIA D. ULIVO

PIAZZA

Mercato di S. Ambrogio

7

BECCARIA

11 San Salvi
GIOBERTI

MACCI

GHIBERTI

VIA ALLEGRI

Casa Buonarroti

ro

DELL'

DE'

AGNOLO

1

VIA GIOTTO

BORGO

VIA D. FICO

VIA DE' PEPI

VIA D. PANDOLFINI

GHIBELLINA

Archivio di Stato (under constr.)

V. LE

V. CIMABUE

VIA FRA. GIOV. ANGELICO

S. Croce

V.D. CONCIATORI

CASINE

VIA P. THOUAR

VIALE D. GIOVINE ITALIA

DUCA D. ABRUZZI

VIALE GIOV. AMENDOLA

VIA ARNOLFO

Sm. d. Croce al Tempio

ra di S. Croce

VIA DI SAN GIUSEPPE

S. Guiseppe

Capp. dei Pazzi

VIA DE' MALCONTENTI

oteca onale

VIA

TRIPOLI

PIAZZA PIAVE

GERI

□ **13**

LUNGARNO D. ZECCA VECCHIA

LUNG. P. GIRALDI

LUNG. D. TEMPIO

ERRISTORI

3

4

Ponte S. Niccolò

PIAZZA GIUS. POGGI

DEI

LUNG

CELLINI

PIAZZA

LUNG.

NICCOLÒ

⊠

Porta S. Niccolò

VIA D FORNACE

F. FERRUCCI

F. FERRUCCI

VIA G. ORSINI

VIALE

GIUS.

POGGI

BASTIONI

VIA

SER

VENTURA

MONACHE

58
□

PIAZZALE MICHELANGELO

MINIATO

AL

MONTE

DEL MONTE

Pal. Caffè

VIA DI SAN

VIA

S. Salvatore al Monte

MICHELANGELO

6

MICHELANGELO

MONTE

ALLE

V.D. CORTI

ALLE CROCI

V.D.

CROCI

GIRAMONTE

S. Miniato al Monte

Monte alle Croci

V. S. BERNARDINO DA SENA

GIRAMONTE

DI

VIALE

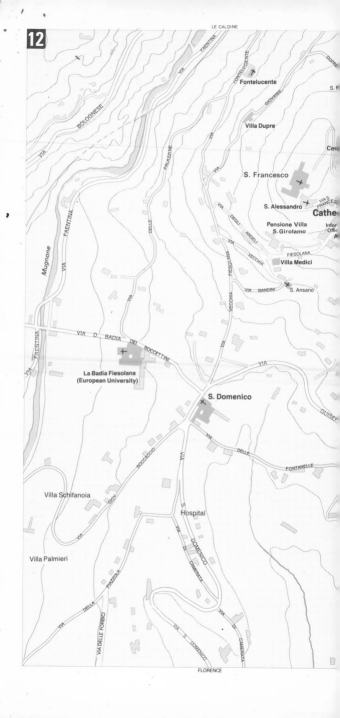

12

LE CALDINE

Fontelucente

Villa Dupre

Cere

S. Francesco

S. Alessandro

VIA S. FRANCESCO

Cathe

Pensione Villa S. Girolamo

Infor
Offic
p

FIESOLANA

Villa Medici

VIA BANDINI

S. Ansano

VIA D BADIA DEI ROCCETTINI

VIA

**La Badia Fiesolana
(European University)**

S. Domenico

GUISEL

VIA DELLE

FONTANELLE

Villa Schifanoia

Hospital

Villa Palmieri

FLORENCE

PIAN DI MUGNONE

Fiesole
and Environs

| 0 yards | 400 |
| 0 metres | 400 |

13

N

VIA RIORBICO

VIA A. COSTA

DELLE MURA ETRUSCHE

VIA BASTIANINI

VIA DEL BARGELLINO

Campo Sportivo

an Theatre
Museum
ni

MARINI P. ZA DEL MERCATO

VIA PORTIGIANI

VIA

PZA GARIBALDI

GRAMSCI

VIA G. MATTEOTTI

VIA FRANCESCO FERRUCCI

Etruscan Tombs

Borgunto

STRADA DEI BOSCONI

Town Hall

SM Primerana

VIA F. POETI

Camping site

VIA CORSICA

FIESOLE

VIA SANT APOLLINARE

VIA ADRIANO MARI

✝ S. Apollinare

GUISE PRE

VIA VERDI

BELVEDERE

VIA MONTE CECERI

VIA GIOVANNI ANGELICO

Villa S. Michele Hotel

MANTELLINI

MONTE CECERI

VIA

Pensione Bencista

Torraccia

VIA BENEDETTO DI

MARINO

Maiano ✝

IL SALVIATINO   PONTE A MENSOLA   SETTIGNANO

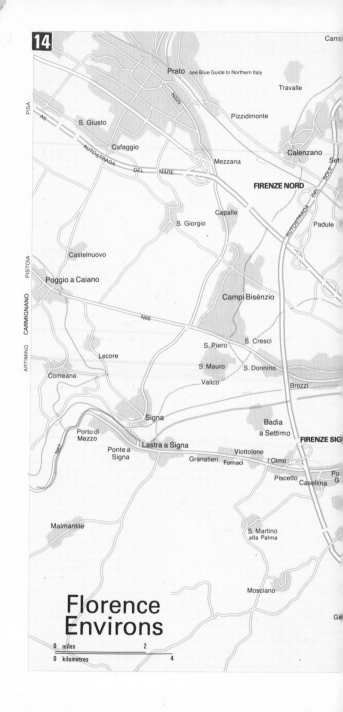

14

Carra

Prato see Blue Guide to Northern Italy

Travalle

Pizzidimonte

PISA

A11

S. Giusto

AUTOSTRADA

Cafaggio

DEL   MARE

Mezzana

Calenzano

Set

FIRENZE NORD

AUTOSTRADA DEL SOLE

Capalle

S. Giorgio

Padule

PISTOIA

Castelnuovo

Poggio a Caiano

Campi Bisénzio

CARMIGNANO

N66

ARTIMINO

Lecore

S. Piero

S. Cresci

Comeana

S. Mauro

S. Donnino

Valico

Brozzi

Signa

Badia
a Settimo

FIRENZE SIG

Porto di
Mezzo

N67

Ponte a
Signa

Lastra a Signa

Viottolone

l'Olmo

Granatieri   Fornaci

Piscetto

Po
G

Casellina

Malmantile

S. Martino
alla Palma

Mosciano

Florence
Environs

Gi

0 miles   2

0 kilometres   4

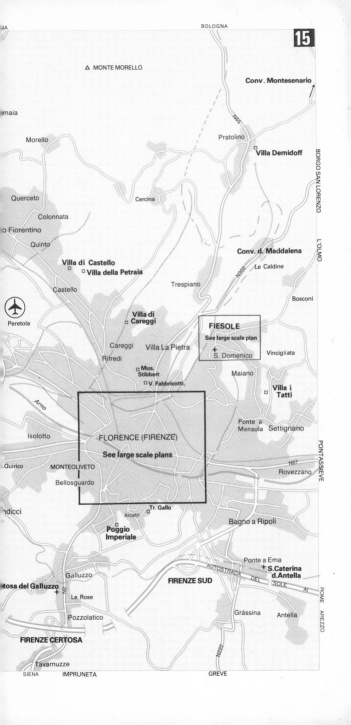

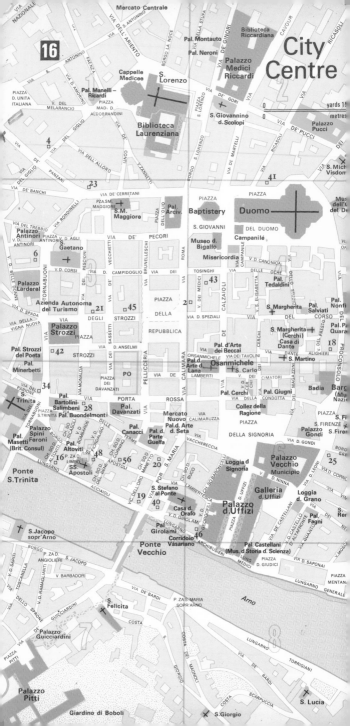